CIVIL WAR AMERICA

Longman History of the United States

The New Republic, 1st edition
Reginald Horsman

America before the European Invasions, 1st edition
Alice Beck Kehoe

Civil War America: Making a Nation, 1848–1877, 1st edition
Robert Cook

CIVIL WAR AMERICA
MAKING A NATION, 1848–1877

Robert Cook

An imprint of **Pearson Education**

London · New York · Toronto · Sydney · Tokyo · Singapore · Hong Kong · Cape Town
Madrid · Paris · Amsterdam · Munich · Milan

PEARSON EDUCATION LIMITED

Head Office:
Edinburgh Gate
Harlow CM20 2JE
Tel: +44 (0)1279 623623
Fax: +44 (0)1279 431059

London Office:
128 Long Acre
London WC2E 9AN
Tel: +44 (0)20 7447 2000
Fax: +44 (0)20 7447 2170
Website: www.history-minds.com

First published in Great Britain in 2003

© Pearson Education Limited 2003

The right of Robert Cook to be identified as Author
of this Work has been asserted by him in accordance
with the Copyright, Designs and Patents Act 1988.

ISBN 0 582 38107 X

British Library Cataloguing in Publication Data
A CIP catalogue record for this book can be obtained from the British Library

Library of Congress Cataloging in Publication Data
A CIP catalog record for this book can be obtained from the Library of
Congress

10 9 8 7 6 5 4 3 2 1

Set in 10.5/12.5pt New Baskerville by Graphicraft Limited, Hong Kong
Printed in Malaysia

The Publishers' policy is to use paper manufactured from sustainable forests.

FOR ANDREA, MARTHA AND DANIEL

CONTENTS

ACKNOWLEDGMENTS

No one foolhardy enough to write an account of the United States in the era of the Civil War can claim to be self-reliant. As readers of the following chapters will be only too aware, I owe a great deal to many renowned scholars for their work on broad and specific aspects of one of the most studied periods in modern history. Their insights are woven into the fabric of this text and my debt to them is readily apparent in the endnotes and bibliography. Two individuals in particular contributed to the genesis of this book. Bill Dusinberre fired me with a fascination for nineteenth-century American history when I was an undergraduate at the University of Warwick. He has continued to do so in numerous ways during the intervening years. The project itself would never have reached the drawing-board without the backing of Peter Parish, who died in the spring of 2002. Professor Parish was the kindest of men as well as being one of the most respected of Civil War historians. His death saddened all who knew him and he is greatly missed.

I wish to express particular thanks to fellow historians who offered incisive comments and criticism on earlier drafts of this book: Richard Carwardine, Peter Coates, Susan-Mary Grant, Bruce Levine, Kathleen Liulevicius, Brian Holden Reid, and the series editor, Mark White. The text is the stronger for their assistance but, regrettably, the inevitable errors of fact, omission, and interpretation are all my own. Librarians have been unfailingly helpful on my research trips to the United States. I am especially grateful to the assistance rendered by Lesley Fields, curator of the Gilder Lehrman Collection at the Pierpont Morgan Library in New York City, and the efficient staff who administer the Southern Historical Collection in Chapel Hill, North Carolina. Essential financial aid, again gratefully acknowledged, came from three sources: the Gilder Lehrman Institute of American History (for a month's research in New York); the United Kingdom Arts and Humanities Research Board, and the University of Sheffield (which, in tandem, allowed me to spend a full academic year researching and writing). The expertise supplied by Wordwise Edit played an important role in preparation of the manuscript at various stages, not least the creation of the index.

My greatest debt, however, is to my closest family for their deeply appreciated love, support, and patience throughout this project. Concluding thanks then to Andrea, Martha, and Daniel, and to my mother, Margaret, and my father, John. I couldn't have reached this stage without them.

The publishers are grateful to the following for permission to reproduce copyright material:

Maps 1, 5, and 6 redrawn from *The American Civil War*, copyright © 1975 by Peter J. Parish, published and reproduced with the permission of Holmes & Meier, New York (Parish, P.J. 1975); Map 2 redrawn from *White Society in the Antebellum South*, © Longman Group Ltd 1985, reprinted by permission of Pearson Education Ltd (Collins, B. 1985); Map 3 redrawn from *For God and Mammon: Evangelicals and Entrepreneurs, Masters and Slaves in Territorial Kansas*, used by permission of The University of Georgia Press (SenGupta, G. 1996); Map 4 redrawn from *Battle Cry of Freedom: The Era of the Civil War* by James M. McPherson, copyright 1988 by Oxford University Press, Inc. Used by permission of Oxford University Press, Inc. (McPherson, J.M. 1988); Map 7 redrawn from *Gold Dust and Gunsmoke: Tales of the Gold Rush Outlaws, Gunfighters, Lawmen and Vigilantes*, used by permission of John Wiley & Sons, Inc. (Boessenecker, J. 1999).

In some instances we have been unable to trace the owners of copyright material, and we would appreciate any information that would enable us to do so.

ABBREVIATIONS

CEHUS	Stanley L. Engerman and Robert E. Gallman, eds, *The Cambridge Economic History of the United States: Vol. 2, The Long Nineteenth Century* (Cambridge: Cambridge University Press, 2000)
CWH	*Civil War History*
CWL	Roy P. Basler, *The Collected Works of Abraham Lincoln*, 9 vols (New Brunswick, NJ: Rutgers University Press, 1953–55)
GLC	Gilder Lehrman Collection, Pierpont Morgan Library, New York City
JAH	*Journal of American History*
JSH	*Journal of Southern History*
LC	Manuscripts Division, Library of Congress, Washington, DC
SHC	Southern Historical Collection, University of North Carolina Library, Chapel Hill, NC

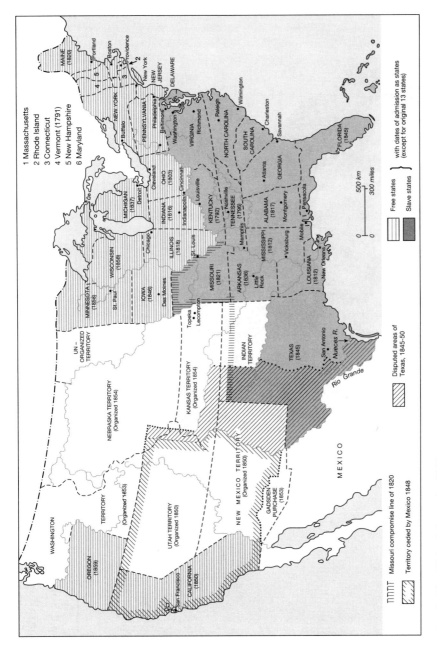

Map 1. The United States in 1860

Source: After Parish, P.J. (1975), *The American Civil War* (pub. New York: Holmes & Meier), pp.18–19. Copyright © 1975 by Peter J. Parish. Reproduced with the permission of the publisher.

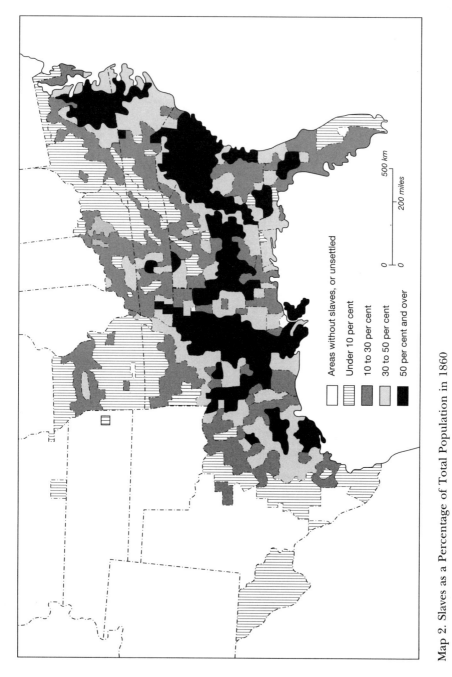

Map 2. Slaves as a Percentage of Total Population in 1860

Source: After Collins, B. (1985), *White Society in the Antebellum South* (pub. Longman), p.194. © Longman Group Ltd 1985, reprinted by permission of Pearson Education Ltd.

Legend:

Areas without slaves, or unsettled

Under 10 per cent

10 to 30 per cent

30 to 50 per cent

50 per cent and over

0   500 km

0   200 miles

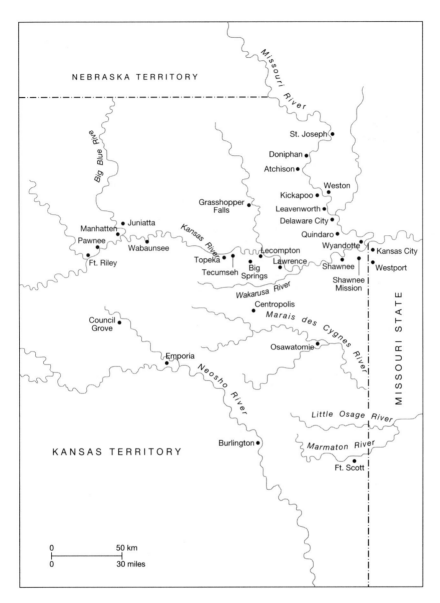

Map 3. Kansas Territory in 1856

Source: After SenGupta, G. (1996), *For God and Mammon: Evangelicals and Entrepreneurs, Masters and Slaves in Territorial Kansas*, 1854–1860 (pub. The University of Georgia Press), p.xiii. © 1996 by The University of Georgia Press, Athens, Georgia 30602. All rights reserved.

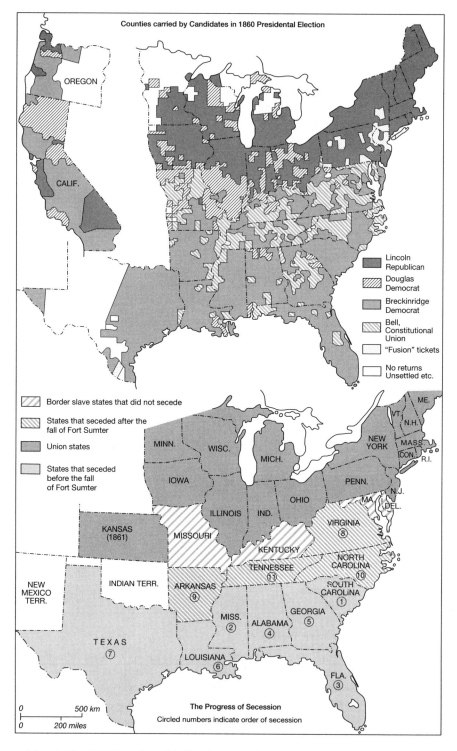

Counties carried by Candidates in 1860 Presidential Election

Lincoln
Republican

Douglas
Democrat

Breckinridge
Democrat

Bell,
Constitutional
Union

"Fusion" tickets

No returns
Unsettled etc.

Border slave states that did not secede

States that seceded after the
fall of Fort Sumter

Union states

States that seceded
before the fall
of Fort Sumter

OREGON

CALIF.

MINN.

WISC.

MICH.

NEW
YORK

ME.

VT.

N.H.

MASS.

CON.

R.I.

IOWA

PENN.

MA

N.J.

DEL.

KANSAS
(1861)

MISSOURI

ILLINOIS

IND.

OHIO

VIRGINIA
⑧

NEW
MEXICO
TERR.

INDIAN TERR.

ARKANSAS
⑨

KENTUCKY

TENNESSEE
⑪

NORTH
CAROLINA
⑩

SOUTH
CAROLINA
①

MISS.
②

ALABAMA
④

GEORGIA
⑤

TEXAS
⑦

LOUISIANA
⑥

FLA.
③

0   500 km

0   200 miles

The Progress of Secession

Circled numbers indicate order of secession

Map 4. The 1860 Presidential Election and the Secession Crisis

Source: After McPherson, J.M. (1988), *Battle Cry of Freedom: The Era of the Civil War* (pub. Oxford University Press, Inc.), p.236. Copyright 1988 by Oxford University Press, Inc. Used by permission of Oxford University Press, Inc.

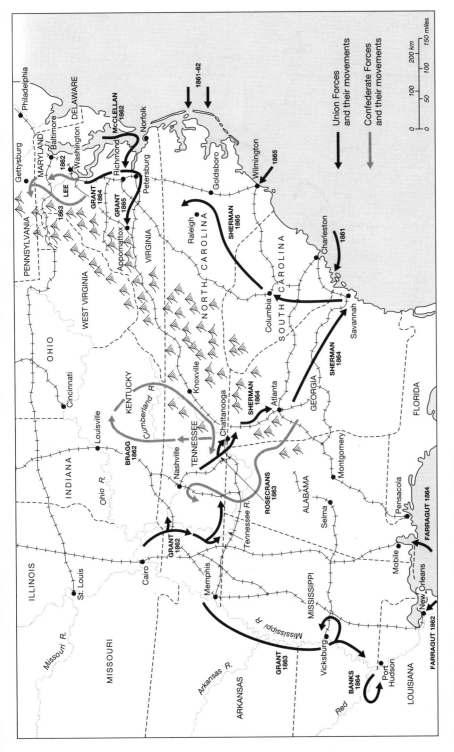

Map 5. Principal Campaigns of the American Civil War

Source: After Parish, P.J. (1975), *The American Civil War* (pub. New York: Holmes & Meier), p.116. Copyright © 1975 by Peter J. Parish. Reproduced with the permission of the publisher.

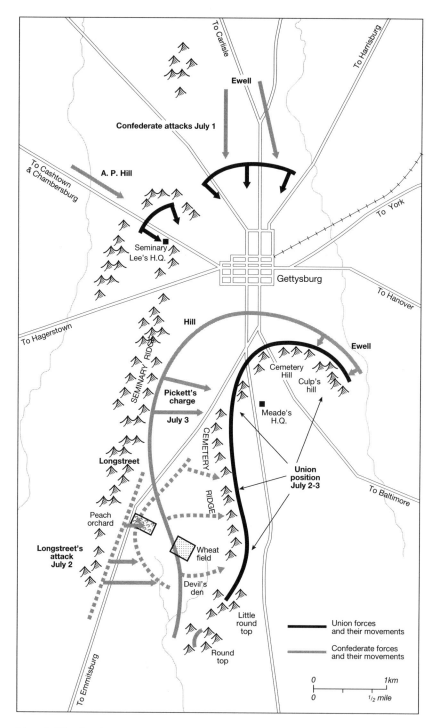

Map 6. The Battle of Gettysburg

Source: After Parish, P.J. (1975), *The American Civil War* (pub. New York: Holmes & Meier), p.289. Copyright © 1975 by Peter J. Parish. Reproduced with permission of the publisher.

Map 7. Gold-Rush California

NOTE ON THE TEXT

Nineteenth-century American spelling was notoriously inconsistent. For the most part I have avoided the use of *sic* in quotations and retained the original spelling. In a very few instances I have added letters and inserted punctuation to improve clarity.

PROLOGUE

INDEPENDENCE DAY, 1854

Maine Yankees began flocking into their state capital, Augusta, on July 3, 1854.[1] They came on foot, on horseback, in farm carts, by train, and on boats along the Kennebec River. Eager to celebrate the city's centennial and the seventy-eighth anniversary of American independence, boisterous youths stayed up into the early hours of the morning firing crackers, blowing on fish horns, and making what one observer called 'other demonstrations of a joyous and patriotic character'. The day itself dawned bright and hot. At sunrise the start of official festivities was signaled by the ringing of Augusta's church bells and a national salute from the United States arsenal. As the city came awake a steady stream of folk converged on Winthrop Street where the main parade was due to assemble. Proceedings were delayed by the late arrival of some fire companies but at eleven o'clock the long column began snaking its way toward the grounds of the state-house.

A cavalcade escort fronted the procession. Behind marched a long line of prominent individuals and groups: the chief marshal, the Augusta band, the mayor, the arrangements committee, the day's orator and poet, the chaplain, the toast master, aldermen, members of the city's common council, city officials, former mayors, mayors from neighboring towns, the Sheriff of Kennebec County, the Governor of Maine, other state officers, members of Maine's congressional delegation, clergymen, justices and officers of the state supreme court, local judges, county commissioners, and registers of deeds and probate. On they came: representatives from the United States military, gnarled veterans of the country's two wars against the British, militia officers, directors of the local school district, Augusta school teachers, the brass band from the coastal town of

Bath, engineers from the fire department, the men of the Atlantic Number 3 and Pacific Number 4 fire companies with their engines, visiting fire companies, Kennebec lumbermen, ship carpenters, and, bringing up the rear, ordinary citizens and 'strangers' from out of town.

The most eye-catching feature of the parade was a colorful group of 20 floats. Each of the carts was bedecked with flowers and represented a specific theme. A local newspaper reporter was especially taken by one marked 'Ship of State'. Drawn by four horses, it was topped by evergreen wreaths that met in the center with what the journalist called those 'glorious words': 'The Union' and, just below, 'These sister states must never be severed'. Although he did not say so, the reporter's eye was doubtless drawn to the young women in the cart. Each one was color coordinated representing not only a state, but also a region. Those representing the northern states wore green, the South blue, the middle states pink, the West 'buff or corn color'. Other wagons bore names such as 'Floral Queen', 'Goddess of Liberty', and 'The Indian Group'. There was even one called 'The Know Nothing', a reference to a new patriotic and anti-Catholic political party which had performed surprisingly well in recent elections.

Gathered in front of a wooden stage erected on the steps of the capitol building, the assembled throng of New England republicans listened solemnly to a national air from the band, a Christian prayer, more music, a reading of Thomas Jefferson's familiar Declaration of Independence and an address by Judge Nathan Weston. The official ceremony concluded with a poem and more music from the band.

Then the procession reassembled and marched proudly to the county court house. Here the fire companies left for their own function while the dignitaries, invited guests, and those who had paid a dollar for the privilege made their way to the rows of dinner tables set out in the open air on Pleasant Street adjoining Montgomery Place. A tall arch at the entrance to the square was surmounted by the motto: 'These Colonies Are, And Of Right Ought To Be Free And Independent States', while its sides were emblazoned with the names of Revolutionary War battles like Bunker Hill.

It was already mid-afternoon, but the diners seemed content to sit through a series of toasts: The Signers of the Declaration of Independence ('They were the chosen instruments through whom, in the darkness of despotism, Deity proclaimed, "Let there be Liberty", and there was Liberty'), General Washington and his Companions in Arms, The Republic ('Better than all the Kingdoms of the world and the glory of them'), The President of the United States, The United States Military ('Foes and friends unite in saying of their past deeds – ENOUGH. May they henceforth keep themselves always ready for action, and "have nothing else to do"'), The State of Maine, The Governor of Maine, The City of Augusta, The Cities and Towns of the Kennebec Valley, Our River, and, finally, Our Women.

More speeches followed. Judge Weston, a busy man this day, looked forward to the growth of Augusta. The Honorable James Bradbury, a well-known Democratic politician, amplified on this theme by lauding the public enterprises of the era. He regarded them all, he said, 'as springing from that *great enterprise* of the Revolutionary Patriots' which secured not only independence but also the Union. The second, he considered, 'was hardly less important to our prosperity as a people than the first. The whole country laid as a wreck upon the water until *the Union* was formed. It was the Union that breathed the breath of life into commerce, manufactures, agriculture, and secured us prosperity at home and respect abroad.' Lavishing praise on the railroads in particular, Mr Bradbury felt another toast coming on. '*The public enterprises of the day*', he proposed, 'While they contribute to the growth, prosperity, and happiness of the people, they strengthen also the bands of the UNION upon which our growth, prosperity, and happiness depend.'

The Reverend William Drew devoted his remarks to one of New England's most famous sons, the late Daniel Webster. After quoting from Webster's stirring Reply to Hayne during the nullification debate of 1830, the minister observed that the 'God-like Daniel' had had his prayer answered, beholding as he did 'what we and all posterity after us ever see, the gorgeous ensign of the Republic full high streaming with not a star or stripe erased'. John W. Chase chose a different subject but ended with another toast: 'Woman's rights. As woman was taken from the hide of man, it is most fitting that she keep her natural position.'

At some point during the festivities (history does not record precisely when) the diners were forced to run for cover by a burst of rain. More showers interrupted both a subsequent contest between the fire companies and the last of the day's official events, a fireworks display at the arsenal. The wet weather, however, did little to dampen the spirits of participants and spectators. As many as 20,000 people had turned out for the occasion, noted one of the local newspapers, yet there had been little drunkenness in the streets. It had been, all things considered, 'a memorable day'.

Note

1.   This account of events in Augusta is based on reports in the *Maine Farmer*, June 29 and July 13, 1854.

I

A ROBBER AND A JAILER: THE ANTEBELLUM REPUBLIC

National development and national identity

Viewed from the perspective of the 1880s the United States was one of the great success stories of the nineteenth century. 'The old nations of the earth creep on at snail's pace,' observed the industrialist, Andrew Carnegie, while 'the Republic thunders past with the rush of the express.'[1] Success came at a high price. Between 1861 and 1865, 620,000 people died in the bloodiest conflict ever fought on the continent of North America. At times it seemed that the United States itself might cease to exist. The Civil War was the great watershed in American history. Without the unity it so dearly bought, Carnegie's express train of a nation might have been derailed on its way out of the depot.

Knowing that the United States was nearly destroyed by the sanguinary events of the early 1860s, it is tempting to conclude that the antebellum Republic was not a viable national entity. Hindsight, however, is a notoriously dangerous tool for historians to deploy. The New Englanders who celebrated Independence Day in Augusta may have been troubled by the fierce congressional debates over the Kansas–Nebraska Act, but patently they had no doubt that the Union was a functioning state to which they were proud to pledge allegiance. The same applied to white southerners who risked their lives fighting for the United States on the battlefields of the Mexican War. It was certainly not unknown for antebellum Americans to use the words 'nation' and 'national' to describe their country. Nor can their preference for terms such as 'Union' and 'Republic' be taken as evidence that they had little sense of national patriotism. In fact Americans were noted during the 1840s for their constant self-promotion – a trait which sometimes annoyed even the Americans themselves. 'I do believe we're the windiest people extant,' remarked the patrician New York diarist, George Templeton Strong, on reading sensational press reports of early military victories during the Mexican War.[2]

In fairness, Americans had plenty of competition in the global bragging stakes and they did indeed have much to brag about. Within the space of a single lifetime their beloved republic, won for them by the exploits of the Revolutionary generation, had been transformed from a satellite of Great Britain confined mainly to the Atlantic littoral to a major regional power capable of crushing the Mexicans in one of the most one-sided wars ever waged in the region. More than that, the United States was rapidly emerging as a significant player on the world stage.

The best evidence for this development was the fact that after the War of 1812 the British began to accept the primacy of the United States in North America. Tensions between the two countries persisted throughout the nineteenth century and several times portended the outbreak of war. But in spite of considerable mutual suspicion at the elite and grassroots levels, British and American leaders worked successfully to limit the damage caused by border disputes, trading rivalries and British antislavery activity. Once President James K. Polk had acquiesced in the 49th parallel as the northwestern boundary line with Canada in 1846 and the Clayton-Bulwer Treaty of 1850 had calmed American fears about British imperialism in Central America, the United States was well placed not only to dominate its own backyard but, with European squabbles confined largely to the Old World, also to continue the task of extending its own influence across the Pacific. Commodore Matthew Perry's bellicose effort to end Japan's trade isolation in 1853 brought few immediate gains. However, it was part of a broader trend toward American economic engagement with the Orient that gathered pace later in the century.

Fundamental to changing external perceptions of the Republic was the steady growth of the American economy. By 1850 the United States had emerged as the world's second largest manufacturing country behind Great Britain. This did not mean that the country had become fully industrialized. As late as 1860 mining, manufacturing, and the hand trades accounted for just 22 percent of aggregated US output compared with contributions of 35 percent from agriculture and 26 percent from commerce.[3] Even excluding the huge amounts of raw cotton exports, the export value of American agricultural commodities exceeded that of semi-finished and finished goods until the twentieth century. The process of industrialization, however, was well underway (and had been since the early decades of the century). The United States lagged well behind Britain in terms of fixed steam power, yet quickly surpassed the former colonial power in terms of railroad mileage. At London's Great Exhibition in 1851 observers were highly complimentary of the 'American System' of standardized production with interchangeable parts that was particularly in evidence in the manufacture of armaments and clocks. Economic development was extensive as well as intensive. The Treaty of Guadalupe Hidalgo which ended the war with Mexico in 1848 added half a million square miles to the national domain and confirmed the United States' existence as a continental power (see Map 1). Commercial cotton and grain cultivation had already moved across the Mississippi by the time the Civil War began. Popular pride in the achievements of the young nation might have been irksome to some, but it seemed fully justified by the material facts.

Historians seeking to explain the carnage of the 1860s often stress the decentralized nature of the antebellum Republic.[4] It is certainly true that the Revolution had imbued Americans with a deep distrust of centralized power. To an extent, their tendency to link power with despotism had been institutionalized by the 1787 federal Constitution, a document revered at least as highly as the Declaration of Independence. The Constitution delegated certain enumerated powers to the central (or federal) government based in Washington, DC, but reserved the rest to the individual states. The intention of the Founding Fathers was to create a balanced federal system in which power was diffused, firstly, between Washington and the states, and secondly, between executive, legislative, and judicial branches of government. Ultimate sovereignty was deemed to rest with the people. Early signs of dysfunctionality were in evidence, but the War of 1812 against Britain revealed the capacity of the United States to protect itself on the world stage and unleashed centralizing forces which further sustained that ability.

Many factors enabled the United States to function and prosper as a sovereign entity before the Civil War. A long tradition of local self-government provided the foundations for a federal system that drew strength from the fact that it was created from the bottom up as well as the top down. This tradition not only imparted legitimacy to the existing polity but also confirmed Americans in their view that they enjoyed a greater degree of liberty than any other people on earth. Yet while Americans were often suspicious of government they did not abjure it altogether at any level. Limited government responsive to the wishes of the people was regarded as beneficial to the smooth operation of society as well as the inexorable march of national progress. Municipal and state governments performed numerous positive functions in the antebellum period. They regulated many aspects of daily life, for example, promoting hygiene and cracking down on criminal and immoral activity. If the federal government itself was not a dominant force in the lives of most Americans in the late 1840s and early 1850s, American citizens were nevertheless affected by its operations in several spheres. Washington, for example, administered the nation's postal service. Every village, town, and city had a federal post office, making that building (and its incumbent postmaster) the most ubiquitous tangible symbols of national authority in the country. The federal government was also by far the nation's largest single landholder. Because Congress had opted for a system of land disposal rather than land management, federal land offices were the main port of call for many Americans seeking to purchase land and settle on the national domain.[5] During the 1850s alone the government sold off nearly 50 million acres, an area roughly one and a half times the size of New York state. Although Jacksonian Democrats railed against the use of national power to promote infrastructural development in the 1830s, the practice of making federal land grants to the states for the purpose of 'internal improvements' was sanctioned by a majority of antebellum politicians. Other vital central functions included national defense, control of external commerce, broad oversight of the money supply, and the administration of the territories (thinly populated areas of the West that were being prepared for full statehood).

A plethora of other centripetal forces existed in the antebellum Republic. The United States was one of the largest free-trade areas on the globe in the nineteenth century. The concomitant growth of a genuinely national market was largely a product of advances in transportation and communications: canals, steamboats, railroads, and the telegraph. These innovations fostered the development of complementary regional economic specializations which provided a solid base for national unity. Whereas the Northeast was the primary center of manufacturing and commercial strength, the South grew raw cotton to satisfy burgeoning demand from the domestic and British textile industries, and the 'West' (what we know today as the Midwest) was fast becoming a mecca for commercial grain farmers.

Religion furnished an important cultural gel. Roughly 10 percent of Americans were members of the main evangelical denominations

(Methodist, Baptist, and Presbyterian) in 1860, rendering evangelical Protestantism 'the principal subculture' of the day.[6] Perfectionist religion was one of the main sources of antebellum voluntarism – the widespread impulse toward civic activism and reform which many observers, Alexis de Tocqueville among them, had singled out as one of the most distinctive features of American life. Although the steady growth of Protestantism was resisted by secular republicans, the pervasive influence of evangelical Christianity joined with economic change to facilitate a metamorphosis of traditional republican values. This fundamental ideological shift transcended region and class and therefore contributed to the creation of a relatively cohesive nation. Hard work, self improvement, personal salvation, and material success may not have been uniquely American values in the Victorian era but they were certainly supralocal ones – as were many of the key institutions (religious newspapers and reform societies, for example) that fueled the expansion of evangelical culture.

Crucial to the development of what Benedict Anderson calls an 'imagined community' was the strong sense among Americans of a shared Revolutionary heritage.[7] Native-born Americans in all parts of the country participated in the kind of ritual festivities that occurred in Augusta on July 4, 1854. National fêtes and parades had been a feature of the Republic since its inception, increasingly popular events that had garnered community-wide participation across the continent. Americans on both sides of the Mason-Dixon Line were taught at home and in school to revere the military exploits of the Revolutionary generation. *Primus inter pares*, of course, was the immortal George Washington, the first president of the United States and the victorious commander of the Continental Army. Mason Locke Weems's *Life of Washington* (1809) was required reading for every child growing up in the early nineteenth century. Its unashamedly hagiographical portrait of the general carried with it an equally unashamedly nationalist message: Washington had fathered a nation that would remain free only as long as its citizens practiced the selfless virtues of the Founders. More scholarly historians such as George Bancroft continued the task of crafting national identity, vaunting American liberty over the despotism and superstition of the Old World. Reading such histories was one way Americans came to define themselves as American. Abraham Lincoln, a keen exponent of Weems, said in 1832 that he hoped 'every man may receive at least, a moderate education, and thereby be enabled to read the histories of his own and other countries, by which he may duly appreciate the value of our free institutions'.[8]

The boastful rhetoric of the 1840s masked a good deal of insecurity. To some extent this was a product of the country's relative youth. As a young people, in terms of both the age profile of the population and the length of the country's existence, the Americans were less than sure of themselves. Culturally they remained shackled to the former metropole, and even in trading and manufacturing terms they remained heavily dependent on economic currents across the Atlantic. Much of the braggadocio noted by observers was compensatory in origin – an outgrowth of fears about the country's lingering dependence on Europe, particularly Britain. But there was more to American insecurity than the fact that the children of Empire had not yet matured to full adulthood. High geographical mobility, a relatively democratic political system, economic change, widespread religious enthusiasm, massive immigration, increasing chronological distance from the Founding Fathers, and sectional tensions generated by the slavery question were at the root of profound uncertainty not only about the individual's role in society but also about the meaning of American identity itself.

National identity, like an individual's social identity, can be seen as a process – an evolving and complex construct built on a variety of overlapping, normally complementary, identities rooted in historical memory, institutional allegiances, a sense of place, ideological attachments, and, in many cases, a perception of group commonality defined in racial or ethnic terms. As Lincoln's comment on reading history revealed, nations, like individuals, often define themselves relationally too; that is, in relation to other people or peoples. The nature of this collective identity shifts over time in response to internal changes, external forces, and events in the way that individual social identity evolves with age, with social interaction, and with landmark changes associated with the life cycle.

For many whites, particularly successful white males, national identity was not a problem. When one of the most renowned white men of his generation, former Union general and president Ulysses S. Grant, sat down to write his memoirs in 1884, he began his narrative with a deceptively simple sentence: 'My family is American, and has been for generations, in all its branches, direct and collateral.'[9] Grant, a true hero of the Republic in spite of his failings as a president, garnered his sense of Americanness from the fact that his forebears had been among the first settlers of Massachusetts and, no less important, that his grandfather had fought against the British throughout the War of Independence. Thousands of Grant's peers could claim a similarly impressive lineage to prove their worth as

Americans. But what of those people who could not lay claim to an ancestor who had fought at Bunker Hill or Saratoga, let alone landed at Plymouth Rock? Between 1846 and 1860 over three million European immigrants flocked to the United States, the majority of them Irish or German Catholics with little in common (or so it appeared to worried Protestants) with respectable native-born Americans. How did an impoverished Irishman living in the slums of New York or Philadelphia manage to define himself convincingly as an American (or even an Irish American) when large numbers of the local population regarded him as something more akin to a 'Negro' or a savage?

And what of the 3.6 million blacks who constituted 15 percent of the country's population in 1850? The free minority of 400,000 could and did insist that their predecessors had played a positive role in the early stages of the Republic, fighting for the United States in the Revolution and the War of 1812. Their claims, however, were disregarded by most white Americans who used experience and scientific racism to equate blackness with slavery, crime, dependency, laziness, and benighted Africa. Skin color was a major determinant of national identity in the antebellum period, a point underlined not only by Chief Justice Roger B. Taney's ruling in the *Dred Scott* case that black people were not citizens of the United States but also by the 1790 Naturalization Law which stated that 'all free white persons' wishing to migrate to the United States and who 'shall give satisfactory proof, before a magistrate, by oath, that they intend to reside therein, and shall take an oath of allegiance, and shall have resided in the United States for one whole year, shall be entitled to the rights of citizenship'.[10] It was this eighteenth-century statute that ultimately helped the European immigrants of the 1840s and 1850s, notably the Irish, to establish their credentials as 'white' and thereby successfully lay claims to American nationality. On the other hand, it was precisely because racial categories were so muddied by the massive antebellum influx of Europeans that free blacks were able to assert their own identity as Americans in contradistinction to the widely despised arrivals from the Old World.

No matter how malleable whiteness may have been as a construct in the mid-nineteenth century, it was clearly central to the meaning of American national identity. All native-born whites thought of themselves as heirs to the republican traditions of the Revolution and vaunted the manifold blessings of living in a country committed to the ideals of liberty, equality, and democracy. Most of the European-born immigrants were no less committed to this image of the United States, even if they were not always welcomed to the New World with open arms. Notwithstanding the growth of xenophobic nativism in the late 1840s and 1850s, the idea that the very strength of the Republic might lie in its ethnic pluralism was a compelling one for some antebellum Americans. Among them was Herman Melville's semi-autobiographical character, the seaman Wellingborough Redburn. 'There is something in the contemplation of the mode in which America has been settled', muses Redburn on observing German migrants waiting to leave Liverpool for the New World, 'that, in a noble breast, should forever extinguish prejudices or national dislikes.'

> You can not spill a drop of American blood without spilling the blood of the whole world ... [O]ur blood is as the flood of the Amazon, made up of a thousand noble currents all pouring into one. We are not a nation, so much as a world ... .[11]

Hindsight reveals that the main obstacle to national unity in the mid-nineteenth century lay not so much in ethnic diversity as in the persistence and growth of strong regional identities. Under normal circumstances personal and local identities bolstered a healthy sense of national community. Under the federal system it was inevitable that strong local attachments would be formed, even more so in an era in which interregional communications were still limited. American identity was thus a compound of multiple and overlapping identities. It embraced loyalty to oneself, the family, local organizations and institutions, one's home town, the state, the region, and the nation. Although these loyalties could and sometimes did conflict, the resulting tensions were normally contained by the built-in flexibility of a system which mandated a fair degree of mutual tolerance. For the most part, then, most native-born whites in the antebellum period thought of themselves not only as Americans but also as, say, Georgians and southerners, or Vermonters and New Englanders. It was precisely because their attachment to place was so profound that their loyalty to the wider nation was strengthened accordingly. Jefferson Davis, the future president of the southern Confederacy, fought bravely against the Mexicans at the battle of Buena Vista in February 1847. He did so for several mutually reinforcing reasons: to further his own status, to improve the prospects for his young family, to boost the reputation of his home state of Mississippi, and for the glory of the United States ('our Republic' as he termed it in July 1846).[12] Multiple identities enabled and emboldened countless other Americans to act as patriots, as they saw it, in the image of the Founding Fathers.

This healthy combination of personal, local, and supralocal identities was tested to the limit in the mid-nineteenth century over one key issue: the place of human bondage in the United States. By 1850 growing numbers of Americans were beginning to sense that slavery (blamed by many for its role in starting the Mexican War) might pose a threat to the nation's welfare. Among them was Margaret Fuller, one of antebellum America's most visible and articulate feminists. Having been on the fringe of the transcendental commune at Brook Farm in the early 1840s, Fuller had begun to write literary and social criticism for Horace Greeley's progressive *New York Tribune* in 1844. Greeley and Fuller shared an interest in communitarian socialism. When Fuller left for Europe to pursue her interest in art and politics, Greeley employed her to send back dispatches for the *Tribune.* Her eighteenth letter, which appeared on January 1, 1848, revealed how rising consciousness over slavery was changing the way some Americans defined their country.

'The American in Europe, if a thinking mind', she wrote from Italy, 'can only become more American.' This was not to say, she continued, that it was not a pleasure in some respects to be in the Old World: 'Although we have an independent political existence, our position toward Europe, as to Literature and the Arts, is still that of a colony, and one feels the same joy here that is experienced by the colonist in returning home.' Politically, however, she found Europe sadly deficient in 'genuine Democracy':

[S]ee this hollow England, with its monstrous wealth and cruel poverty, its conventional life and low, practical aims ... see Russia with its brutal Czar and innumerable slaves; see Austria and its royalty that represents nothing, and its people who, as people, are and have nothing!

This was predictable fare. Many Americans at this juncture in their history denigrated Europe in this fashion in order then to extol the virtues of their democratic republic. At the close of the Mexican War, however, Fuller could not bring herself to do this. She took pride in America's liberty of the press 'and that checks and balances naturally evolve from it which suffice to its government. I may say the minds of our people are alert, and that Talent has a free chance to rise. It is much.' But, she wrote, Americans had found no antidote to the evils of commercialism and rampant individualism.

Then there is this horrible cancer of Slavery, and this wicked War that has grown out of it. How dare I speak of these things here? I listen to the same arguments against the emancipation of Italy, that are used against the emancipation of our blacks; the same arguments in favor of the spoliation of Poland as for the conquest of Mexico. I find the cause of tyranny and wrong everywhere the same – and lo! my Country the darkest offender, because with the least excuse, foresworn to the high calling with which she was called, – no champion of the rights of men, but a robber and a jailer; the scourge hid behind her banner; her eyes fixed, not on the stars, but on the possessions of other men.[13]

Such blistering indictments of the United States at this stage of its history were atypical but not uncommon. Fuller's denunciation and others like it boded ill for those southern whites whose economic livelihood depended on the maintenance of chattel slavery. In just over a decade after Fuller's tragic death at sea in 1850, billowing controversy over the fate of slavery would snap the attachment that many southerners felt toward the wider national community. In order to understand why slavery posed such a threat to the white Republic at a time when the majority of its inhabitants had little interest in the welfare of blacks and seemed set fair to dominate the globe, we must investigate the sources of interregional friction.

Slavery and the antebellum South

Even before the Civil War began, commentators argued that some kind of conflict between the two dominant regions (or 'sections') of the United States was inevitable, given the very different labor systems on which the economies of the North and South were based. Modern leftist historians have built on antebellum notions of an 'irrepressible conflict' between free and slave labor to insist that southerners and northerners were becoming two different peoples, primarily because their social relations were grounded in antipodal economies.[14] Southerners, they argue, dwelt in a pre- or noncapitalist slave society, while northerners were building a genuinely modern section increasingly dependent on capitalist labor relations. There is no doubt that the imperative to protect slavery was the central factor in the South's decision to secede (and since that decision was contested forcibly by the North then slavery must be regarded as an important cause of the war itself). Yet southern slaveholders were quite prepared to fight alongside nonslaveholders for the United States in the late 1840s. In other words, if there were fundamental differences between the sections they did not necessarily mean that domestic strife had to occur.

Economic and social conditions in the United States were diverse. Slavery, a remarkably varied and surprisingly flexible form of labor, was one very important element in an increasingly integrated and specialized national economy responsive to the dictates of the developing domestic and global market. Cotton was the antebellum Republic's most valuable export. High demand in Great Britain – specifically from Lancashire textile mills – brought good prices, fueling the expansion of plantation agriculture into the Southwest and strengthening southern whites' commitment to slave labor. The United States dominated the global market for high quality short-staple cotton. During the Civil War southerners assumed that an embargo on cotton exports could be used to secure Great Britain's intervention on the side of the Confederacy. They were wrong but their mistake was understandable given the sheer volume of the trade. For almost 40 years during the mid-nineteenth century Britain was dependent on its former colony for more than three-quarters of its raw cotton supplies, while by 1860 the value of cotton exports represented two-thirds of America's total exports.[15] By the end of the 1850s the United States was exporting well over one thousand million pounds of raw cotton per year, most of it to Britain. It was little wonder that as the sectional crisis began to deepen, many southerners began to sense that they possessed the wherewithal to plow a separate furrow.

Just over 3.2 million slaves resided in the southern states in 1850, a figure which had risen to nearly 4 million (roughly a third of the total population of the 15 slave states) by the eve of secession. At mid-century 1.8 million of the 2.5 million slaves laboring in the agricultural sector worked on farms that produced primarily cotton. The remainder cultivated other staple crops: 350,000 were engaged in tobacco production, 150,000 in sugar, 125,000 in rice, and 60,000 in hemp. In marked contrast to the Caribbean, most of them did not work on very large plantations. On the eve of secession less than 3 percent of American slaveholders 'owned' 50 or more slaves and only 25 percent of slaves lived on such large holdings.[16] The most extensive plantations were located in the low country of South Carolina and Georgia and the lower reaches of the Mississippi River where the principal staples were rice and sugar respectively. The vast majority of slaves resided on small farms and small to medium-sized plantations where they had some limited opportunity to develop their own distinctive, if syncretic, African-American folkways.

American slaves were bound to their masters by a combination of factors. Proslavery propagandists maintained that their workers were the happy beneficiaries of a system designed to raise them up from African barbarism, but there is no evidence that more than a tiny minority of blacks were content with their position. In a society in which all the cards of power were stacked heavily in favor of whites, North American slaves seldom rebelled in large numbers like their peers in the Caribbean where blacks were usually in a clear majority. What they did do was seek to undermine slavery by running away from the plantations, by damaging farm tools and machinery, and often by working as inefficiently as the system would allow.

American slavery was not just about physical coercion, though the threat and reality of white violence certainly underpinned it. Southern law and southern church leaders sought to hold masters to minimum standards of treatment, while high slave prices before the Civil War meant that it made little economic sense to mistreat human chattels. Some masters, to a greater or lesser extent, imbibed the paternalist strain of proslavery ideology which evolved in response to external attacks on the peculiar institution. Eugene D. Genovese has argued that paternalism was practice and not just rhetoric.[17] Masters and slaves, he suggests, were caught in a complex tangle of interpersonal relations and reciprocal obligations. On the one hand, the masters demanded labor from their slaves; on the other, the slaves expected (and sometimes received) beneficent treatment from their owners. Unfortunately there is no accurate method of determining the number of paternalistic slaveholders. For every kind master in the historical record, there is at least one monster like Charles Manigault, a wealthy Georgia rice planter whose compulsive efforts to minimize spending and maximize workloads resulted in the loss of 90 percent of all slave children born on his plantation.[18] What is clear is that even the most benevolent of slaveholders were forced to sell their charges to service debts and found it difficult to limit mortality rates in the slave quarters. Although American slaves may have been materially better off than their peers in other New World slave societies, the shackles that bound them were tight enough, more so perhaps in the deep South than in the upper South and border states where the system was looser.

Paternalists depicted a cohesive society in which employers and bonded workers lived in harmony with one another. The reality was less impressive. The interstate slave trade broke up tens of thousands of black families in the antebellum South. Michael Tadman suggests that in the upper South (the main slave-exporting region during the antebellum period) roughly one first marriage in three was broken by involuntary separation and nearly half of all children were separated from at least one parent.[19] Use of the whip as a punishment for poor work or disciplinary infractions was frequent and untold numbers of black women were raped by their white masters. Such factors were among the reasons why so many southern churchmen, fearful of God's impending judgment upon a sinful people, implored their fellow whites to improve their treatment of slaves. If paternalism was so integral a factor in southern life, one wonders why prominent local ministers were so loud in their calls for reform.

The controversy over paternalism has fed into the heated scholarly debate over the extent to which the South differed from the modernizing, capitalist North. Much depends here on how one defines capitalism, a notoriously slippery term at the best of times. John Ashworth, for example, has embraced Marx's definition of capitalism as a specific set of social relations between the owner of capital and his wage-earning employee.[20] Since the South's principal working class – the slaves – did not normally work for wages, the region was clearly not a capitalist one. But compare this definition with that preferred by Richard D. Brown. For Brown, capitalism can be used to describe 'a money economy where market dictates prices and where private, profit-seeking patterns of ownership and investment operate, whether or not these patterns are rational, efficient, or innovative'.[21] If one employs a non-Marxist definition of capitalism, the notion that the South was some kind of semifeudal society begins to vanish before one's very eyes.

The slave South was both similar to and different from the rest of the country. Precisely because of slavery it was less economically developed than parts of the North, especially the Northeast. Aside from larger port cities such as New Orleans and centers of genuine industrial activity in the upper South, the southern states lacked the kind of dominant commercial bourgeoisie which was coming to the fore above the Mason-Dixon Line. The region did have an urban middle class, consisting of merchants, lawyers, teachers, clergymen, and other professionals, but in terms of size and influence it was dwarfed by its northern equivalent. This was largely a result of the South's slow pace of urbanization. Only a tenth of its people lived in places containing more than 2,500 inhabitants in 1860 compared with just over a quarter in the free states.

This is not to say, however, that slaveholders stood at the apex of a backward society. The group of large slaveholders which exercised disproportionate influence in the region was not the barrier to nineteenth-century progress that some external critics of slavery believed. John C. Calhoun, for example, the South Carolina cotton planter often regarded as the godfather of secession, was a staunch advocate of progressive agriculture and heavily involved in local and regional railway promotion. Some of his fellow slaveholders were less enthusiastic about running up public debts to pay for what they regarded as grandiose schemes of internal improvement, though many shared Calhoun's enthusiasm for railroads. While slavery limited industrial growth in the deep South by channeling surplus capital into land and slaves, the generally high returns on cotton and other staple products indicate that most planters were motivated primarily by the desire to make money. In common with the commercial and manufacturing elites of the North, they usually sought to maximize profits, they invested a portion of their wealth in status-enhancing goods such as houses and furniture, and they adhered to most of the commonplace nineteenth-century ideas of progress. While it is true that they did not always act as rational economic beings, they were nevertheless enmeshed in the developing capitalist system.[22] They participated frequently in the domestic labor market for slaves, relied heavily on external sources of investment capital, and were almost entirely dependent for their wellbeing on outside demand for their staple products. Although the slave South may have been a hybrid society, only partly capitalist, its dominant elite was as ruthlessly entrepreneurial in its own way as any northern ironmaster or railroad magnate.

The fundamental Americanness of the planter class was most visible when its representative men encountered societies outside the United States. On the grand tour of Europe they were generally as enraptured by the architecture and landscape of Italy as other visitors from home, but no less appalled by the poverty and decrepitude that they found – flaws that they ascribed to the baleful effects of Roman Catholicism and authoritarian monarchical rule. The southern reaction to Mexico was very similar. Jefferson Davis, a rich Mississippi cotton planter, insisted that if the Mexicans had had the right to dispossess the Aztecs because the latter had not cultivated the land properly, the same argument justified the United States taking land from the Mexicans. The Mexicans, he told the Senate in March 1847:

produce little to that which the country is capable of yielding; and year by year the amount is steadily decreasing. The country is going to waste, villages are depopulated, fields once highly productive in all that nature in her bounty yielded to the industry of man, now lie uncultivated, and marked only by the remains of the irrigatory ditches by which they were formerly watered.[23]

Such remarks bore an uncanny similarity to northern descriptions of the South during the 1850s. Slavery, ran the free-soil critique, was both morally and economically retrogressive. Southerners like Davis found such attacks not only insulting but also mystifying for the simple reason that their region was patently not laggard when compared with virtually every country in the world. Only Great Britain, the Low Countries and parts of the North surpassed the South in terms of urbanization and economic development. As southern responses to other societies and cultures reveal, it makes little sense to see the planter class as anything other than quintessentially American: Protestant, individualistic, acquisitive, and deeply committed to the values of republican government. Yet while it is easy to exaggerate the differences between North and South, it is true that slavery did produce a mindset that was different from that of the North in one critical respect: an overriding preoccupation among southern whites with the maintenance of the existing race-based social order. Herein lay the seeds of secession and civil war.

Just 12 percent of the 350,000 slaveholders resident in the South at the time of secession qualify for the description of planter under the conventional modern definition of this term: someone who owned 20 or more slaves. Although only a quarter of southern white families possessed slaves, slave ownership was relatively widespread in the fertile 'black belts' of those states at the forefront of the secession movement in 1860–61 (see Map 2). In South Carolina, Mississippi, Alabama, and Georgia between 35 and 50 percent of white families held slaves.[24] Further north large numbers of slaveholders resided in the staple growing districts of states like Tennessee, Kentucky, and Virginia.

Inevitably, friction often characterized relations between planters, small slaveholders, and nonslaveholders (a diverse group which included most urban dwellers and much larger numbers of propertyless whites and yeoman farmers, both landholders and tenants). None of these groups were themselves monolithic. Planters disagreed with one another on virtually every topic. Louisiana sugar planters, for example, favored high tariffs to protect the domestic sugar industry, whereas cotton planters were normally inveterate freetraders (because of their high consumption of externally manufactured goods and their need to export cotton to Britain). Small slaveholders and nonslaveholders were riven by class, status, and ethnicity. A well-to-do lawyer in Savannah, one of the South's principal cotton entrepôts, certainly had little in common with an Irishman working on the docks. The relatively self sufficient inhabitants of the upland areas of the region, such as the hills of northern Alabama and Georgia and the mountains of East Tennessee and western North Carolina and Virginia, chafed at the rule of slaveholding and commercial elites based in the more economically mature areas of their states. The urban bourgeoisie often clashed with that portion of the planter class which sometimes opposed its developing plans for 'reform' (a catch-all term which included calls for public schools, manufacturing, and tighter moral discipline). Planters worried about the possibility that their dominance might be challenged seriously by those who did not have a major financial stake in slavery. For all these deep social fissures, however, southern whites had one thing in common. By 1850 they could all agree that slavery was the mainstay of southern society. As William H. Trescott, a South Carolina cotton planter, put it: 'Slavery informs all our modes of life, all our habits of thought, lies at the basis of our social existence, and of our political faith.'[25]

For several decades after the Revolution there had been strong signs that southern whites might be ready to abolish slavery. Washington and Jefferson were famously ambivalent about the institution and a state constitutional convention in Virginia seriously considered the possibility of abolition as late as 1830–31. The enormous profits to be garnered from slave-grown staples and the emergence during the Jacksonian era of a strident abolitionist movement in the North which vilified southern whites as moral reprobates put an end to any chance that slavery could be destroyed from within. While some critical voices could still be heard in some of the border states, notably Kentucky, the white South closed ranks from the late 1830s onwards. Increasingly, slavery was hailed as a positive good and those who criticized it were ostracized, exiled, or physically attacked. When middle-class reformers called for economic diversification and state-funded public schools in the 1850s, they did so within the context of a relatively mature slave society which they assumed to be permanent. None of the Presbyterian divines who called for improved treatment of slaves in the same decade considered the possibility that slavery itself might be dismantled. Why should they have done? Slavery underpinned white privilege, for their color was the most important thing that southern whites had in common. General emancipation would not only deprive the slaveholders themselves of the principal source of their elevated position in society (not to say millions of dollars worth of investments), but it would also rob nonslaveholders of the precious material and psychological benefits from being neither black nor enslaved. As William Cooper has observed, southern whites of all classes understood that slavery was the foundation of their own liberty.[26] They simply could not contemplate a future in which large numbers of blacks lived among them as free citizens.

The point applies as much to white women as to white men. In common with all American women, the lives and identities of female southerners were conditioned by gender, class, and race relations. Like their northern peers they were legally second-class citizens – deprived of the vote, equipped with only limited property rights and, at least in ideological terms, restricted to the private sphere by a pervasive cult of domesticity. What was unique about their situation was that slavery generated a resolutely patriarchal society in which the male-dominated household was the primary unit of production and reproduction and thus the regnant model for the wider world.[27] While the possibilities for unorthodox behavior did exist – particularly at the lower reaches of the social scale – slavery imposed on southern women a degree of conformity to patriarchal norms that did not prevail even in the undeniably sexist (but more plural) North. Plantation mistresses sometimes railed against the penchant of southern men – their faithful husbands excepted – for sexual relations with female slaves, but the vast majority of them adhered to the view of Louisa S. McCord, a well-to-do South Carolinian, that women should submit to the rule of their husband-protectors, eschew ambition and, by no means coincidentally, regard blacks as a biologically inferior species.

We know far more about slaveholding women like McCord than we do of white females belonging to the yeomanry or the widely despised stratum of poor whites. Many non-elite women could be found working on the land as well as engaging, like most plantation mistresses, in household production. Almost certainly they shared McCord's racial views and attachment to the existing racial order. Had they not done so one might have expected to see some evidence of southern women becoming involved in reform movements of all kinds during the years preceding the Civil War. Such evidence does not exist. Living in a rural slave society, southern white women lacked not only the urban networks essential for the promotion of social reform, but also the will. Whereas local charitable activity was widely practiced by evangelical women, the imperative to preserve slavery resulted in northern reform movements such as abolitionism and women's rights being labeled entirely disreputable. Even the homegrown temperance movement, heavily reliant on female involvement, had fizzled out by the 1850s.

Wealthy cotton lords such as John C. Calhoun had no compunction in using the defense of slavery to promote regional political unity in the face of perceived northern aggression. Writing to a Marylander in August 1847, Calhoun pulled no punches in his description of a post-emancipation South. Any moves to contain and abolish slavery, he wrote, would threaten the South with a 'whole train of calamities':

> You will be penned in with your black population, as every other slave State will be, while the non slave holding States will never cease their agitation until blacks are placed in all respects on an equality, politically & socially with their former masters; when they would govern us and our posterity through our former slaves, and their posterity. Think not, I look too far ahead, or that I am deceived. I see the future thus far, if we do not meet & repel the attack, as clearly, as I do the rising of the sun tomorrow.[28]

Slavery did not guarantee that southern whites would agree on everything. Far from it. Common whites were tenacious defenders of their rights and, away from some of the established plantation areas where slaves were numerous, they contested the gentry's claims to authority. However, as members of a *herrenvolk* society, one in which whiteness engendered self-respect, power, and profit, they often shared Calhoun's dark fears of emancipation and clung to slavery as the fount of their liberties.

The political power of the plantocracy testified to the fact that nonslaveholding farmers and landless whites were not unwilling to defer to the rule of wealthy men. In 1860 in North Carolina, for example, 85 percent of state legislators were slaveowners despite the fact that less than a third of white families possessed slaves. Only 3 percent of white families belonged to the planter class, yet more than a third of the lawmakers in the Tarheel state came from this elite social group.[29] Even though planter domination was less evident

elsewhere apart from South Carolina, slaveowners of all kinds dominated state political office throughout the deep South. Perhaps,
as Bruce Collins asserts, slaveholders failed to inspire organized
opposition precisely because they did not act as a cohesive unit.
However, their political visibility alone is suggestive of the inordinate
influence they waged in a region where the social order was conditioned by the existence of black slavery.[30]

Life in the 'free states'

By the late 1840s growing numbers of southerners agreed with
Calhoun's contention that the northern, nonslaveholding states posed
a concrete danger to the social stability of the South. The main
source of this perceived threat was a belt of states running from
thickly wooded Maine on the northeastern border with Canada
through the manufacturing areas of southern New England and the
mid-Atlantic region to the breadbasket of the rapidly developing
Midwest. Although the Mexican War vastly extended the domain of
the United States, the mineral-rich lands of the Far West remained
only thinly settled at mid-century.[31]

The North did not exist as a formal political entity in 1850 any
more than the South, though some antislavery men had already
started to call for unity in the face of what they saw as mounting
southern aggression. The free states (or 'nonslave states' as Calhoun
preferred to call them) contained two-thirds of America's total
population. They embraced a disparate collection of subregions,
each of them distinguished by a particular ethnic and social mix
and increasingly specialized contributions to the national economy.
New England, once the center of Puritanism in the New World,
was the most urbanized and ethnically homogeneous of these areas,
though its coastal towns and cities (especially the large cultural and
commercial center of Boston, Massachusetts) attracted more than
their share of Irish immigrants. Economically, however, it was diverse,
with the southern portion of the region being significantly more
developed than the north. Whereas industrialization had begun to
take hold in the form of factory production in towns such as Lowell,
Waltham, Worcester, Springfield, and Providence, small farmers
dominated the rocky soils of Vermont and New Hampshire. Much
of Maine was still a wilderness. Timber, fish, and ships numbered
among its most profitable exports. The whaling industry centered in
salty places like Nantucket and New Bedford remained an important

source of employment in the region but the industry was already on the verge of terminal decline.

The mid-Atlantic states stood at the core of American economic, political, and cultural life throughout the nineteenth century. New York was already emerging as a global metropolis before the Civil War. A vibrant, cosmopolitan city with a population of just under a million, it was the nation's leading banking hub as well as its most important trading port and a major manufacturing center.[32] Largely due to its magnificently situated harbor, the entrepreneurial drive of its merchants, and the construction of the Erie Canal which channeled midwestern farm products to the port via the Great Lakes and the Hudson River, New York's economic preeminence helped to make it the literary center of the United States. Although the patrician elites of Boston would continue to dispute this latter position until the end of the century, New York's publishing houses were bigger and its newspapers, notably Horace Greeley's *Tribune*, more influential. Young writers and poets keen to celebrate the democratic thrust of the era found Manhattan irresistible – a churning mass of humanity embracing European immigrants, free blacks, and native-born workers clustered in squalid tenements, a burgeoning middle class eager to consume new mass-produced goods at fancy department stores like Alexander Stewart's Marble Palace, and the super-rich elite of Vanderbilts and Astors who were busy building their mansions uptown. The city was intolerant of myopic provincialism and Old World pretension. When the volatile but talented scribbler, John L. O'Sullivan, chose to remove his talismanic journal, the *Democratic Review*, from the decidedly provincial environs of Washington, DC, in 1841, it was almost inevitable that he would choose to relocate in New York. As well as brilliantly articulating the Anglophobic and expansionist desires of the late Jacksonian period, O'Sullivan's magazine directly and indirectly fostered the talents of new writers such as Walt Whitman and Herman Melville. The raw energy of their work was, at least in some measure, an outgrowth of their immersion in the sights and sounds of Manhattan and its ambitious neighbor Brooklyn (itself the third largest city in the country).

Rivaling, and in some respects surpassing, the New York area as an industrial hub was Philadelphia, a center for the metal trades and the North's thriving textile manufacturing sector. Like New York, the City of Brotherly Love was growing rapidly in size and diversity. The population of over half a million in 1860 included large numbers of Irish, Germans, and free blacks who competed for employment with native-born white workers, a fact which did nothing to promote working-class solidarity. Philadelphia's industrial growth owed most to its broad, highly skilled artisan base which was ably exploited by entrepreneurs like Matthias Baldwin, a former jeweler's apprentice and toolmaker whose interest in developing machinery for textile production soon led him into building steam engines. After successfully designing a railway locomotive in 1831–32, he entered into a partnership to construct engines for the nascent American railroad market. By mid-century his Broad Street locomotive works employed around 400 smiths, boilermakers, patternmakers, molders, carpenters, and other specialist craftsmen.[33] Baldwin's employees were unusual in that they labored for good wages in a relatively large manufacturing plant. Over two-thirds of the city's working people continued to toil in small shops lacking the steam engines and water wheels commonly found in the textile sector and heavy industries.[34]

What Charles Sellers has called 'the market revolution' had penetrated the mid-Atlantic states to a greater extent than any other region of the United States.[35] However, in terms of population, the fastest growing area of the North was the Midwest, accurately described by an enthusiastic British observer as embracing 'probably the greatest tract of fertile land on the surface of the globe'.[36] Barred to slavery by the Northwest Ordinance of 1787, the flat prairie lands north of the Ohio River were being peopled swiftly by native-born and European migrants. Border state southerners, New England Yankees, Pennsylvanians and New Yorkers swept across the region during the first half of the nineteenth century. The aim of most of them was to secure a farm on which they could lead prosperous and independent lives. Roughly $500 and ready access to credit was normally reckoned to be the minimum requirement for setting up a farm in the antebellum West, unless, that is, one had received a federal land bounty certificate in return for military service.[37] This was a not inconsiderable sum of money and one that placed farming out of the reach of most common laborers and urban artisans.

Most of those who purchased unimproved land from individual speculators, land companies, or directly from the federal government were themselves farming folk who had not only the money but also the skills needed to turn prairie grass into marketable crops of wheat and corn. While subsistence farming persisted in parts of the lower Midwest, the majority of these migrants sensed the material benefits likely to accrue from involvement in the market. By 1850 commercial agriculture had begun to dominate counties astride the rivers and railroads of Ohio, Indiana, and Illinois – most of the corn, wheat, and pork exported from the region being produced on family-owned farms. Involvement in supralocal trade incurred dependence on market forces. However, buoyant domestic and foreign demand for American grain and widespread use of evolving technology such as the reaper-mower made midwestern farming a prosperous enterprise in the late 1840s and 1850s. When the Crimean War broke out in 1854 American farmers as far west as Iowa benefited from the resulting increase in demand for foodstuffs.

The rapid growth of commercial farming in the region was accompanied by significant urban and industrial development. Forward-looking cities such as Cleveland, Cincinnati, and that miracle of the prairies, Chicago, functioned not only as transportation hubs for their rural hinterlands but also as processing centers for local grain and pork. These substantial urban places (as well as smaller towns dotted along the rivers) were a magnet for European-born as well as American-born migrants seeking work along the region's watercourses, railroads, and lakesides and in its abundant small-scale packing houses and flour mills. Many of the Europeans did settle in the countryside, often founding their own separate rural communities, but from the late 1840s onwards the Germans and Irish congregated in large numbers in the port cities of the upper Mississippi and the Great Lakes region. In 1860 foreign-born migrants made up 50 percent of the population of Chicago and 60 percent of that of St Louis.[38]

Some evangelical leaders regarded the accompanying spread of Roman Catholicism in the Mississippi Valley as a major threat to republican liberty, and rushed to meet the challenge with a combination of thunderous jeremiads and feverish missionary activity. Most contemporaries, however, equated the West with opportunity. Even if they might condescendingly regard it as a land without the basic trappings of nineteenth-century civilization and were divided over how to distribute the precious resources of the region, easterners saw it as the hope of America. For some it represented a safety valve for overpopulation in the crowded Northeast. For others it offered fulfillment of Thomas Jefferson's agrarian dream – a nation of independent yeoman farmers stretching from the Atlantic to the Pacific.

Western settlers, rough hewn though their manners may have been, tended to be perpetual optimists. Some entertained the possibility that their section might be able to mediate between North and South. Was it not true, after all, that their region encapsulated the expansionist dynamic at the heart of national life? And was not the Midwest in particular an ethnic and cultural crucible where

Europeans learned how to become Americans and where northerners and southerners came together as members of the same national community? Such hopes were readily comprehensible in the highly charged political atmosphere of the late 1840s when local politicians such as Stephen A. Douglas of Illinois were able to yoke the expansionist rhetoric of Manifest Destiny to the cause of national unity. Yet ultimately they proved to be illusory. The Midwest could not rise above the sectional conflict for it had become, economically, a satellite territory of the Northeast. Because the slave South was largely self sufficient in food, the Midwest exported most of its farm goods to the relatively urbanized Northeast and to Great Britain. Although some of this trade still went down the Mississippi to New Orleans, the network of canals and railroads radiating out from the mid-Atlantic states fed the bulk of it away from the South. New Yorkers and Philadelphians consumed western food products, while western farmers increasingly relied on credit and manufactured commodities supplied from the Northeast.[39]

The developing East–West axis grounded in interregional trade and communications was strengthened by the fact that southern migrants were becoming a smaller element of the West's population over time. As settlers from New England, the mid-Atlantic states and Europe poured into the region, southern-born whites found their influence confined mainly to the lower Midwest. Tellingly, the folkways of those who inhabited areas like southern Illinois and Indiana – a fondness for corn and sweet potatoes, low levels of literacy, and a seeming inability to build adequate farm buildings – attracted widespread criticism from New England Yankees whose puritanical and commercial zeal often knew no bounds. Slowly the various American and even European cultures of the region did begin to blend, but in these early decades of settlement the Midwest was less a melting pot than the site of an ongoing *Kulturkampf.*

Apart from the obvious economic indicators, perhaps the clearest sign that the North was becoming a recognizably modern society was the emergence throughout the section of both a wage-earning working class and a confident urban bourgeoisie. Both were spawned by the advent of a full-blown capitalist economy in the United States. Wage labor spread rapidly during the 1840s and 1850s. This distinctively modern mode of economic relations had once been despised by republicans as 'wage slavery' – as corrosive of independence. Now it was in the process of being legitimized as 'free labor'.[40] Efforts to draw a telling contrast between northern free labor and southern slavery had met with sharp opposition from northern working men in the Jacksonian period. By 1850 workers were beginning to come to terms with a system which (and here the contrast with slavery was critical) guaranteed a regular income and allowed for some possibility of job mobility. Of course, the periodic economic downturns that were the bane of industrial capitalism furnished potent ammunition for those cynics who questioned the virtues of contract. Fortunately for the devotees of commerce and industry, such disasters seemed to be a thing of the past in the late 1840s. The happy combination of abundant and affordable land, free labor and internal free trade appeared to have delivered the possibility of upward social mobility to large numbers of northern whites by 1850.

The antebellum northern working class was ethnically diverse. Indeed, a major fault line existed between American skilled workers and European-born or non-white unskilled laborers. By contrast, the amorphous middle class was predominantly native-born. In the representative Hudson River town of Kingston, New York, for example, native-born Americans dominated all the main professions as well as the higher categories of property ownership. Poor Americans certainly could be found in Kingston but as many as 90 percent of the town's adult Irish males were probably wage earners, the vast majority of them poorly paid unskilled workers.[41] While laboring people in the urban North participated actively in the public sphere by joining voluntary groups such as fire and military companies, by participating in street parades, by voting regularly and enthusiastically in elections, and sometimes by organizing unions and promoting strike action, local power was wielded primarily by the wealthier and (in residential terms) more persistent middle class. In the Kingston area, more than 70 percent of key party offices were occupied by men with high-ranking occupations. Lawyers, merchants, and other white-collar professionals furnished 57 percent of village and town officeholders and more than three-quarters of county officers.[42] Farmers remained a significant force in northern legislatures but, whereas wealthy planters continued to wield a disproportionate amount of political power in the antebellum South, northern political life was falling increasingly under the influence of the section's urban middle class.

There was, of course, a heavily gendered aspect to the distribution of political power in the North. Because women could not vote, all politicians were men. Fading notions of republican motherhood and more modern middle-class and evangelical notions of domesticity helped to place heavy constraints on antebellum American women.

However, it would be wrong to assume that all northern women were thus confined to hidden lives in the nominally private sphere of home and family. Some non-elite women may have assimilated such allegedly feminine virtues as piety and submission, yet their hard lives as mothers, wives, and wage earners (large numbers of black and foreign-born women were forced to take poorly paid jobs as domestic servants or seamstresses) left them with little time, let alone money, to contemplate buying soft furnishings from one of the new shopping emporiums. Not that middle-class women themselves were necessarily splendid exemplars of true womanhood. Eastern and midwestern farm women played a critical role in household affairs: milking cows, churning butter, processing slaughtered animals, cooking food, and making and mending clothes. Elite urban women with a working husband came closest to the ideal, but they too suffered grievously (sometimes fatally) at childbirth, were injured by discriminatory laws that made it difficult for them to control their own property, found divorce hard to secure when trapped in an unhappy marriage, and were prisoners of the latest ridiculous fashion.

Most bourgeois women did value respectability and status and discovered in religion, especially evangelical Protestantism, an important source of solace and stoicism. However, they were not necessarily passive occupants of a discrete and largely feminine private sphere. Crucial here was the reformist impulse that derived from the act of Christian benevolence. American social norms conceded women's right to engage in charitable activities. The latter were regarded as a fit extension of woman's innate moral sensibility. In marked contrast to their southern counterparts who were constrained by the existence of slavery, some women in the antebellum North found their Christian desire for individual perfection spilling over into semipolitical efforts to secure social change. Even without the vote, thousands of northern women played a crucial role in promoting temperance, antislavery, and female education – one of their principal defenses being that such efforts stemmed from their sex's duty to protect and improve the home. By the late 1840s a minority of the most radical reformers, their consciousness raised especially by involvement in the abolitionist movement, had concluded that women were scarcely less oppressed than slaves and that it was time to contest their own political and legal oppression.

In 1848 two highly literate women reformers with links to the antislavery movement, Lucretia Mott and Elizabeth Cady Stanton, called a national meeting to discuss all aspects of women's oppression. The resulting Seneca Falls convention held in upstate New York on July 19–20 was attended by 200 women and more than 40 men. The meeting passed a series of resolutions (including a demand for the suffrage) and a 'Declaration of Sentiments and Resolutions' that averred 'all men and women are created equal'.[43] The convention's work was too radical for some of the delegates, let alone the majority of middle-class northern women who adhered to more conservative views. However, Stanton was in no mood to accept criticism from hypocritical opponents who contended that the cause of women's rights was contrary to the teaching of the Bible. When taken in 'its true spiritual meaning', she and a fellow coworker insisted publicly after the convention, the Bible was 'the great charter of human rights ... Why[,] the self-styled Christians of our day have fought in and supported the unjust and cruel Mexican war, and have long held men, women, and children in bondage.'[44] Such outspoken views (which were sometimes accompanied by calls for dress reform) were not typical of the majority of northern women at this juncture of American history, and judged by the most conventional definition of politics women remained marginal actors throughout the 1850s. However, even more conservative female activists such as Catharine Beecher insisted that women should become more positive agents within the putative domestic sphere. Beecher herself was a tireless campaigner for women's education and by the time of the Civil War had contributed significantly to the drift of northern women into a once male-dominated teaching profession.

Notwithstanding the coalescence of discernibly modern classes and values, the extent to which the free states were economically developed in 1860 should not be exaggerated. As intimated above, the North could be more accurately described as an industrializing than an industrialized society. Just like the South, the North's importance in the global economy lay in its capacity to produce agricultural products for the European, particularly the British, market. Whereas the South exported cotton, the North traded wheat and wheat flour. Because of the United States' low *ad valorem* duties on a wide range of imported goods, British manufactures such as woolens, high-grade cotton items and railroad iron poured across the Atlantic in return, often forcing American capitalists into niche markets.[45] As a result economic development was uneven across the section. Textiles and iron led the way in technological innovation and factory production. But industrial productivity growth in the 1850s was primarily a result of the continuing expansion of small-scale manufacturing. Farming remained a principal mainstay of the northern economy, even if the trend away from agriculture was clearly visible. Two-thirds of northerners were living in rural areas at the outbreak of the Civil War.

When Ralph Waldo Emerson, one of the most eminent American thinkers of his generation, went to lecture in Great Britain in 1847–48 he found a society operating at a much faster pace than his own. 'The buildings are on a scale of size and wealth out of all proportion to ours', he gasped at one point of his visit.[46] While it is true that Emerson was a resident of small-town Massachusetts, even the great cities of the North were still in the early stages of spatial expansion. New York, for example, had not fully colonized Manhattan, let alone the city's modern-day hinterlands in the outer boroughs, suburban New Jersey and Long Island. George Templeton Strong took an idyllic horse ride across the Hudson one hot summer afternoon in 1847. '[T]he by ways and back roads of New Jersey,' he noted in his diary, 'are paths of pleasantness, shady and quiet, and not without glimpses of real picturesqueness at times – views of the river and of Newark meadows and so on.'[47] Another diarist, an Englishman named Henry Bright, arrived in New York five years later and was moved to describe the view from Broadway as reminiscent of the genteel Warwickshire spa town of Leamington.[48] The North was changing quickly but these observations suggest we should not overestimate the extent of that development in 1860.

As well as being engines of modernity, northern cities were notoriously turbulent places. Frontier conditions and slavery helped to make the South a more lawless society than the Northeast, but the urban North witnessed rising crime rates as well as sporadic mob violence in the late 1840s and 1850s. Most of the mob action was less a result of racism and anti-abolitionist feeling (as it had been in the Jacksonian period) than a combustible mix of identity politics and class and ethnic friction. One of the most sensational outbreaks of disorder occurred in Manhattan on May 10, 1849 when a large group comprised of mainly Irish toughs from the Bowery disrupted an elite theater performance given by the renowned English trage-dian, William Macready, and were met with the full force of the militia. Twenty-two people died in the ensuing bloodbath. The Astor Place Riot shocked New Yorkers, particularly upper-class residents who feared social unrest and were unsympathetic to attempts by the Anglophobic Irish underclass to act like patriotic Americans. Arriving at Astor Place two days after the riot, George Templeton Strong described something akin to a scene from the Mexican War. Everything 'looked much in earnest –', he observed with evident relish:

guns loaded and matales lighted – everything ready to sweep the streets with grape at a minute's notice, and the police and troops well disposed to do it whenever they should be told. The mob were in a bitter bad humor but a good deal frightened ... Some of the cavalry were badly hit with paving stones, but as soon as the Unwashed were informed that unless they forthwith took themselves off they would be treated with a little artillery practice, they scampered.[49]

Disease represented a deadlier threat than urban violence to the people of the antebellum North. What reliable information we have on mortality during the first three-quarters of the nineteenth century indicates that there was no significant reduction in death rates before the Civil War. The positive effects of rising real income per capita and steady economic growth after 1840 appear to have been offset by large-scale immigration, poor working conditions, and inadequate municipal services (for example, housing, refuse collection, water provision, and sewerage).[50] There were, moreover, no major breakthroughs in medical knowledge during the mid-nineteenth century. The results were grim. Indians, blacks, the poor, the young, and the elderly were most at risk from diseases such as yellow fever, typhoid, cholera, malaria, and tuberculosis, but these indiscriminate killers were no respecters of class or race. With disease so prevalent and most doctors unable to distinguish between lethal poisons and effective curatives, a growing number of middle-class northerners turned in desperation to alternative remedies. Probably the most effective was 'hydropathy', a holistic lifestyle change requiring the patient to eat in moderation, abstain from all drugs, take frequent walks in the outdoors, and, perhaps most importantly of all, consume vast quantities of water (which did at least have the effect of flushing quack medicines from the system).

If most individuals were somewhat less prepared for their passing than Mary Moody Emerson, the philosopher's aunt who carried her shroud with her at all times, the awful frequency and suddenness with which death visited the antebellum northern family highlights the limits on progress in the North and also helps to explain the influence of evangelical religion in nineteenth-century America. The loss of children was particularly hard to accept but, in a culture heavily infused with sentimentality, it was at least possible for mothers and fathers to view the transition of an innocent soul from earthly cares to heavenly bliss with some degree of resignation.

Death and disease were as familiar to malaria-prone southerners as they were to northerners. So too were many other basic features of antebellum life. The majority of the white inhabitants of both regions shared a profound respect for the nation's Revolutionary heritage, a prosperous farming sector devoted to the export of valuable staples, whiteness, language, evangelical Protestantism, and a commitment to nineteenth-century ideas of progress. Slavery was at the heart of the differences, perceived and actual, between them but it did not have to separate them. Most northern whites clearly valued the Union over the liberty of black people, and bonded labor complemented free labor by cultivating the raw cotton that fed northern textile mills. Slavery did possess the potential to divide Americans along sectional lines. This was evident during the fierce debates over the Gag Rule and Texas annexation in the late 1830s and 1840s. Both the Methodist and Baptist churches, moreover, had split over the issue of slavery. The nation, however, seemed safe enough as long as the existing political system was able to contain the inevitable tensions created by the existence of the peculiar institution.

The second party system

While the fragmented nature of power in antebellum America played into the hands of slaveholders so too, for the most part, did the operations of the political system. Two parties had dominated the political landscape of the Jacksonian era: the Democrats and the Whigs.[51] Slaveholders played a leading role in both organizations, each of which attracted significant support from large numbers of southerners and northerners. Crucially, then, the 'second party system' (a term invented by modern political scientists) was a genuinely national system. Because most northern Whigs and Democrats required some incentive to alienate their respective southern wings, they tended to suppress any doubts which they might have harbored over slavery or, at the very least, to subordinate reservations and grievances over the issue to more pressing topics.

This was especially the case in the early years of the system when the Democratic and Whig coalitions had solidified primarily over governmental responses to the cycle of recession, recovery, and depression that dominated American political life in the late 1830s and early 1840s. On the whole Whig strategists benefited enormously from the Van Buren administration's conservative response to the economic downturn, mobilizing large numbers of voters on the back of calls for positive government. Henry Clay's 'American System' – a national bank, federal aid for infrastructural development, and high import tariffs to promote domestic manufactures – proved an alluring alternative to the Democrats' emphasis on *laissez-faire*, states' rights and hard money. Indeed, the existence of a coherent program of federally sponsored economic development did much to secure victory for the Whigs in the 1840 presidential contest, their first success at that level.

Although the refusal of President John Tyler, a states' rights Virginian, to embrace Clay's project helped the Democrats to reassert their Jacksonian-era dominance, the Whigs remained competitive in most areas of the country during the 1840s. Still dismissed by the opposition as the tool of patrician elites, they had gone a long way toward embracing the new democratic politics which had been spawned by the Revolution, spatial expansion, economic change, and the spread of grassroots evangelical religion. The very rich on both sides of the Mason-Dixon Line did tend to exhibit a preference for the Whigs who claimed to represent the values of an ordered and respectable society, but the same was true of large numbers of up-wardly mobile folk, many of them Godfearing evangelicals, who lived their lives further down the social scale yet were keen to embrace the emerging Victorian values of the middle class. The Whigs' distinctive evangelical base imbued the party with a reformist tinge, though its predominantly conservative leaders generally hesitated to embrace 'moral' causes for fear of alienating crucial segments of the wider electorate.

Whiggery was especially popular in areas penetrated by the market revolution – the quickening process of economic change evident in the United States after the War of 1812. Large-scale planters, manu-facturers, northeastern merchants, the urban middle classes, and significant numbers of evangelical farmers and artisans tended to be Whigs. So too did many upcountry southerners desirous of better roads and railways and jealous of wealthy Democratic elites in states like Virginia and Tennessee. There was also a strong regional, ethnic, and religious cast to Whiggery. Old Congregationalist (and Federal-ist) bastions such as coastal Maine and eastern Massachusetts were staunchly anti-Democratic, as were areas like the Western Reserve of northern Ohio that had been settled by New England Con-gregationalists and Presbyterians. British-stock immigrants preferred to vote Whig in part because the organization inherited some of the Federalists' pronounced Anglophilia.

The Democrats' vigorous advocacy of democracy, states' rights, limited government, and religious toleration appealed to a rather different set of constituencies, some of which (like those of the Whigs) overlapped. The Democrats' core voters were subsistence farmers, urban working men, Irish and German immigrants, yeoman farmers and slaveholders throughout the South, and those belonging to denominations which inclined toward ritualistic forms of worship and theological conservatism (for example Episcopalians, Catholics, Lutherans, and anti-Mission Baptists). These groups not only looked askance at Yankee moralizing and excessive government interference in society but were also often aggressive supporters of the white Republic and proslavery expansion.

In addition to the party's southern bias there was a decidedly antidevelopmental tinge to much Democratic rhetoric and policy-making. Voters took seriously the claims of leading Jacksonian politicians that credit, banks, paper money, and high tariffs threatened the very fabric of the Republic, producing concentrations of economic power, boom–bust cycles in which ordinary people suffered the most, and an unhealthy dependence on market forces beyond the control of the individual citizen. It would be too much, however, to claim that the Democratic party was opposed to capitalism. Like all large political organizations it was a broad coalition. Conservative Democrats in almost every state supported Whiggish economic legislation such as government aid for internal improvements and banks. The *laissez-faire* policies favored by radicals, moreover, often redounded to the benefit of capitalists by loosening the shackles of an over-regulated society. What Democrats of all stripes really despised was special privilege. Unlike the Whigs they expressed boundless faith in the people, believing that the Republic would prosper only if individuals were left as free as possible to govern their own lives. By 'people', the Democrats meant primarily white males of all social classes. As prosperity began to return to the United States in the early 1840s, the party's emphasis began to shift from economic issues to those concerning spatial expansion and race.

Essentially the second party system bolstered the existence and even expansion of slavery. It did so for several reasons. Firstly, although southern Whigs and Democrats often differed over slavery-related issues, they shared a commitment to southern values and institutions and often vied with one another to proclaim themselves the most reliable defenders of human bondage – for example by trying to link the opposition to antislavery elements in the North.[52] Secondly, sufficient numbers of leading northern Democrats disregarded the moral aspects of the slavery question and embraced territorial expansion (with or without slavery) as a great national issue that would prove popular with the voters. Thirdly, even though a majority of northern Whigs and large numbers of northern Democrats disliked slavery for a wide range of reasons, political realities often served to suppress their qualms on the issue. This was particularly true at the time of presidential elections when northern and southern wings of each party came together every four years to nominate a presidential standard bearer and then campaign for his election the following November. No man could receive a national party nomination in the 1840s if he was known to be an opponent of slavery. Southern Whigs and Democrats simply would not have accepted it. Besides, party strategists demanded nominees who could garner votes in both sections – hence the quadrennial search for an 'available' candidate who could transcend narrow sectional prejudices and campaign as a genuinely national figure.

Internal party factionalism and the related struggle for federal patronage also served to complicate matters. Most politicians entered political life for a variety of motives, not only a commitment to a certain ideology and specific policies but also a thirst for jobs and power. Control of state and national governments could bring major financial rewards to individuals in the form of a monopoly on the printing of government documents or an appointment as a federal postmaster or tax assessor. Ordinary Whigs and Democrats sought such rewards by linking their cause to that of a leading local politician who, in turn, sought advancement in part on the basis of job promises to his supporters (as well as on wider appeals to the electorate). While there was often an ideological fit between the contracting parties, this was not always the case. A person holding certain views on topics such as slavery might at times be forced to put those views to one side in order to obtain preferment from a more powerful person whose own career was dependent on satisfying a large and diverse number of individuals and groups. Disappointed office seekers could either lick their wounds in private or attach themselves to other issues or politicos more likely to further their aims. If these 'soreheads' were newspaper editors (who, along with lawyers, were the mainstays of antebellum politics) their shifts of allegiance might well have lasting effects on a party's appeal to the voters. Factional groupings grounded in patronage struggles developed within the sectional wings of both major parties in the 1840s. At times these struggles could push moderate men to adopt extreme positions in order to outflank opponents. At others, they could lead radicals to moderate their views for the same reason.

As long as the second party system continued to mobilize the voters along party rather than sectional lines, slavery was safe within

the Union. The real danger, for slavery and the Union, lay
fundamental reorientation of politics along a North–South
During the 1840s there were worrying signs that this trend was
underway. Renewed controversy over the annexation of Texas,
however, highlighted the system's capacity not merely to contain the
tensions generated by slavery-related issues but actually to promote
the expansion of slavery.

Annexation was opposed in many parts of the North because
Texas was a slaveholding republic. When the Texans had fought
for independence against Mexico in the mid-1830s the outspoken
northern Whig, ex-President John Quincy Adams, had denounced
the war as a Slave Power conspiracy to expand the domain of the
peculiar institution (and increase the influence of the South within
the Union). Annexation was deeply unpopular with members of
the Liberty party, a new third party devoted to bringing about the
abolition of slavery through political means. Influential primarily in
parts of New England and pockets of the Midwest settled by New
England migrants, the Liberty men acted mainly as a pressure group.
They won few elections but in close races sometimes induced mainstream politicians in the North to adopt more extreme positions
on slavery issues than they might otherwise have chosen to uphold.
Their efforts helped to radicalize Whig candidates and office holders
in constituencies containing significant numbers of antislavery voters
(often Quakers or Yankee evangelicals). Charged by antislavery Whigs
and Liberty men with doing the bidding of the South, some northern
Democrats in turn were forced into establishing their independence
from the powerful southern wing of their party. In 1840, for the first
time ever, more northern Democrats voted against than for the Gag
Rule, first adopted by the House of Representatives in 1836 to prevent
proper consideration of abolitionist petitions.[53]

The subsequent debate over Texas annexation brought the slavery
issue to the center stage of American politics. In the spring of 1844
US Secretary of State John C. Calhoun released a copy of a letter he
had sent to Richard Pakenham, the British minister in Washington.
Calhoun denounced the antislavery British for supposedly trying to
turn Texas into a satellite territory, hailed the virtues of slave labor
and advocated annexation as the best means to protect domestic
slavery and promote the national good. By depicting annexation as
a proslavery measure Calhoun set off a storm of criticism in parts of
the North. Both leading candidates for the White House, Henry
Clay and ex-President Martin Van Buren, issued public statements
indicating their opposition to immediate annexation. Clay secured

the Whig nomination but Van Buren's hopes were dashed at the Democratic convention in Baltimore. Southerners played a major role in invoking the rule (first adopted in 1836) requiring any nominee to secure two-thirds of the convention vote. Unable to secure the necessary level of support, Van Buren was passed over in favor of a relatively obscure Tennessee politician, James K. Polk. Polk was a wealthy slaveholder committed to a policy of continental-ism: the expansion of the United States to the Pacific coast. He saw Texas annexation as the first step in a program that would eventually bring the prize Mexican possession of California into the Union.

Although Polk's nomination was far from popular with Van Buren's supporters, his aggressive advocacy of Manifest Destiny won him plaudits from many northern Democrats who appreciated the nationalist strain of his rhetoric. Polk won a narrow victory in November in large measure because defections to the Liberty party had lost Clay the critical state of New York. Although three-quarters of northern Democrats voted to terminate the Gag Rule the following month, only the embittered Van Burenites joined the Whigs in opposing the administration's Texas annexation treaty when it came to a vote in the House early in 1845. The admission of Texas to the Union vastly increased the pressure on the Mexicans. While Polk would have been happy to buy his way to the coast, he was quite prepared to use stronger methods. When the Mexicans refused to negotiate over the sale of their northern territories, American troops were dispatched to the disputed international border along the Rio Grande in January 1846. Mexico resisted, Polk had a *casus belli* and within two years the United States had defeated its weaker southern neighbor on the battlefield. The president secured his continental empire but the consequences of the Mexican War would provide the second party system with its greatest test.

Notes

1. Andrew Carnegie quoted in Richard Sylla, 'Experimental Federalism: The Economics of American Government, 1789–1914' in *CEHUS*, pp.489–90.

2. Allan Nevins and M.H. Thomas, eds, *The Diary of George Templeton Strong: Young Man in New York 1835–1849* (New York, 1952), p.277.

3. Robert E. Gallman, ed., 'Economic Growth and Structural Change in the Long Nineteenth Century' in *CEHUS*, p.50.

4. For an insightful discussion of the strengths and weaknesses of the antebellum Union (which comes down decisively on the side of the former) see Donald Ratcliffe, 'The State of the Union, 1776–1860' in Susan-Mary Grant and Brian Holden Reid, eds, *The American Civil War: Explorations and Reconsiderations* (Harlow, 2000), pp.3–38.

5. Thomas Le Duc, 'History and Appraisal of US Land Policy to 1862' in Howard W. Ottoson, ed., *Land Use Policy and Problems in the United States* (Lincoln, Neb., 1963), pp.3–27.

6. Richard J. Carwardine, *Evangelicals and Politics in Antebellum America* (New Haven, Conn., 1993), p.xv.

7. Benedict Anderson, *Imagined Communities: Reflections on the Origin and Spread of Nationalism* (1983: revd edn, London, 1991).

8. Quoted in William C. Davis, *Lincoln's Men: How President Lincoln Became Father to an Army and a Nation* (New York, 1999), p.3.

9. Ulysses S. Grant, *Personal Memoirs of U.S. Grant* (1885: repr. New York, 1999), p.5.

10. Quoted in Matthew Frye Jacobson, *Whiteness of a Different Color: European Immigrants and the Alchemy of Race* (Cambridge, Mass., 1998), p.22.

11. Herman Melville, *Redburn* (1849: Harmondsworth, 1986), pp.238–9.

12. James T. McIntosh, ed., *The Papers of Jefferson Davis: Vol. 3, July 1846–December 1848* (Baton Rouge, La, 1981), p.8.

13. Margaret Fuller, *'These Sad But Glorious Days': Dispatches from Europe, 1846–1850*, ed. Larry J. Reynolds and Susan Belasco Smith (New Haven, Conn., 1991), pp.161–5.

14. See e.g. Eugene D. Genovese, *The Political Economy of Slavery: Studies in the Economy and Society of the Slave South* (New York, 1965) and John Ashworth, *Slavery, Capitalism, and Politics in the Antebellum Republic: Vol. 1, Commerce and Compromise, 1820–1850* (Cambridge, 1995). William H. Seward referred to 'an irrepressible conflict' between slavery and free labor in a Senate speech of 1858.

15. Jim Potter, 'Atlantic Economy' in Leslie S. Pressnell, ed., *Studies in the Industrial Revolution* (London, 1960), pp.240–1.

16. Peter Kolchin, *American Slavery 1619–1877* (New York, 1993), p.101.

17. Eugene D. Genovese, *Roll, Jordan, Roll: The World the Slaves Made* (New York, 1974).

18. William Dusinberre, *Them Dark Days: Slavery in the American Rice Swamps* (New York, 1996), p.51.

19. Kolchin, *American Slavery*, pp.125–6.

20. Ashworth, *Slavery*, pp.82–3.

21. Richard D. Brown, *Modernization: The Transformation of American Life 1600–1865* (New York, 1976), p.9.

22. Works depicting slaveholders as capitalists include James Oakes, *The Ruling Race: A History of American Slaveholders* (New York, 1982) and Robert W. Fogel, *Without Consent or Contract: The Rise and Fall of American Slavery* (New York, 1989), esp. pp.17–198. Although Eugene Genovese is the most well-known exponent of the opposing point of view, it should be noted that he has refined his views over time. In *Roll, Jordan, Roll* and more recently *The Slaveholders' Dilemma: Freedom and Progress in Southern Conservative Thought* (Columbia, SC, 1992) he contends that the planter class was not opposed to capitalism *per se*, but rather to the liberal, wage labor variant evolving in the North.

23. McIntosh, ed., *Papers of Jefferson Davis*, 3, p.286.

24. Bruce Collins, *White Society in the Antebellum South* (London, 1985), pp.15–16.

25. Quoted in Parish, *Slavery*, p.124.

26. William J. Cooper, Jr, *Liberty and Slavery: Southern Politics to 1860* (New York, 1983), pp.30–2, 117–19, 136–7, 179–81, 208–9, 219–21, 267–8, 282–3, 285.

27. Elizabeth Fox-Genovese, *Within the Plantation Household: Black and White Women of the Old South* (Chapel Hill, NC, 1988), pp.38–9.

28. Calhoun to Charles James Faulkner, Aug. 1, 1847, in Clyde N. Wilson and Shirley Bright Cook, *The Papers of John C. Calhoun: Vol. 24, 1846–1847* (Columbia, SC, 1998), p.481.

29. Paul D. Escott and Jeffrey J. Crow, 'The Social Order and Violent Disorder: An Analysis of North Carolina in the Revolution and the Civil War', *JSH* 52 (1986), pp.378–9.

30. Collins, *White Society*, pp.22–4.

31. For an account of the development of the Far West see Chapter 8 below.

32. This and other urban population statistics in this section are taken from Raymond A. Mohl, *The New City: Urban America in the Industrial Age, 1860–1920* (Arlington Heights, Ill., 1985), p.15.

33. John K. Brown, *The Baldwin Locomotive Works 1831–1915* (Baltimore, 1995), pp.1–27.

34. Bruce Laurie, *Working People of Philadelphia, 1800–1850* (Philadelphia, 1980), p.15.

35. Charles Sellers, *The Market Revolution: Jacksonian America, 1815–1846* (New York, 1991).

36. James Caird, *Prairie Farming in America with Notes by the Way on Canada and the United States* (London, 1859), p.31.

37. Clarence Danhof, *Change in Agriculture: The Northern United States 1820–1870* (Cambridge, Mass., 1969), p.89.

38. Mohl, *New City*, p.20.

39. Albert Fishlow, 'Antebellum Interregional Trade Reconsidered', *American Economic Review* 54 (1964), pp.352–64.

40. Eric Foner, 'Free Labor and Nineteenth-Century Political Ideology' in Melvyn Stokes and Stephen Conway, eds, *The Market Revolution in America: Social, Political and Religious Expressions, 1800–1880* (Charlottesville, Va, 1996), pp.99–127.

41. Stuart M. Blumin, *The Urban Threshhold: Growth and Change in a Nineteenth Century American Community* (Chicago, 1976), pp.87, 89.

42. *Ibid.*, p.181.

43. Quoted in Ann D. Gordon, ed., *The Selected Papers of Elizabeth Cady Stanton and Susan B. Anthony: Vol. 1, In the School of Anti-Slavery, 1840 to 1866* (New Brunswick, NJ, 1997), pp.77–8.

44. Elizabeth Cady Stanton and Elizabeth W. McClintock to the Editors of the *Seneca County Courier* [after July 23, 1848] in *ibid.*, p.89.

45. Potter, 'Atlantic Economy', pp.236–80.

46. Quoted in Robert D. Richardson, Jr, *Emerson: The Mind on Fire* (Berkeley, Cal., 1995), p.441.

47. Nevins and Thomas, eds, *Diary of George Templeton Strong*, p.295.

48. Anne Henry Ehrenpreis, ed., *Happy Country This America: The Travel Diary of Henry Arthur Bright* (Columbus, Ohio, 1978), p.71.

49. Nevins and Thomas, eds, *Diary of George Templeton Strong*, pp.352–3.

50. Michael R. Haines, 'The Population of the United States, 1790–1920' in *CEHUS*, p.171.

51. The following discussion of party ideology in the 1840s draws heavily on Daniel Walker Howe, *The Political Culture of the American Whigs* (Chicago, 1979), John Ashworth, *'Agrarians' & 'Aristocrats': Party Political Ideology in the United States, 1837–1846* (London, 1983), and Harry L. Watson, *Jacksonian Politics and Community Conflict: The Emergence of the Second American Party System in Cumberland County, North Carolina* (Baton Rouge, La, 1981).

52. This theme is developed in William J. Cooper, Jr, *The South and the Politics of Slavery 1828–1856* (Baton Rouge, La, 1978).

53. Leonard L. Richards, *The Slave Power: The Free North and Southern Domination, 1780–1860* (Baton Rouge, La, 2000), p.38.

2

BITTER FRUIT OF AN UNJUST WAR: THE POLITICS OF SLAVERY EXPANSION, 1848–52

One did not have to be a famous savant to foresee that the United States would defeat its weak southern neighbor and that the resulting victory would bring new problems. However, it was the 'Sage of Concord', Ralph Waldo Emerson, who summarized most memorably the likely consequences. The conquest, said Emerson, would result in disaster: 'it will be as the man who swallows the arsenic, which brings him down in turn. Mexico will poison us.'[1] The debate over whether slavery should be allowed to expand into the vast slice of territory likely to be seized from Mexico thrust sectional issues to the top of the political agenda, polarizing debates in Congress and destabilizing the nation's two main parties. The persistent strength of American nationalism at mid-century was highlighted by the passage of a series of measures known collectively as the Compromise of 1850. However, while the Compromise staved off a genuine secession crisis, those who celebrated the country's salvation (and there were many) soon found that a once secure political landscape was shifting alarmingly under their feet. By the time Franklin Pierce was inaugurated as president in March 1853, the second party system was already in a state of advanced decay.

The political impact of the Mexican War

The Mexican War of 1846–48 presents historians with an apparent paradox. Those who played a leading role in bringing on the unequal conflict, President James K. Polk and his expansionist allies in the Democratic party, had good reasons for supposing that territorial aggrandizement at the expense of an unloved and widely despised neighbor would pave the way for victory in the 1848 presidential election, assuage Jacksonian anxieties about Britain's role in the Far West, and promote their own dreams of a great commercial and agrarian empire reaching out across the Pacific to China and Japan. The war itself was costly in financial terms and led to the deaths of 13,000 American soldiers, mostly from disease. Yet, overall, the military campaigns went well for the Polk administration. US troops reached Mexico City within 16 months of the war's outset. The conflict produced a fresh stock of national martyrs and new republican heroes in the form of Generals Zachary Taylor and Winfield S. Scott. The Treaty of Guadalupe Hidalgo, which ended the war in March 1848, brought California and the modern Southwest into the Union (see Map 1). Why, in view of these gains, did the Democrats and the country have cause to regret the adventure?

There is no denying the fact that the Mexican War instilled what the historian Henry Nash Smith called 'a yeasty nationalism'.[2] The rapid progress of American arms across the high plains and mountains of Mexico thrilled millions of ordinary people. During the early months of the war, the national mood was jingoistic. The belated news of victories at Palo Alto and Resaca de la Palma was greeted with enormous relief and both battles were soon enshrined in the popular culture of the day. The mood became more cynical over time but Taylor's victory at Buena Vista and Scott's subsequent entry into Mexico City continued to fire the national imagination. Although regular army generals like Taylor and Scott were singled out for praise, particular pride was felt in the achievements of the volunteers – mostly untrained citizen-soldiers who had laid aside their daily chores for the higher duty of protecting their common country. Much of the fighting was done by southerners who had no compunction asserting their patriotism. 'We entered [Mexico City] two days since after hard fighting', the Mississippi officer and future secessionist John A. Quitman told his wife in September 1847: 'Our arms & our country covered with glory.'[3]

It was not all one-way traffic. Fierce opposition to the Mexican War soon developed. Abolitionists condemned it not only as naked aggression against a defenseless neighbor but also because they judged it to be what the radical reformer William Lloyd Garrison called a 'cowardly pro-slavery war' fought by the dominant slave-holding influence in the government to wrest yet more territories for its own purposes.[4] Several prominent intellectuals condemned the war for similar reasons, although Emerson was probably right to label as gesture politics the decision of his friend, Henry David

Thoreau, to spend a night in jail rather than help finance the bloodshed through payment of his poll tax. There was also condemnation of the war from many northern clergymen, especially from Congregationalists and Presbyterians living in New England or in areas of the upper Midwest settled by New Englanders. Some ministers were genuinely concerned that such an aggressive and unequal contest was corrupting the moral fabric of the Republic. 'Never have I so much feared the judgments of God on us as a nation', wailed the New York Presbyterian minister James W. Alexander.[5]

The notion that an unjust war was perverting America's republican experiment by promoting Roman-style Caesarism and imperial overstretch was widespread in the North. So too was blame of the South for starting the war in the first place. Southerners, it was claimed (not just by abolitionists), were attempting to augment their own power inside the Union by spreading slavery beyond its existing boundaries. Horace Greeley's *New York Tribune* claimed that for years 'a spirit has been rampant in our public affairs, styling itself "the South," and demanding that the whole nation should fall down and worship whatever graven images it chooses to set up'.[6] Such views were part of a dangerous trend on the part of some northerners to define American nationality in strictly northern terms. Inevitably, southerners found criticism of their role in the war insulting and began to question their own relationship to the North. Were southerners like Taylor and Quitman not fighting to strengthen the Union and expand republican liberties at the expense of Mexican despotism? Were they not risking their lives so that carping, hypocritical northerners could inhabit a mightier nation stretching from coast to coast?

Sectional disagreement over the purpose and consequences of the Mexican War was encapsulated in bitter political strife over the Wilmot Proviso. First introduced into the House of Representatives in August 1846, the Proviso declared that slavery should be prohibited in any Mexican territory ceded to the United States as a result of the conflict. The measure had its origins not only in interparty competition (northern Democrats understood that a proslavery stance would render them vulnerable to Whig assaults at home) but also in the ongoing factional strife within the Democratic party.[7] David Wilmot was an obscure Pennsylvania Democrat who had been put up to the job of introducing the Proviso by the supporters of Martin Van Buren. On assuming office, Polk had awarded important cabinet and other federal appointments to opponents of the former president. The Van Burenites were outraged and sought to retaliate by hitting at slavery, widely regarded as the main source of southern power inside the Union and the national Democratic party. Carving out more slave states from the Mexican lands would simply increase this malign influence and further reduce the Van Burenites' influence inside the party of Jackson.

The sectionally divisive impact of the Proviso was immediately apparent. Northerners voted 83–12 in favor, southerners 67–2 against passage. Entrenched southern power in the Senate (where each state had two delegates) ensured that the Proviso would not become law – neither this time nor on the other two occasions (in 1847 and 1848) when the House again passed the measure. However, the controversy over the status of slavery in the territory taken from Mexico became the focal point for political debate in the late 1840s. The resulting strain on the second party system was enormous.

The more successful the progress of American arms, the more pressing became the debate over the humiliating territorial settlement which Polk's hawkish administration seemed determined to impose upon the enemy. Slavery had been barred under Mexican law since 1825. The Wilmot Proviso was intended to uphold the status quo in any territory purchased from Mexico on the basis of language taken from the federal Ordinance of 1787 (which banned slavery from the Old Northwest). Because many southerners did not expect slavery to take root in the Far West, several leading figures, Zachary Taylor among them, initially dismissed the measure as a political irrelevance. There was, after all, little chance that it would ever be passed by the Senate. Unfortunately, radicals on both sides of the Mason-Dixon Line were reluctant to let the matter rest. On February 19, 1847 Senator John C. Calhoun of South Carolina introduced four resolutions on the Proviso when it came up for debate in the upper house. Acting on the premise that the territories of the United States were the common property of the several states, Calhoun demanded that Congress had no right to discriminate between the states and that

> the enactment of any law which should directly, or by its effects, deprive the citizens of any of the States of this Union from emigrating with their property into any of the territories of the United States, will make such a discrimination, and would, therefore, be a violation of the Constitution, and the rights of the States from which such citizens emigrated, and in derogation of that perfect equality which belongs to them as members of this Union, and would tend directly to subvert the Union itself.[8]

Calhoun's reasons for stirring the pot of sectional strife are impossible to determine with absolute precision. His main aim was probably to increase southern unity to the disadvantage of his rivals enmeshed in a national party system that, from his vantage point, was an unreliable bulwark against persistent antislavery activity. Personally, the powerful senator regarded the Wilmot Proviso as less of a direct threat to the stability of southern life than attempts by incendiaries to undermine slavery in the states, for example through the passage of state laws designed to secure the rights of blacks accused of being fugitives from slavery.[9] But Calhoun knew that most southern whites, particularly those outside the border slave states where runaway blacks had a better chance of escaping to the North than those who worked the plantations of the lower South, were as yet unconvinced by secessionist claims that their personal property and security were under immediate threat from abolitionists. Mobilizing the region's voters on the basis of opposition to the Wilmot Proviso made obvious political sense in that the measure could be depicted convincingly as a more general blow to southern rights, power and honor. The South's prominent contribution to the Mexican War merely enhanced the potency of his resolutions. Southerners had risked their lives in the cause of American expansion. Why, in all equity, should they not be rewarded for their patriotism and be allowed to take their human property into the Far West?

Calhoun's resolutions threatened to exacerbate the sectional divisions caused within both major parties by the Wilmot Proviso, a measure which, notwithstanding its introduction by a Pennsylvania Democrat, had already been warmly welcomed by many northern antislavery Whigs as a necessary antidote to southern influence in the nation's councils. Few northerners were abolitionists, but men on both sides of the party divide above the Mason-Dixon Line were beginning to rue the impact of slavery on economic growth (southern Democrats were consistent opponents of protective tariffs intended to promote manufacturing) and America's image abroad. If they were northern Democrats, they were likely to favor the containment of slavery largely because they wanted to promote the Jacksonian project of a white settler nation. 'I have no squeamish sensitiveness upon the subject of slavery, nor morbid sympathy for the slave', said David Wilmot when reintroducing his proviso in December 1846, 'I plead for the cause of the rights of white freemen. I would preserve for free white labor a fair country, a rich inheritance, where the sons of toil, of my own race and own color, can live without the disgrace which association with negro slavery brings upon free labor.'[10] If they were northern Whigs, they were likelier to regard slavery as a moral evil which perverted the original intentions of the Founding Fathers. It was not surprising, therefore, that there was widespread support for the Proviso in the North, especially in areas like New England where suspicion of southern power and genuine (and related) hostility to slavery had been a constant factor in local politics since the days of the Federalists.

Resolutions adopted by a local Whig meeting in Maine five days after the Proviso's debut in Congress reflected the strength of sectional feeling among many northeastern Whigs. The delegates to the Cumberland County convention in Portland in August 1846 condemned the Mexican War as 'one designed for the ultimate subjugation of the free States' and declared it the duty of northerners 'to assume an attitude of independence'. In his acceptance speech the successful congressional nominee reiterated this theme. 'I wish the whole North, *irrespective of party*,' said J.S. Little in a blatant bid for Liberty support in the upcoming election, 'could be roused to act as unitedly against the grasping encroachments of the slave power, as the South does in its support. The time has come, when all, who believe the spirit and evil influences of slavery should be resisted, should act, shoulder to shoulder and side by side in harmony, in the great contest between freedom and slavery.'[11]

While only a minority of northerners would have endorsed such comments at this stage of the country's history, the Wilmot Proviso was generally as popular in the North as it was unpopular in the South. Even though issues unrelated to slavery continued to play an important role in American politics during 1847, it was imperative for national party leaders to maintain party unity across the sections before the crucial 1848 presidential election (and before the Proviso sectionalized debate along the worrying lines staked out by antislavery men and Calhounite radicals). Predictably, their responses differed. Several leading southern Democrats and northern 'doughface' Democrats sympathetic to southern fears – men such as Polk's secretary of state, James Buchanan – favored extending the existing Missouri Compromise Line of 36°30′ to the Pacific.[12] This option had two advantages but one major drawback. It was conservative and national in the sense that it built on existing policy and gave both sections a roughly equal stake in territorial expansion. Unfortunately, it was unacceptable to the Van Burenites because it ran counter to the Wilmot Proviso. The Proviso was their signal to northern voters and to southerners inside the party that they were not, as their Whig and abolitionist opponents often claimed, lackeys of the South. Without a viable alternative, large numbers of northern Democrats were bound to adhere to the measure.

It is a testimony to the strength of the second party system and the resourcefulness of contemporary politicians that an alternative was devised. Labeled 'popular sovereignty' by its supporters and 'squatter sovereignty' by its detractors, this option was developed by Lewis Cass, an elderly Democratic presidential aspirant from Michigan. Seizing on comments made initially by Vice President George Dallas, Cass suggested (in a public letter written to the Tennesseean, A.O. Nicholson, in 1847) that the settlers of a territory should have the right to decide the status of slavery for themselves. Adroitly circumventing the Wilmot Proviso, this solution seemed to be entirely consistent with Jacksonian emphases on western expansion and popular self-government. In addition, as long as the precise point at which slavery could be banned in the governing process remained unclear, northerners and southerners could choose to believe that it operated to their advantage.

Crucially, influential Democratic politicians on both sides of the Mason-Dixon Line moved to endorse popular sovereignty as the party's solution to the problem of slavery expansion. In the North leading figures such as Senators Stephen A. Douglas of Illinois and Daniel S. Dickinson of New York were swift to embrace what they saw as a truly national policy likely to find favor with the majority of patriotic voters in their section. In the upper South popular sovereignty offered local Democrats a means of simultaneously maintaining links with their northern counterparts and sustaining their image as reliable supporters of the existing racial order. Senator Andrew Johnson of Tennessee told Nicholson that the policy offered slavery much greater protection than the demand of fiery states' rights men like William Lowndes Yancey of Alabama that the federal government must protect the property rights of slaveholders in the territories. 'It seems to me', wrote Johnson in January 1848, 'for the south to admit that the federal Government has the power to establish slavery where it does not now exist ... is conceding all that the most ultra Wilmot proviso man desires – for if the Government can establish Slavery, in a territory now free, it can abolish it in a territory where it does exist.' Popular sovereignty, added Johnson, was the ideal *via media*: as well as being 'the safest position for the south[,] it is the most defensible for the democracy of the north, whilst at the same time we steer clear of impracticable Yanceyism on the one hand and Wilmot Provisoism on the other'.[13]

By no means all southern Democrats felt this way, especially in the deep South where the majority of them, Jefferson Davis included, would have preferred to see the party endorse extension of the Missouri Compromise Line. In the North, moreover, the Van Burenites adhered to the Wilmot Proviso and carried out their threat not to support the regular ticket. At the national convention in June, however, moderate northern and southern Democrats joined forces to nominate Cass on a platform endorsing traditional Jacksonian policies. An attempt by Yancey to align the party behind federal protection for slave property in the territories failed miserably.

The Whigs found it just as difficult to maintain their cohesion after the Wilmot Proviso had been introduced into Congress. In large measure, this stemmed from the heavily evangelical northern wing's discernible moral hostility toward slavery – a serious but, as it turned out, not insurmountable barrier to continued cooperation across sectional lines. The party's first response to the danger posed by the Proviso was to resist the acquisition of any territory from Mexico. Few antislavery Whigs preferred this solution to an outright ban on slavery expansion, but it was endorsed during 1847 with varying degrees of enthusiasm by northern conservatives such as Daniel Webster (like Cass, another presidential hopeful) and influential southern Whigs such as the Georgians Alexander H. Stephens and Robert Toombs. The obvious drawback with the 'No Territory' policy was its supreme irrelevance once the United States had formally secured possession of Mexico's northern provinces. When the Senate ratified the Treaty of Guadalupe Hidalgo in February 1848, no one doubted that the Whigs had to fashion a new response to slavery expansion if they were to surprise everyone, including themselves, and emerge triumphant in the presidential race.

The Whigs found their solution in the candidate rather than making new policy. What was required, wrote one prescient politician, was someone who could 'unite whatever there is left amongst the people of the popularity of the Mexican war and also the opposition to the mode of prosecuting it by the present administration'.[14] The man who benefited from this strain of thought was Zachary Taylor, the unprepossessing people's soldier whose victories in northern Mexico had made him a genuine military hero with real political potential. For much of 1847, it seemed possible that the wealthy Louisiana cotton planter might run as an independent candidate drawing support from voters who deprecated the office seeking, wire pulling, and corruption so endemic in American political life. A number of Whig strategists, however, quickly realized that the general offered their party the best hope of transcending its divisions over slavery. Taylor was certainly a slaveholder but, more critically, his 'no-party' image and unimpeachable republican credentials held out the hope of holding the core of the Whig party together and of reaching out to Democrats and previously unaffiliated voters in the presidential election. Loyal Whigs who resided in states where the Democrats reigned supreme were particularly anxious to draft Taylor, regardless of their position on slavery.[15] A group of proslavery southern Whigs which included Stephens and Toombs led the movement in Congress to nominate Taylor, but it was also supported actively by several isolated northern moderates, Abraham Lincoln of Illinois among them.

In spite of fierce opposition from those who disliked Taylor for his nonpartisan stance, his slaveholding, his military station, or his apparent suspicion of European immigrants, the efforts of the 'Young Indians' bore fruit at the national convention in June. At a packed gathering in the Chinese Theater in Philadelphia almost unanimous southern support combined with roughly 40 percent of the northern Whig delegates to nominate Taylor on the fourth ballot. Opposition to the general was strong but his predominantly northern detractors failed to unite behind a single candidate, of whom the party's long-time standard-bearer, Henry Clay, was by far the most prominent. Significantly, the convention avoided action on the Wilmot Proviso by declining to produce a platform. This was not an oversight. Silence on the Proviso would enable the Whigs to run a double-headed campaign: antislavery in the North, proslavery in the South.

The actions of the Whig and Democratic conventions in 1848 highlighted the ambiguous impact of the Mexican War. On the one hand, it stirred the national imagination as no other contest since the War of 1812. On the other, it countered many of the centripetal forces unleashed by raising centrifugal doubts about the very meaning of the republican experiment in America. Both mainstream parties attempted to deal with the divisive slavery issue in their own distinctive way. The electorate would judge how successful their efforts had been.

The presidential election of 1848

Late in 1846 Charles Sumner, one of Boston's most committed antislavery lawyers, penned a letter to a like-minded Cincinnati attorney named Salmon P. Chase. Though by no means free from the racial prejudices of the day, both men were genuine supporters of human freedom as well as being typically ambitious politicians. While Sumner was a Whig and Chase a former Democrat who had become one of the leading Liberty men in Ohio, it was clear from the tone of the communication that they had much in common. 'I hope', wrote Sumner, 'the time will come, – (I wish that it had come) – when the Friends of Freedom may stand together. There must be very soon a new chrystallisation of parties, in which there shall be one grand Northern party of Freedom. In such a party I shall hope to serve by yr side. Meanwhile, the opponents of Slavery should aim at Union together.'[16] In less than a decade after this letter had been written, the northern antislavery party for which Sumner yearned had not only come into existence but also come close to winning a presidential election. The process that resulted in the formation of the Republican party, the single most important factor in the coming of secession and civil war, was a lengthy one. Its immediate origins, however, lay in the summer of 1848 when antislavery elements in the North united to contest the stranglehold exerted by the major parties over American political life.

Rightly remembered by one of its founding members as 'a new and significant departure in party politics', the Free Soil party was a disparate antisouthern coalition made up primarily of renegade Democrats, antislavery Whigs, and Liberty activists who shared Sumner's desire for a broader front against slavery and its doughfaced minions.[17] The critical event in the formation of the Free Soil party was the June 1848 Democratic national convention. Free soil 'Barnburners' – predominantly Van Burenites alienated by Polk's patronage policy – went to the Baltimore convention to demand that they should be recognized as the legitimate representatives of the New York Democratic party. When the convention refused to seat them at the expense of their 'Hunker' rivals, they deserted the party, thereby making them an obvious target for the coalition (or 'fusion') strategy of political antislavery men like Chase. The Whigs' decision to nominate a slaveholder for president released more potential recruits, especially in areas like the Western Reserve of Ohio where there was pronounced grassroots hostility toward the South and its peculiar institution. With Chase at the forefront of political maneuvers, the Free Soilers finally came together in Buffalo, New York, in the second week of August.

An estimated 20,000 people attended the inaugural gathering of the new party but the main business was conducted away from the gigantic tent that had been erected in the city park. More than 450 elected 'conferees' representing the three main factions met at a nearby church to ratify a bargain forged between Barnburner and Liberty leaders on the night before the convention. The crux of this deal was that the abolitionists would help secure the presidential nomination of the Barnburners' candidate, Martin Van Buren, in return for the renegade Democrats' support for a strong antislavery platform. The latter, drafted primarily by Salmon Chase, addressed several issues. As well as calling for a range of economic initiatives including free land for western settlers, a tariff for revenue only, and federal support for internal improvements, it adhered strictly to the Wilmot Proviso and incorporated Chase's firmly held belief that the federal government should divorce itself completely from slavery 'wherever that government possesses constitutional power to legislate on that subject and is thus responsible for its existence'.[18] While the platform denounced further truckling to the Slave Power, it diluted Liberty objectives by guaranteeing the existence of slavery in the states and ignoring the rights of free blacks.

Events proceeded entirely to plan. The platform was accepted without debate by the conferees and the crowd. Van Buren was nominated on the first ballot, largely because Chase announced the withdrawal of Judge John McLean, leaving Whig delegates with no alternative except the Liberty men's choice, Senator John P. Hale of New Hampshire, who stood no chance of taking votes away from the major parties in November. In spite of predictable tensions, most of those present were satisfied, if not positively pleased, with the work of the convention. Even the black abolitionist Frederick Douglass, fast moving away from his Garrisonian apprenticeship, gave the party a qualified endorsement in his newspaper, the *North Star.*

Many observers were less impressed. Garrison himself took time off from partaking of the water cure to disparage what he saw as the essential conservatism of the new movement and to underline his own conviction that the cause of emancipation would be served best if the free states severed their ties to the South.[19] More significant was the decision of leading politicians in both major parties to remain aloof from a party that could not possibly triumph in November. These included free-soil Democrats like Hannibal Hamlin of Maine but more especially antislavery Whigs such as Horace Greeley, Thaddeus Stevens, and Hamlin's fellow downeaster, William Pitt Fessenden, whose own father was an outspoken abolitionist. These politicians felt little enthusiasm for either Cass or Taylor but their political sixth sense mingled with residual party loyalty to make them disinclined to venture into the wilderness.

Before the Buffalo convention the powerful Delaware Whig, Senator John M. Clayton, made a last-ditch attempt to remove the slavery issue from political debate by introducing a bill to devolve final arbitration of the status of slavery in the territories onto the US

Supreme Court. Too many northern and southern members of the senator's own party, however, feared that this measure would redound to the benefit of the other section and that a vote in its favor would cost them support at home. The so-called Clayton Compromise passed the Senate on July 27, 1848, mainly with Democratic support, but was derailed in the House the following day by the decision of a small bloc of southern Whigs to vote with the bill's northern opponents from both parties. The Free Soilers remained the only party formally committed to the containment of slavery, a fact which impelled northern Whigs and Democrats alike to insist that their respective organizations were actually the most reliable obstacle to the spread of human bondage. Meanwhile their copartisans in the South vied with one another in its defense.

If slavery expansion was clearly the dominant issue on politicians' minds during late 1848, it was by no means the only one. After a poor start to Taylor's campaign the Whigs were able to capitalize on their traditional economic issues when the first signs of a recession began to appear in the fall. This was especially true in states such as Pennsylvania where industrial workers were generally the first to suffer from adverse fluctuations in the Anglo-American trading relationship. They also pointed out the dangerous consequences likely to ensue from Cass's virulent hatred of Britain and continued to gnaw on the remaining bones of the Mexican War by contrasting Taylor's military glories with Polk's high-handed conduct of hostilities. The Democrats countered by posing as the architects of peace (had they not ended the war with the Treaty of Guadalupe Hidalgo?) and, with rather more conviction, of republican greatness.

Much to the surprise of many of his copartisans, Taylor triumphed in the presidential race.[20] He secured only a plurality of the popular vote (his margin of victory over Cass was just over 200,000 out of roughly 3 million cast) and won primarily by holding onto areas of core Whig support and carrying states such as Georgia which Clay had lost narrowly in 1844. Turnout was relatively low – at 73 percent it was 6 percentage points down on the figure for 1844. Southerners seemed to be especially apathetic, probably because they could discern little difference between the parties on slavery. In spite of widespread concerns over their potential influence, the Free Soilers did not affect the overall result, attracting as they did voters from both of the main parties – Whigs in Ohio, Massachusetts, and many parts of the Midwest, Democrats in large numbers in New York. Even though leading southern Whigs were Taylor's most ardent supporters, his victory was clearly not a sectional one: roughly 60 percent of his electoral college votes came from the free states, 40 percent from the South. In fact, Van Buren's failure to exert a decisive impact on the campaign might well be seen as evidence that the Mexican War's overall influence on the country was a positive one. This, however, would be to ignore the fact that the problem of slavery expansion not only remained unsolved but also continued to divide the parties along sectional lines. One event above all others, the discovery of gold in California in January 1848 (with its consequent need to extend American governance over the new land), demanded urgent action from Washington and kept the slavery issue at the top of the political agenda.[21]

The Compromise of 1850

The election of Zachary Taylor as president offered the country hope but no guarantees for the future. A slaveholding nationalist in the mold of George Washington, Taylor seemed to many Americans to transcend the bitter divisions of party and section unleashed by the expansionist urges of the 1840s. This was certainly Old Rough and Ready's own perception of himself. At best a nominal Whig, the new president acted swiftly to reward his backers with important cabinet posts at the expense of party regulars who had leaned toward Henry Clay. His long-term aim was to broaden the base of his support by reaching out to Democrats and antiparty men rather than appealing to the Whigs' electoral core on the basis of traditional economic issues such as federal aid for internal improvements and high tariffs.

As well as strengthening his own position in the White House, Taylor genuinely believed that this strategy would benefit the nation as a whole. The same was true of his action on the slavery issue. Seeking to build on policy outlined by Polk and encapsulated in bills introduced into Congress by Democratic Senator Stephen Douglas of Illinois and the Virginia Whig, William B. Preston, in the winter of 1848–49, the president planned to admit the entire Mexican Cession to statehood. As he saw matters, this would have several advantages. It would circumvent the Wilmot Proviso, the source of growing murmurs of secession in the South. It would prevent the expansion of slavery, which remained the goal of most northerners regardless of partisan allegiance. Most importantly of all, it would secure the Union by removing the slavery issue from national political debate.

At first, events seemed to be moving in Taylor's direction. John C. Calhoun seized on the opportunity presented by the Wilmot Proviso controversy and other evidence of antislavery sentiment in Congress to try to break the second party system's hold on southern politics. His objective was radical yet not quite secessionist: the creation of a unified southern party which could exercise a permanent veto over antislavery legislation by governing as a 'concurrent majority' within a loose Union of sectionally divided states. On December 21, 1848 the northern-dominated House of Representatives passed an inflammatory resolution calling for slavery to be banned from the Mexican Cession and permitting slaves and free blacks to vote in a popular referendum on the continuation of slavery in Washington, DC. Slavery, declared the resolve, was 'a reproach to our country throughout Christendom and a serious hindrance to the progress of republican liberty among the nations of the earth'.[22]

Incensed, 69 southern Congressmen acquiesced in Calhoun's call for a special caucus which met in the Senate chamber the following day. The caucus appointed a committee to formulate an immediate response to the House assault. The South Carolinian's subsequent Southern Address offered nothing new but his determination to play on the racial fears of southern whites portended only evil for the Union. Unless southerners united to staunch abolitionist attacks on the peculiar institution, wrote Calhoun, they would soon find themselves subjugated by abolitionists and emancipated blacks – 'a degradation greater than has ever yet fallen to the lot of a free and enlightened people'.[23]

Fortunately for Taylor, southern Whigs remained confident that a slaveholder in the White House represented a more than adequate bulwark against abolitionism. They had no intention of allowing an ambitious rival to destroy the fruits of their recent electoral triumph. Only 39 percent of southern congressmen signed the Address when it finally saw the light of day on February 4. Only two of the 48 signatories were Whigs. While a majority of southern Democrats did sign, the president-elect must have been encouraged by the size of the minority that did not. These included Democrats like Howell Cobb of Georgia and Linn Boyd of Kentucky who were reluctant to surrender control of events to Calhounite radicals at home. The two men were among the authors of a trenchant critique of the Address issued to their constituents on February 26. An adherence to the national Democratic party, they insisted, was the only effective means of countering the overt abolitionist tendencies of northern Whiggery. Secession could not be ruled out completely but those who courted it actively could only damage the institution they professed to protect. In a patriotic conclusion that must have been music to the ears of Zachary Taylor, Cobb, Boyd, and their southern Democratic allies pressed the hope that the final settlement of the territorial issue would be marked by 'a spirit of liberality and justice':

> The sincere attachment felt by the people of all sections to this Union of our fathers, cemented as it was by their blood, and consecrated by their wisdom, forbid the idea that its existence and perpetuity will be wantonly endangered by an act of gross and palpable injustice upon any portion of the confederacy. This Union is the rock upon which the God of nations has built his political church, and we have been summoned to minister at its holy altars. Let us not prove unworthy of the high mission to which we have been called.[24]

Calhoun's defeat at the hands of southerners belonging to both major parties augured well for the future but unfortunately for Taylor his plans soon began to unravel. The Whig party, badly factionalized at the outset of his presidency, was further divided by an injudicious patronage policy which offered too little to orthodox Whigs thirsting for federal jobs. Some regulars were able to forge a close relationship with the new administration. These included the charming William H. Seward, a progressive antislavery politician who dominated the New York Whig party in tandem with Thurlow Weed, the Machiavellian editor of the *Albany State Register*. Seward's ingratiating manner enabled him to develop ties with most of Taylor's cabinet members and the president himself, much to the dismay of Seward's New York rival, Vice President Millard Fillmore, who found his predominantly conservative allies left out in the cold when the spoils of office were distributed. Other loyal Whigs were demoralized by the administration's apparent reluctance to dismiss Democrats, particularly in states such as Pennsylvania where there seemed to be a real chance of fostering a new cross-party Taylor Republican organization. The cabinet's inept handling of patronage distribution fostered a multiplicity of internal grievances which would destabilize the Whig party during a critical phase of its existence.

Equally serious, for Taylor and the country, was the absence of a binding solution to the slavery question. The Thirtieth Congress adjourned for the last time in March 1849 without legislating decisively on the issue, the main stumbling block being the determination

of northern congressmen from all parties to apply the Wilmot Proviso to the chief proposals under discussion. Its successor would not
convene until November. President Taylor, therefore, was left free to
pursue his own executive strategy of bypassing the territorial stage
of organization in the Mexican Cession. To this end, federal envoys
were dispatched to the Far West in order to foster rapid applications
for statehood from California and New Mexico. Because the president
knew that such interventionist activities would be controversial in the
country at large, he sought to keep them as secret as possible. Most
Whigs outside the cabinet therefore remained unaware of the administration's intentions and were consequently handicapped in their
efforts to compete successfully in the state elections of 1849. So
desperate were northern Whigs to combat antislavery attacks
emanating from Democrats and Free Soilers, that the president
was forced to come to their aid in the summer by expressing his
confidence that slavery would not be able to expand into the new
territories. Such unguarded comments merely alarmed Taylor's
southern Whig allies and failed to help his party recover its electoral
fortunes. Internally divided, deprived of their traditional economic
issues, and dangerously exposed in both sections on the slavery
question, the Whigs won only 30 percent of the year's congressional
races compared with 57 percent in 1848.[25]

The new Congress opened amid a sense of impending crisis. In
September 1849 the Californians had written a free-state constitution and applied for admission to the Union without embracing
the Utah Mormons as Taylor had wished. New Mexico had set up a
territorial government thereby undermining the administration's
policy of promoting immediate statehood in the Mexican Cession.
Even more seriously, in a move that was engineered by Calhoun,
Mississippi Democrats had called on southerners to meet in convention at Nashville in June 1850 to devise a common defense against
antislavery aggression. Southern Democrats' hawkish line on slavery
during the election campaign forced their local Whig opponents to
adopt an increasingly uncompromising line on southern rights.

Particularly galling for the likes of the Georgia Whigs, Stephens
and Toombs, was the president's failure to announce a satisfactory
plan for the Far West – one that would allow them to counter Democratic jibes that they were soft on those who sought to interfere in
southern affairs – and the vociferous support given to the Wilmot
Proviso by their northern counterparts. Sectional tensions within
the Whig organization became apparent at the very beginning of
the Congress when Stephens, Toombs, and four other southern

Whigs bolted a party caucus when they failed to secure guarantees that no attempt would be made to impose the Proviso on the Mexican Cession or to abolish slavery in the District of Columbia. Internal divisions within both major parties then resulted in a prolonged, fractious struggle to organize the House of Representatives, a contest that was not resolved until the sixty-third ballot when the moderate Georgia Democrat, Howell Cobb, was finally elected speaker.

Once Zachary Taylor had finally made public his desire that Congress should admit California and New Mexico to the Union as states, leading politicians in Washington labored to fashion a coherent response. Although, as the president emphasized in his special message to the legislature in January 1850, his policy had the advantage of circumventing the Wilmot Proviso, southerners from both parties knew the final result would be the same: the exclusion of slavery from what they regarded as the common property of the several states. Not only did this exclusion strike at their sense of pride and honor, but it also reduced the chances that the South could sustain its influence in national affairs by carving out additional slave states in the West. Many southern whites also believed that a ban on slavery expansion would make it harder to diffuse the manifold blessings of slaveownership (with adverse consequences for class relations within their section) or shared Calhoun's fear that imposition of the Proviso would increase the risk of slave rebellions at home.

The response of some southern leaders was to begin organizing for secession. Prominent among them was James Henry Hammond, a South Carolina planter who drew on his network of regional contacts to promote support for the Nashville convention – a meeting that he expected to initiate the process of disunion. Fears of Yankee domination and slave emancipation impelled him to act. 'We will be in a clear minority when California comes in,' he told Calhoun on March 6,

> & in twenty or thirty years there will be ten or more free states west of the Mississippi & ten more north of the St. Lawrence and the Lakes ... Long before the North gets this vast accession of strength she will ride over us rough shod – proclaim freedom or something equivalent to it to our Slaves & reduce us to the condition of Hayti. She would not even do what England did to Jamaica. She would do what the Constitutional Assembly did to Hayti. If we do not act now we deliberately consign our children ... to the flames. What

a holocaust for us to place upon the Altar of that Union
for which the South & West have had such a bigoted &
superstitious veneration.[26]

Hammond's allies were under no illusions about the likely consequences of secession agitation. 'Do you agree with me, that war
must follow disunion[?]', asked one Charleston radical candidly. As
the North would not acquiesce in peaceable secession, 'ought not
some agreement be made secretly between the leaders, as to the
preparations for war[?]'[27]

Fully aware of the threat to the Union posed by southern
hotheads and the North's determination to adhere to the Wilmot
Proviso, Henry Clay introduced eight resolutions into the Senate at
the end of January. The measures were conceived as a 'comprehensive scheme' which the veteran Kentucky statesman believed would
produce a final settlement of the slavery issue.[28] The first provided
for the admission of California as a state without reference to slavery.
The second provided for the establishment of territorial governments
for New Mexico and Utah. Again, no mention was made of slavery
because, maintained Clay, the peculiar institution did not exist in
the Cession under Mexican law and was unlikely to be introduced.
The third and fourth, said Clay, were linked: they proposed a substantially reduced boundary for Texas (which was then claiming
a large portion of New Mexican territory) in return for federal
assumption of Texas's pre-annexation debt. The fifth resolve deemed
it inexpedient to abolish slavery in Washington, DC, unless
Marylanders agreed and willing owners were compensated. The sixth
proposed to ban the capital's embarrassing slave trade. The seventh
called for a more effective fugitive slave law that would curtail
southern outrage at the way northern states such as Pennsylvania
sought to evade their constitutional duty to return runaways to their
masters. A final resolution denied any intention on the part of
Congress to interfere with the interstate slave trade.

Clay spoke to his plan beneath an expectant and crowded Senate
gallery on February 5–6. Central to his argument was his insistence
that a combination of Mexican law and an arid climate represented
insuperable obstacles to the spread of slavery into the Far West.
Northerners should therefore recognize that the only consequence
of the Wilmot Proviso was to stir up sectional antagonism. 'Elevate
yourselves from the mud and mire of mere party contention', he
told them. Act 'as lovers of liberty, and lovers, above all, of this
Union.'[29]

Clay's compromise measures played well in the country at large. However, opposition from radicals on both sides of the Mason-Dixon Line was intense. While the new Free Soil senator from Ohio, Salmon P. Chase, denounced the measures as 'sentiment' for the North and 'substance' for the South, many southern Democrats sensed that the Great Pacificator's long-term aim was a Union without slavery. In spite of being a slaveholder himself, Clay was a well-known advocate of gradual emancipation coupled with the colonization of blacks in Africa. His many admirers, Abraham Lincoln among them, held this position to be the only stance that a progressive nationalist could adopt without endangering the Union.

On balance, Clay's compromise measures offered relatively little to the South in terms of meaningful gains.[30] California would be admitted as a free state. The failure to apply common law to a region in which slavery had been prohibited already almost certainly meant that New Mexico and Utah would also be free. The slave state of Texas was to have its boundaries significantly reduced. Abolition of the capital's slave trade was a long-time abolitionist goal. All the South would gain would be the symbolic absence of the Wilmot Proviso as well as uncertain promises on the security of slave property and the continuation of the domestic slave trade. It was little wonder, then, that southern Democratic senators were quick to condemn Clay's proposals. In separate remarks Jefferson Davis of Mississippi insisted that under the Constitution slavery must follow the flag and warned that any failure to protect southern rights in the Far West would lead to secession. Virginia senator James M. Mason read out a speech by the dying Calhoun in which the South Carolinian similarly urged Congress to sustain southern rights as the price for maintaining the Union of the Founders.

President Taylor was unimpressed with Henry Clay's rival plan and appalled by the treasonous utterances of southern radicals. He gleaned little more satisfaction from the contributions of two other powerful senators. On March 7 Daniel Webster gave his backing to Clay's compromise measures in a characteristic setpiece oration which sought to strengthen the hands of the nationalists. 'I wish to speak today,' intoned the powerful Whig leader, 'not as a Massachusetts man, nor as a northern man, but as an American ... I speak today for the preservation of the Union. "Hear me for my cause." '[31] In his speech, Webster was at pains to criticize northern abolitionists for their role in destabilizing the country. The move disgusted antislavery supporters in New England. Four days later Senator William H. Seward parted company from Taylor by reiterating his support for the Wilmot Proviso. God, he said, had a divine purpose for the Far West. Therefore, when his stewards came to consider slavery they owed allegiance to 'a higher law' than the Constitution. While the positions advanced by Webster and Seward were not unrepresentative of their personal views on slavery, they were also rooted in political expediency. Webster was courting the center ground as a precursor to running for president in 1852. Seward wanted to bolster his influence within the New York Whig party in which his own predominantly antislavery allies were engaged in a power struggle with the more conservative friends of Vice President Fillmore. Taylor was especially infuriated by Seward's failure to endorse his statehood proposals and told his ally, Alexander Bullitt, to attack the New Yorker in the administration's Washington organ.

From mid-February onward anti-Taylor supporters of compromise began to coalesce and then gain the initiative in Congress. These moderates (who were generally opposed by Proviso advocates led by the fiery Jacksonian warrior, Thomas Hart Benton) included Senator Stephen Douglas, chairman of the committee on territories, who was determined for personal, partisan, and civic reasons to insure that popular sovereignty was embedded in any settlement. Also prominent among this nascent bipartisan bloc were Alexander Stephens and Robert Toombs who walked out of the Whig caucus in December and were savaged by the president as traitors. Both men appear to have been ready to endorse popular sovereignty as the *quid pro quo* for acquiescing in California's admission as a free state. As long as its backers did not specify the stage at which slavery could be prohibited from a territory, popular sovereignty allowed for the possibility (however remote) of slavery expanding into the West. This might be just enough for them to beat off proslavery attacks on their flank at home and enable them to benefit from the substantial unionist feeling which still existed in Georgia. Their fellow Georgian, the Democratic Speaker of the House, Howell Cobb, aligned himself with the compromise bloc for similar reasons. Signs of southern support for compromise drove secessionists like Hammond to despair. The people of the South, he told the author William Gilmore Simms at the end of March, 'are wholly provincial in feeling – will not sustain anything Southern – not even Slavery I fear. If we cannot infuse more of the manufacturing & commercial spirit into them – more vim in every thing they are gone. You see there is to be a regular back out at Washington. All will be surrendered to party.'[32]

The decisive breakthrough came on April 8, when Henry Clay announced his acceptance of a proposal, first made by Henry S.

Foote of Mississippi, to combine his measures into an 'omnibus bill'. Combination, he said, would prevent passage of individual measures and not others and provide some insurance against an executive veto from the hostile Taylor. The Senate set up a select committee to discuss all the measures relating to slavery and the territories. Headed by Clay, it reported on May 8. Three proposals were announced. The first, the omnibus, linked California's admission as a free state with (a) provision for territorial governments in New Mexico and Utah and (b) settlement of the Texas–New Mexico boundary question and federal assumption of the Texas debt. The omnibus slightly increased the size of Texas and, contrary to Douglas's reading of popular sovereignty, denied the right of territorial legislatures to prohibit slavery at any stage of the territorial process. It also abjured territorial lawmakers from passing legislation replacing the existing (Mexican) prohibition of slavery. Two separate items were appended: a fugitive slave law (slightly amended to take into account the objections of antislavery critics) and a recommendation for the abolition of the slave trade in Washington.

In spite of the fact that most Americans breathed a sigh of relief when delegates to the Nashville convention in June agreed to adjourn and reconvene in November when Congress had come to some decision, the Union remained in real peril during the summer of 1850. Free-soil senators who demanded the application of the Wilmot Proviso to the territories and proslavery southern Democrats who despised Clay's original proposals sought desperately to undermine the work of the committee against a background sharpened by the growing prospect of war between Texas and New Mexico over their border dispute. Then, on July 9, President Taylor died suddenly, probably as a result of acute gastroenteritis. His opposition to any plan except his own had represented a major barrier to compromise. Now the supporters of sectional peace had a new ally in Millard Fillmore, a patriotic Whig whose factional struggles with Seward and determination to solve the boundary problem before the Texans began a shooting war with federal troops in New Mexico inclined him to favor the moderate bloc. Centrists were further buoyed by the explicit insertion of popular sovereignty into the omnibus. As Douglas had intended from the outset, territorial legislatures were now empowered to prohibit or allow slavery subject only to a gubernatorial veto or disavowal by Congress.

Although the omnibus unraveled worryingly in three roll-call votes on the Texas boundary measure at the end of July, Douglas and his allies in the House successfully piloted the individual bills through Congress. Southern Whigs, northern Democrats, and a minority of pro-Fillmore northern Whigs supplied a nationalist core which enabled the Senate to pass the various compromise measures individually. Sectional ultras provided the margin of victory, voting for or against the separate bills as they chose. Fillmore's strong backing for an immediate and satisfactory settlement of the Texas boundary played a decisive role in the House's passage of the so-called 'little omnibus' which provided generous compensation, in terms of land and money, for Austin's decision to abandon its claims over a portion of New Mexico. The other bills were pushed quickly through the lower chamber along the same lines as they had been passed in the Senate and then signed into law by a relieved president.

Passage of the Fugitive Slave Act, however, illustrated the absence of a genuine consensus. The measure was extremely controversial. Not only did it intensify federal government involvement in what antislavery northerners regarded as the sordid business of manhunting but it also implicated them personally by empowering federal marshals to call out civilian posses to track down fugitives. Southerners, on the other hand, demanded its enactment to provide greater security for their property, to counterbalance the loss of California, and to ensure that northerners abided by the dictates of the Constitution. When the measure came to a vote in the House, it passed by 109 votes to 76. Less than a third of the votes in favor were cast by northerners and all but two of these were Democrats. Nearly all those northern Whigs who voted in the final roll call opposed the bill. The 20 who chose not to vote at all did so primarily because of their reluctance to counter a bill that had such strong backing from their own president. In other words, a measure that was central to the overall settlement failed to garner anything resembling majority support from northern representatives.

Yet, for all its undeniable political and moral flaws, what David Potter has termed 'the Armistice of 1850' was a major legislative achievement.[33] If the actual voting patterns provided little evidence of sectional cooperation beyond the Fillmoreite/northern Democrat/southern Whig axis essential to its passage, it nevertheless pulled the rug from beneath the feet of secessionists and antislavery radicals alike. A majority of Americans rejoiced wildly at the nation's salvation, only dimly aware that the seeds of destruction remained embedded in the legislation their leaders had agreed to endorse.

The Democrats ascendant, 1850–52

The deliberations of power elites in Congress had an immediate and direct impact on one of the country's most marginal groups. Early in October 1850 a large crowd of free black men and women gathered at the Belknap Street church in Boston to formulate a response to the new Fugitive Slave Law which placed all of them at the mercy of southern manhunters. They were angry folk, determined to assert their identity as Americans. Several of the leaders spoke in relatively conservative terms, anxious to combat emigrationist sentiment kindled by the Act. William C. Nell, a self-taught Garrisonian abolitionist, had no doubt that blacks had a place in the United States. Keenly aware of the role that his people had played in the War of Independence and the War of 1812, he exclaimed that 'The example of the Revolutionary Fathers is a most significant one to us, when MAN is likely to be deprived of his God-given liberty.' Charles L. Remond, another black antislavery activist, agreed. Any suggestion that blacks should prepare to leave the country was, he said, a mistaken one: Massachusetts 'should be our Canada'; Bunker Hill the people's model for action.

Others were similarly convinced that blacks should stay and secure their rights but even more inclined to use the Revolutionary heritage to support militant action. One speaker was minuted as saying that 'it was with the United States Government they were to contend, and that their position in resisting this obnoxious law was that of rebels, – a name which he did not hesitate to accept, if loyalty to the constitution made him false to humanity'. When a patently alarmed William Lloyd Garrison urged his listeners to pursue moral suasion rather than physical resistance, one respondent told the veteran abolitionist that he 'would not be quietly led like a lamb to the slaughter'.[34] In spite of some differences of opinion between Garrisonians and non-Garrisonians over the use of force to defy the law, the crowd was united in its contempt for colonization, its defiance of slavery, and the need for constant vigilance on the part of everyone in the community, dock laborers and washerwomen included. If President Fillmore expected the country to rally behind the Compromise, it was evident from this event and others like it across the North that free blacks would not heed him.

Hatred of the Fugitive Slave Act mobilized whites as well as blacks. Once the new US commissioners appointed under the law began to exercise their powers with the help of federal officers, many abolitionists such as the outspoken Unitarian minister, Theodore Parker, inclined toward force as the only way to resist what they saw as slavery's tightening grip on the nation. Parker headed the interracial Vigilance Committee in Boston which tried in vain to prevent the rendition of an alleged fugitive slave, Thomas Sims, in April 1851. Ralph Waldo Emerson himself, hitherto suspicious of political radicalism, was appalled by the government's vigorous efforts to prosecute a defenseless black youth. It was time, he told readers of Garrison's *Liberator*, for every lover of human freedom to 'enter his protest for humanity against the detestable statute of the last congress'.[35]

Harriet Beecher Stowe, another politically moderate northerner and a member of the North's growing number of women writers, was similarly radicalized by high profile cases involving the enforcement of the Fugitive Slave Act. As well as personally harboring runaway blacks and urging her fellow Beechers to oppose the measure, she began writing essays for the *National Era*, the Free Soil party's chief organ in Washington, DC. In the spring of 1851, she told the paper's editor, Gamaliel Bailey (an Ohioan closely allied to Salmon Chase), that she had begun work on a much bigger antislavery project. 'Up to this year', she wrote revealingly, 'I have always felt that I had no particular call to meddle with this subject, and I dreaded to expose even my own mind to the full force of its exciting power. But I feel now that the time is come when even a woman or a child who can speak a word for freedom and humanity is bound to speak.'[36] Based heavily on her brother Charles's stories of his experiences in Louisiana as well as firsthand accounts of slavery provided by the black abolitionist, Frederick Douglass, and her own domestic servant, Eliza Buck, Stowe's dramatic tale of flight from, and suffering under, slavery was serialized weekly in the *Era* from June 1851. It was finally published as a novel, *Uncle Tom's Cabin*, in the spring of 1852. Shot through with romantic racism and Christian sentimentalism, the book was a remarkable success. Ten thousand copies were sold in the first week alone and 300,000 had been bought by the end of the first year.[37] Such phenomenal domestic sales testified not only to Stowe's talents as an author, but also to the widespread unpopularity of the Fugitive Slave Act in the North.

Normally, dislike of the Act did not translate into political action. Although many northerners were uneasy about certain aspects of the Compromise, the majority were prepared to accept it for the sake of national harmony. Apart from blacks and white abolitionists, the only elements in the North to remain publicly opposed to the Compromise were the Free Soilers (now vastly reduced in number owing to the Barnburners' decision to return to the Democratic fold) and the much larger number of antislavery Whigs.

The national Whig party, in fact, was seriously riven by the sectional accord. Southern Whigs generally rallied behind the Compromise during late 1850 and early 1851 but in the deep South they tended to merge with like-minded Democrats to form Union coalitions that could not be tarred by an association with politicians like Seward. Northern Whigs were deeply divided. A minority wing, anchored by powerful commercial elements in New York City, strongly supported President Fillmore's efforts to present the Compromise as a final settlement of the slavery question. Most of these conservatives deprecated the persistent attempts of sickly sentimentalists in their party to promote the rights of black people. Such efforts undermined the Union and allowed the Democrats to beat them by playing the race card. 'We must either break down the negro party in this city, or all be painted black', wrote one agitated Fillmoreite from New York where Sewardites and conservative 'Silver Greys' were still competing furiously for control of the spoils in the early 1850s.[38] Antislavery northern Whigs rejected such arguments, representing, as most of them did, evangelical constituencies in which hostility toward the Fugitive Slave Act ran deep. Yet unsympathetic though they were to the Compromise, even their opposition was tempered by an awareness of the strength of nationalist feeling in the country. Individual Whigs continued to campaign for reform of the Fugitive Slave Act in spite of the president's insistence on 'finality', but only in Vermont did the local party actually pass a new 'personal liberty law' designed to protect the rights of alleged fugitives and guaranteed to infuriate the South.

While the Whigs fought among themselves, the Democratic party gathered itself for the 1852 presidential election campaign. Factional splits continued to burden the party in several states, particularly in the deep South where pro-Union Democrats had coalesced with Whigs in support of the Compromise. The general trend within the party as a whole, however, was toward unity. Several events made it clear to most southern Democrats that a majority of their constituents were willing to abide by the Compromise – at least conditionally. In November 1850 the Nashville convention disbanded without promoting secession. The following month Georgia nationalists led by Stephens, Toombs, and Cobb formed the state Union party at Milledgeville. The organization's platform pledged that Georgia would adhere to the Compromise as 'a permanent adjustment' as long as northerners abided by the terms agreed in Washington, especially the Fugitive Slave Law. Local Democrats, such as ex-Governor George Towns whose secessionist urges sprang from the rich soil of the plantation belt, converted themselves into Southern Rights men but soon found their radicalism disavowed at the polls. In 1851 Cobb was elected governor with 60 percent of the popular vote and Unionists dominated the congressional and legislative contests. Secessionists met a similar fate in other areas of the South, again primarily because of cooperation between black-belt Whigs and upcountry Democrats. In Mississippi, Jefferson Davis was persuaded to resign his Senate seat and run for governor as a Southern Rights candidate. He lost narrowly to the Unionist Henry S. Foote. In neighboring Alabama, Unionists were victorious in state and congressional elections. South Carolina, the engine room of secession, delivered its verdict in November when cooperationists, the supporters of the Compromise, triumphed easily over the radicals whose leader, Robert Barnwell Rhett Sr, sensibly left Charleston for Europe before the results were announced.

As it became clear that the Compromise had trumped secession, southern Democrats began to return to the fold, their passage eased by the party's decision to nominate Franklin Pierce for president in June 1852. Pierce was sympathetic to southern concerns yet possessed a political record obscure enough to allow even free-soil Barnburners like David Wilmot to consider him trustworthy on the slavery issue. A handsome, likeable man too fond of strong drink for his own good, he triumphed at the national convention in Baltimore primarily because his stronger rivals, Stephen Douglas and James Buchanan, failed to secure the two-thirds majority necessary for nomination, thereby forcing the convention to draft a dark-horse candidate who could draw votes from the major candidates. The delegates were divided by many things apart from the presidency, not least factional disputes involving the return of the prodigal Barnburners and the merits or demerits of popular sovereignty. However, they managed to unite on a platform that restated the party's Jacksonian faith in limited government and strong opposition to congressional interference with slavery. Significantly, they also pledged to uphold the Compromise measures, the Fugitive Slave Law included.

While the Democrats closed ranks, the Whigs entered the 1852 presidential election campaign in something close to disarray.[39] The Compromise had divided the party in the North and sundered many of the bonds between northern and southern Whigs. Equally seriously, the return of national prosperity in the late 1840s and early 1850s (mainly as a result of California gold, large-scale British investment in US railroads, and buoyant European demand for American grain) had deprived the party of many of its traditional economic issues. What use was Henry Clay's American System now that business was booming without the aid of federal intervention in the economy? At the state level, pragmatic Democrats had stolen the Whigs' clothing by softening their stance on credit provision, supporting government aid to railroad corporations, and sponsoring general incorporation laws to promote business.

Worse still, northern Whigs in particular were being buffeted by a raft of divisive issues generated by the latest wave of European immigration. With many of the new immigrants entitled to vote for the first time in 1852, the Whig party was confronted with the choice of competing with the Democrats for their support or fanning the flames of nativism to win over American Protestants. Matters were made especially complicated by the fact that Whigs at the grass roots could not agree whether state and local governments should prohibit sales of liquor. Although social drinking was generally popular among the Irish and Germans, many evangelicals regarded drink as a threat to family welfare as well as to the development of self discipline and individual responsibility in the sight of God. Whig strategists were thus faced with several unpalatable options. They could yield to the demands of temperance advocates and surrender the immigrant vote to the Democrats; oppose prohibition and witness the proliferation of independent prohibition candidates at the local level; or sit on the fence and risk alienating everyone. By early 1852 the absence of a clear party line on prohibition – or indeed any other issue – had begun to erode still further an already weakened party.

Matters came to a head in the spring and summer. In April a large majority of northern Whigs in Congress voted against a motion in the House declaring the Compromise a final settlement of the slavery issue. Subsequently, they rejected a similar measure in caucus. Those southern Whigs who had not abandoned the party for Union coalitions were appalled and, encouraged by President Fillmore, redoubled their efforts to secure a pro-Compromise platform at the national convention in Baltimore. Antislavery Whigs, however, understood that this would not only negate their own appeal in areas where hostility toward the South was pronounced but also play into the hands of conservative National Whigs against whom they were generally arrayed in struggles to control the patronage. Their objective was to repeat the successful strategy of 1848 and nominate a popular military hero for president. Their choice on this occasion was General Winfield Scott whose forces had captured Mexico City in September 1847.

At a tumultuous convention in the Hall of the Maryland Institute in Baltimore, the Whigs struggled to find common ground. Lacking a majority, the antislavery forces were outmaneuvered on the platform issue by conservatives who were divided between the supporters of Fillmore and Daniel Webster. The resulting document declared the party's willingness to acquiesce in the Compromise of 1850 (no exception was made for the Fugitive Slave Law) and denounced 'all further agitation of the question thus settled, as dangerous to our peace'.[40] The Scott men divided roughly evenly over the Compromise plank, indicating a reluctance among many delegates to maintain even a semblance of internal unity. Their efforts to secure the nomination, however, bore fruit when Scott was nominated on the fifty-third ballot. The friends of Webster clung stubbornly to their favorite, thereby preventing the southerners from nominating their own standard-bearer, Fillmore.

The decision of both major parties to support the Compromise and their failure to adopt distinctive positions on other issues turned the election into a vacuous contest over personality. Scott might have altered matters by appealing to nativist sentiment in the country at large. However, the lure of immigrant votes proved too much for party strategists. The candidate bid openly for Irish support in the fall, a politically unwise move that left the growing numbers of nativists with little stomach for the fight. In spite of being disparaged as 'the hero of many a well fought bottle', Pierce (an unremarkable commander in the Mexican War) triumphed easily in the November election, winning 85.8 percent of the electoral college vote and carrying 27 states to Scott's four.[41] Apathy prevailed everywhere, primarily to the detriment of the Whigs. Alarmed by their candidate's close ties to Seward and disappointed by his lack of enthusiasm for the party's pro-Compromise plank, southern Whigs found little reason to vote for a man they feared might prove another abolitionist tool like Taylor. Northern conservatives who had placed their faith in Fillmore or Webster were similarly unimpressed by the general, and stayed away *en masse* from the polls in several states. With Whigs suffering additional defeats in state gubernatorial races, many of their number (radicals and conservatives) were ready to pronounce the party at an end.

In the short term, the Union had survived the political trauma induced by the introduction of the Wilmot Proviso and southern attempts to resist its implementation. The sheer tedium of the 1852 campaign (as well as the poor showing of the anti-Compromise Free Soilers who won only 5.1 percent of the popular vote) indicated that Unionist politicians from both parties had taken some of the heat out of the slavery question.

Henry Clay died in June of the election year, four months before Webster himself surrendered his presidential ambitions to the ages. Shortly after Clay's death, the Kentucky senator's embalmed body, encased in a heavily ornamented cast-iron coffin, was transported by railroad and steamboat through the great cities of the United States. Thousands came to look upon his corpse and to reflect upon the debt owed to him by the nation. Many wept openly, disbelieving that the political world could go on without the greatest statesman of the age and fearful perhaps that his work might unravel. 'Who shall now guard,' lamented one inexpert eulogist,

> The helmet and the destiny of state
> When storms and darkness wildly hover round,
> with such a gallant hand?[42]

Such patriotic concerns were entirely justified. History records that Henry Clay, arguably the principal architect of the Whig party and the Compromise of 1850, died just in time. Within two years of his sad demise, both of his achievements lay in ruins.

Notes

1. James H. Schroeder, *Mr. Polk's War: American Opposition and Dissent, 1846–1848* (Madison, Wis., 1973), p.117.

2. Henry Nash Smith, *Virgin Land: The American West as Symbol and Myth* (1950: repr. Cambridge, Mass., 1978), p.84.

3. Quitman to Eliza Quitman, Sept. 18, 1847, Quitman Family Papers, SHC 616.

4. Garrison to Richard D. Webb, March 1, 1847, in Walter M. Merrill, ed., *The Letters of William Lloyd Garrison: Vol. 3, No Union With Slaveholders 1841–1849* (Cambridge, Mass., 1973), p.470.

5. Quoted in Richard J. Carwardine, *Evangelicals and Politics in Antebellum America* (New Haven, Conn., 1993), p.146.

6. Quoted in Susan-Mary Grant, *North Over South: Northern Nationalism and American Identity in the Antebellum Era* (Lawrence, Kan., 2000), p.71.

7. Michael A. Morrison, *Slavery and the American West: The Eclipse of Manifest Destiny* (Chapel Hill, NC, 1997), pp.44–5.

8. Calhoun, 'Speech and Resolutions on the Restriction of Slavery from the Territories', Feb. 19, 1847, in Clyde N. Wilson and Shirley Bright Cook, *The Papers of John C. Calhoun: Vol. 24, 1846–1847* (Columbia, SC, 1998), p.175.

9. Calhoun to Henry W. Perroneau, Sept. 28, 1847 in *ibid.*, p.580.

10. Quoted in Leonard L. Richards, *The Slave Power: The Free North and Southern Domination 1780–1860* (Baton Rouge, La, 2000), p.152.

11. *Portland Evening Advertiser*, Aug. 13, 1846.

12. In March 1820 Congress had admitted Missouri to the Union as a slave state but excluded slavery from the rest of the Louisiana Purchase north of the line 36°30′N, the southern border of Missouri.

13. Johnson to A.O. Nicholson, Jan. 18, 1848, GLC 4628.

14. C.W. Hester quoted in Michael F. Holt, *The Rise and Fall of the American Whig Party: Jacksonian Politics and the Onset of the Civil War* (New York, 1999), p.317.

15. *Ibid.*, pp.285–90.

16. Sumner to Chase, Dec. 12, 1846, in Beverly Wilson Palmer, *The Selected Letters of Charles Sumner*, 2 vols (Boston, 1990), 1, p.180.

17. George W. Julian, *Political Recollections 1840 to 1872* (Chicago, 1884), p.56.

18. Quoted in Frederick J. Blue, *The Free Soilers: Third Party Politics 1848–54* (Urbana, Ill., 1973), p.75.

19. Garrison to Edmund Quincy, Aug. 10, 1848, in Merrill, ed., *Letters*, 3, pp.581–2.

20. For a close analysis of the 1848 presidential campaign and election results see Holt, *Rise and Fall*, pp.368–81.

21. For a discussion of the California gold rush see pp.272–4 below.

22. Quoted in Irving H. Bartlett, *John C. Calhoun: A Biography* (New York, 1993), pp.364–5.

23. Quoted in *ibid.*, p.365.

24. Howell Cobb *et al.*, *To Our Constituents* (printed pamphlet, n.p., n.d.) [1850], p.8, GLC 6070.

25. Holt, *Rise and Fall*, p.455.

26. Hammond to Calhoun, March 6, 1850, James Henry Hammond Papers, LC (mic).

27. J.M. Walker to Hammond, Feb. 25, 1850, Hammond Papers.

28. Quoted in Robert V. Remini, *Henry Clay: Statesman for the Union* (New York, 1991), p.731.

29. Quoted in *ibid.*, p.736.

30. Holt, *Rise and Fall*, pp.479–80.

31. Charles M. Wiltse, ed., *The Papers of Daniel Webster: Speeches and Formal Writings: Vol. 2, 1834–1852* (Hanover, NH, 1988), pp.515–16.

32. Hammond to Simms, March 26, 1850, Hammond Papers.

33. David Potter, *The Impending Crisis 1848–1861* (New York, 1976), pp.90–120.

34. 'Declaration of Sentiments of the Colored Citizens of Boston on the Fugitive Slave Bill', (printed broadside, n.p., n.d.) [1850], GLC 5345.

35. Quoted in Robert D. Richardson, Jr, *Emerson: The Mind on Fire* (Berkeley, 1995), p.496.

36. Quoted in Joan D. Hedrick, *Harriet Beecher Stowe: A Life*, (New York, 1994), p.208.

37. *Ibid.*, pp.218–20, 222–3.

38. Holt, *Rise and Fall*, p.595.

39. The most reliable and insightful accounts of the 1852 election are *ibid.*, pp.673–764, and William E. Gienapp, *The Origins of the Republican Party 1852–1856* (New York, 1987), pp.13–35.

40. Quoted in Holt, *Rise and* Fall, p.717.

41. Larry Gara, *The Presidency of Franklin Pierce* (Lawrence, Kan., 1991), pp.38–9.

42. Anne Henry Ehrenpreis, ed., *Happy Country This America: The Travel Diary of Henry Arthur Bright* (Columbus, Ohio, 1978), p.240.

3

POLITICAL CRISES OF THE 1850s

Franklin Pierce's election appeared to signify that the Union was safe from destruction. The Democratic party may have been threatened by the same political currents as the Whigs but, unlike the opposition, it remained a plausibly national organization. Whereas the strength of moral antislavery feeling among northern Whigs severed the ties to their proslavery copartisans in the South, the Democrats' continued commitment to states' rights and cultural pluralism enabled them to hold onto their core constituencies in all regions of the country. Radicals on both sides of the Mason-Dixon Line, eager for a sectional reorientation of politics, had seen their hopes dashed. It was Stephen A. Douglas, ironically one of the most patriotic devotees of Manifest Destiny in Congress, who, unwittingly, set in train a series of events that was to lead to secession and civil war. Douglas's bill to organize the remaining portion of the 1803 Louisiana Purchase on the basis of popular sovereignty produced a groundswell of anger in the North that ultimately enabled an entirely new party to supplant the Whigs as the main opposition to the Democratic party. The process by which the antislavery and antisouthern Republican coalition came together was complicated by an unexpected surge of political nativism in the mid-1850s but a serious outbreak of sectional violence in Kansas rendered 'fusion' close to completion by the time of the 1856 presidential election. Although the Democrats won that race, the Republicans emerged victorious in most of the northern states. For the first time, a majority of southern whites felt their slave-based society to be under immediate threat. Secession, their response to the election of a Republican president in 1860, would bring on civil war.

The Kansas-Nebraska Act

No sooner had Franklin Pierce's political career reached its apogee than tragedy struck. Just weeks before the inauguration ceremony Pierce was traveling with his family on the Boston to Concord railroad when the train careered off the tracks and tumbled down an embankment. His young son, Bennie, died in the accident. His wife, Jane, never really overcame her grief and the president-elect was consumed by powerful feelings of guilt that exacerbated his natural indecisiveness.

Pierce was inaugurated on March 4, 1853. With snowflakes eddying down around him, he told listeners that he would pursue the Jacksonian tradition of territorial expansion (ideally peacefully), maintain the rights of the states and adhere rigidly to the Compromise of 1850. His efforts to bolster both the Democratic party and the Union resulted in a patronage policy designed to attach as many key leaders and factions to his administration as possible. Unfortunately for Pierce, his inclusive policy alienated as many Democrats as it attracted. The decision of his old acquaintance Jefferson Davis to become secretary of war looked to be a major boon, for Davis was one of the most influential southern rights men in the party. However, the appointment alienated southern Union Democrats such as Howell Cobb of Georgia. Appointing the Barnburner John A. Dix to the lucrative post of assistant collector at the port of New York made similar sense in that it offered an olive branch to northern free-soilers who chafed at southern influence within the party, but it had the negative effect of angering 'hardshell Hunkers' like Senator Daniel S. Dickinson who wanted the Barnburners marginalized for their apostasy in 1848. The overall result of the president's well-meaning policy was thus to disillusion many of those Democrats who had been most supportive of the Compromise. Pierce's policy initiatives during 1853 did little to improve matters. Many northerners in the party were perturbed especially by his favoritism toward southern schemes of expansion and infrastructural development and by his public condemnations of antislavery agitation. Many free-soil Democrats remained at best conditional supporters of the administration or at worst, in states such as Maine where factionalism and prohibition had blurred existing party lines, preferred to cooperate actively with like-minded Whigs and political abolitionists.

The disastrous consequences of the president's failure to unite either the country or the party became clear during the early months of 1854. On January 4, Stephen Douglas, chairman of the Senate committee on territories, reported a bill to organize Nebraska

Territory. Nebraska constituted the unorganized portion of the 1820 Missouri Compromise and, lying north of the line 36°30′, was generally understood by northerners to be barred to slavery. Using language taken directly from the territorial provisions of the 1850 Compromise, the bill provided that any states formed in the region should be admitted with or without slavery and empowered the territorial legislature to deal with all rightful subjects under the Constitution (including slavery). In his accompanying report, however, Douglas seemed to imply that the Missouri Compromise restrictions would retain the force of law until the territorial government acted.

The 'Little Giant' had several motives for introducing the most fateful piece of legislation ever brought before the United States Congress. Although he relied heavily on the profits of his late wife's Mississippi cotton plantation, his intention was not to spread the peculiar institution. His main aim was to secure southern support for a bill designed to pave the way for a Pacific railroad. A staunch nationalist as well as loyal party man, Douglas believed not only that this ambitious project would do a better job of reuniting the Democrats than had Pierce's patronage policy but also that it would greatly enhance the country's power by binding California to the East and furthering the Democrats' goal of promoting trade with Asia. In the previous session, southern senators had opposed a bill to provide federal backing for a transcontinental railroad, primarily because the designated route was a central rather than southern one. (Several leading southerners, Secretary of War Davis among them, favored the building of the road but insisted that it should link New Orleans and San Diego.) Douglas therefore knew that if he wanted to organize Nebraska as a necessary precondition for the construction of a railway along a more northerly route, he would have to make the relevant act palatable to southerners. Prodded by southern Democrats determined to maximize the property rights of slaveholders, he made it absolutely clear a few days later that the bill did permit the territorial legislature to decide the status of slavery if it so desired. Popular sovereignty, the quintessential embodiment of republican self-government as Douglas liked to brand it, was thus enshrined in the bill in an attempt to bridge the differences between northern and southern Democrats.

An article in the proslavery *Washington Sentinel* on January 14 revealed that the senator from Illinois had not gone far enough. Further agitation of the slavery issue, insisted the *Sentinel*, could only be damaging to the country. Therefore, that portion of the Missouri Compromise relating to slavery in Nebraska should be 'directly and positively repealed'.[1] If Douglas had any doubts about how he should react, Archibald Dixon, a Tennessee Whig, helped to force his hand. Eager to attract bipartisan support for his forthcoming reelection bid at home, Dixon told the Senate on January 16 that he was planning to introduce an amendment to the bill, one that would make both the Missouri Compromise and popular sovereignty inapplicable to Nebraska. This induced southern Democrats to radicalize their demands, which in turn forced Douglas to give more ground to his copartisans. At a highly irregular Sunday morning gathering at the White House, Douglas joined several leading proslavery men – Jefferson Davis among them – in gaining the president's consent to an explicit repeal of the Missouri Compromise. On January 23, the Illinoisan introduced a revised bill to the Senate, dividing the land to be organized into two territories (Kansas and Nebraska), applying popular sovereignty to both of them, and declaring the Missouri Compromise 'inoperative and void' (see Map 1). Douglas had fashioned a bill acceptable to the South but at what cost to national unity?

Congressional Free Soilers were quick to respond. Throughout the early weeks of 1854, they worked to convince northerners that Douglas's measure was the latest and most serious attempt in a long-running design by the Slave Power to erode the liberties of free white men. Their Washington organ, the *National Era*, took the lead in setting the terms of the debate. '[T]he conspiracy of the Slavery Propagandists', it averred, was 'to abrogate the Missouri Compromise, to make all the territory, west of our border States, Slave Territory, out of which to erect a cordon of Slave States around the Free West!'. The planter class and its doughface allies thus sought to exclude poor southerners, landless Yankees and impoverished foreigners from the land of opportunity 'and cover it, as they have covered the fertile plains of the South, with plantations of overgrown landlords, and hordes of squalid slaves'.[2]

The Free Soilers' arguments were brought together in a powerful 'Appeal' to the people drafted largely by Salmon Chase and disseminated rapidly after its initial appearance in several newspapers, the *Era* included. The Kansas-Nebraska bill was condemned as 'part and parcel of an atrocious plot' to spread slavery into a vast area reserved for settlement by free men under the terms of the venerated Missouri Compromise. 'Whatever apologies may be offered for the toleration of slavery in the States,' contended the 'Appeal', 'none can be urged for its extension into Territories where it does not exist ... Let all protest earnestly and emphatically ... against this enormous crime.'[3]

The 'Appeal' was an astute piece of political propaganda artfully designed to play on the inchoate fears and prejudices of the electorate. Americans knew the lessons of history. Republics were fragile entities constantly under threat from evil men and institutions conspiring to concentrate power and wealth in their own hands. The Revolution itself had taught the people that eternal vigilance was the only sure safeguard against encroaching tyranny. Chase and his allies in Congress were longstanding opponents of slavery – on humanitarian as well as political grounds – but they knew their audience well. The aim of the 'Appeal' was simple: to broaden the coalition against slavery, hitherto marginalized by the Compromise of 1850, by promoting a fundamental realignment of politics along sectional lines. What better way to do this than shake northern voters out of their lethargy by providing clear evidence that their own rights were under threat from a malign coterie of southern slaveholders who allegedly exercised a dominant influence over the Republic with the assistance of dupes like Stephen Douglas? The latter, then, had unwittingly presented his radical antislavery opponents with an opportunity to break the stranglehold of a party system that traditionally had operated to protect slavery. 'My soul sickens at the names Whig & Democrat', wrote the Massachusetts Free Soiler Charles Sumner privately. 'The North must be united, & take the control of Govt., or we shall sink under the despotism of the Slave-Power.'[4]

Aided by outraged abolitionists and antislavery clergymen throughout the North, the Free Soilers succeeded in their efforts to whip up a storm of popular protest. At first, the prospects for a full-scale realignment of politics seemed bright. Anti-Nebraska meetings took place across the North and the bill, its author, and the South were condemned in the harshest terms. Antislavery Whigs, free-soil Democrats and political abolitionists made common cause at many of these gatherings. Such cross-party action also occurred in northern state legislatures in the early months of 1854. In Maine, William Pitt Fessenden, an antislavery Whig, was elected as US senator by a combination of Whigs, Democrats, and Free Soilers, much to the consternation of loyalists in both major parties. In Congress itself, the bill widened the divisions between northern and southern Whigs. Nine out of ten southern Whigs voted in favor of the bill when it passed the Senate on March 4 by a vote of 37–14. No northern member of the party voted in favor. In the House, where the bill was approved 113–100 on May 22, southern Whig support made the difference between success and failure. Northern Whigs, again, opposed passage in large numbers.[5]

No less encouraging for the supporters of realignment were signs that the bill had split the northern wing of the Democratic party. The Pierce administration used its patronage powers to secure crucial support from hardshells whose disgruntlement with the generous treatment of the Barnburners had initially inclined them to oppose Kansas-Nebraska. When the bill passed the House northern Democrats were divided 44 in favor and 43 against. A majority of New Englanders and New Yorkers in the party refused to back the measure.

Seizing the moment, Free Soilers promoted their realignment strategy at every level of the federal system, urging the bill's opponents in the states and in Washington to abandon their attachments to existing parties in order to form a new organization dedicated solely to thwarting the ambitions of the Slave Power. More than seven weeks before the Kansas-Nebraska Act finally passed the House, Iowa Free Soilers indicated their commitment to cause over party by withdrawing their own gubernatorial nominee in favour of James W. Grimes, a New England-born Whig who successfully demonstrated his antislavery credentials to the state's political abolitionists.[6] The fusionist drive also bore fruit in Congress in May when a multiparty gathering of northern representatives endorsed the formation of a sectional organization dedicated to the containment of slavery.

Over the next few months fusion conventions were called in several northern states.[7] The first of these occurred in Michigan where local Free Soilers and Whigs overcame their mutual differences in time to meet in mass convention at Jackson on July 6. The delegates nominated a balanced ticket for the state elections and adopted the label 'Republican', a name strongly advocated by the New York editor, Horace Greeley, who was one of the North's leading advocates of fusion. Anti-Nebraska men journeyed to a similar convention in Madison, Wisconsin, the following week and set about the task of organizing a state Republican party to contest upcoming elections. Ohioans mobilized by Douglas's perfidy met on the same day, July 13, in Columbus and endorsed a fusion 'People's' or 'anti-Nebraska' ticket. Significantly, however, they adopted a relatively moderate platform. Unlike their peers in Wisconsin, the Ohioans omitted any demand for repeal of the Fugitive Slave Law, in favor of less controversial calls for the restoration of the Missouri Compromise and a ban on slavery expansion.

Unfortunately for the self-styled devotees of freedom, the fusion process was destined to be complicated by a variety of factors. In spite of its early appearance in parts of the Midwest, the Republican party did not cohere as a national force until the beginning of 1856.

Republican organizations came into being at different times in different states, their emergence entirely dependent on the interplay of local political conditions and state and national issues. Particularly worrying to men like Chase and Sumner was the reluctance of many leading politicians to abandon their traditional allegiances in states where their own party remained competitive. Many conservative Whigs simply did not want to cooperate with persons they regarded as dangerous radicals bent on destroying the Union. Rather more surprising was the determination of large numbers of antislavery Whigs to keep their distance from the fusionists. A strong residual loyalty to the party of Clay and Webster goes some way to explain why men like Abraham Lincoln in Illinois and William Seward in New York eschewed coalition for so long. Even more important was the hardheaded conviction that Whigs could actually utilize the anti-Democratic animus generated by Kansas-Nebraska to their own advantage. Only when the election results of 1854 and 1855 made it clear that Whiggery could not monopolize or at least control the opposition to the Democrats, did the vast majority of its adherents finally decide to jump ship. One event above all others ended lingering hopes of a Whig revival: the rapid emergence of a new party devoted primarily not to containing slavery but to answering the concerns of grassroots nativism.

Politics in flux

The Know-Nothing or American party transformed the domestic political landscape in the mid-1850s. The principal source for the growth of the nativist movement was the arrival of more than 2.9 million European immigrants in the United States between 1845 and 1854. The majority of these newcomers were Irish and German Catholics who settled predominantly, though not exclusively, in the growing urban centers of the eastern seaboard and Midwest. Many, especially among the Irish, were poor. Native-born Protestants regarded these interlopers with great suspicion. Not only did they compete with the immigrants for jobs at the lower end of the social scale but they also resented their clannishness, social drinking, and allegiance to a foreign prelate, the Pope. Roman Catholicism appeared to be the antithesis of Protestant republicanism. As the Americans' recent experience in the Mexican War surely revealed, Catholicism fostered a host of Old World evils, among them aristocracy, political oppression, licentiousness, and grinding poverty.

Although the sheer size of the European influx does much to explain the sudden surge of nativism, it was the immigrants' dramatic entry into politics that particularly disturbed their hosts. Legally entitled to the suffrage as soon as they had completed the five-year process of becoming naturalized US citizens, adult male immigrants were already voting in significant numbers by the early 1850s. The relatively democratic and egalitarian nature of the Republic's political system was one of its prime attractions for Old World migrants, even if the latter's own corporatist beliefs often existed in tension with the liberal, individualistic values they found in America. Thus, they quickly became important players in local and national politics. With the Democrats embracing the Irish and Germans with great enthusiasm, pragmatic Whigs recognized the need to compete aggressively for the same votes. As governor of New York in the early 1840s, William Seward was noted for his interest in immigrant education. In the 1852 presidential election campaign Winfield Scott lavished flattery on the Irish in a desperate bid for support. When established politicians like these made matters worse by ignoring the increasingly shrill (and organized) grassroots demands for the prohibition of liquor sales, native Protestants began to fear that the political system was no longer responsive to their needs. Ever watchful for signs of republican declension, they sensed that the immigrants were a source of serious domestic corruption and cast around for a vehicle that would truly satisfy their requirements.[8]

The Know-Nothing party offered anxious Americans genuine hope of reform as well as a conduit for unalloyed anti-Catholic bigotry. Beginning life as a shadowy and secretive fraternal order in New York City in the mid-1840s, the Know-Nothings first emerged as a genuinely competitive political organization in the North's state and congressional elections of late 1854.[9] Anti-Nebraska coalitions performed well in the Midwest and in upper New England even in states where many Whigs resisted cooperation with refugees from other parties. In the rapidly urbanizing Northeast, however, where greater numbers of immigrants had settled, it was a different story. In Pennsylvania, Know-Nothing support was the critical factor in the reelection of a nominally Whig governor, and nativist candidates made huge inroads into Whig strength in the state's congressional and legislative contests. In Massachusetts, where antislavery Whigs balked at combining with Free Soilers (the latter having traditionally cooperated with the local Democrats), the Know-Nothings won control of the legislature and elected their own gubernatorial candidate, Henry J. Gardner, on a prohibitionist and anti-Nebraska platform.

Gardner, a Boston merchant, gained an impressive 63 percent majority in a four-horse race compared with the Whig nominee's paltry 21 percent. In New York, where both the Whigs and Democrats were still deeply split by factionalism, the emergence of the Know-Nothing movement threw politics into even greater confusion. Pro-Seward antislavery Whigs sought to maintain their party identity by rejecting a merger with local Free Soilers but were forced to nominate a prohibitionist and Know-Nothing, Myron Clark, for governor in order to defeat their conservative Whig opponents who themselves had already backed a nativist for the same position. Although Clark won a narrow plurality, the fact that Scott supporters in 1852 divided roughly evenly between the Sewardite and Silver Grey candidates revealed the elusiveness of Whig unity in the Empire State.

There were three losers in the confused elections of 1854. The Democratic party lost two-thirds of its congressional seats in the North, a severe blow not only to the floundering Pierce administration but also to the sectional balance inside the party. Already widely denigrated for its alleged southern bias, the Democracy took on an even more pronounced southern character as more of its northern constituents yielded to the counter-attractions of nativism and anti-slavery. For all their problems, however, at least the Democrats held onto their core support among southern whites, Catholic immigrants, and farmers in the lower Midwest.

The Whig party had ceased to exist. Operating under a political system in which new parties could be formed simply by printing their own ballot papers, the Whigs had been eclipsed by anti-Nebraska fusionists in the Midwest and Know-Nothings in the Northeast.[10] Their own divisions over slavery and temperance had done much to weaken their position, preventing as they did a reunification of the party in the wake of the Kansas-Nebraska Act. 'We are utterly wrecked', commented a Buffalo newspaper disconsolately after the electoral debacle of 1854, 'It is altogether idle to think of a reconstruction of the Whig party. It is past all surgery, past all medicine.'[11]

The third loser, at least temporarily, was the cause of antislavery fusion. While Salmon P. Chase and his allies could look to the Midwest as a source for much optimism and rightly understood that the election results were, in large part, a repudiation of the Kansas-Nebraska Act, the sheer scale of the nativist assault in the Northeast indicated that realignment was going to be anything but smooth. Even if one regarded the Know-Nothings as little more than intolerant bigots, their evident popularity made it essential that they be treated with respect. 'I confess', commented Chase to a Free Soil editor in Ohio in November 1854,

> I feel more uneasiness about the probable influences of the Order on our movement than I did when I saw you last: but I still think that it is best not to say any thing against them. Wait until it becomes necesary & it may never become necessary. What is objectionable may cure itself. Meantime Antislavery men should be constantly warned of the importance of keeping the Antislavery idea paramount. There is danger of its being shoved aside.[12]

The only clear winners in the winter of 1854–55 appeared to be the Know-Nothings. Large numbers of Americans had registered their disaffection with the two main parties. Even in the South, where the numbers of foreign-born residents were small outside the border states, the order appeared to be on the increase – its attractions obvious to the majority of local Whigs left homeless by the demise of the national party. It was this latter development, the intersectional growth of political nativism, as well as the Know-Nothings' surprisingly strong showing in the elections, that convinced conservative unionists on both sides of the Mason-Dixon Line that they could use the order to serve their own patriotic ends. Prominent among those who recognized the cohesive potential of Know-Nothingism was former president Millard Fillmore whose own political ambitions were far from satiated. During the winter, Fillmore urged his New York allies to enter the order *en masse* with a view to controlling its operations. In January 1855 he took the secret oath himself and wrote a confidential letter announcing his support for Know-Nothing goals. His aim of saving the Republic from sectional destruction, however, was heavily dependent for success on persuading southern nativists that their northern peers had no interest in meddling with slavery. This problem had wrecked the Whig party. It remained to be seen whether the Americans could steer their ship safely through the shoals.

Any attempt to transform the Know-Nothing party into an agent of Unionism was heavily dependent on the maintenance of sectional peace as well as the creation of common ground between northern and southern nativists. Unfortunately for conservatives like Fillmore their efforts to fashion a viable national party organization occurred against a background of growing sectional strife in Kansas Territory. Ultimately, the slavery question destroyed what chances there had been of saving the Union with an injection of red-blooded patriotism.

By the summer of 1854, settlers were moving into Kansas and Nebraska in ever increasing numbers. The preponderance of free-state migrants made proslavery advocates nervous. In July Senator David Rice Atchison of Missouri, a leading states' rights Democrat, received an urgent letter from William Walker, the self styled 'provisional Governor of Nebraska'. Southerners, wrote Walker, 'must be up and stirring' in order to prevent the territory from becoming 'the unwilling receptacle of the filth and scum and offscourings of the East and Europe – to pollute our fair land, to dictate to us as a government, to preach Abolitionism and dig underground R[ail].R[oa]ds'.[13]

Atchison was quick to respond. Disturbed by news that meddle-some Yankees had already chartered an aid society to spur free-state settlement of the newly opened region, he and other proslavery Missourians moved rapidly to stem what they saw as the rising tide of abolitionism on their western border, specifically in Kansas, the southernmost of the two new territories. The senator assumed the leadership of the new Platte County Self-Defensive Association and during the second half of 1854 stumped the western portion of his own state organizing 'blue lodges' to encourage proslavery settlement in Kansas. In September, he told Secretary of War Jefferson Davis that he had advised Kansas settlers and Missourians 'to give a horse thief, a robber, or homicide a fair trial, but to hang a negro thief or abolitionist, without judge or jury ...'.[14] In the spring of 1855 Atchison led his Missourians across the border in a blatant effort to control the elections to the first Kansas legislature (see Map 3). In spite of evidence that over three-quarters of the votes in the contest had been cast illegally, Pierce's territorial governor, Andrew Reeder, allowed the result to stand. Jubilant proslavery men at Lecompton, the ramshackle capital, then enacted Missouri's slave code to secure the territory for southern interests. By late 1855, however, free-state settlers, already in a clear majority in Kansas, had set up their own rival government based at Topeka. Midwestern free-soil Democrats (who outnumbered antislavery New Englanders among the northern migrants) had no intention of allowing haughty southern planters to pollute the land with their black chattels.

At first, the Know-Nothings appeared undaunted by these developments. In the spring of 1855 they built on their successes of the previous year by winning crushing victories in Rhode Island, Connecticut, and New Hampshire. Large-scale Whig defections in all three states revealed what most people already knew: that the Whig party was now defunct. By this time, moreover, Know-Nothings had emerged as the main opposition to the Democrats in the South, its membership in Virginia alone estimated at 60,000 out of a total electorate of 170,000.[15] Here, surely, were signs that an intersectional unionist party could be built on the ashes of Whiggery. A glance at the election in New Hampshire, however, suggests that Millard Fillmore's hopes of converting the nativist movement into an agent of national unity were likely to be dashed by the strength of anti-southern and antislavery feeling among northern Know-Nothings.

By January 1855 virtually every town in New Hampshire possessed a Know-Nothing lodge. The state attracted relatively few foreign immigrants, yet an influx of Irish laborers seeking jobs at the Amoskeag textile mill in Manchester had greatly heightened tensions during the previous summer. Running battles between nativists and Irish had broken out in Manchester (as in several other New England towns), stimulating support for the new movement. Well organized by the winter, local Know-Nothing activists campaigned on a platform that combined nativism and social reform with antislavery. Calling for an expansion of the state's public school system, judicial change, and restrictions on immigrants' voting rights and access to public office, New Hampshire Know-Nothings also launched scathing attacks on the South and the Slave Power. The voters liked what they heard. Turnout in the March 1855 gubernatorial election was an impressive 82 percent. The Know-Nothing candidate, Ralph Metcalf, an anti-Nebraska, anti-administration Democrat, won a narrow majority in a four-way race and nativists triumphed spectacularly in congressional and state legislative contests. Crucially, Metcalf's triumph was, like Gardner's in Massachusetts, as much an antislavery victory as a nativist one. His predominantly urban coalition was made up of Free Soilers, antislavery Whigs and anti-Nebraska Democrats who could only have been heartened by the governor's annual message in which he demanded repeal of the Kansas-Nebraska Act as well as other reforms such as a prohibitory liquor law.[16] If watching conservatives had any doubts about the meaning of Metcalf's victory, they must have been removed completely by the nativist-dominated legislature's decision to reelect the veteran Free Soiler, John P. Hale, to the US Senate.

While the number of northern state Republican organizations grew during the course of 1855, near total fusion on a sectional basis required northern Know-Nothings to abandon nativism for antisouthernism. Two things enabled this to happen: firstly, a disastrous split within the Know-Nothing movement over slavery expansion and, secondly, the growing seriousness of the crisis in Kansas which strengthened the appeal of the Republicans' message.

In June 1855 northern and southern Know-Nothings convened in Philadelphia. The southerners were concerned by what they perceived as evidence of antislavery leanings on the part of their peers above the Mason-Dixon Line. Even before the New Hampshire election had taken place, the nativist-dominated Massachusetts general assembly had elected an antislavery politico, Henry Wilson, to the Senate. Equally seriously, on the assumption that southern support for the Kansas-Nebraska Act freed northerners from any obligations under the Compromise of 1850, the same legislators passed a new personal liberty law intentionally designed to obstruct enforcement of the Fugitive Slave Act. In May Governor Henry Wise of Virginia, a sharp political operator, had used these developments to halt the Know-Nothing charge at home by tarring his opponents as abolitionists. The southern delegates in Philadelphia therefore had good political reasons for wanting reassurances on the slavery question from their northern brethren.

The northerners differed over the wisdom of such reassurances. Most conservatives were prepared to give them out of deference to southern opinion. Moderates such as Governor Gardner of Massachusetts and some conservatives feared that this strategy would only render them vulnerable to the Republicans who had already begun to capitalize on the Kansas issue. They favored taking no action at all on slavery in order to remain competitive. Radicals among the northern bloc rejected such a craven response to southern opinion. Split between crypto-Republicans like Henry Wilson who were plotting to destroy the nativist movement from within and those who wished to build a northern-based coalition around the issues of nativism, slavery expansion and prohibition, they leaned toward demanding a restoration of the Missouri Compromise and an even more incendiary ban on the admission of further slave states to the Union.

Matters came to a head when the platform committee produced a majority report bent to the will of the southern delegates. Section Twelve upheld the Kansas-Nebraska Act, declaring the National Council's willingness 'to abide by and maintain the existing laws upon the subject of Slavery, as a final and conclusive settlement of that subject, in spirit and in substance'.[17] It also denied the right of Congress to prevent the entry of slave states into the Union, to prohibit slavery in a territory or to abolish slavery in the District of Columbia. A minority report, secretly written by Henry Wilson's close confederate, Samuel Bowles (a Massachusetts journalist who was not even a Know-Nothing), defiantly called for restoration of the Missouri Compromise, protection for genuine settlers in Kansas and the admission of both Kansas and Nebraska as free states. After the defeat of the minority report, eleven northern conservatives aided passage of Section Twelve by a vote of 78–63. The majority of northerners then responded by gathering at a nearby hotel to announce their refusal to abide by this section of the platform. The Know-Nothing movement, thought some of its antislavery critics, now stood on the verge of collapse.

During the second half of 1855, election results in several import-ant northern states provided mixed messages for Republicans and Know-Nothings. In Ohio, where Salmon Chase treated local nativists with circumspection, Chase himself was elected as the state's first Republican governor on a platform devoted almost entirely to opposing slavery expansion and proslavery violence in Kansas.[18] The Know-Nothing grand council had endorsed Chase not only because of the split at Philadelphia but also because of adverse publicity stemming from nativist involvement in a deadly riot in Cincinnati in April. The Republicans, however, had recognized the inherent strength of the Ohio Know-Nothings by filling the rest of the ticket with members of the order. Chase ran several thousand votes behind all of them.

In New York, where anti-Nebraska feeling and Thurlow Weed's adept use of patronage had secured Seward's reelection to the US Senate over the objections of the predominantly pro-Fillmore Know-Nothings, the state's antislavery Whig leaders finally threw in their lot with the Republican movement. Yet antislavery fusion, finally achieved at Syracuse in September, did not guarantee success at the polls. Know-Nothing candidates triumphed in the summer's state elections, most of their support apparently coming from conservative Whigs. Republican parties were also formed in other northeastern states, notably in Pennsylvania, Massachusetts, and Maine. There, divisions among the anti-Democratic opposition and the refusal of many conservative Whigs to support the new party resulted in more defeat at the polls. While a combination of the Kansas-Nebraska Act and the activities of 'border ruffians' in Kansas had spurred the formation of state Republican organizations across the North, it had not yet allowed the new party to monopolize the opposition to the Democrats.

Events in the winter of 1855 finally shifted the balance between Republicans and Know-Nothings in favor of the former. A low-level guerrilla conflict (the so-called 'Wakarusa War') broke out between antislavery and proslavery settlers in December. This conflict was politicized significantly in January when those acting under the banner of the Topeka constitution elected a rival free-state governor

(Charles Robinson) and legislature. An essentially local contest over land and power, in which both parties claimed to be fighting tyranny in the image of Revolutionary patriots, was then transformed into an immensely damaging struggle by outsiders responding, for various motives, to the Kansans' urgent cries for help.[19]

David Atchison led the South's response to the worsening situation in Kansas. When it seemed that the free-soilers were about to resist efforts by proslavery officials to arrest one of their number, the territorial secretary appealed to Missourians for help. Atchison crossed the border with 200 riflemen in mid-December but decided against a full-scale attack on the town of Lawrence when the northerners backed down. He then threw himself into the task of galvanizing southern whites into resisting Yankee efforts to make Kansas a free state. In January he dispatched an urgent appeal to a Georgia newspaper urging young southern men to bring their weapons to the West. 'I do not see how we are to avoid civil war;' he wrote, 'come it will. Twelve months will not elapse before war – civil war of the fiercest kind – will be upon us. We are arming and preparing for it. Indeed, we of the border counties are prepared. We must have the support of the South. We are fighting the battles of the South.'[20]

When President Pierce branded the free-state Topeka movement as revolutionary on January 24, 1856, it appeared to many northerners that the United States government had taken sides with the South. While free-state officials called desperately for northern state aid, Republican politicians in Washington seized the opportunity to excoriate the administration as a tool of the Slave Power. They did so not only because they genuinely believed that Pierce was a contemptible doughface but also because they realized that the violence in Kansas would hasten the process of fusion on an antislavery rather than a Know-Nothing basis and increase the pace of defections from the northern wing of the Democratic party. Republican strategists knew that the more they could operate in a landscape polarized between freedom and slavery, the better the party's chances would be in the forthcoming presidential election campaign. Kansas, in short, was their ticket to power.

Galvanized by developments in the West, the Republican party emerged as a sectionally dominant force in February 1856.[21] Several events brought this about. Firstly, after a long battle, Republicans in the House of Representatives secured the election of their candidate, Nathaniel P. Banks of Massachusetts, as speaker. Although Banks had few commitments to any political aim besides his own advancement, his skin-deep antislavery and nativist credentials enabled his Republican campaign managers to package him as the only reliable friend of freedom on the list of candidates. A substantial group of northern Know-Nothings rallied to Banks's support, providing the difference between defeat and victory and presaging the final denationalization of the American party. Later that month, on Washington's Birthday, somewhere between 700 and 800 delegates assembled in Lafayette Hall in Pittsburgh to attend the first national convention of the Republican party. They oversaw the creation of a national committee to coordinate fund raising for the upcoming campaign, fixed a date in June for a presidential nominating convention, and then adopted resolutions demanding the containment of slavery and the immediate admission of Kansas as a free state. There was no mention of nativism. The majority of those present saw no reason to kowtow to Know-Nothings (and thereby alienate potential foreign-born voters) at a time when sectional forces were predominant. A northern walkout from the nativists' national nominating convention in Philadelphia seemed to prove the wisdom of their actions.

The crisis in Kansas intensified during the spring of 1856. On May 5, shortly after a Republican-dominated congressional committee had begun hearings in the territory, a grand jury indicted several free-state leaders and recommended action against the free-state headquarters and press in Lawrence. The grand jury acted on the instructions of the territory's supreme court justice, Samuel Lecompte, a Pierce appointee whose sympathies lay with the proslavery government. On May 21 the federal marshal led a large posse to the outskirts of Lawrence. Free-soil leaders promised to comply with the law but a high-handed sheriff, against the advice of men like Atchison who realized the likely political repercussions of proslavery aggression, led the posse into the town where they set about destroying the Free State Hotel and other buildings.

The next day, over a thousand miles away in Washington, a South Carolina congressman named Preston Brooks strode manfully into the upper chamber and delivered a ritual caning to the Republican senator, Charles Sumner, as he struggled to rise from his desk. In the course of a typically learned and interminable speech entitled 'The Crime against Kansas', Sumner had made personal attacks on Brooks's kinsman, Senator Andrew Butler, and belittled the history of South Carolina as inferior when set beside Kansas's valiant struggle for freedom. Determined to resent these insults and uphold the honor of both Butler and his home state, Brooks administered the beating with a view to humiliating a man he regarded as a miserable coward.

Together these two sensational events, the 'Sack of Lawrence' and the caning of Charles Sumner, enabled Republicans to convince growing numbers of northerners of the essential barbarism of slavery and the reality of the Slave Power threat to fundamental American liberties such as freedom of speech.[22] Southerners had a different perspective on events. As far as they were concerned Yankee organizations such as the New England Emigrant Aid Society and the American Missionary Association were attempting to make Kansas a free state in their own image, their long-term aim being to place an abolitionist stronghold on the South's northwestern border. Kansas would thus become a conduit for fugitive slaves, and society in the plantation areas would be destabilized. For most southern whites, Charles Sumner embodied the Yankee threat in Kansas. To them he was the epitome of the arrogant, meddling, and hypocritical northern abolitionist. He surely deserved the beating administered to him by Congressman Brooks. Excited meetings and angry newspaper editorials across the South applauded Brooks's noble deed while northerners simultaneously deplored what they saw as unquestionable evidence of the slavedriver's brutality.

Stirred furiously by Republicans and southern radicals, the pot of sectional hatred neared boiling point. In Kansas a hitherto obscure, middle-aged New England abolitionist, John Brown, decided to avenge the attack on Lawrence in true Old Testament style. With seven men from his volunteer free-state militia company, four of them his own sons, he put to death five proslavery settlers at their cabin on Pottawatomie Creek. This grizzly event brought on full-scale guerrilla war in the territory, resulting in desperate efforts by Governor Wilson Shannon to end hostilities with the use of federal troops. Critically, however, his actions were seen to favor the Lecompton forces. On July 4 US dragoons dispersed the free-state legislature at Topeka which had been forbidden to meet by a presidential proclamation. This proved to be a major blunder for it served to confirm northern suspicions that the federal government was in league with the Slave Power. Militant abolitionists redoubled their efforts to funnel arms into Kansas, their activities aided covertly by Republican politicians in the neighboring state of Iowa. A few outraged New Englanders traveled to the war zone determined to fight for freedom. Among them was Thomas Wentworth Higginson, a Unitarian minister from Massachusetts, who insisted that Yankees like him were ready to take on the United States. It would, he said, 'be necessary to do it, first or last', and that when was 'a mere question of policy'.[23] In fact, Higginson did not have to put his treasonous words into practice. President Pierce's wise decision to replace Shannon with a more neutral executive, the Pennsylvania Democrat John W. Geary, had helped to pacify the territory by September. However, neither Higginson nor other leading abolitionists were willing to give up the fight against slavery.

The sectional tensions unleashed by events in Washington and Kansas destroyed whatever chances remained of the Know-Nothings emerging as the principal opposition to the Democrats in the North. At their national nominating convention in Philadelphia in February 1856, the nativists had repealed Section Twelve but tacitly endorsed the Kansas-Nebraska Act by calling for 'the maintenance and enforcement of all laws constitutionally enacted until said laws shall be repealed, or shall be declared null and void by competent judicial authority'.[24] Together with the nomination of Millard Fillmore, this move had prompted most of the antislavery delegates from the North to withdraw from the convention. After some debate, the bolters had then called for their own nominating convention to meet in New York on June 12. The subsequent growth of sectional tension meant that when the 'North Americans' did gather in the summer most of them were already favorably disposed toward a coalition with the Republicans. Thus, when their June nominee, Nathaniel Banks, withdrew (as planned in advance) in favour of the Republican presidential candidate, John C. Frémont, the majority of antislavery nativists fell into line and backed the Republicans in the 1856 election campaign.

Political nativism had taken the country by storm two years earlier, its meteoric rise attributable in large part to the Know-Nothings' compelling and multifaceted analysis of the problems confronting the American Republic. Two years of nativist success at the polls, however, had wrought fewer policy achievements than many voters had hoped (the party's chief demand for a 21-year naturalization law remained unfulfilled) and the movement was disliked by many politicians and voters for its intolerance and complicity in periodic outbreaks of urban violence. Most damagingly of all, the party had proved unable to persuade a majority of voters in either section that religious-based patriotism would effectively protect republican government from those seeking to undermine it. As the forthcoming presidential election campaign was about to prove, events had persuaded Americans that they dwelt in a political world polarized primarily by freedom and slavery, not Protestantism and Catholicism.

The Republican threat

The Union was saved in 1856 by the election of another Democratic president. Throughout the difficult years of his presidency, Franklin Pierce struggled to hold together a party that he regarded as the only guarantee of national unity. Unhappily for Pierce, his own pro-southern sympathies and extensive southern influence within the party itself played into the hands of those who sought to benefit from mounting sectional tensions. The repeal of the Missouri Compromise and the administration's support for the proslavery Lecompton government may have been necessary to ensure the continued loyalty of powerful southerners, but such actions provided fertile soil for Republicanism and brought about the defection of thousands of northern Democrats from the party.

The Pierce administration's foreign policy did nothing to stem this trend. In October 1854 three American envoys in Europe, well aware that the president was eager to gain control of the Spanish slave island of Cuba, signed the so-called Ostend Manifesto which recommended that the United States should seize Cuba if the authorities in Madrid failed to sell this choice slice of Caribbean real estate to Washington. The North's reaction to such blatant evidence of proslavery policymaking was so vociferous that the cabinet had little option but to repudiate the report in order to prevent further seepage from the Democratic party. Although expansionists condemned this apparent betrayal of their cause, they continued to fuel sectional prejudices by undertaking illegal 'filibustering' activities in Central America.

In May 1855 'Colonel' William Walker, a quixotic Tennesseean, led a small band of mercenaries to Nicaragua with the backing of Cornelius Vanderbilt, a wealthy New York entrepreneur whose Accessory Transit Company had already built a railroad across the isthmus. Walker quickly installed a new president of Nicaragua whose puppet regime was then granted official recognition by the Pierce administration early in 1856. By this time Walker had managed to alienate Vanderbilt and was attracting strong support from mercantile interests in New Orleans who regarded Nicaragua as a potential source of tropical, slave-grown produce. On September 22 the colonel delighted his southern friends by sanctioning the reintroduction of slavery into his fiefdom. In spite of the fact that the Central American states temporarily derailed his career by ousting him from power, the filibustering issue deepened the conviction of many northerners that Democrats were trying to expand the peculiar institution. Belatedly President Pierce had begun to realize the disastrous consequences of this perception. In the summer of 1856 he refused to receive one of Walker's emissaries. And in December he instructed John W. Geary, his new Kansas governor, 'that whatever others may do, absolute impartiality is required at your hands. You are to know no North no South among the citizens of the Territory ... .'[25] By then, however, the damage had been done.

Three parties fought the election of 1856.[26] At their national convention in Cincinnati, the Democrats dumped Pierce ignominiously in favor of the experienced Pennsylvania Democrat, James Buchanan, whose recent posting as minister to the Court of King James at least ensured that he was untainted by developments in Kansas. The platform upheld the Compromise of 1850 and the Kansas-Nebraska Act (much to the disgust of many free-soil Democrats) and offered no clarification of the stage at which a territorial government could prohibit slavery (a move which ensured that popular sovereignty Democrats like Stephen Douglas could continue to cooperate with southern rights men).

After convening as a national party for the first time in Pittsburgh in February, the Republicans held their inaugural delegate convention at Philadelphia early in the summer. In spite of strong support for the two antislavery heavyweights, Chase and Seward, the delegates nominated a candidate with more widespread appeal. John C. Frémont was young, self made, and wrapped in the irresistible garb of the Far West where his various explorations and military exploits had won him a national reputation as 'the Pathfinder'. Described by William Gienapp as 'a political cypher' (his only experience was one undistinguished term in the California senate), he lacked the controversial antinativist and antislavery baggage carried by the frontrunner, Seward.[27] Equally importantly, the candidate was politically well connected. Married to Jessie Benton Frémont, the daughter of Senator Thomas Hart Benton of Missouri, Frémont was also linked closely to the powerful Blair family whose power base lay in the western gateway city of St Louis. He therefore seemed likely to attract votes from significant numbers of disaffected antislavery Democrats whose support was essential if the new party were to expand from its Whig–Free Soil core.

Before Frémont's nomination, the Philadelphia convention enthusiastically endorsed the national platform, reported from committee by the ubiquitous David Wilmot. This document made it clear that the party's primary goal was not abolition but the restriction of slavery. It deemed Congress to have 'sovereign powers' over slavery in the territories and denied all levels of government the authority to defy what Chase had long viewed as the Founding Fathers' intention to rid slavery from the national domain. The Pierce administration was condemned for its policies over Kansas and Cuba and there was a specific demand for Kansas to be admitted as a free state. Fear of alienating former Democrats resulted in a general absence of any economic planks beyond support for federal aid to internal improvements, including the construction of a Pacific railroad. Nativist issues were largely ignored but there was no explicit condemnation of Know-Nothings. The Republicans hoped to attract German Protestants *and* nativists into the fold – a neat trick if they could pull it off.

Ranged against the Democrats and Republicans was the Know-Nothing party, now a shadow of its former self owing to the loss of large numbers of Old Line Whigs in the North. Its candidate Millard Fillmore saw his hopes of riding into power on a tide of popular unionism dashed by the nomination of Buchanan at Cincinnati. For all his limitations (and time would prove he had many), Buchanan was a stalwart conservative who could claim convincingly to be the only true representative of both sections in the race. The willingness of so many northern nativists to either join or cooperate with the Republicans meant that most of Fillmore's support was likely to come from the South, particularly the border slave states where fears for the future of the Union were intense and where many former Whigs, unable to stomach Republicanism or Democracy, had had little choice but to join the Know-Nothings.

Essentially two election campaigns took place during the second half of 1856. In the North the Republicans provided the main opposition to Buchanan, their lack of funds and organization counterbalanced by the strength of their popular appeal on the slavery issue. Although Fillmore did run in the North, his party was most effective below the Mason-Dixon Line where the Republicans declined to campaign. While the latter hammered home their message about the dangers posed by the Slave Power, their opponents attacked them relentlessly as disunionists and abolitionists. The Democrats in particular were able to draw on a reservoir of white settler and working-class racism, persistently linking 'Black Republicanism' to white fears of black emancipation. Some ex-Democrats within the Republican coalition responded with racist attacks of their own, insisting, for example, that the Democrats were trying to infect the territories with their black bondsmen and women. The existence of antislavery humanitarians in the party, however, served as a powerful counter-weight to these appeals and enabled such Democratic taunts as 'Fremont! Free Niggers!' to hit home. The Know-Nothings, mean-while, struggled to get their patriotic message across to the voters. In the deep South, they were again undone by the taint of associ-ation with antislavery radicals. In the North they were frustrated by the willingness of many northeastern Republicans to cooperate openly with prominent nativists.

Buchanan won the election in November in spite of failing to win a majority of the popular vote. His electoral college victory of 174 to 114 over Frémont was substantial enough but, remarkably in their first national contest, the Republicans emerged as the strongest party in the North with 45.2 percent of the region's popular vote. Had they carried Pennsylvania and nine more electoral votes in the North they would have won the election and, quite possibly, given the hos-tility with which they were regarded in the deep South, precipitated a full-blown secession crisis. Although Fillmore performed reasonably well in the South, his strength lay primarily in the border slave states. His real problem was in the North where Whig desertions (princip-ally to Frémont) meant that only 13.4 percent of voters in that section gave him their support.

James Buchanan and other leading Democrats welcomed the election result as a triumph of nationalism over sectionalism. In truth, the message of the poll was more ambiguous than that. Notwithstanding considerable despondency among Republicans after their defeat, the contest revealed that a powerful new force had arrived on the American political stage. The reasons why the Republicans proved attractive to so many northern voters in the second half of the 1850s are easier to assess than the extent of the threat that they posed to the South. Combining moral opposi-tion to slavery with a pronounced concern for the rights of white men, Republicans appealed to a broad, cross-class constituency through-out the North. Many of their core supporters were evangelicals who previously had belonged to the Whig or Free Soil parties – not only New England Congregationalists and New School Presbyterians but also most Quakers, Free Will Baptists, and large numbers of Methodists. Even if these denominational voters often found the Republicans' readiness to temporize on pressing issues such as slavery, nativism, and prohibition intensely frustrating, they rightly sensed that the party's worldview was heavily infused with a strong spirit of Protestant reformism.

A majority of leading Republicans were political pragmatists but most were well aware that the party's survival depended on retaining the allegiance of men (and women) who sought to perfect American society in the eyes of the Lord. Although this millennial strain of Republicanism would come to the fore during the Civil War years, it was evident in the mid-1850s when several northern state parties assumed dangerously radical ground on slavery, liquor drinking, and Sabbatarianism. The close relationship between Republican politics and religion was manifest in the 1856 presidential election campaign. The party's first national convention at Philadelphia was reminiscent of the 1848 Buffalo Free Soil gathering in the sense that it reminded one participant of a Methodist conference rather than a political meeting. Henry Wilson, the Massachusetts antislavery leader who had entered the nativist movement with a view to sectionalizing it, contended that with a national platform that 'embraces freedom, humanity and Christianity ... all that is required is that we organize the Christian Democratic spirit of America, and place that ticket in power'.[28]

There was more to the Republican cause than religion. After the 1856 defeat, party strategists recognized that they would have to broaden the base of their coalition if they were to win in 1860. Due deference was still given to the exponents of moral reform, but in the late 1850s greater stress was placed on economic questions. Conventionally depicted as a vehicle for northern capitalism, Republicanism was initially shunned by most American businessmen (especially those engaged in banking and commerce) because of its potentially destabilizing influence. Generally responsive to changes in popular mood, party leaders seldom repeated the Whigs' common mistake of aligning themselves too closely with unpopular corporations. When midwesterners began to chafe at the growing political influence of railroad companies and the higher taxes required to pay for the construction of track, local Republicans were quick to set aside their initial support in favor of countermeasures. Predictably, perhaps, there was often a significant gap between their public and private activities. In July 1856, for example, Governor James Grimes of Iowa was happy to condemn 'the sometimes monopolizing tendencies of powerful corporations' and then, just over a year later, accept a private loan of $20,000 from the Detroit railroad entrepreneur, James F. Joy.[29]

Notwithstanding the lack of initial support from northeastern business interests and their pragmatic recourse to Jacksonian-style rhetoric, Republicans were broadly supportive of Whiggish economic policies such as federal aid for internal improvements, a well-organized and flexible banking system, and higher tariffs to promote domestic manufactures. The party's most potent contribution

to industrial development in the United States, however, may well
have been its swingeing critique of slavery. Drawing on a wide range
of authorities including the Whig economist Henry Carey, the Republicans condemned slavery as economically regressive, contrasting
it unfavorably with the 'free labor' society of the North. This critique
was disseminated in numerous speeches, pamphlets, newspaper
articles, and books during the late 1850s. Some of the best of this
work emanated from the pen of Frederick Law Olmsted, a highly
talented Jack of all trades who possessed direct links with the free-
state party in Kansas. After making two trips to the South earlier in
the decade, Olmsted wrote up his firsthand observations of slavery
in several books and newspapers. Although he had not embarked
on his travels as an antislavery radical, he found abundant evidence
to support the view that the peculiar institution was a disaster for
the nation, the South, and even the slaves themselves. The system,
he contended, provided no incentives for the bonded laborers and
resulted in laziness and low productivity. White southerners looked
on manual labor as beneath them, and slaveholders and slaves alike
were brutalized by the coercion that underpinned their mutual relations. Such views typified the way northerners thought about slavery
in the years immediately preceding the Civil War. While they seldom
led directly into outright support for abolitionism, they joined with
perceptions of southern aggression in helping to mold the Republicans' distinctly sectional (that is to say, northern) conception of
American national identity.[30]

The Republicans' use of bipolar language to posit a dichotomy
between freedom and slavery served an important function by
smoothing the transition to a full-blown capitalist economy in the
United States. At a time when many northern working people were
anxious about their growing dependence on the market, Republican
politicians alleviated their fears by arguing that 'free labor' was central
to the development of a genuinely meritocratic society. Southern
slavery, in contrast, fostered unhealthy concentrations of wealth and
power, thereby promoting the growth of an avowedly un-American
planter aristocracy that rode roughshod over the rights of ordinary
white people in both sections of the Republic. As the political crises
of the 1850s imparted cumulative substance to the notion of a
slaveholders' conspiracy to expand the peculiar institution into all
corners of the Union (and beyond), the concept of the Slave Power
emerged as 'the master symbol of the Republican party'.[31] The use
of this concept had at least two advantages. Firstly, it enabled pragmatic Republican politicians to disclaim any suggestion that they

were either hostile to ordinary southern whites or obsessed with promoting the rights of black people. Secondly, the idea of a Slave Power design imparted urgency to the Republicans' efforts to gain control of the national government. If the North could not free itself from the shackles of the planter class (whose political influence was exerted through the medium of the Democratic party), it would – sooner rather than later – surrender both its freedoms and its economic dynamism.

Given the close links that developed between businessmen and Republican politicians, it is tempting to suggest that the party's stress on free labor and trumpeting of a Slave Power conspiracy were intended to promote the triumph of capital over labor. While this suggestion may not be entirely unwarranted, most antebellum Republicans would have balked at the idea that they were trying to build the kind of corporate-dominated society which emerged in the United States at the close of the nineteenth century. Their objective was to fashion a competitive, forward-looking and prosperous nation in the image of the North – a country in which those who worked hard and utilized their skills effectively reaped the material rewards. Economic growth was clearly one of their central aims but they assumed, like the Whigs before them, that the benefits of the market would be widely distributed. Their societal model derived primarily from the fluid small-town and commercial farm economy of the rural North where wealth tended to be less concentrated than in either the South or the urban Northeast. As the most famous product of this relatively meritocratic milieu, Abraham Lincoln, put it during a speech in New Haven, Connecticut, in March 1860: 'When one starts poor, as most do in the race of life, free society is such that he knows he can better his condition; he knows there is no fixed condition of labor for his whole life.'[32] As a number of modern scholars have pointed out, moreover, the notion of a Slave Power conspiracy was not simply a product of wily politicking (or downright paranoia).[33] The antebellum United States *was* the most powerful slavetrading nation on earth. Southern slaveholders may not have been conspiring to deprive white Americans of their liberty, but the proslavery South did exercise a disproportionate influence on the country's affairs by dint of the three-fifths clause of the Constitution and its persistent domination of the Democratic party.

The Republicans' main policy initiative, the containment of slavery, represented the lowest common denominator of thought on the peculiar institution within the party which, like all political organizations, embraced a broad range of constituencies.[34] As well

as political abolitionists and antislavery Whigs, the organization contained large numbers of free-soil Democrats, conservative Old Line
Whigs, former Know-Nothings, and even some German radicals ('red
Republicans') who had fled their homelands after the abortive
revolutions of 1848. Of these groups only former political abolitionists
and a minority of the antislavery Whigs hated slavery because of its
impact on the slaves. Forming what can be described loosely as the
radical wing of the Republican party, they tended to represent areas
containing large numbers of Yankee evangelicals: parts of New England itself, western New York, the Western Reserve of Ohio around
Cleveland, and the upper Midwest. Although few of them were bold
enough to call publicly for the immediate abolition of slavery, most
were prepared to destabilize the institution by supporting passage of
state personal liberty laws to protect runaway slaves and by countering the activities of proslavery forces in Kansas. Some of them understood that white racism was a central prop to the slave system in
the United States and tried to promote civil rights for northern free
blacks. The radicals' efforts to secure black suffrage were of great
concern to pragmatic party leaders because white supremacy was
one of the Democrats' most potent weapons in the late 1850s. However, the need to retain the support of its crusading wing induced
several Republican-controlled states to hold popular referenda on
local black suffrage before the Civil War. The fact that a majority of
white voters in Iowa, Minnesota, and New York rejected the reform
by large margins certainly indicated the strength of cross-party racism.
However, even the relatively small percentages in favor of black suffrage proclaimed the existence of a vocal minority of northerners
who were willing to rock the foundations of the white Republic.

Moderate Republicans (mostly antislavery Whigs and free-soil
Democrats) held the balance of power inside the party. They frowned
on persistent lobbying for black rights because they had a negative
view of the innate capabilities of black people and readily accepted
the party's official position that slavery had every right to exist in the
states. Nonetheless, even they were prepared to grant that free blacks
should enjoy the basic rights enshrined in the Declaration of Independence. The latter's ringing claim that 'all men are created equal'
gave the Revolution's central text limited purchase in the slave
South (particularly compared with the Constitution). However, it
had deepening resonance among antebellum northerners who were
beginning the difficult task of redefining the nation. Its radical
potential in the context of rising hostility between North and South
and the Republicans' ongoing attempts to promote the causes of

free labor and meritocracy can be seen in the way moderates insisted on its application to free blacks. As Abraham Lincoln exclaimed in August 1858, he had no desire to secure the political and social equality of the races, 'but I hold that ... there is no reason in the world why the negro is not entitled to all the natural rights enumerated in the Declaration of Independence – the right to life, liberty and the pursuit of happiness'.[35]

By the time he delivered these words, Lincoln was a wealthy corporate lawyer. Yet few men better epitomized the self-made, self-educated Republican ideal than he did and few could doubt that his social vision was more inclusive than that of the average southern planter. As he contended at New Haven in 1860, 'I want every man to have the chance – and I believe a black man is entitled to it – in which he can better his condition – when he may look forward and hope to be a hired laborer this year and the next, work for himself afterward, and finally to hire men to work for him!'[36]

Most ex-Democrats in the Republican coalition had no stomach for abolition or black rights. Their complaint against slavery was not that it deprived blacks of their liberty and dignity, but rather that it augmented the political power of the South at the expense of the North. Politicians such as David Wilmot of Pennsylvania and Francis P. Blair of Missouri resented the arrogance of high-handed southerners. Indeed, they had spent much of their political lives battling against southern domination of the Democratic party. After participating in the Barnburner revolt in 1848 and then returning to the fold, former Van Burenites had left the party of Jackson again in the wake of the Kansas-Nebraska outrage. Staunch upholders of white supremacy, they were determined to defend the liberties of white settlers in the territories, liberties that they believed to be threatened by Douglas's flaccid popular sovereignty doctrine and proslavery violence.

While these former Democrats were suspicious of Whig-Republicans and their fondness for government intervention in the economy, their love of the federal Union and dislike of the Slave Power were shared by conservative Whigs within the Republican coalition. Some Old Line Whigs had gravitated toward the Know-Nothing or Democratic party in 1856 as the only viable means of saving the Union, yet many had been genuinely affronted by the repeal of the Missouri Compromise and southern aggression in Kansas. Their leading representatives agreed with the likes of Olmsted that slavery was an obstacle to American economic progress. Like the Democratic-Republicans, they usually had little time for abolitionists, regarding them at best as impractical do-gooders.

A congressional ban on slavery was the one policy initiative on which each of these factions could agree. Although some northern free blacks were encouraged by the formation of the Republican party, most were appalled by the organization's apparent readiness to trade justice for votes. Frederick Douglass, one of the North's most prominent black abolitionists, was highly critical of leading New York Republicans for failing to campaign actively in favor of black suffrage in the state referendum of August 1860. Southern slaveholders, however, saw the party in a very different light. To them, Republicanism was the embodiment of everything they feared and despised about the North: material greed, puritanical moralizing, and hypocritical abolitionism. If they exaggerated the party's commitment to emancipation, they were certainly right to see it as a powerful counterweight to southern influence in the Union. Republicanism was the political ideology of a region that was self-confident enough to believe itself in the vanguard of national (and human) progress yet paradoxically consumed with doubts about the impact of slavery expansion on the nation's future. A Republican triumph in 1860 would consign domestic slavery to the sidings of history. Southerners knew it and were prepared to respond defiantly.

The eclipse of national Democracy and the election of Lincoln

A Democratic administration in Washington was all that stood between the Republic and disaster. Southern rights men were willing to adhere to the Union as long as their proslavery views received national sanction through the medium of the Democratic party. When it became clear that their traditional partisan allegiance would not protect them from northern power, they chose (sometimes reluctantly) to sever their ties to a Union which, in their eyes, had been taken over by the enemies of the Constitution.

The wealthy Pennsylvania bachelor, James Buchanan, was not the most dynamic of politicians, but his wealth of experience in the domestic and international arenas suggested he could avoid the pitfalls that ruined his predecessor. Unfortunately, although a much more accomplished political operator than Pierce (he was notably intolerant of the African slave trade as well as William Walker's filibustering activities in Central America), Buchanan was another doughface president. At a time when northern defections were strengthening southern power inside the Democratic party and when states' rights men were toughening their stance on slavery, evidence of further southern influence in the White House was bound to exacerbate northern concerns about the activities of the Slave Power. A series of events in the late 1850s finally put paid to the president's hopes of saving the Union. The *Dred Scott* decision of March 1857 fueled Republican concerns that a proslavery conspiracy was underway. The Lecompton crisis of 1857–58 resulted in a damaging feud with the most popular of all northern Democrats, Stephen Douglas. In 1859 John Brown's raid on Harpers Ferry heightened southern fears of a direct abolitionist attack. By the time of the following year's Democratic convention, the only national party in existence had split disastrously along sectional lines.

James Buchanan's cabinet choices betrayed his predilection for southerners as well as the South's domination of the Democratic party in the wake of northern defections in the 1856 election. The appointees, who included the states' rights Mississippian Jacob Thompson, were virtually all southern men or northerners sympathetic to the needs of slaveholders. Buchanan also followed Pierce's lead in largely ignoring the patronage requirements of Senator Stephen Douglas whom he resented as an ambitious contender for the presidential succession.

The new president took the oath of office from Chief Justice Roger B. Taney on March 4, 1857. In his inaugural address, he was optimistic about the nation's prospects and expressed confidence that the Supreme Court would soon decide the stage at which territorial legislatures could act on slavery. Buchanan had good reason to believe that the Court was about to rule on slavery in the territories, because he had been involved in a thoroughly irregular correspondence with two of the justices. The subject of these communications was a complex case, *Dred Scott v. Sandford*. Scott, an obscure slave who resided in St Louis, was suing for his freedom having spent several years of his life at army posts in the North. Several Missouri cases appeared to operate in Scott's favor, the doctrine established being 'once free, always free'. However, although a lower court in Missouri originally ruled in his favor, the decline of interstate comity resulted in a reversal of this decision by the proslavery state supreme court in March 1852.

When Scott's lawyers appealed this ruling to the US Circuit Court for the district of Missouri, the attorneys working for John F.A. Sanford (the brother of Scott's current mistress) introduced a plea in abatement asking the court to deny jurisdiction over the case. Scott, read the plea, was 'a negro of African descent' and not a citizen of

Missouri – thus, he could not bring suit in a federal court. Judge Robert W. Wells dismissed the plea with a broad interpretation of the diverse-citizenship clause of the federal Constitution. Citizenship, he ruled, implied simply residence in a designated state and the right to own property. However, he upheld the judgment of the state court that Scott's return to Missouri rendered the black man a slave. The case was then appealed to the US Supreme Court where in May 1856 a decision was postponed until the following term and reargument scheduled on two questions. Firstly, was the plea in abatement properly before the Court? Secondly, if it was, had Judge Wells been correct to decide that blacks did have the right to sue in federal court? The following winter counsel for both parties argued over four days not only on these points but on two others: Had Scott become a free man by living in the free state of Illinois? If not, had he become free by virtue of his residence in Wisconsin Territory, a region barred to slavery by the Missouri Compromise of 1820?

Initially, antislavery activists paid little attention to the case, perhaps expecting that the Court would simply uphold the Missouri decision in line with recent precedent. For a while this was precisely what some of the nine judges expected to do. However, at some point in mid-February 1857 the five southern justices on the Court, all Democrats, decided to turn the case into a political stick with which to beat the Republicans. Taking the lead was the chief justice himself. An elderly Maryland Democrat and former slaveholder who had served in Andrew Jackson's cabinet, Taney was a staunch opponent of those he regarded as dangerous antislavery radicals. With the aid of his fellow southern justice, John Catron of Tennessee, he solicited the help of Buchanan to put pressure on the president's fellow Pennsylvania doughface, Judge Robert Grier. The objective was to secure some northern support on the Court for the forthcoming decision – without such an endorsement, the southerners knew the ruling would lack all legitimacy. Buchanan's efforts bore immediate fruit. 'I am anxious', wrote Grier of the forthcoming decision, 'that it should not appear that the line of latitude should mark the line of division in the court.'[37]

Taney delivered his verdict to a packed courtroom on March 6. After a lengthy historical review suffused with racial prejudice, he averred that when the Constitution had been drawn up black people were regarded as 'so far inferior' that they 'had no rights which the white man was bound to respect'.[38] Although individual states could confer local citizenship upon them, blacks were not citizens of the United States. They were included neither within the purview of the Declaration of Independence nor in the citizenship clauses of the Constitution. Having denied Scott's right to sue in federal court, Taney boldly entered the realm of sectional controversy by assailing the Republicans' containment policy on two counts. Congress, he ruled, derived no power to govern the territories from Article 4, Section 3, which authorized the legislature 'to dispose of and make all needful rules and regulations respecting the territory or other property belonging to the United States'. This section, he opined, applied only to land owned by the Republic in 1789. Secondly, he took the Calhounite view that there was no difference between slavery and any other form of property. The right of southerners to take their slaves into the territories, therefore, was protected under the Fifth Amendment. Although the other judges differed on specific aspects of the judgment, it is clear that in overall terms Taney had voiced the view of the majority.

If Taney and Buchanan concurred with the *Philadelphia Pennsylvanian* that the decision would be 'the funeral sermon of Black Republicanism', they were soon apprised of their mistake.[39] In spite of being genuinely affronted by the decision, Republican leaders drew comfort from the fact that they could only gain from such outrages. As Chase told a recuperating Charles Sumner, while the Slave Power would undoubtedly receive 'a positive gain' from the decision, 'to us must accrue the incidental benefit of exposure of its purposes & arrogant demands and the arousing of a more determined resolve to withstand them'.[40] Radical antislavery men focused primarily on the verdict's impact on free blacks. One Maine newspaper, for example, denounced the 'monstrous doctrine' that denied local black citizens 'the ordinary justice which the meanest individual of any other race of foreign people may obtain among us'.[41] Far more typical, however, of the general Republican response was the cry that Taney's judgment was a product of sectional bias. Taking their lead from the dissenting opinions of the two non-Democrats on the Court, Justices John McLean and Benjamin Curtis, they condemned the invalidation of the Missouri Compromise as *dictum* (the gratuitous opinion of a politically biased Court). Crucially, the case was depicted as further evidence of Slave Power machinations. Buchanan's alleged whisperings with Taney on inauguration day were regarded in a particularly sinister light, though not absurdly so in view of what we now know to have been the president-elect's collusion with Grier and Catron. Moderates like Abraham Lincoln in Illinois insisted that the ruling was part of an ongoing plot to nationalize slavery. It was only a matter of time, they argued, before the Court decided that slaveholders could take their property into the free states.

Unwittingly the president was soon adding to the Republicans' bill of indictment against his administration. During the summer and fall of 1857, pressured by southerners in the cabinet, proslavery forces on the prairies labored to make Kansas a slave state. Against the wishes of the free-state majority, Buchanan allowed an unrepresentative constitutional convention in Lecompton to draw up a proslavery state constitution for submission to Congress. He then sanctioned a referendum in which settlers could vote not to rid Kansas of slaves but only on the question of whether or not to exclude more slaves from coming into the area. Even though his own placeman, Governor Robert J. Walker, warned him of the undemocratic nature of the statehood process, Buchanan ignored his advice and urged Kansans to vote in the referendum on December 21. The free-staters turned a deaf ear and boycotted the event, allowing the Lecompton constitution to be ratified by the proslavery minority.

Buchanan's acute sensibility to southern concerns provoked a near fatal split in his own party. Pilloried by Republicans at home in the run-up to his Senate reelection campaign and determined to stake out a viable and distinctive position on slavery in time for the 1860 presidential contest, Stephen Douglas broke publicly with the president on December 9. In a blistering speech, he criticized the government's Kansas policy as a negation of popular sovereignty and the democratic process. An incensed Buchanan then sought to destroy his rival's career by deploying his patronage powers and by intervening against Douglas in the 1858 Illinois Senate race. His efforts succeeded in dividing northern Democrats but failed to secure their objective. Douglas was reelected by the Springfield legislature after a high-profile series of local debates against the Republican candidate, Abraham Lincoln. In the course of these debates the 'Little Giant' proved as skillful as any other antebellum Democrat at manipulating grassroots prejudice against blacks to browbeat his Republican opponent. However, Lincoln subjected him to fierce cross-examination on the extent to which popular sovereignty could be salvaged in the wake of the *Dred Scott* decision.

Almost as an aside, Taney had ruled that because Congress was powerless to prevent slavery from entering a territory, it could not delegate that power to a territorial legislature. During the debate at Freeport on August 27 Lincoln asked Douglas whether a territorial legislature could do anything to prevent slavery expansion. Douglas's so-called 'Freeport Doctrine' – that territorial governments could outlaw slavery by using their police powers to pass unfriendly legislation – came as no surprise to Lincoln (for his opponent had made the same point in June 1857), but the question served to highlight the growing rift within the Democratic party. Douglas was further embarrassed by Lincoln's persistent efforts to paint him as an inveterate doughface, just another northern dupe in the Slave Power conspiracy. These arguments helped the Republicans to achieve a plurality of the votes cast in the elections for state office. However, 13 holdover senators enabled the Democrats to retain a 54–46 majority in the legislature. Douglas was reelected by a strict party vote in January.[42]

Although Republicans tried to exploit the Lecompton issue during 1858, Douglas's decision to break with the administration blunted their attack. Some eastern leaders of the party, Horace Greeley among them, even considered drafting Douglas for the presidency (much to the disgust of Illinois Republicans like Lincoln). Effectively, moreover, the Kansas issue was taken out of national political debate by the summer of 1858. Once Republicans and Douglas Democrats had combined to reject the Lecompton Constitution in the House of Representatives, the administration placed its weight behind a face-saving compromise, the English bill, designed to delay a decision on Kansas statehood by coupling a vote on the proslavery constitution with a plebiscite on a vastly reduced grant of public land to the state. But although Kansans terminated the possibility of immediate statehood in August by voting overwhelmingly against the revised land grant, the Republicans continued to thrive in the North, their cause aided by the effects of a sharp regional recession which allowed them to supplement their Slave Power thesis with local economic initiatives. At the same time (and very ominously), some southern rights Democrats such as Albert Browne of Mississippi moved to counter what they saw as the twin threat posed to slavery by Republicanism and popular sovereignty by demanding positive federal protection for slavery in the territories.

The divisive debate over slavery which had turned Congress into an armed camp by early 1858 assumed an even more threatening appearance late the following year. In October 1859 the revolutionary abolitionist John Brown reemerged onto the national stage with a dramatic raid on the federal arsenal at Harpers Ferry, a deceptively picturesque town located in the mountains of western Virginia. This audacious venture, intended to spark off a general slave revolt in the South, was funded by the 'Secret Six', a group of well-connected northeastern abolitionists including Thomas Wentworth Higginson,

Theodore Parker, and Gerrit Smith. The attack on the armory by Brown's tiny group of conspirators caused initial panic but was swiftly contained by the Virginia militia and a squad of federal troops under the command of Lieutenant Colonel Robert E. Lee. Several of the conspirators died in a fierce firefight at the engine house in which Brown and his men had taken refuge with a handful of hostages. Brown was captured alive and incarcerated in the jail at Charlestown. With what many northerners regarded as unseemly haste, he was then convicted by a Virginia court and sentenced to hang on December 2.

Several interested parties struggled for control of John Brown's body. Abolitionists were quick to realize that the old man was more valuable to the antislavery cause dead than alive. 'Let Virginia make him a martyr!' cried the popular evangelical minister, Henry Ward Beecher, 'Now he has only blundered ... But a cord and gibbet would redeem all that, and round up Brown's failure with a heroic success.'[43] Brown agreed. Writing 'good' above a press report of Beecher's comments, he proceeded to act out the part demanded of him by his northern allies. No longer God's instrument of vengeance on the sinful South, he bore his captivity in the manner of Christ before his crucifixion. Abolitionists helped to manufacture a groundswell of criticism by holding sympathy meetings across the North on the day of his judicial killing. Plans to parade the corpse were seriously considered, then shelved in favor of generating a heavily sentimentalized image of Brown through the rapid diffusion of books, poems, paintings, lithographs, and photographs. The fact that middle-class abolitionists identified so positively with John Brown not only as Christ but also as a Cromwellian man of action testified to the extent to which the antislavery cause had been radicalized by the Kansas-Nebraska Act, the violence in Kansas, and ongoing federal efforts to enforce the hated Fugitive Slave Law. Even William Lloyd Garrison, a confirmed pacifist, began to consider that violence might be the only way to purge America of its most grievous sin.

The Republican response to the raid was mixed. Although many radicals privately sympathized with Brown (a few actually had some advance knowledge of Brown's plans), moderates and conservatives feared that their opponents would try to implicate them in this blatant assault on the rights of sovereign states. Eschewing the Union-saving meetings favored by Democrats, nonradical Republicans generally tried to distinguish between Brown's unconstitutional and violent actions and his apparently more altruistic motives. Others insisted that Brown was simply a madman, much to the annoyance of Virginia's populist governor, Henry A. Wise, who needed Brown as much as Brown needed him. Eager to secure his home base before making a bid for the Democratic presidential nomination in 1860, Wise resisted all pleas for clemency that were based on the claim that his prisoner was a 'monomaniac' on the subject of slavery and therefore certifiably insane. His presidential chances would hardly benefit if white southerners saw him display leniency toward a man who engaged in the most heinous criminal act they could imagine.

Republican concerns about the political consequences of the raid seemed fully justified at the outset of the Thirty-sixth Congress in December 1859. Democrats tried to link John Sherman, the Republican candidate for speaker of the House of Representatives, to Harpers Ferry by denouncing his public backing for a digest of Hinton Rowan Helper's *Impending Crisis*. Published in 1857, Helper's book had depicted slavery as a disaster not primarily for black slaves but more especially for nonslaveholding southern whites. By allegedly trying to flood the South with antislavery trash of this kind, Sherman had, claimed southern Democrats, played his part in encouraging abolitionists to foment slave insurrection in their section. Sherman was forced to withdraw from the contest and a conservative Republican, William Pennington, was finally elected speaker after a bitter, sectionally charged debate that had lasted two months.[44]

Ordinary southern whites, particularly those living in blackbelt plantation areas where slaves were present in large numbers, were appalled by both the raid and the extent of northern popular mourning after Brown's death. Schooled by their political representatives to be watchful for abolitionist attempts to stir up a Haitian-style black uprising, they regarded Harpers Ferry as the stuff of nightmares. The first signs of a genuine crisis of fear were evident in several areas. In South Carolina a grassroots vigilance movement developed in the aftermath of the raid. Committees of safety were established at public meetings across the state, most of the gatherings attended by lower-class whites and planters in a show of racial unity. Each committee cracked down on the movement of blacks in its locality and monitored the actions of white outsiders deemed to be acting suspiciously. Free blacks across the South, a marginal group at the best of times, were worst hit by the knee-jerk white reaction to Harpers Ferry. Cave Johnson, a Nashville Democrat, reported in December 1859 that Tennessee whites were 'much excited' and that the legislature was discussing proposals to drive free blacks from the state or reenslave them.[45]

The raid did nothing to aid the floundering cause of national unity. 'There are thousands upon ... thousands of men in our midst', contended one Virginia newspaper, 'who, a month ago, scoffed at the idea of a dissolution of the Union as a madman's dream, but who now hold the opinion that its days are numbered, its glory perished.'[46] However, while the invasion convinced most southern whites that the dark specter of Republicanism lurked behind John Brown, conservatives in the region were at least able to point to northern Union meetings and anti-Brown editorials in Democratic papers like the *New York Herald* to show (allegedly) that a majority of northerners had no sympathy for his aims. South Carolina secessionists discounted such evidence but found their efforts to promote a southwide response to Harpers Ferry thwarted by persistent southern unionism and the contention of local politicians like Henry Wise that salvation lay with the Democratic party. As the mood of hysteria began to abate in the early months of 1860, southerners girded themselves for the most critical presidential election in the young nation's history.

The winner of the ensuing contest, Abraham Lincoln, remains one of the most elusive of American historical figures. His character is obscured not only by layers of national myth-making after his assassination but also by the efforts of both himself and his campaign managers to turn an able midwestern politician into real presidential timber. A lank, awkward figure whose capacity for self-deprecation, tendency toward melancholy, and lifelong fondness for folksy humor belied his strong self-reliance, driving ambition, and innate intellect, Lincoln had been born in 1809 in the slave state of Kentucky and reared in poverty in the free state of Indiana. During the 1830s and 1840s, his tireless commitment to self-improvement enabled him to leave the drudgery of farm labor behind and establish himself as a successful corporate lawyer and Whig politician in Springfield, Illinois. In common with many other Whigs operating in states controlled by the Democrats, his political fortunes had been rescued by the realignment of the mid-1850s. By the end of 1855 he had abandoned the party of his idol, Henry Clay, and hooked his political career to the rising star of Republicanism.

A predestinarian Baptist by upbringing but a deist by inclination, Lincoln developed a fatalistic view of the world that typified the thoughtful American mind in an age in which liberal ideals of progress struggled to find equilibrium with older notions of Christian faith. A Calvinistic denial of free will, however, did not breed in Lincoln a passive personality. He adhered strongly to the utilitarian

notion that human beings acted out of self-interest and had no compunction in doing so himself.[47] While this understanding of human
'motives' gave him considerable empathy for slaveholders, he was
under no illusions about the immorality of slavery itself. The Founding Fathers, he insisted, had placed the institution on the road to
extinction and he was as determined as any Republican to ensure
that this policy was not reversed.

By the late 1850s Lincoln had emerged as a credible presidential
candidate largely through his efforts to convince the northern
public that there were fundamental differences between Republican
policy on slavery expansion and the Douglas Democrats' popular
sovereignty. The latter's relationship to self-government, claimed
Lincoln, was beguiling yet illusory. It was 'the miner and sapper' of
the republican form of government established by the Founders.
'Now, what is Judge Douglas's Popular Sovereignty?', he asked an
audience in Columbus, Ohio, in September 1859. 'It is, as a principle,
no other than that, if one man chooses to make a slave of another
man, neither that other man, nor anybody else has a right to object.'[48]
Although his unionism prevented him from becoming an abolitionist,
he frequently injected a note of cautious morality into his speeches
– primarily because he believed morality went to the heart of the
distinction between Republicans and Democrats. Whereas the latter
regarded slavery in a positive or neutral light, the former considered
it, quite simply, wrong.

Lincoln secured the Republican nomination at Chicago on May
18, 1860. Held in a temporary wooden auditorium nicknamed the
'wigwam', the convention had been expected to nominate William
Seward for president. Lincoln's managers, however, took care to
isolate Seward's overconfident supporters from undecided state
delegations, and the New York senator proved unable to shed the
antinativist and higher law baggage which had scuppered his chances
four years earlier. Unlike Seward or his other main rivals, Salmon
Chase and Edward Bates, Lincoln was marvelously 'available'. Located
in the vital center of the party, he made no secret of his dislike of
human slavery yet claimed only to uphold the principles of the
Revolutionary generation. He was known to be honest at a time when
scandals had revealed the Buchanan administration to be unpalatably
corrupt. He hailed from the great West, the object of northerners'
hopes and fears for the future. A refreshingly direct, if somewhat
high-pitched, speaker, he had already proved his ability to communicate effectively with the voters. Once the convention had nominated
Lincoln and adopted a broad platform that intelligently combined

moderate antislavery with economic development, the Republicans, better organized than they had ever been before, were set to make a strong bid for victory in November.

Their chances of success had already been increased by a damaging split at the Democrats' national convention in Charleston, South Carolina, in early May. Determined to destroy Douglas's hopes of securing the presidency, southern rights men including William L. Yancey demanded federal protection for the territories as the price of their continued cooperation with northern Democrats. When their efforts were thwarted by Douglas's allies, a bolt by deep South delegates ensued. Douglas was then denied the nomination by a procedural ruling and the remaining delegates partly dispersed after agreeing to meet again in the less pressurized environment of Baltimore. When this gathering took place in mid-June, the majority voted to admit several pro-Douglas delegations from the South and rejected attempts by the Charleston bolters to regain their places. Douglas was the near unanimous choice of the convention which committed itself to the Union and popular sovereignty. The next day anti-Douglas Democrats met nearby at the Maryland Institute Hall to nominate the Kentuckyan, John C. Breckinridge, for president on a proslavery southern rights platform that made no mention of secession. By the time the Democrats had completed their bitter deliberations, worried conservatives (mostly Old Line Whigs unassimilated by political realignment) had already formed the Constitutional Union party with Senator John Bell of Tennessee as their chosen standard-bearer.

Fought in an atmosphere of growing sectional tension, the 1860 campaign was won by the Republicans rather than lost by the Democrats. Republican strategists wrote off the South and targeted the populous northern states that Frémont had lost relatively narrowly in 1856. Industrial workers in Pennsylvania, for example, were wooed specifically with the protariff plank in the Chicago platform, while the convention's support for western homestead legislation was used to appeal to would-be settlers in Illinois and Indiana. Lincoln, meanwhile, was packaged expertly as 'Honest Abe' and (a reference to his teenage years spent chopping fences) 'the Railsplitter'. He was the perfect antidote to Democratic corruption and the living embodiment of the Republican vision of a successful meritocratic society built on the solid foundations of free labor.

Notwithstanding widespread fears that a Republican victory would prompt secession, Lincoln won a comfortable victory in the electoral college owing to his strong performance across the North, especially outside the major cities. Although he won only a plurality of the popular vote (39 percent), he carried every northern state except New Jersey (see Map 4). This general strength throughout most of the Midwest and the Northeast ensured that he would probably have triumphed even if the Democrats had retained their cohesion during the summer. Breckinridge won the lion's share of votes in the deep South, yet failed to gain a majority of the popular vote in the slave states as a whole. Douglas and Bell, the only credible national candidates, performed respectably in certain areas. Douglas was competitive in most of the northern states but proved incapable of securing the kind of popular majorities that might have brought him victory in the electoral college. Indeed, Bell actually won more electoral college votes because his support was concentrated more effectively – primarily in the border states where residual Whiggery found solace in conservative unionism. For the most part, though, the election result represented the triumph of sectionalism over nationalism. With the help of some inept policymaking in Washington and a series of fateful events, the realignment of the previous decade was at an end. Some Americans rejoiced that the confusion of the 1850s appeared to be over: that the North finally had found the political will to stand up to the exactions of the Slave Power or, conversely, that the South was at last in a position to defend itself effectively against northern assaults on slavery. The price of certainty, however, was high. Secession and civil war now beckoned.

Notes

1. Quoted in William E. Parrish, *David Rice Atchison of Missouri: Border Politician* (Columbia, Mo, 1961), p.145.

2. *National Era*, Jan. 12, 1854, p.6.

3. 'Appeal of the Independent Democrats' in William E. Gienapp, ed., *The Civil War and Reconstruction: A Documentary Collection* (New York, 2001), pp.33–4.

4. Sumner to Amasa Walker, April 26, 1854, in Beverly Wilson Palmer, ed., *The Selected Letters of Charles Sumner*. 2 vols. (Boston, 1990), 1, p.407.

5. William E. Gienapp, *The Origins of the Republican Party 1852–1856* (New York, 1987), pp.77–8.

6. Robert Cook, *Baptism of Fire: The Republican Party in Iowa, 1838–1878* (Ames, Ia, 1994), p.47.

7. On fusion efforts in the immediate wake of the Kansas-Nebraska Act see Gienapp, *Origins*, pp.103–27.

8. Michael F. Holt, *The Political Crisis of the 1850s* (New York, 1978), pp.162–5.

9. Detailed analyses of the important 1854 election results can be found in Michael F. Holt, *The Rise and Fall of the American Whig Party* (New York, 1999), pp.879–908, and Gienapp, *Origins*, pp.129–66.

10. Michael F. Holt, 'The Mysterious Disappearance of the American Whig Party' in *idem, Political Parties and American Political Development from the Age of Jackson to the Age of Lincoln* (Baton Rouge, La, 1992), p.255.

11. *Buffalo Democrat* quoted in Gienapp, *Origins*, p.161.

12. Chase to Edward S. Hamlin, Nov. 21, 1854, in John Niven, ed., *The Salmon P. Chase Papers: Vol. 2, Correspondence, 1823–1857* (Kent, Ohio, 1994), p.389.

13. Quoted in Parrish, *Atchison*, p.161.

14. Quoted in *ibid.*, p.164.

15. Holt, *Rise and Fall*, p.926.

16. Lex Renda, *Running on the Record: Civil War-Era Politics in New Hampshire* (Charlottesville, Va, 1997), pp.54–5.

17. Quoted in Tyler Anbinder, *Nativism and Slavery: The Northern Know-Nothings and the Politics of the 1850s* (New York, 1992), p.168.

18. William E. Gienapp, 'Salmon Chase, Nativism and the Formation of the Republican Party in Ohio', *Ohio History* 93 (1984), 5–39.

19. Nicole Etcheson, ' "Our Lives, Our Fortunes and Our Sacred Honors": The Kansas Civil War and the Revolutionary Tradition', *American Nineteenth Century History* 1 (2000), 62–81.

20. Quoted in Parrish, *Atchison*, p.187.

21. Gienapp, *Origins*, pp.189–303, details the coalescence of the Republican Party in late 1855 and early 1856.

22. William E. Gienapp, 'The Crime Against Sumner: The Caning of Charles Sumner and the Rise of the Republican Party', *CWH* 25 (1979), 218–45.

23. Quoted in Cook, *Baptism of Fire*, p.63.

24. Anbinder, *Nativism*, p.207.

25. Pierce to Geary, Dec. 12, 1856, GLC 375.

26. Useful studies of the 1856 election include Roy F. Nichols and Philip S. Klein, 'Election of 1856' in Arthur M. Schlesinger, Jr, ed., *History of American Presidential Elections 1789–1968.* 9 vols. (New York, 1985), 3, 1007–33, and Gienapp, *Origins*, pp.375–448.

27. *Ibid.*, p.317.

28. Quoted in Richard J. Carwardine, *Evangelicals and Politics in Antebellum America* (New Haven, Conn., 1993), pp.263–4.

29. Cook, *Baptism of Fire*, pp.98, 107–10.

30. This theme is explored more fully in Susan-Mary Grant, *Northern Nationalism and American Identity in the Antebellum Era* (Lawrence, Kan., 2000).

31. William E. Gienapp, 'The Republican Party and the Slave Power' in Robert H. Abzug and Stephen E. Maizlish, eds, *New Perspectives on Race and Slavery in America: Essays in Honor of Kenneth Stampp* (Lexington, Ky, 1986), p.53.

32. *CWL*, 4, p.24.

33. Gienapp, 'Republican Party and the Slave Power', p.73; Don E. Fehrenbacher, *The Slaveholding Republic: An Account of the United States Government's Relations to Slavery* (Oxford, 2001), p.118.

34. Eric Foner, *Free Soil, Free Labor, Free Men: The Ideology of the Republican Party Before the Civil War* (New York, 1970), esp. pp.103–225, remains the fullest account of the antebellum Republican coalition.

35. Harold Holzer, ed., *The Lincoln–Douglas Debates: The First Complete Unexpurgated Text* (New York, 1993), p.285.

36. *CWL*, 4, pp.24–5.

37. Quoted in Don E. Fehrenbacher, *The Dred Scott Case: Its Significance in American Law and Politics* (New York, 1978), p.312.

38. Quoted in *ibid.*, p.347.

39. Quoted in *ibid.*, p.419.

40. Chase to Sumner, May 1, 1857, in Niven, ed., *Correspondence*, 2, p.450.

41. *Bangor Whig and Courier* quoted in Fehrenbacher, *Dred Scott Case*, p.429.

42. Allen C. Guelzo, *Abraham Lincoln: Redeemer President* (Grand Rapids, Mich., 1999), p.226.

43. Quoted in Paul Finkelman, 'Manufacturing Martyrdom: The Antislavery Response to John Brown's Raid' in *idem*, ed., *His Soul Goes Marching On: Responses to John Brown and the Harpers Ferry Raid* (Charlottesville, Va, 1995), p.42.

44. My thanks to David Brown for alerting me to the connection between Harpers Ferry, Helper's *Impending Crisis* and the speakership contest. See his biography of Helper (forthcoming, Louisiana State University Press).

45. Johnson to P.G. Washington, Dec. 6, 1859, GLC 02823.

46. *Richmond Whig* quoted in David Potter, *The Impending Crisis 1848–1861* (New York, 1976), p.384.

47. Guelzo, *Lincoln*, pp.117–20.

48. *CWL*, 3, p.405.

4

THE DISUNITED STATES: SECESSION AND CIVIL WAR

The secession crisis brought on by the Republican triumph in 1860 signaled the failure of the existing political system. However, it did not necessarily mean that 620,000 Americans had to die in a vicious civil war. Many southern whites who voted for secession in the winter of 1860–61 did not expect the North to respond with military force. States' rights leaders often went out of their way to reassure potential supporters that secession was an intrinsically conservative act, fully justified by the abolitionists' seizure of power and entirely legitimate under the terms of the federal Constitution. Their optimism was sadly misplaced. While large numbers of northerners yearned for peace, they did not do so at the expense of the Union. Opinion toward the South hardened considerably after the foundation of the Confederacy in February 1861: Lincoln's ensuing call for troops after the bombardment of Fort Sumter was met by widespread enthusiasm above the Ohio. Both sides then became locked in a progressively brutal conflict in which the South desperately sought to counter the North's vast economic and demographic resources through the application of superior operational virtuosity and fighting capabilities. Several times during the war the Confederates came close to securing their goal of independence. Indeed, southern whites harbored hopes of success as late as the summer of 1864, arguably the nadir of the Union cause. Remorselessly, however, the North began to grind down the enemy on all fronts. By the spring of 1865 the would-be Confederate nation lay in ruins.

Secession and the outbreak of war, 1860–61

The secession movement which gripped the lower South in the days after Lincoln's election succeeded because political radicals in the area were quick to capitalize on a general feeling of profound crisis – one that they had done much to create. South Carolina led the way as it had done in 1832–33 and 1850 but, critically, on this occasion its maneuvers attracted widespread regional support. Even before Lincoln's triumph, Palmetto state residents had begun to form military companies and elected a secessionist general assembly. Governor William Gist, moreover, had dispatched letters to fellow slave state executives urging them to join South Carolina in leaving the Union. When it became clear that none of the other states was prepared to precipitate secession, Gist redoubled his efforts to initiate the process of disunion as soon as Lincoln's election had been confirmed. To call for a southwide conference to discuss a common response to the Republican victory, he told Governor John J. Pettus of Mississippi on November 8, would only promote delay because some states, particularly those in the upper South, were bound to counsel patience. Mississippians, he insisted, should follow Carolinians and summon a state convention to discuss secession.[1]

Two days later the Columbia legislature provided for elections to a secession convention on December 6. The convention met for the first time on December 17. Virtually all of its 169 members owned slaves and over a hundred of them were planters. Because of fears of a smallpox epidemic in the capital, the delegates quickly adjourned to the radical stronghold of Charleston where Robert B. Rhett's fireeating *Mercury* bombarded them with secessionist appeals. Three days later, amid great excitement on the streets, the convention gathered in St Andrew's Hall to pass an ordinance of secession by a vote of 169–0. South Carolina no longer regarded itself as part of the federal Union.

Steven Channing's description of the secession of South Carolina as 'an affair of passion' applies with equal force to the other cotton states, even if there were signs of less unity in some of them.[2] Radicals elsewhere understood Gist's impatience. Only one decisive strike was necessary to take their states out of the Union but success was dependent on prompt action and the maintenance of tension. Just as in South Carolina, therefore, secessionists across the deep South maneuvered swiftly to hold elections to secession conventions and then to elect reliable delegates to those gatherings. Mississippians went to the polls on December 20 and the resulting convention adopted a secession ordinance on January 9, 1861. Over the next two days similar bodies in Alabama and Florida took the same action. By the time a Confederate government had been organized in Montgomery in February, the three remaining states of the deep South – Louisiana, Texas, and Georgia – had left the Union (see Map 4).

Secessionists generated a plethora of newspaper editorials, speeches, political pamphlets, and sermons to influence the voters. These outpourings marshaled a wide range of arguments to persuade anxious southern whites that their interests were under imminent threat. The need to protect the existing racial order from newly empowered Yankee abolitionists constituted the primary theme. 'The Republican party is a standing menace', claimed the Alabama states' rights Democrat, Jabez L.M. Curry, in a speech at Talladega on November 26. 'Its success is a declaration of war against our property and the supremacy of the white race.'[3] Lincoln's election, insisted a New Orleans newspaper, was a declaration that northerners meant to implement 'their destructive and aggressive policy' against slavery, a policy that could threaten the future prosperity and security of the South.[4] For years proslavery ideologues and southern rights politicians had been telling local whites that slavery was a positive good: that it promoted harmony among whites of all classes and brought civilization to inferior blacks. Abolitionism would wreck the region's economy in the same way that emancipation had allegedly destroyed the prosperity of the British West Indies. Even more seriously, it would destabilize southern society. According to the *Columbia South Carolinian*, abolitionism (widely held to be synonymous with Republicanism) 'is at the bottom of every raid upon the South; it incites to the murder of her citizens, whether at home, amid the quiet of domestic life, or in neighboring States demanding the restoration of property stolen away by those who covenanted to respect it and to restore it ... .'[5]

Secessionists everywhere talked of defying 'subjugation' and protecting southern rights against northern attack. It was not they, but the Republicans, who had disobeyed the Constitution – by passing personal liberty laws, abetting fugitive slaves, and encouraging evildoers like John Brown. Leaving the Union, they claimed, was a lawful act, for the Founding Fathers had created a voluntary federation, not a 'consolidated' nation. Beneath all the talk of honor and constitutional bluster, however, lay deep fears of fundamental social change from which all southern whites, not only slaveholders threatened with the loss of valuable investments, would suffer as a result of emancipation. Although disunionists differed over the mechanisms by which the Republicans would seek to undermine slavery, they agreed that Lincoln's election signaled the end of normal politics. Southerners had not voted for a Republican president, went the argument. Therefore they did not have to abide by the result.[6] Self-preservation alone seemed to demand an immediate separation from Yankeedom. For Lincoln and his victorious party such reasoning on the part of an aggrieved minority smacked of sour grapes and, more critically, threatened to plunge the country into political and social chaos.

In an atmosphere thick with suspicion, hatred, and fear, large numbers of whites in the deep South – convinced that 'Black Republicans' would promote abolition with all the means at their disposal – were caught up in the excited stampede toward secession. Even if they remained concerned about the South's leap into the dark, they responded positively to secessionist rhetoric. Frances Kirby Smith, a well-to-do inhabitant of St Augustine, Florida, fulminated in mid-December that her state was '*ripe* and *ready*' for secession. Although she confessed that no-one knew the consequences of hasty action, hard times were a better option than

> insult[,] injury[,] loss of property – little did or do the northern abolitionists, fanatics, atheists, socialists, devils own (excuse me) know what a spirit they have raised in the South. Our people say that in the end it will be much better for us, that we have within us the means of support but it must take some time to get organized[,] our crops in, our manufactures established and mean time we must remember what our forefathers underwent in those times when they sought freedom from the oppressors.[7]

Three weeks later, Kirby Smith wrote more confidently of 'the excitement which prevails among all classes, all ages, women as well as men. Our *cause* is a *just* one, and I fully believe Providence will smile upon us – if we pass thru it without a baptism of *blood* and fire shall we not have reason to thank God with our whole hearts.'[8] It was a big 'if'. The following week she told her son that a large flag, made by the local women, was now waving in the town square. The central device on a blue background was a stately palmetto (in honor of South Carolina), an eagle bearing a hemisphere, and two stars with the motto, 'Let Us Alone'. The 'ladies', she also noted, were preparing a hospital.[9]

Wealthy slaveholding planters, lawyers, and merchants dominated the secession conventions in the deep South, indicating the grip that political elites exerted over the radical movement in the cotton states. Although it has been argued that rich southerners acted precipitately in the wake of Lincoln's election because they feared that a Republican administration would exacerbate existing class divisions in the region, there is little hard evidence that slaveholders were motivated primarily by such concerns.[10] White society in the deep South was certainly not monolithic, but common folk in the plantation counties needed little persuading that their interests were threatened directly by the accession of an antislavery and antisouthern party to national power. Even those areas, such as the hill country of northern Alabama and Georgia, well known for their opposition to the inordinate political influence of the black belt, failed to elect unconditional unionists as delegates to their state conventions.

The chief faultline within the lower South conventions lay not between American and southern nationalists but between immediate secessionists and so-called 'cooperationists'. Whereas the former wanted to get their states out of the Union as quickly as possible, their opponents (many of whom were former Whigs) favored a coordinated southwide response to the Republican triumph. Essentially the cooperationists, who occupied more than one point on the continuum between secession and union, adopted the Calhounite approach of the late 1840s: exhibit a united southern face to the North in the hope of meaningful concessions, while maintaining secession as a last but viable resort. Secessionists won majorities of varying size during the winter's elections, their votes coming mainly from counties containing the largest numbers of slaves. Against a background of minimal Republican concessions in Washington, they were able to pass secession ordinances in each of the cotton states against only limited opposition. Even the Georgia convention, where cooperationist strength was greatest, resolved to leave the Union by a vote of 208–89 on January 19, 1861.

In order to limit the dangers of separate state action, secessionist politicians in the deep South acted to maintain regional cooperation by appointing state-to-state commissioners. These envoys relied heavily on racial themes to make their point. John McQueen of South Carolina told the Texas convention that Republicans sought 'the abolition of slavery upon this continent and the elevation of our own slaves to an equality with ourselves and our children'.[11] An Alabaman, Stephen Hale, was even more blunt in a letter to Governor Beriah Magoffin of Kentucky. Lincoln's election, he wrote, constituted

a solemn declaration, on the part of a great majority of the
Northern people, of hostility to the South, her property, and
her institutions; nothing less than an open declaration of war,
for the triumph of this new theory of government destroys the
property of the South, lays waste her fields, and inaugurates all
the horrors of a San Domingo servile insurrection, consigning
her citizens to assassinations and her wives and daughters to
pollution and violation to gratify the lust of half-civilized
Africans ...

If the policy of the Republicans is carried out according to
the programme indicated by the leaders of the party, and the
South submits, degradation and ruin must overwhelm alike all
classes of citizens in the Southern States. The slave-holder and
non-slave-holder must ultimately share the same fate; all be
degraded to a position of equality with free negroes, stand side
by side with them at the polls, and fraternize in all the social
relations of life, or else there will be an eternal war of races,
desolating the land with blood, and utterly wasting and
destroying all the resources of the country.[12]

It matters little whether or not Hale actually believed this
hellish vision of Republican rule. The important point is that
such racial fears were so widespread in the region that – at the very
least – he believed arguments like this would further the cause of
secession.

A major step on the road to disunion occurred on December 13
when 30 cotton state members of Congress, Senator Jefferson Davis
of Mississippi among them, met together in Washington. They
declared all hopes of a compromise extinguished and called for the
formation of an independent Confederacy. Less than two months
later delegates from each of the seven seceded states met in
Montgomery, Alabama, to organize a provisional government and
draw up a constitution for the new nation. Jefferson Davis was chosen
to be the first president of the Confederacy – his cause abetted by
his battlefield exploits in the Mexican War, his cabinet experience
in the early 1850s, and his reputation as a leading disciple of Calhoun
after the great man's death. A staunch supporter of southern rights,
Davis had stayed loyal to the United States as long as he did not
perceive that entity to subvert his own material interests and political
values. The strength of secessionist feeling at home and the refusal
of Republicans in Congress to offer concrete concessions to the

South, now led him to sunder all ties to the Union for which he had once fought so nobly.

In his inaugural address delivered before a crowd of several thousand on February 18, Davis invoked the Founding Fathers, insisting that in America governments rested upon the consent of the governed. He also said that the establishment of the Confederacy was justified because the Union 'had been perverted from the purposes for which it was ordained'.[13] His listeners – their core values rooted in localism, family, and white supremacy – could have had little complaint with their president's reasoning.

Jefferson Davis was a practical man. He preferred peace but knew, firstly, that civil war was likely and, secondly, that the Confederacy's chances of ultimate success were slim as long as the states of the upper South declined to secede. He realized violence was probable because the Republicans had failed to offer the kind of concessions that might have kept the cotton states in the Union. Although Buchanan, vacillating fatally in the final days of his presidency, had called on Congress to solve the crisis with another set of compromise measures, the incoming Republicans evinced little desire to risk their internal cohesion by capitulating to proslavery opponents whose high-handed activities had done much to secure Lincoln's election in the first place.

Initially, most congressional Republicans presumed that southern threats to secede were mere bluster. Consequently they braved substantial compromise sentiment in the North, evident most clearly among northeastern commercial interests, Democrats and Old Line Whigs, and voted consistently against the only piece of comprehensive legislation that might have satisfied southern desires. Introduced into the Senate by John J. Crittenden of Kentucky, this bill embraced a range of measures designed to quell southern fears. The first and most important of these initiatives extended the Missouri Compromise Line to the Pacific Ocean. Crucially, it also permitted the establishment of slavery in any territory south of the line currently owned or 'hereafter acquired' by the United States.[14] Had the South been assured of its own distinct sphere of influence with which it could counter the acquisition of further free states, its leaders might just have been willing to abandon secession. The inclusion of future territory in the bill, however, angered many Republicans precisely because it appeared to open the way to proslavery expansion in Mexico, Central America, and the Caribbean, thereby thwarting their party's fundamental objective of containing slavery within its existing limits. The Crittenden bill came to a vote on several occasions in

THE DISUNITED STATES: SECESSION AND CIVIL WAR

the two congressional committees that were created to devise a compromise solution to the crisis. On no occasion did a single Republican vote for it.

Republicans were not entirely united on how to react to secession, especially in the confused early weeks of the crisis when influential figures like Horace Greeley and Thurlow Weed urged peaceable separation or, at the very least, a more positive approach to compromise. However, after the passage of secession ordinances and the formation of the Confederacy, most party members, regardless of their ideological or factional orientation, rallied behind the president-elect's strategy of no significant departure from the Chicago platform.

Throughout the winter of 1860–61, Abraham Lincoln remained at home in Springfield. He was determined to say nothing publicly that could be twisted by his enemies but worked privately to ensure that Republicans held firm against their opponents' attempts to destroy the party before the inauguration ceremony in March. The most that Lincoln and some of his allies were willing to concede was a constitutional amendment guaranteeing the existence of slavery in the states where it existed already, repeal of the personal liberty laws that most northern states had passed after the Kansas-Nebraska Act, and a bill that might have resulted in the admission of New Mexico as a slave state. The majority of Republicans objected to even these concessions and only a constitutional amendment (the Corwin amendment) denying that the United States had any intention of interfering with slavery ever saw the light of day.[15]

The main reason that Republican leaders offered any olive branch to the South was their conviction that procrastination would prevent the upper South from seceding and allow unionists in the cotton states to reassert themselves. William H. Seward, Lincoln's choice for secretary of state, was the foremost exponent of this policy. Convinced, just as he had been in 1848, that he could treat the party's successful presidential nominee as a cypher, the New Yorker worked hard to prevent civil war. He did so firstly by supporting concessions like the Corwin amendment (which he authored) to retain the allegiance of key upper South states like Virginia and secondly by secretly persuading southern emissaries that he was in charge in Washington. Initially it appeared that his strategy (the first prong of which Lincoln supported) was paying dividends. After the secession of Texas at the beginning of February, the rebel movement seemed to lose momentum. Voters in Tennessee and North Carolina opposed the calling of a state secession convention, and unionists dominated elections to the state conventions summoned in Virginia and

Arkansas. Of the border slave states only Missouri held a convention to consider secession. Unionists outnumbered secessionists in this body by three to one. In Kentucky, where slaves made up a fifth of the population, lawmakers refused to act on Governor Beriah Magoffin's call for secession.

The North Carolina vote on February 28, 1861 was close. The voters opposed calling a convention by a majority of only 661. However, just over 60 percent of the delegates selected were unionists – a fairly clear indication that secession was less popular in states where two-party competition had been vigorous in the 1840s and 1850s.[16] Even though secessionists insisted that Republicans sought to abolish slavery, impose black social and political equality, and degrade the white man, local unionists in the central and upper piedmont responded that bloody civil war would extinguish all constitutional rights in the state. To good effect, they also condemned neighboring South Carolina for its rashness and insufferable arrogance toward their own state where society was somewhat less in thrall to the planter aristocracy. David Schenck, a Gaston County secessionist, was appalled by the result of the convention election and blamed it on 'the tories of 76'. Personally, he remained defiant. The 'Revolution', he confided in his diary, still has 'my hearty approval. I do not want Abe Lincoln to drive me from my native soil. I am for resistance to the death by means legal if possible but illegal if necessary ... "Free negro equality" or resistance is the issue.'[17]

If the stalling of secession in the border and upper South meant that two-thirds of southern whites remained within the Union at the time of Lincoln's inauguration, the conditional nature of these subregions' attachment to the Union was everywhere apparent.[18] Many moderates in states such as Virginia and North Carolina were prepared to accept a Republican administration only as long as it refrained from interfering with slavery and, even more crucially, declined to coerce the seceded states back into the Union. The problem was that most Republicans were not prepared to see the work of the Founding Fathers destroyed by what they regarded as an unrepresentative clique of slaveholding aristocrats. The only hope of avoiding a general war and preventing the secession of the upper South seemed to be to eradicate all points of possible friction between the two sections.

By the second week of January 1861 two federal forts – Sumter in Charleston harbor and the more defensible Pickens off the coast of Pensacola, Florida – had emerged as the likeliest flashpoints.

Southern state and subsequently Confederate authorities sought the removal of US troops from these installations but refrained from a full-scale assault because of the need for greater military preparedness and the Buchanan administration's informal promise that no attempt would be made to reinforce the existing garrisons. The president, his stance toughened somewhat by southern resignations from his cabinet and the hardening of northern popular opinion, declined to accede to the southerners' demands for a federal withdrawal. However, his overriding concern remained the outbreak of civil war. He continued to hope that a political solution to the crisis could be found, if not in Congress then by a peace convention that assembled in Washington's Willard Hotel on February 4 at the behest of the Virginia legislature. Again, sectional ultras ruined his hopes. No delegate from the deep South was present at the convention and Republicans like Salmon Chase attended only to observe. When the convention finally passed a modified version of the Crittenden Compromise, Republicans in Congress ensured that it did not come to a vote. In the early morning of February 23 Lincoln slipped furtively into Washington in order to avoid the possibility of assassination by secessionists en route through Baltimore. Major Robert Anderson in command at Fort Sumter was rapidly running out of supplies but at least the Republicans were now free to deal with the crisis in their own way.

The new president delivered his eagerly awaited inaugural address on March 4, having incorporated some of Seward's suggestions the previous day. Sharpshooters were positioned around the unfinished capitol building to ensure his safety. Remembered today for its magnificent peroration, the speech fused Lincoln's uncompromising unionism with Seward's urgent desire to encourage voluntary reconstruction. There were no new concessions. Lincoln repeated his oft-expressed intention not to meddle with slavery in the states as well as his belief that the government should enforce the Fugitive Slave Act (with proper guarantees for the rights of free blacks). Much more important was his unbending insistence that 'the Union of these States is perpetual' and that it was his duty to ensure that national laws were enforced in all the states. The South's refusal to accept the election result was, he claimed, to place democracy on the road to anarchy. Surely, southerners could see that the breakup of the Union was physically and emotionally impossible. 'In *your* hands, my dissatisfied fellow countrymen, and not in *mine*', he concluded, is the momentous issue of civil war. The government will not assail *you*. You can have no conflict, without being yourselves the aggressors. *You* have no oath registered in Heaven to destroy the government, while *I* shall have the most solemn one to 'preserve, protect and defend' it.

I am loth to close. We are not enemies, but friends. We must not be enemies. Though passion may have strained, it must not break our bonds of affection. The mystic chords of memory, stretching from every battle-field, and patriot grave, to every living heart and hearthstone, all over this broad land, will yet sway the chorus of the Union, when again touched, as surely they will be, by the better angels of our nature.[19]

Notwithstanding their obvious attraction to diehard nationalists, Lincoln's mnemonic appeals to a common Revolutionary heritage had little impact on the deep South. How could it have done when secessionists themselves appealed to the same heritage to justify their decision to abandon the Union? Lincoln's inaugural, argued the *Richmond Dispatch* on March 5, 'inaugurates civil war ... The Demon of Coercion stands unmasked. The sword is drawn and the scabbard thrown away.'[20]

That same day, his first full day in office, the new president learned that if action were not taken immediately the garrison at Fort Sumter would be starved out. Seward immediately brought his influence to bear.[21] His allies General Winfield Scott and Colonel Joseph Totten told Lincoln that the fort could not be reinforced effectively. In cabinet, the secretary advised that Anderson and his men should be evacuated. And behind the president's back he told the southern-born Supreme Court Justice, John A. Campbell, to assure Jefferson Davis that the garrison would be pulled out. Campbell and Confederate commissioners seeking to treat with the new administration were convinced that Seward spoke for the government and informed the authorities in Montgomery that the United States would not make a stand at Sumter. Like Seward, Jefferson Davis required time. An uneasy peace prevailed as the Confederate president hoped for peace and prepared for war.

Two missions to Charleston in the third week of March induced Lincoln to show his hand. Gustavus V. Fox, a former naval officer whose plans to relieve Sumter by sea had won only limited approval among members of Buchanan's cabinet, met with Anderson on March 21. He found the anxious commander opposed to any scheme that might lead to civil war and adamant that he could not survive in post beyond April 15. Three days later two of Lincoln's most trusted Illinois friends, Stephen A. Hurlbut and Ward Hill Lamon, arrived in Charleston incognito and soon discovered that unionism was a spent force in South Carolina. Once in possession of these facts, Lincoln told a critical cabinet meeting on March 29 that Sumter should be reprovisioned rather than reinforced with troops. This masterstroke held out the possibility of avoiding an immediate clash with the Confederate authorities without relinquishing national sovereignty or, a worst case scenario, of leaving the southerners to take the responsibility for initiating civil war. He found vigorous support for some form of relief expedition from Secretary of the Treasury Salmon Chase, Secretary of the Navy Gideon Welles, and Postmaster General Montgomery Blair. Seward opposed any expedition to Charleston harbor and, seeking to buy more time, argued that the government should focus on holding remote Fort Pickens at Pensacola. The latter, he argued, might be reinforced more efficiently and with even less likelihood of initiating all-out war. Caleb B. Smith, the new secretary of the interior, and Attorney General Edward Bates concurred.

Sufficiently emboldened, Lincoln ordered Fox to outfit an expeditionary force to Sumter at the Brooklyn Navy Yard. Seward, fast losing control of events, then composed a desperate memorandum suggesting that the administration create a wave of patriotic sentiment on both sides of the Mason-Dixon Line by threatening to go to war with Spain and France over Cuba. Sumter, he advised again, should be evacuated and Pickens and other minor forts on the Gulf reinforced. Irked at Seward's accompanying insinuations that the administration lacked direction and that the secretary of the state was the man to provide it, Lincoln noted (in a letter that may never have been sent) that it was his job to determine policy. Yet, in his desire to avoid war if possible, he sanctioned Seward's plan for an expedition to Pickens and may even have offered to withdraw the garrison from Sumter if the Virginia secession convention agreed to disperse.[22] Conflicting objectives led to confused policymaking. The warship *Powhatan* was assigned to the Pickens-bound relief force after it had already been included in the flotilla that Fox was fitting out for Sumter.

It made no difference. The Confederates had run out of patience. On April 8 Governor Pickens of South Carolina received word from Lincoln that an attempt would be made to resupply Fort Sumter 'and that, if such attempt be not resisted, no effort to throw in men, arms, or am[m]unition' would be made without further notice.[23] On receipt of this news, President Jefferson Davis and his cabinet concurred that national self-respect and self-preservation demanded the immediate surrender of the installation. Only the former Georgia Whig, Robert Toombs, disagreed. 'You will wantonly strike a hornet's nest which extends from mountains to ocean', he warned, 'and legions, now quiet, will swarm out and sting us to death. It is unnecessary; it puts us in the wrong; it is fatal.'[24]

In the early hours of April 12 the Confederate commander in Charleston, Brigadier General Pierre G.T. Beauregard, implemented his orders and began the bombardment of Anderson's troops at Sumter. Fox's expeditionary force arrived on the scene later that day but it was too late. Anderson surrendered the battered installation on April 14 and the next day, amid a general clamor for action, Lincoln called on the states to provide 75,000 ninety-day militiamen to suppress the rebellion against federal authority. Southern impatience and a tenacious determination to save the Union had finally inaugurated civil war (see Map 5).

The chimera of victory, 1861–62

Lincoln's call for troops to put down the Rebellion ended Jefferson Davis's residual hopes that a swift attack on Fort Sumter combined with magnanimous treatment of its defenders might persuade the North that southerners were in earnest and that the latter should be left alone to forge their own destiny. But while hindsight reveals that war signaled the fate of the Confederacy and its slave-based society, the initial outbreak of hostilities brought the South important short-term gains. Arkansas, Tennessee, North Carolina, and Virginia all seceded in the wake of Lincoln's move and disunionists in Kentucky, Missouri, and Maryland redoubled their efforts to take these border slave states into the Confederacy.

Amid the infectious *rage militaire* that induced tens of thousands of young men to enlist in the armed forces of the United States and the Confederacy at the outset of the Civil War, many observers believed that one quick and decisive victory on the battlefield would end the conflict in favor of North or South.[25] This view proved illusory but the truth was – if Union morale held out – that the Confederacy's best hope lay in a brief war. Some scholars have suggested that the superiority of the strategic defensive brought about by the advent of the long-range rifled musket and the Minié bullet required the South to fight cautiously. Confederates, they argue, needed only to wage a defensive war to survive as an independent people, whereas northerners had to occupy the South if they were to secure their ultimate aim of reunifying the country.[26] In actual fact the yawning gulf in resources between the two sides meant that the South's chances of winning were likely to recede as northern mobilization gathered pace.

Because slavery had depressed industrialization, urbanization, and immigration, the Confederacy went into the war at a decided disadvantage to the enemy. The Rebel states contained only one-ninth of the antebellum Republic's manufacturing capacity. Ninety percent of the United States' boot and shoe production, 93 percent of its pig iron output, and 97 percent of its production of firearms was located in the North.[27] The demographics were no more encouraging to southern leaders. Nineteen million people lived in the North in 1860 compared with 12 million in the slave states. Even this telling comparison inflates the size of the Confederacy's potential manpower pool, for the border slave states were lost to the Union in the first year of the war and a third of the South's population were enslaved blacks. In fact President Davis could draw on a white military-age population that was less than a third as large as the one on which Lincoln theoretically could depend. To have any chance of winning, the South would have to mobilize quickly and more effectively than the North. Fluctuating troop mobilization ratios in the early stages of the war show that the Confederacy initially outpaced the North in its ability to put men in the field. During the spring and early summer of 1861 the North–South ratio approached parity. In January 1862 it was 1.6:1; at the end of June 1862 it had fallen to 1.3:1; but by the end of the year it was 2:1. Thereafter the North always enjoyed the luxury of having substantially more men in uniform. The ratio at the end of the war was as high as 2.2:1.[28]

Confederate leaders were aware that time was on the side of the biggest battalions. This fundamental realization helps to explain why the South adopted, in the words of Jefferson Davis, the 'offensive–defensive' – a flexible yet relatively aggressive grand strategy by which the government would seek to protect the Confederate heartland while simultaneously seizing any opportunity to inflict a decisive and morale-sapping military defeat on the North.[29] Union strategy at the outset of the war was grounded in the erroneous assumption that it would not take too much effort to defeat the Rebels. General Scott's 'Anaconda Plan' eschewed the idea of a damaging full-scale invasion of the South in favor of a coastal blockade and a combined army and navy operation along the Mississippi. The result, argued the elderly Mexican War hero, would be to sever the South's external links and strangle the Confederacy at birth. The plan was not without merit but it ignored the impatience of ordinary northerners to get to grips with the enemy. Once the Confederates had moved their capital to Richmond in May, only 100 miles separated the two national capitals from one another. 'On to Richmond!' was a popular cry that the Union high command could ill afford to ignore.

Under intense pressure from President Lincoln to take the initiative, Brigadier General Irvin McDowell advanced west from Washington to engage a raw Confederate force of 24,000 under Beauregard at nearby Manassas Junction in northern Virginia. In the wake of his 36,000-strong army traveled a motley collection of journalists and other civilians keen to observe the destruction of the Rebels. McDowell got more than he bargained for. After running into Confederate resistance at Blackburn's Ford on July 18, he opted to launch a surprise attack on the enemy's weaker left flank. Two days of tarrying at Centreville awaiting supplies allowed the Confederates to reinforce their position. Acting with commendable speed, General Joseph E. Johnston deceived a covering army of Federals in the Shenandoah Valley and transported his force of 11,000 men by rail to the point of concentration near Bull Run creek. There they played a critical role in the outcome of the ensuing battle.

At around 8.30 am on July 21, Confederates spotted the Union flanking column in the morning sun. Poor planning had slowed the movement, allowing the Rebels to rush troops to meet the advancing threat. After fierce fighting north of the Warrenton Turnpike, the outnumbered southerners were forced back across the road to high ground on Henry Hill. A complacent McDowell assumed victory was all but won and stopped to regroup. When Union assaults did begin they were undertaken in piecemeal fashion. The Confederate defense on the hill was ably undertaken by Colonel Wade Hampton's eponymous Legion and the Virginia Brigade of General Thomas J. Jackson whose actions this day would earn him the legendary sobriquet, 'Stonewall'. Southern resistance was ferocious. Charging up the hill in one of the many unsuccessful Federal assaults, boys of the 2nd Wisconsin thought they heard the Virginians cry, 'Kill them! Mow them down, the Northern Abolitionist sons of bitches!'[30] By mid-afternoon McDowell's offensive, confused in part by the fact that some of his troops were wearing gray like the Confederates, had become totally uncoordinated. When Beauregard deployed his reinforcements in a general counterattack the Union soldiers broke. Chaos ensued as terrified boy soldiers mingled with panic-stricken civilians desperate to reach the safety of Washington. Luckily for those in retreat, the exhausted Confederates were unable to launch a decisive pursuit and the vanquished Federals were left to lick their wounds.

By the standard of later battles casualties were light: 1,500 Federals were killed or wounded compared with just under 2,000 Confederates. The scenes on the battlefield after the Union rout, however, were ghastly enough and would be repeated many times over before the war's end. One victorious Rebel described how he found 'dead men in every conceivable position, mangled, dismembered, disemboweled – some torn literally to pieces. Some, in their death struggles, had torn up the ground around where they fell.' Another found a wounded Federal dying at the base of a tree. 'You can do one thing for me ... ,' asked the poor man, 'for God's sake, take your bayonet and run me through, kill me at once and put an end to this.'[31]

First Manassas marked an early turning point in the war. The day after the battle, Abraham Lincoln signed a bill providing for the enlistment of half a million three-year soldiers. On July 26 McDowell paid the price of failing to use his resources effectively (less than half his available force had actually participated in the battle) and was replaced by another West Pointer, George B. McClellan. At 35 years of age McClellan had an outstanding service record, both as a member of General Scott's staff during the Mexican War and as the commander who had secured the unionist stronghold of western Virginia during the first weeks of the Civil War. Lincoln knew the general personally during the latter's career as vice president of the Illinois Central Railroad and rightly regarded him as an effective organizer and motivator. Three days later the president added to the impression of urgency by authorizing a call for another half a million troops. For the first time, the North seemed prepared to fight fire with fire.

The Confederates, meanwhile, passed up the opportunity to follow up their dramatic victory with a decisive campaign in the Washington area. While their failure to assault the Federal capital after Manassas was understandable given the ferocity of the fighting and the inexperience of the men involved, their reluctance to take advantage of the momentum generated by the victory may have been less forgiveable. At a meeting with Jefferson Davis on October 1, a number of Confederate generals urged an immediate attack on Federal forces around Washington. While Beauregard called for an offensive in Maryland, Major General Gustavus W. Smith urged a concentrated attack in northern Virginia. 'Success here at this time saves everything', he said excitedly. 'Defeat here loses all.'[32] Davis demurred. The country's lack of men and arms, he insisted, would ensure the failure of such operations. Besides, he added, as president he had to take into account the defense of the whole Confederacy, including the western theater. If there really was a window of opportunity at this juncture of the war, the shutters had closed.

The lack of a follow-up campaign after Manassas gave the Federals the respite they required. Most of the small-scale skirmishing that characterized the fighting during late 1861 took place in the strategically important border slave states. Here the Federals began to gain the upper hand. In Maryland the unionist sympathies of Governor Thomas Hicks and tough action by Federal commanders helped to secure the state for the Union by September 1861. Kentuckyans, having sought salvation in a desperate bid for Swiss-style neutrality, saw the western part of their state invaded on September 3 by a Confederate army under the fighting bishop, General Leonidas Polk. This rash move (which was quickly countered by the local Union commander, Ulysses S. Grant) caused the legislature to declare in favor of the United States. A secession convention nominally took Kentucky out of the Union in November but the Confederates were left in control only of the southwest corner of the state.

In Missouri decisive action by the hot-headed Federal commander Nathaniel Lyon against secessionists in St Louis and the surrounding area seemed a mere preliminary to clearing the state of traitors. However, a combined Rebel force of Arkansans, Louisianans, and Texans (under Confederate General Ben McCulloch) and proslavery Missourians (commanded by Major General Sterling Price) defeated Lyon's army of US regulars, Iowans, Kansans, and pro-Union German-Americans from St Louis in a savage engagement at Wilson's Creek on August 10. Having lost Lyon in the battle, the battered Federals retreated and the town of Lexington surrendered to Price the following month. By late 1861, however, renewed Union pressure and McCulloch's preference for a defensive strategy had confined Confederate forces to southern Missouri. Although the state was dogged by some of the worst guerrilla fighting of the Civil War and, like Kentucky, sent delegates to the Confederate Congress, it lay clearly within the Union's sphere of influence and would remain so for the rest of the war.

For several reasons, the loss of the border slave states was a serious blow to the Confederacy.[33] Firstly, around 200,000 border state whites fought for the Union cause (compared with 90,000 for the Confederacy). Secondly, the area was the most industrialized region of the Old South; the Rebels could ill afford to sacrifice large manufacturing centers such as Baltimore and St Louis to the enemy. Thirdly, and perhaps most importantly, the loss was preeminently a strategic one. The Union secured access to vital communications links such as the Ohio River and the Baltimore and Ohio Railroad. Its armies were ideally placed to thrust deep into the Confederate heartland from points that were well south of the Mason-Dixon Line.

No-one understood the importance of securing the border slave states better than President Lincoln. His initial decision not to alienate slaveholders in this region by pursuing a policy of emancipation was deeply unpopular with many members of his own party (who believed that abolition was the path to victory) but it made good sense in terms of the bigger picture. Strategic gain was all very well, however. What the North required above all else was a military commander who could make telling use of that advantage.

Initially, General George McClellan lived up to the vast expectations invested in him. Largely by dint of his own charismatic personality and force of will, he molded his raw troops in and around Washington into an adequately supplied, disciplined, and well-trained fighting force. The Army of the Potomac was destined to suffer a series of reverses on the battlefield, owing in large measure to the inadequate leadership provided by its generals. Although this problem was itself part of McClellan's legacy, the Army's durability was a crucial factor in the Union's eventual success. For this fact alone the justifiably maligned McClellan deserves his share of the credit.

During late 1861 and early 1862 Confederate strength appeared to wane. Leonidas Polk's unwise decision to ignore Kentucky neutrality made more Federals than it uncovered secessionists. The Confederate commander of the vast new Department No. 2 in the west, Albert Sidney Johnston, found his lines seriously overextended and failed in his efforts to recruit large numbers of Kentuckyans to the southern cause. Union naval supremacy also began to bite as the Federals not only initiated a full-scale blockade of the South but also seized a number of beachheads on the Atlantic and Gulf coasts. Although the occupation of Port Royal in November 1861 and of Roanoke Island, New Berne, and Beaufort in the early months of 1862 caused consternation in the Carolinas, the most damaging reverse suffered by the Confederacy was the loss of its principal port, New Orleans, to a Union fleet under David G. Farragut in April 1862.

By this time Confederate affairs in the west had deteriorated. In February a Union force under the overall command of Major General Henry Halleck, the head of the Department of Missouri, oversaw a brilliant riverine campaign that forced the surrender of two strategically important Confederate fortifications. Somewhat reluctantly, Halleck had assented to a bold plan put forward by his subordinate, Brigadier General Ulysses S. Grant. Grant, a shabbily dressed West Pointer and Mexican War veteran who had spent the 1850s struggling to make a living in the Midwest, joined Flag Officer Andrew H. Foote in contending that Union forces should mount an attack on Fort Henry. This low-lying Confederate outpost on the Tennessee River, they argued, was the weak spot in General Johnston's defense line in Kentucky. Capture it and the way would be open into the heart of the Confederacy.

After a fierce artillery duel with Federal gunboats, Fort Henry surrendered on February 6. The local Rebel commander sent his small garrison to Fort Donelson on the neighboring Cumberland River. Rashly, Johnston chose to reinforce Donelson with 12,000 men and retreat with his main force to Nashville, Tennessee. Initial Union attacks on the heavily defended fort were unsuccessful. The entrenched defenders fought off probing land attacks and Foote's ironclad gunboats were damaged by shelling from the enemy's floating artillery batteries. A Rebel breakout attempt on February 15, however, was thwarted and the garrison surrendered the following day. Grant's bold thrust into Tennessee below the Confederate forces in Kentucky proved to be one of the first major turning points of the war. The state was now secure for the Union and west and central Tennessee lay open to Union invasion. Don Carlos Buell, commander of the Department of the Ohio, immediately occupied Nashville while Grant took his 39,000-strong army down the Tennessee River in pursuit of Johnston's army which had transferred its base to northeastern Mississippi. As the Confederates proceeded to concentrate their forces around the railroad center of Corinth, one of the bloodiest battles of the Civil War ensued.

At dawn on April 6 Johnston launched a preemptive attack on the outnumbered Federals at Pittsburg Landing on the west bank of the Tennessee River. Union troops under Grant and his subordinate, William Tecumseh Sherman, an experienced soldier who had suffered a nervous breakdown after the debacle at Bull Run, paid dearly for Grant's decision to reject Halleck's orders to entrench. Initially the Confederates enjoyed great success, driving back Sherman's inexperienced midwestern troops on the Union right toward Shiloh Church and enveloping the Union left. Thick woods and a sunken road anchored the Federal center and only fierce fighting eventually dislodged battered Union regiments from the aptly named 'Hornet's Nest'. The Rebels' obsession with the Union center cost them dear. Sidney Johnston, Jefferson Davis's favorite general, was killed in the assault and the defenders in the Hornet's Nest bought their side crucial time. Grant reorganized his forces along the bluff overlooking Pittsburg Landing and, during a soaking night, was reinforced by four divisions from Buell's army and one from his own force, led by Major General Lew Wallace. Bolstered by these fresh troops, Grant ordered a decisive counterattack and the Confederates, exhausted and now outnumbered, were forced to retreat.

The murderous battle of Shiloh nearly cost Grant his career, for the Union losses were staggering for this early stage of the war. The figure of 13,000 killed, wounded, or missing represented 22 percent of the total force engaged. President Lincoln, however, drew consolation from Grant's determination to fight and resisted calls from leading politicians that he should be dismissed (or worse). It was one of the best decisions of his life. For all his tactical errors at Shiloh, Grant had won a narrow strategic victory for the Union. The Confederates had suffered heavy losses themselves: over 10,000 in total (roughly a quarter of their own force). Even more significantly, they had lost control of the central Mississippi Valley. Shiloh was 'a must win for the South'.[34] Failure to destroy Grant's army marked the beginning of a long war of attrition that ultimately could only benefit the North.

The Confederacy suffered another reverse in the winter of 1861–62. During the early months of the war many southerners harbored expectations that the two great European powers, Britain and France, would intervene to ensure the independence of the Confederate nation. To secure this end they initiated an informal embargo on cotton exports, the assumption being that Britain in particular was so dependent on southern cotton that it would be forced to aid the Confederacy in order to prevent or alleviate distress at home. This was a serious mistake. Cotton was a vital resource but its value lay primarily in its capacity to earn specie through export or to serve as collateral for foreign loans. Withholding supplies merely irritated the British who, besides, enjoyed the luxury of healthy stockpiles of cotton as well as alternative supplies from India and Egypt. By the time serious economic distress had taken hold of Lancashire in

1862, it was far from clear that the Confederacy would achieve its independence.

To secure outside help the Confederates needed to do more than simply withhold cotton exports. They had to convince London and Paris that they had made a nation. Although both governments would have shed few tears over the dissolution of the United States, neither of them was willing to risk war against the North to achieve it. The Lincoln administration, in the guise of Secretary of State Seward, made it plain that any attempt to aid the Rebellion would be regarded as a *casus belli*. The Liberal prime minister Lord Palmerston had little reason to think that picking a fight with the United States would enhance Britain's interests, especially as the Union had the support of Russia. Napoleon III, the flashiest of nineteenth-century monarchs, was more inclined to rashness but had no desire to act without the involvement of the Royal Navy. The most the western European powers were willing to do during the early stages of the war was to recognize the Confederacy as a belligerent – a status in international law empowering the Rebels to secure loans, buy weapons, and commission ships with the right to search and impound on the high seas.

Confederate efforts to secure full recognition of the South as an independent nation proved abortive even in the wake of its triumph at First Manassas. This was partly a consequence of the growing effectiveness of the Union blockade of Confederate ports which President Lincoln had proclaimed formally on April 19, 1861. Over 260 Federal warships were on patrol by the end of the year, severely restricting the South's ability to trade with the outside world. It was also a result of the inadequate diplomatic skills of commissioners such as William Lowndes Yancey – a fact which prompted Secretary of State Robert M.T. Hunter to send two more able politicians as fully fledged ministers plenipotentiary to Britain and France. On November 8, 1861 the two envoys, former US senators James Mason of Virginia and John Slidell of Louisiana, were intercepted by a US naval vessel en route for Europe. Captain Charles Wilkes believed he had accomplished a major coup. In fact he had caused a grade-one diplomatic crisis, for Mason and Slidell were traveling on board the British mail packet, the *Trent*. Whitehall bristled at the North's infringement of neutral rights on the high seas (historically one of the Americans' most treasured causes). Palmerston's foreign secretary, Lord John Russell, demanded an immediate apology from Washington and British troops were sent to bolster the Canadian garrison. The French also made known their outrage at the incident.

Southern hopes of European intervention rose accordingly in late 1861, only to be dashed by Lincoln's wise decision to disavow Captain Wilkes's actions and release the captured southern ministers. Although Mason, Slidell, and other Confederates would labor intensively on the other side of the Atlantic to gain recognition for their cause, the *Trent* affair showed clearly that sympathy alone would not secure their ends. What was required was a decisive military victory over the North.

Such a result seemed a long way off in mid-March 1862 when a Union force numbering around 100,000 men began to arrive by sea on Virginia's Yorktown Peninsula. Harried repeatedly by an impatient president, who was himself under pressure from antislavery radicals within his own party, the cautious McClellan had finally chosen to take the offensive. Having little respect for Lincoln (in his view an ignorant midwesterner deficient in gentlemanly virtues), the general had refused to reveal his strategic plans until the White House had issued formal orders for the Army of the Potomac to advance. In a move reminiscent of Scott's 1847 amphibious expedition to Vera Cruz and the Allies' landing in the Crimea, McClellan transported his troops down Chesapeake Bay, landed them at Fort Monroe, and began to move west along the Peninsula toward Richmond. Unfortunately for the Union cause, 'the Young Napoleon' was habitually inclined to overestimate the strength of his opponents. He therefore allowed his invading host to be pinned down in the vicinity of Yorktown by a much smaller Confederate force, thereby allowing Joseph E. Johnston's Army of Northern Virginia to organize a defense of the southern capital.

Meanwhile McClellan's familiar calls for reinforcements were put into perspective by a brilliant diversionary campaign in Virginia's Shenandoah Valley launched by Confederate general Stonewall Jackson. Running southwest to northeast in the Appalachians, the fertile valley represented one of the South's most advantageous physical features, for it took Union forces away from the Confederate capital and gave southern troops a backdoor entry into the Washington area. In the spring of 1862 this 'dagger at the heart of Yankeedom' witnessed five impressive victories by Jackson's hard-marching, hard-fighting men over three separate Union armies.[35] The puritanical Jackson, a master of the art of maneuver, repeatedly concentrated his forces against those led by McDowell and two incompetent political generals, John C. Frémont and Nathaniel P. Banks. His successive victories against superior numbers gave the Confederacy a real hero at a critical juncture in its young history.

By the end of May units of the Army of the Potomac were only five miles from Richmond. McClellan's ponderous advance up the Peninsula had forced the Confederates not only to evacuate the port of Norfolk but also to destroy their ironclad ship, the *Virginia* (formerly the *USS Merrimac*), which in March had been engaged in a bizarre duel in Hampton Roads with the Union's own metal monster, the *Monitor*. These actions largely surrendered control of the local rivers to Union gunboats. Then, just when the fall of Richmond seemed inevitable, fate intervened. McClellan unwisely divided his force on both sides of the Chickahominy River. Heavy rains separated two Union corps on the south side from three on the north. On May 31 Johnston, spotting the opportunity, launched a massive but poorly coordinated attack on the Fourth Corps of Brigadier General Erasmus D. Keyes. In the ensuing battle of Seven Pines, the Confederates inflicted 6,000 casualties on an enemy hampered by its apparent inability to undertake a mobile defense. But in the process they lost even more of their own men, among them Johnston himself, who was seriously wounded in his right shoulder by shell splinters. With his troops imperiled outside the fortifications of Richmond, President Davis appointed his chief military aide, General Robert E. Lee, to head the Army of Northern Virginia. A war that had seemed on the verge of a conclusion was about to take a new and startling turn.

At 54 Lee, a resolute, dignified Virginia slaveholder who lived in the shadow of his erratic father, 'Light Horse Harry' Lee (a disgraced Revolutionary War hero), might well have presumed his military career to be on the wane in the spring of 1861. The secession crisis, however, saw North and South bidding keenly for his services. His impressive Mexican War record and experience as commandant at West Point caused President Lincoln to offer him the overall command of Union forces, but Lee had no sympathy for Black Republicanism and sided with his home state when it seceded after Fort Sumter. After a short period in the wilderness, Jefferson Davis brought him to Richmond as his chief military adviser. Lee quickly established good working relations with his aloof superior. He deferred to Davis when necessary and, in marked contrast to Joseph Johnston who chafed at his subordinate rank in the Confederate military hierarchy, took every opportunity to consult with him over military strategy. Lee's own thoughts about the war during the summer of 1862 dovetailed neatly with Davis's own views. Both men understood the limited nature of Confederate resources and the fatal consequences that would ensue if they allowed McClellan to bulldoze his way into Richmond. Born of desperation, Lee's plan to take the offensive made good strategic sense. Davis therefore concurred with his general's suggestion that the Confederates should concentrate their forces on the Peninsula by ordering Jackson back from the Shenandoah Valley. If all went well, Jackson's confident soldiers would smash into Union troops south of the Chickahominy and drive the bluebellies back into the sea.

In a series of fluid engagements between June 25 and July 1, Jackson's men belatedly combined with Lee's forces and pushed the Federals away from Richmond. McClellan evaded disaster in the Seven Days' Battles only by moving his supply base to the southern side of the Peninsula. With the aid of a Federal rearguard action at the battle of Malvern Hill, he stabilized his new position at Harrison's Landing on the James River. The week's slaughter was appalling. More than 30,000 men were killed and wounded in the Seven Days' Battles. The Confederates lost as many men in fierce fighting at Gaines's Mill on June 27 as they had lost in two days at Shiloh. 'The ground was covered with dead and wounded men and horses', wrote one Union private after Malvern Hill. 'Many of the latter had been disembowelled completely by shell exploding under them. Soldiers of both sides lay in all the orchards, sheds and barns, torn, mangled, dead and dying.'[36]

While Confederate losses were huge and significantly greater than those suffered by the enemy, Lee had stalled the Federal advance on Richmond. An ordinary commander might have paused for breath at this point. Lee, however, was determined to grasp the initiative and take the war to the Yankees. Aware that another substantial Union force, the Army of Virginia under Major General John Pope, was being organized and that the newly appointed Union general in chief, Henry Halleck, had ordered a withdrawal from the Peninsula to facilitate concentration of US forces around Washington, he decided to take the offensive. He dispatched Jackson's wing of the hastily reorganized Army of Northern Virginia to combat Pope and Banks – a task that it partially accomplished at the battle of Cedar Mountain on August 9. Lee then joined General James Longstreet and the main body of his army as it hastened north in an effort to concentrate Confederate strength in northern Virginia. His aims were simple, but ambitious: to relieve the pressure on Richmond; to enable the Confederates to augment their area of food supply; and to defeat Pope before McClellan's army arrived in force.

Fortunately for the Confederates, Pope talked a better battle than he fought and the Federals failed to reunite their forces more speedily than their opponents. Although he thwarted an initial attempt to turn his left flank, Pope soon found Jackson in his rear in the vicinity of Manassas Junction. Worse still, he failed to detect the arrival of Longstreet's troops at the second battle of Manassas on August 30. As the Union troops advanced on Jackson's position they were mown down by concealed Rebel artillery on their left and forced back by a counterattack ordered by Longstreet.

Lee did not stop there. Eschewing a direct attack on Washington, by now one of the most heavily fortified cities in the world, he opted to raid north into the slave state of Maryland. Southern troops, Lee told the president, were inadequately equipped for such a movement: 'Still, we cannot afford to be idle, and though weaker than our opponents in men and military equipments, must endeavor to harass, if we cannot destroy them.'[37] Although this expedition was fraught with risk, more supplies could be gathered in Maryland and large numbers of local people, allegedly suffering under the iron heel of Yankee despotism, might welcome the southern troops as liberators. General Braxton Bragg had similar hopes of Kentuckyans as his Army of Tennessee began a simultaneous offensive in the west. In September 1862 Confederate forces were on the move across a broad front more than 600 miles long. Hopes were raised that victory was in sight and that the European powers would soon recognize the Confederacy.

The Maryland campaign began well. Stonewall Jackson captured 12,500 Union troops at Harpers Ferry on September 15. By this time, however, McClellan had learned of Lee's plans for the invasion of Maryland and begun to contemplate the defeat of the entire southern army. A member of Lee's staff had carelessly wrapped some cigars with his commander's orders and left them to be found by Federal troops. But Little Mac failed to make the best of his good fortune. It took him three and a half days to maneuver his forces into position just east of Antietam Creek near the backwater village of Sharpsburg in western Maryland. His near fatal lack of celerity gave Jackson time to cross the Potomac and rejoin the main body of Lee's army. Nearly 5,000 Americans died in the course of the clumsy Federal assault on September 17, the bloodiest single day of the entire Civil War. Some of the worst carnage occurred in the 'Bloody Lane', a sunken road in the center of the Confederate line where the dead were piled high as the battle reached a crescendo. Outnumbered by nearly two to one, Lee used his interior lines to prevent a potentially decisive Federal breakthrough. Although the Confederate center eventually collapsed, McClellan remained cautious and failed to exploit the opportunity presented. Troops under Stonewall Jackson on the Rebel left held firm. It was late in the day when Union regiments under the overall command of Ambrose E. Burnside finally fought their way across the narrow creek on the Confederate right. Their success was short-lived. A forced march from Harpers Ferry enabled Rebel troops led by A.P. Hill to launch a ferocious counterattack. By nightfall, the Federals were back across the creek. With stalemate on the field, both sides exhausted and McClellan unwilling to use his reserves, Lee opted to disengage and return to Virginia.

The strategic Union victory at Antietam had an important political consequence. On September 22 President Lincoln used the narrow battlefield success to signal his waning attachment to a soft-war policy on slavery. Moderate and radical Republicans had been clamoring for decisive action against the peculiar institution for at least a year. Confronted with a formidable foe (who relied heavily on slaves to build fortifications, serve as hospital orderlies and teamsters, and grow food), Lincoln issued his preliminary Emancipation Proclamation in which he announced his determination to declare free, on January 1, 1863, all slaves held in Confederate territory. The Rebels had just over three months to come to their senses and rejoin the Union with their constitutional property rights intact.

As well as threatening to use emancipation as a weapon of war, Lincoln intended his Proclamation to have diplomatic effect. Placing the Union on the side of freedom, he felt, might forestall southern hopes of European recognition. In fact, far from persuading transatlantic politicians that Union resolve was unbroken, Antietam and the emancipation edict convinced southern sympathizers abroad that arbitration was necessary to prevent further killing on the battlefield as well as a bloody slave rebellion. On October 7 Britain's Chancellor of the Exchequer W.E. Gladstone made a premeditated policy speech in Newcastle-upon-Tyne in which he opined that the Confederates 'had made a nation' and intimated that the ministry was about to extend full diplomatic recognition to the South.[38] Gladstone spoke without authorization from Palmerston. However, he found an important ally in the shape of Foreign Secretary Lord John Russell, who made the case for a joint offer of mediation by the Powers in a strongly worded memorandum for discussion by the cabinet. But by November British support for intervention in the American Civil War had receded. Secretary for War Sir George Cornewall Lewis consistently argued that the Union would reject mediation, thereby provoking a general conflict that could only harm British interests.[39]

Palmerston, the key figure, had similar fears and refused to counsel an offer of arbitration unless it had the support of the Russians. Since the Tsar was a close ally of the Union, cooperation from St Petersburg was never likely to ensue. And because France would not take action without the British, the Confederacy could expect no unilateral aid from Paris. Napoleon momentarily abandoned his interest in mediation and proceeded with his own plans to capitalize on the Civil War and launch a French invasion of Mexico. By the time the emperor renewed his proposals for arbitration the following year, Lincoln could be fairly sure that Britain would not support these as long as the armed forces of the United States held the upper hand.

By the end of 1862 the war had ground to a stalemate on the eastern front. Lee's Maryland campaign had thwarted a full-scale assault on Richmond and cost McClellan his job. Popular with his troops yet widely disparaged by Republicans for his cautious strategy and conservative views on slavery, the general was finally dismissed on November 5. His bewhiskered replacement, Major General Ambrose E. Burnside, did not turn out to be an improvement. On December 13 he attempted to take the direct route to Richmond by ordering a frontal assault on Confederate trenches overlooking the Rappahannock River at Fredericksburg, Virginia. The result was slaughter on a dreadful scale. The Federals suffered 12,653 casualties compared with the 5,309 men lost by the defending Rebels. A bemused Lee was moved to comment famously: 'It is well that war is so terrible – we should grow too fond of it.'[40] However, he failed to organize a decisive counterattack that might have routed the Army of the Potomac. Burnside's self-confidence, never strong at the best of times, drained away in the face of growing opposition from the ranks of his own officer corps. He stayed on long enough to supervise the 'Mud March', a disastrous attempt to outflank the Confederates. Then he resigned, to be replaced by one of his more capable commanders, Major General Joseph Hooker. Union troops settled into winter quarters north of the Rappahannock, their morale at its lowest ebb since the war began.

There was better news for the Union cause further west. Bragg's push into Kentucky was halted by Buell's Army of the Ohio at the inconclusive battle of Perryville in October 1862. After then moving into central Tennessee the luckless Confederate general had a chance to crush the Federals at Stones River in December, but his efforts to secure a decisive victory were stymied by dogged resistance from the Army of the Cumberland under the command of General William

S. Rosecrans and his able subordinate, George H. Thomas, a Virginia unionist. In northern Mississippi Federal forces under Ulysses S. Grant drove back Sterling Price's Rebels at the battle of Iuka and then defeated another large Confederate army under Earl Van Dorn outside Corinth. Although Union commanders passed up opportunities to pursue their opponents aggressively, these two victories prepared the ground for Grant's subsequent thrust toward Rebel strongholds on the Mississippi River. Breakthrough would eventually be achieved in the western theater but during the winter of 1862–63 neither Union nor Confederate leaders could be in any doubt that it would be a long, hard slog to victory.

The triumph of Union arms, 1863–65

The Union was saved in two more years of hideous slaughter that cut swathes through the ranks on both sides between January 1863 and April 1865. Death and mobilization placed huge strains on the warring societies. North and South resorted to conscription to help fill the yawning gaps that resulted, and growing numbers of young volunteers supplemented the battle-hardened and increasingly cynical veterans who had volunteered in the early stages of the war. The Davis administration, aided in part by state officials and in full by talented generals like Robert E. Lee, prolonged the fight as long as it could, often utilizing interventionist strategies to make the most of the South's available manpower as well as its limited industrial and commercial potential under the Union blockade.

The Confederacy's primary wasted resource was its slaves. As noted above, Rebels used bonded labor to build fortifications and work farms. However, until the final weeks of the war they made no effort to utilize slaves as soldiers. Lincoln's Emancipation Proclamation signed, as promised, on New Year's Day, 1863, announced that the North would not only regard as free all slaves held outside the Union-occupied South but also begin recruiting black soldiers into the United States armed forces. Once wary of angering loyal slave-holders and northern conservatives, Lincoln now believed that 'The colored population ... is the great *available* and yet *unavailed* of, force for restoring the Union.'[41] By the end of the conflict 196,000 blacks had served – mostly under white officers – in the Union army and navy. Although they generally fought well when required and played a significant role in Grant's eastern campaigns of 1864–65, their main contribution to the Union war effort may have been their extensive use on garrison duty in the Mississippi Valley.[42] This presence freed up experienced white soldiers to fight the Confederates in the western theater where the decisive Federal breakthrough was made. Making emancipation official government policy and sanctioning the employment of blacks as soldiers greatly expanded the racial dimension of the war. Black expectations of permanent freedom and equal citizenship were heightened accordingly, but so too was Confederate hatred of Yankee oppression.

The Emancipation Proclamation exemplified the mounting determination of the Union high command to make southern civilians feel the 'hard hand of war'.[43] Confederate resistance was so tenacious that McClellan's conservative view that war should be confined to competing armies was no longer tenable. In the spring of 1863 Halleck told Grant that as well as seizing slaves he should 'live on the enemy's country as much as possible'.[44] It was another indication of a more ruthless Union strategy that would eventually secure the defeat of the Confederacy.

Nearly two years into the war there was little sign of a northern victory. 'Fighting Joe' Hooker had done much to revive morale among the soldiers of the Army of the Potomac. In search of the decisive victory that had eluded his predecessors, he then planned and skillfully implemented a bold three-pronged attack on Lee's army stretched out below the Rappahannock. Union troops crossed the Rapidan and Rappahannock Rivers above Fredericksburg in great force. Thick woods in the area known locally as the Wilderness hindered their progress, but by May 1, 1863 they were ready to inflict a massive blow on elements of the Army of Northern Virginia moving westward to counter the Union threat near the hamlet of Chancellorsville. Lee was too quick for them. Using an obscure trail through the forests, Stonewall Jackson led 26,000 men into position for a massive flank attack on the Union right. Taken largely by surprise in the early evening of May 2, the Federals were driven back in confusion. Jackson was mortally wounded in the operation, shot mistakenly by his own troops. The Confederate cavalry commander, 'Jeb' Stuart, sustained the attack, allowing Lee to reinforce his right wing that was now being assailed by Union troops in the vicinity of Fredericksburg. Confronted by an aggressive and confident foe, the Federal commander John Sedgwick retreated to the north bank of the Rappahannock. By May 6 Hooker's entire force was back across the river, its losses over 17,000 compared to the Confederate casualty list of 12,821. Even though Jackson's death a week later was a grievous blow to the southern cause, Chancellorsville provided further evidence that the Rebels' objective of nationhood remained tantalizingly within their grasp. Robert E. Lee, however, was not a man to rest on his laurels. Deeply concerned about his country's waning resources, he began to prepare for another bold incursion above the Mason-Dixon Line, one that might finally convince northerners that their government would never subdue the South.

The costly defeats at Fredericksburg and Chancellorsville had a predictably deflationary effect on northern morale. Even the patriotic poet Walt Whitman, who spent much of the war visiting wounded soldiers in Washington, found his commitment to the Union cause severely tested during this period. 'I say stop this war, this horrible massacre of men', he blurted out in a discussion with his landlord, William O'Connor, and the Unitarian minister William Ellery Channing. When O'Connor retorted that slavery had not yet been abolished, the good, gray poet betrayed his past as a free-soil Democrat by ejaculating, 'I don't care for the niggers in comparison with all this suffering and the dismemberment of the Union.'[45]

While the strain was telling on northerners, that spring the Confederacy probably came as close as it ever did to proving itself a separate nation. Southern efforts to achieve self-sufficiency in war production and supply seemed to be bearing fruit, even though impressment, inflation, hoarding, and distribution problems placed huge demands on the civilian population. For the first time, the Davis administration launched an all-out offensive against the enemy's transatlantic commerce. Fast-paced raiding ships, several of them built at British yards, began to attack US merchant vessels on the high seas. The most effective of them, the CSS *Alabama* commanded by Raphael Semmes, captured or destroyed nearly 64 northern ships in a career that lasted until its destruction in June 1864. The French banking company, Erlanger & Co., was sufficiently impressed by the drift of events that it agreed to loan Richmond approximately $14.5 million, the sum guaranteed by prospective cotton sales. By this time Napoleon III had renewed his support for mediation. With French troops now occupying Mexico, he seemed well placed to pressurize the Union into agreeing to European arbitration. President Davis, however, was under no illusions that the Emperor would act without the concurrence of the British who remained content to await the judgment of Mars.

Just as the Confederate cause was reaching high tide, the prospects of ultimate success began to ebb away. The chief destroyer of Rebel hopes was Lincoln's western commander, Ulysses S. Grant. Having skillfully flushed out the Confederates from the central Mississippi

Valley, his next objective was one of the principal elements of the Anaconda Plan: complete Federal control of the Mississippi River. Lying between Grant and the accomplishment of this task was the last stretch of the river still in Confederate hands. Guarded by imposing fortifications at Vicksburg in the north and Port Hudson in the south, this mainly low-lying, marshy territory was the scene of abortive Federal operations during the winter of 1862–63. Sherman managed to maneuver his forces into position for an attack on Vicksburg but was rebuffed after a bloody assault at Chickasaw Bluffs in late December. Well aware that his country's flagging cause required him to sustain momentum, Grant (the most politically astute of Union commanders) persevered with his efforts to reach the high ground on the east bank of the Mississippi. From there, he believed, his forces could envelop Vicksburg from the south, thereby achieving the strategically important and morale-boosting victory the North required.

After more vain attempts to threaten Vicksburg in early 1863, Grant conceived the idea of running Union transports and supply barges past the Rebel stronghold. His troops would march south down the dry Union-occupied west bank of the river and cross the Mississippi on the transports. After he had completed this phase of the operation successfully on April 30, Grant revealed his daring by opting to advance rapidly from his base of supplies and swing into the interior of Mississippi before moving against Vicksburg. Striking out northeast from their landing point near Port Gibson, his troops took Jackson, the Mississippi state capital, on May 14 and then, turning westward back toward the Big Black River, defeated a combined Confederate force in a critical engagement at Champion's Hill two days later. By May 19 the Federals were in front of Vicksburg. After two ill-judged frontal assaults, Grant opted to lay siege to the town. Without reinforcements, General John C. Pemberton's outnumbered defenders could not hold out indefinitely.

Aware that Vicksburg's fall would be a disaster for the Confederacy, President Davis had already dispatched one of his most senior generals, Joseph Johnston, to take charge of operations in the western theater. Johnston immediately sought and secured reinforcements from Braxton Bragg who was left in command of the Army of Tennessee. In Washington Lincoln and Halleck were appalled at the prospect that the Confederates might be able to concentrate their forces against Grant. The president's response to news that Bragg was supplying Johnston with reinforcements was therefore to urge his commander in Tennessee to do anything 'short of rashness' to prevent further transfer of troops.[46] At first General William S. Rosecrans, methodical as ever, declined suggestions that he should move speedily against Bragg. Not until June 24, weeks after Grant had most needed help, did he finally respond to constant prodding from his superiors and take the offensive. To his credit, when the Army of the Cumberland did advance, it did so effectively. Taken by surprise when Union troops moved south from their base at Murfreesboro, Bragg – beleaguered by supply problems and incompetent, squabbling corps commanders – chose to withdraw across the barren Cumberland plateau to the high terrain around Chattanooga on the Tennessee River. The Union success in the Tullahoma campaign benefited more from Grant's operations in Mississippi than Grant himself drew succor from Rosecrans's belated offensive. Nevertheless, it expelled the Confederates from central Tennessee, improving the prospects for a successful Federal thrust into the mountainous eastern portion of the state where large numbers of unionists were held in check only by the strength of Confederate arms.

With Vicksburg and Port Hudson besieged and Bragg on the defensive in Tennessee, Confederate hopes in the summer of 1863 were pinned primarily on Lee's eastern army. The Army of Northern Virginia began to advance through western Virginia in early June. Hooker was not slow to spot the move but, having been persuaded by Lincoln to confront Lee rather than descend on Richmond, he hesitated to strike when the Confederates crossed the Potomac and was replaced swiftly by one of his corps commanders, George G. Meade. Meade, an irascible though able soldier, then struggled to locate the enemy force as its hard-bitten troops poured through the mountain gaps of western Maryland into the rich farmland of Pennsylvania. General Lee, too, had his problems. His extrovert cavalry commander, Jeb Stuart, burdened with vague orders, lost contact with the main body of the army at a crucial stage of its march, depriving Lee of valuable reconnaissance.

On July 1 lead units of the two great armies accidentally ran into one another at the small town of Gettysburg (see Map 6). After initial fighting in which John Buford's Federal cavalry division delayed the advancing Confederates long enough to allow Meade to organize a defense on Seminary Ridge, Rebels under General Richard Ewell threatened the Union flank from the north. Still awaiting the arrival of their main force, the Federals took up a new and more defensible position on Cemetery Hill, just south of the town. Lee ordered Ewell to press home his advantage 'if practicable' but, perhaps for sound tactical reasons, his subordinate chose not to attack.[47] That night the two armies maneuvered into position for what, potentially, was the decisive battle of the Civil War. By sunrise on July 2 roughly 75,000 Confederates were arrayed along Seminary Ridge. On the high ground to the east, the Army of the Potomac, around 88,000 strong, was deployed in an inverted fishhook formation, over three miles long. Its northern shank curved around Culp's Hill and Cemetery Hill while the eye stretched out to the south toward a hillock named Little Round Top.

Lee's trusted subordinate, James Longstreet, observed the strength of the Union position through his field glasses. Why not disengage, he suggested, and interpose the army between the Federals and Washington? This would allow the southerners to select better ground and force their opponents to attack a well-defended position. The Confederate commander would have none of it. Supremely confident in his own abilities as well as in the fighting capacity of his men, he decided to attack. Having bested the Army of the Potomac on several occasions in the past year, he had good reasons for supposing it to be vulnerable, particularly in the immediate wake of Hooker's dismissal. '[T]he enemy is there', said Lee pointing toward Cemetery Hill, 'and I am going to strike him.'[48]

Unhappily for the South, its most able general had underrated the tenacity of his opponents. Lee made several mistakes at Gettysburg. One of the most serious occurred on the morning of July 2. Wrongly believing that the Federal line was at its strongest along the Emmitsburg Road running south from Gettysburg, he ordered Longstreet to turn the enemy with a devastating attack on the exposed Union left. The Confederates would then roll up the Union line along the turnpike. In part because he lacked confidence in the plan, Longstreet took time to get his troops into position. At around 4 pm thousands of southern troops shouting the blood-curdling 'Rebel Yell' drove toward a vulnerable salient occupied by troops belonging to Daniel E. Sickles's III Corps. Contrary to explicit orders Sickles had moved his men forward from low ground at the southern edge of Cemetery Ridge into a more defensible position amid a group of boulders known as Devil's Den. An adjoining peach orchard now became the scene of desperate fighting. Although the Confederates pressed the Federals back, their relative inaction at other points on the line allowed Meade to reinforce his embattled left wing. When the Rebels did come close to turning the Union flank by ascending Little Round Top they met their match in the 20th Maine which had been rushed into position to hold the line. Commanded by a quick-thinking college professor named Joshua Lawrence Chamberlain, the New Englanders undertook one of the war's rare bayonet charges to drive them back. When units in the Confederate center did advance, the Union army's II Corps under Winfield Scott Hancock repulsed them too.

After movement on the Union right scotched plans for an attack on this flank early on the morning of July 3, Longstreet again urged Lee to disengage. The latter demurred. Committed to the tactical offense, he resolved to launch a massive thrust against Meade's center. It was probably the worst tactical error he made in his entire military career. At around 1.45 pm, after a ferocious but largely ineffectual artillery bombardment of the Union lines, 14,000 of Longstreet's troops advanced in close formation across half a mile of open ground toward the enemy center. 'Pickett's Charge' (so named because one of the division commanders involved was Major General George E. Pickett of Virginia) was magnificent enough to move contemporaries and future generations alike but the men involved paid heavily for Lee's aggression. Showered by shot, canister, and gunfire from Federal positions on the ridge, the southern line grew progressively thinner as it hastened forward. Only a few Rebels reached the Union center and there, after some moments of close-quarter fighting, they were cut down by the defending troops.

General Meade failed to order a decisive counterattack after the Confederates were put to flight. To Lincoln's great disappointment, he allowed Lee time to regroup and withdraw from the field the following day. Although the Union commander had just fought the deadliest single battle of the Civil War (the Army of the Potomac had lost 23,000 men in three days – a quarter of its total strength), the Confederates had suffered even more grievously, losing over one third of their force (28,000 killed, wounded and missing). Meade, however, had too much respect for his opponent to chase after him. When, finally, he did launch a belated pursuit, Lee's army had already recrossed the Potomac back into Virginia. Yet if he erred badly, there was no denying that Gettysburg represented a vital strategic success for the Union. The Confederates would never again be in a position to raid north in such strength and the morale of the Army of the Potomac was greatly increased. Public doubts about Meade's conduct, moreover, were overshadowed by news from the west. On July 4, Vicksburg surrendered to Grant's besieging troops, its demise followed almost immediately by the fall of Port Hudson. Northerners rejoiced that with Union forces in complete control of the Mississippi River the nation appeared close to salvation.

It was not over yet. In mid-September the Federals suffered a potentially disastrous defeat at the battle of Chickamauga. Prodded again by Lincoln to maintain the pressure on Braxton Bragg, Rosecrans had maneuvered his forces across the Tennessee River while Burnside's smaller Army of the Cumberland advanced toward Knoxville. Wrongly believing the Rebels to be in retreat, Rosecrans found Bragg ready for him. Reinforced by rail with two divisions of Longstreet's crack troops from the east, the Confederates launched a poorly coordinated counterattack on the Federals in thickly wooded country near Chattanooga. On the second day of the conflict, September 20, confused orders from Rosecrans opened up a breach in the Union ranks allowing Longstreet to achieve a decisive, if somewhat fortuitous, breakthrough. Only characteristically dismal work by Leonidas Polk on the Confederate right and a ferocious rearguard action by troops under George H. Thomas, 'the Rock of Chickamauga', allowed Rosecrans's battered army to reach the relative safety of Chattanooga. Occupying the high ground to the east, the Confederates immediately laid siege to the city. A beaten man, behaving (in Lincoln's inimitable words) 'like a duck hit on the head', Rosecrans was replaced swiftly by Thomas.[49] In overall charge now was Grant, appointed by Lincoln to command the new Department of the Mississippi.

Grant wasted no time in attempting to lift the siege. Buoyed by the receipt of 23,000 reinforcements from the Army of the Potomac (Hooker's men traveled more than 1,000 miles by rail in nine days), he opened a supply route to Chattanooga and then rapidly deployed his forces in the immediate environs of the city. By daylight on November 24, with Longstreet's divisions having been dispatched to combat Burnside at Knoxville, Sherman's troops had crossed the Tennessee River on pontoons and were ready to assault the right flank of Bragg's army at the northern end of Missionary Ridge.

Hooker, meanwhile, led his bluecoats toward the enemy's left. Forcing the Confederates from the spectacular heights of Lookout Mountain, they closed slowly on the Rebels' main force the following day. Sherman's troops attacked from the north and Thomas's men in the center advanced on Rebel defenses at the base of Missionary Ridge. It was the latter who made the crucial breakthrough. Thomas's assaulting brigades cleared the Rebels out of their rifle pits and then, contrary to orders, drove on up the Ridge. Because Bragg had failed to order the construction of adequate defenses on the heights, the Union soldiers were able to close quickly with their opponents and then, aided by Hooker's men to the south, to roll up the Confederate line. Owing partly to stiff resistance by troops commanded by General Patrick R. Cleburne, one of the South's most effective generals, the Army of Tennessee was able to make good its escape. The defeat at Chattanooga, however, was a major blow to the Rebel cause, for the way was now open for a concerted Union push into the state of Georgia. Braxton Bragg paid the price of failure, surrendering his post to Joseph Johnston.

The constant draining away of its limited manpower resources meant that by the winter of 1863–64 the South's only realistic hope of success was to hold out long enough to achieve a collapse in northern willpower. Many Confederates, Lee included, placed great hopes in the North's presidential election contest scheduled to take place in November 1864. President Lincoln himself, under huge strain at this juncture of the conflict, was under no illusions about the task still facing the Union at the outset of 1864, but he remained determined to finish the job if the people allowed him to do it. Ever the consummate politician, he knew that his own fortunes (more closely than ever linked to those of the nation) would rise or fall with results on the battlefield. In March he placed his own future, together with that of the United States, in the hands of his most competent general, Ulysses S. Grant. Once assured that his potential rival had no political ambitions, Lincoln appointed Grant to the prestigious rank of lieutenant general, a title held previously only by George Washington. The new general in chief of the country's armed forces was summoned immediately to the capital where he met the president for the first time.

By April 1864, after consulting with Henry Halleck, the chief of staff, and Edwin Stanton, the secretary of war, Lincoln and Grant concurred on Union strategy for the forthcoming campaign season. The Federals would seek 'concentration in time' – that is, they would attack all along the line in order to prevent the Confederates from reinforcing their armies at individual pressure points. In the western theater, Sherman would harry the Army of Tennessee with a view to destroying Johnston's force and taking Atlanta. In the east, Grant would personally oversee the operations of the Army of the Potomac with Meade remaining at its head. His task was to engineer a decisive victory over Lee as quickly as possible. Other forces were to help to constrain Confederate mobility (as Lincoln put it, 'Those not skinning can hold a leg').[50] Each of these forces, unfortunately, was commanded by a political general who owed his high position to patronage requirements, not military competence. One, commanded by the German-American Franz Sigel, would operate in the Shenandoah

Valley. Ben Butler's Army of the James was ordered to advance on the Peninsula, cut the Petersburg to Richmond railroad and threaten the enemy capital from the south. Grant also wanted Nathaniel Banks to open a third front by attacking Mobile, Alabama (one of the few remaining ports in Confederate hands) from his base in Louisiana. Lincoln, however, wanted Banks to strike out northwest up the Red River in order to encourage Texas separatism and signal Union intentions to Napoleon's army of occupation in Mexico. Although the Massachusetts Republican set off quickly enough, his expedition was brought to an abrupt halt on April 8 at the battle of Sabine Crossroads – an embarrassing rout which soon turned into a full-scale retreat. It was not the last time Grant would rue his chief's tolerance of political generals, for Sigel proved as incompetent as Banks. The German-American hero advanced slowly up the Shenandoah Valley but was then forced to retreat after being defeated at New Market on May 15. Meanwhile, Butler's Army of the James proved too small to be effective and was soon stalled below Richmond.

Grant's own efforts to get at Lee quickly ran into trouble. After crossing the Rapidan in force on May 4 the Army of the Potomac was shortly engaged in savage fighting in the Wilderness, the same wooded area near Chancellorsville in which Hooker's men had been defeated a year earlier. Lee's efforts to counter the movement nearly came to grief on the Orange Plank Road where A.P. Hill's III Corps was severely mauled by General Hancock's troops on the Union left. Luckily, Texans from Longstreet's I Corps arrived on the field just in time to prevent a complete collapse and the bewildered Federals were driven back in disorder. Had Longstreet not been wounded by gunfire from his own men, a southern flank attack on Hancock might well have turned the tables completely.

Unlike his predecessors in the east, Grant chose not to regard the massive casualties suffered by his army as a good reason to disengage. Instead, he continued to harry the Army of Northern Virginia, confident that while his own command had its problems, Lee's force – smaller, less well supplied and more vulnerable to desertion than his own – could ill afford too many repetitions of the battles in the Wilderness. Pressing on to the southeast, Union troops were intercepted again by Lee in the vicinity of Spotsylvania Court House. Another vicious general engagement ensued, culminating in a massive Union attack on a Confederate salient on May 12. After an initial breakthrough at the 'Bloody Angle', relative inaction by Grant's corps commanders at other points on the line allowed Lee to stabilize the situation by throwing in reinforcements. Union and Confederate casualties at the Wilderness and Spotsylvania were fearful. The Army of the Potomac lost roughly 36,400 killed, wounded, and missing between May 4–21; the Confederate forces lost approximately 21,400.

Grant refused to rest. Failing to tempt Lee into an attack on his divided army in the wake of Spotsylvania, he drove southward with a series of bold flanking movements. After more desperate fighting on the North Anna River, the Federals crossed the Pamunkey to find the Confederates entrenched at Topopotomy Creek less than ten miles northeast of Richmond in the immediate vicinity of the battlefields where McClellan had been frustrated two years earlier. Although the Rebels were tired, hungry, and outnumbered by nearly two to one, their morale remained high. Believing otherwise, Grant allowed Meade to launch a frontal assault on Lee's defensive positions at Cold Harbor on June 3. After hours of senseless killing in which the Federals lost 7,000 men compared with the Confederates' total of less than 1,500, Grant (who admitted that the attack had been a serious mistake) opted to disengage. Determined to maintain the pressure on Lee, the chastened Union commander then engineered a brilliantly conceived and executed crossing of the James River between June 13 and June 15.[51] Although the Confederates failed to take advantage of the crossing, they managed to stall the ensuing Federal drive on Petersburg. The damage, however, was done. The Army of the Potomac was now encamped to the south and east of this strategically vital railroad center – just 20 miles below the enemy capital at Richmond. Well provisioned from their new supply base at nearby City Point, Grant's men laid siege to Lee's defending army, their efforts to pierce or outflank the entrenched Confederates repeatedly stymied throughout the second half of 1864.

Stalemate on the eastern and western fronts that summer brought about another severe dip in Union morale. The country's financial situation was deteriorating rapidly. William Pitt Fessenden, the new secretary of the treasury, found military expenses and interest payments on a soaring national debt running at a ruinous $2.25 million per day.[52] Matters were made worse by a Confederate raid down the Shenandoah Valley and across the Potomac ordered by Lee to reduce pressure on Petersburg. Only smart rearguard action by troops under General Lew Wallace at the battle of Monocacy permitted an effective defense of Washington against Rebel troops commanded by Jubal A. Early. President Lincoln himself seemed convinced that he could not be reelected in November and that his only service thereafter would be to help his successor, probably General McClellan, salvage the Union.

The stalemate was finally ended from the west. Commanding the vast Military Division of the Mississippi was Grant's trusted lieutenant, William T. Sherman. An irritable, cynical Ohioan with excellent political connections, Sherman had grown in confidence during the Vicksburg and Chattanooga campaigns. Whatever defects he had as a battlefield tactician were more than compensated for by his broader strategic insight. He understood the need to wage an aggressive war and was perfectly prepared to make ordinary Confederates suffer to bring an end to the conflict as soon as possible. Atlanta, one of his objectives in the spring of 1864, was a major industrial and commercial center in a state that continued to furnish essential supplies for Lee's Army of Northern Virginia. Sherman's combined force in the Chattanooga area, numbering around 100,000 men, was made up of three armies: George Thomas's Army of the Cumberland, James B. McPherson's Army of the Tennessee, and, the smallest of the three, John M. Schofield's Army of the Ohio. Each of these units was in capable hands and morale was high. Ranged against the Federals was the Confederate Army of Tennessee, still riven by factionalism under its new leader, Joseph Johnston. Johnston remained a cautious commander who had little awareness of the urgent political need not to surrender more territory to the enemy. Easily outnumbered until reinforced by Leonidas Polk on May 11, he rejected Jefferson Davis's repeated requests for him to move on Chattanooga. Instead, he waited on events at his base at Dalton in the hill country of northwest Georgia.

The Federals made the decisive opening move of the Atlanta campaign on May 8. Entering Snake Creek Gap to the west of Dalton, McPherson's troops caught Johnston by surprise. Inconclusive fighting ensued but the Confederate commander realized his position was untenable and withdrew south along the line of the Western & Atlantic Railroad connecting Atlanta with Tennessee. Sherman spent the next two months outmaneuvering Johnston who sought to concentrate and entrench at every opportunity. Using three striking columns to good effect, he wisely eschewed direct engagements in favor of broad flanking movements that forced Johnston back toward the defenses of Atlanta. On the one occasion when Sherman did order a frontal attack – at Kennesaw Mountain on June 27 – Union forces suffered severe casualties. By the second week of July, however, another grand flanking movement had taken the Federals across the Chattahoochee River to the outskirts of Atlanta.

When Jefferson Davis began to suspect that Johnston might abandon the city without a fight, he replaced him with a more aggressive soldier, John B. Hood. The new Rebel commander immediately tried to gain the initiative before the Union guns reduced Atlanta to rubble. Repeated attacks on the Union lines brought the Confederates little joy and high casualties. The Federals, however, did lose McPherson in fierce fighting in the battle of Atlanta on July 22. Shortly afterwards Sherman swung around to the west, tore up railroad tracks and then, at the end of August, defeated the Rebels in two days of fighting near the town of Jonesboro. Facing the prospect of entrapment and total defeat, Hood ordered a withdrawal, thereby allowing the nearly deserted city to fall into the hands of the enemy on September 2. In combination with Rear Admiral Farragut's important Union naval victory at Mobile Bay earlier in the month and General Philip Sheridan's defeat of Early's troops at Opequon Creek (Third Winchester) in the Shenandoah Valley on September 19, this decisive event infused new confidence into the northern war effort at a time when it was sorely needed. Crucially, it virtually guaranteed Lincoln's reelection in November. The incumbent president was a relieved victor in this contest, his popular majority of half a million secured with the help of 78 percent of the soldiers who voted in the field.[53]

The end of the Rebellion was now in sight. Even before Lincoln's reelection, Sherman had told Grant of his determination to make southern civilians feel the full force of Union military power. 'I propose we break up the railroad from Chattanooga', he wired in early October, 'and strike out with wagons for Savannah. Until we can repopulate Georgia, it is useless to occupy it, but the utter destruction of its roads, houses, and people will cripple their military resources. By attempting to hold the roads we will lose 1000 men monthly, and will gain no result. I can make the march, and make Georgia howl.'[54] Although his superiors had reservations about his proposal to cut loose from his supply base and live off the land, they allowed him to go ahead with his plans. Sherman's men left Atlanta in two large columns in mid-November and reached the cotton port of Savannah on December 22. Six days previously George Thomas's Federals had inflicted a decisive defeat on Hood's weakened Army of Tennessee, driving north in a desperate bid to ease the pressure on the Confederates in Georgia, at the battle of Nashville. In the course of their 'March to the Sea', Sherman's soldiers left civilian lives intact but destroyed huge amounts of public and private property, sapping Georgia's ability to contribute significantly to the Confederate cause and signaling to the world, as Sherman had predicted, that an independent South was no longer a viable entity.

Reveling in the fear that his army struck in the hearts of the slaveholding aristocracy, Sherman had no desire to tarry on the coast. In January 1865, having persuaded Grant to allow him to continue his advance northward, the Ohioan led his avenging Federals northward to punish the planter class of South Carolina for their leading role in the Rebellion. On February 17 he did little to prevent the largely accidental destruction of the state capital, Columbia, by fire, an event that would dog him for the rest of his life but one that privately he had little reason to regret. His troops headed further northward to wreak more havoc through the Carolinas and in mid-March repulsed what was left of the Rebels' western army, now commanded by the hapless Johnston, at the battle of Bentonville, North Carolina.

With Sherman preparing to link up from the south, Grant finally achieved the necessary breakthrough to end the ten-month siege of Petersburg. Thwarting a desperate attempt by Lee to penetrate the Union line at Fort Stedman on March 25, the Federal commander found his ability to turn Lee's right flank increased by the arrival of Sheridan's cavalry from the Shenandoah Valley. On April 1 a combined infantry and cavalry force under Sheridan's command overcame entrenched Confederate positions at Five Forks, to the west of Petersburg. Confederate officers including George E. Pickett had left the front for a picnic, thereby allowing the Federals to exploit an uncoordinated defense. Grant seized his chance and ordered a full-scale assault along the Petersburg front. The next day Horatio Wright's VI Corps breached the Confederate defenses close to the South Side railroad, Petersburg's main supply route. The Federals then rolled up the Confederate line, their attack culminating in a bloody and protracted struggle to take the imposing Rebel redoubt of Fort Gregg. While ultimately in vain, the Confederate defense of Fort Gregg (and neighboring Fort Whitworth) allowed Lee to pull his troops out of Petersburg and nearby Richmond that night. On April 2–3 the Army of the Potomac began the task of enveloping Lee's shrunken and dispirited army as it fled westward. Cut off by Sheridan's cavalry and having lost a sizeable part of his supply trains, Lee found escape to be impossible. The Rebel general surrendered to Grant at Appomattox Court House on April 9, leaving President Davis and other high Confederate officials (who had already left the capital) to flee for their lives. Although desultory fighting continued in the trans-Mississippi theatre and Sherman had yet to receive Johnston's surrender in North Carolina, to all intents and purposes the Rebellion was over.

Historians differ as to whether or not the American Civil War was the first modern war. Those who argue in the affirmative point to the salience of railroads, ironclads, and telegraph lines, the primacy of the defense, and the growing complexity of supply operations as evidence that it foreshadowed developments in the twentieth century. Their detractors observe the relatively unsophisticated state of the weaponry involved, the stolidity of tactical thinking and the transitional nature of the mobilization process to argue the opposite. In truth, it matters little. What was important to contemporaries was that it secured the continental supremacy of the United States. Internal developments in the North and South, however, ensured the emergence of a rather different nation from the one that went to war with itself in 1861.

Notes

1. Gist to Pettus, Nov. 8, 1860, GLC 02266.

2. Steven A. Channing, *Crisis of Fear: Secession in South Carolina* (New York, 1970), p.282.

3. John L. Wakelyn, ed., *Southern Pamphlets on Secession: November 1860–April 1861* (Chapel Hill, NC, 1996), p.46.

4. *New Orleans Daily Crescent*, Dec. 14, 1860, in Dwight L. Dumond, ed., *Southern Editorials on Secession* (New York, 1931), pp.331–2.

5. *Columbia Daily South Carolinian*, Aug. 3, 1860, in *ibid.*, p.154.

6. Of course, nearly four million blacks had not voted for slavery but white supremacists had no reason to consider the implications of this inconvenient fact.

7. Smith to Edmund Kirby Smith, Dec. 13, 1860, Edmund Kirby Smith Papers, SHC.

8. Smith to E.K. Smith, Jan. 7, 1861, Kirby Smith Papers, SHC.

9. Smith to E.K. Smith, Jan. 16, 1861, Kirby Smith Papers, SHC.

10. Michael P. Johnson, *Toward a Patriarchal Republic: The Secession of Georgia* (Baton Rouge, La, 1977).

11. Charles B. Dew, *Apostles of Disunion: Southern Secession Commissioners and the Causes of the Civil War* (Charlottesville, Va, 2001), p.48.

12. Hale to Magoffin, Dec. 27, 1860, in *ibid.*, pp.97–8.

13. Lynda L. Crist, ed., *The Papers of Jefferson Davis: Vol.7, 1861* (Baton Rouge, La, 1992), p.47.

14. David Potter, *The Impending Crisis 1848–1861* (New York, 1976), p.531.

15. Michael Vorenberg, *Final Freedom: The Civil War, the Abolition of Slavery, and the Thirteenth Amendment* (Cambridge, 2001), pp.20–1.

16. Mark W. Kruman, *Parties and Politics in North Carolina, 1836–1865* (Baton Rouge, La, 1983), pp.211–12.

17. Shenck Diary, March 18, 1861, SHC 652.

18. William W. Freehling, *The South vs. the South: How Anti-Confederate Southerners Shaped the Course of the Civil War* (Oxford, 2001), p.41.

19. *CWL*, 4, pp.264, 271.

20. *Richmond Dispatch*, March 5, 1861, in Dumond, ed., *Southern Editorials*, p.475.

21. For accounts of the Fort Sumter crisis see Brian Holden Reid, *The Origins of the American Civil War* (London, 1996), pp.310–67, and Maury Klein, *Days of Defiance: Sumter, Secession, and the Coming of the Civil War* (New York, 1997).

22. David H. Donald, *Lincoln* (London, 1995), p.290.

23. *CWL*, 4, 323.

24. Quoted in Klein, *Days of Defiance* (New York, 1997), p.399.

25. James M. McPherson, *For Cause and Comrades: Why Men Fought in the Civil War* (New York, 1997), pp.16–17.

26. See e.g. Grady McWhiney and Perry D. Jamieson, *Attack and Die: Civil War Military Tactics and the Southern Heritage* (Tuscaloosa, Ala, 1982).

27. James M. McPherson, *Battle Cry of Freedom* (New York, 1988), p.318.

28. Joseph L. Harsh, *Confederate Tide Rising: Robert E. Lee and the Making of Southern Strategy, 1861–1862* (Kent, Ohio, 1998), p.13.

29. Gary Gallagher, *The Confederate War* (Cambridge, Mass., 1997), pp.115–16.

30. Quoted in JoAnna M. McDonald, *'We Shall Meet Again': The First Battle of Manassas (Bull Run) July 18–21, 1861* (New York, 1999), p.137.

31. John Opie and McHenry Howard quoted in *ibid.*, p.174.

32. Quoted in William C. Davis, *Jefferson Davis: The Man and His Hour* (New York, 1991), p.363.

33. For an insightful discussion of this issue see Freehling, *South vs. South*, pp.47–64.

34. Larry Daniels, *Shiloh: The Battle that Changed the Civil War* (New York, 1997), p.317.

35. Richard M. McMurry, *Two Great Rebel Armies: An Essay in Confederate Military History* (Chapel Hill, NC, 1989), pp.16–17.

36. Robert Knox Sneden, *Eye of the Storm: A Civil War Odyssey*, ed. Charles F. Bryan, Jr and Nelson D. Lankford (New York, 2000), p.97.

37. Quoted in Emory M. Thomas, *Robert E. Lee* (New York, 1995), p.256.

38. H.G. Matthew, *Gladstone, 1809–1874* (Oxford, 1988), p.133.

39. Howard Jones, 'History and Mythology: The Crisis over British Intervention in the Civil War' in *The Union, the Confederacy, and the Atlantic Rim*, ed. Robert E. May (West Lafayette, Ind., 1995), pp.48–52.

40. Quoted in Thomas, *Lee*, p.271.

41. Quoted in Freehling, *South vs.South*, p.121.

42. *Ibid.*, pp.150–4.

43. On this theme see esp. Mark Grimsley, *The Hard Hand of War: Union Military Policy Toward Southern Civilians, 1861–1865* (Cambridge, 1995).

44. Quoted in Stephen E. Ambrose, *Halleck: Lincoln's Chief of Staff* (1962: repr. Baton Rouge, La, 1990), p.119.

45. Quoted in Roy Morris, Jr, *The Better Angel: Walt Whitman in the Civil War* (Oxford, 2000), p.119.

46. Quoted in Steven E. Woodworth, *Six Armies in Tennessee: The Chickamauga and Chattanooga Campaigns* (Lincoln, Neb., 1998), p.17.

47. Quoted in McPherson, *Battle Cry*, p.654.

48. Quoted in Carol Reardon, *Pickett's Charge in History and Memory* (Chapel Hill, NC, 1997), p.5.

49. Quoted in Donald, *Lincoln*, p.457.

50. Quoted in McPherson, *Battle Cry*, p.722.

51. Brian Holden Reid, 'Another Look at Grant's Crossing of the James, 1864', *CWH* 39 (1993), 291–316.

52. Robert Cook, '"The Grave of All My Comforts": William Pitt Fessenden as Secretary of the Treasury, 1864–65', *CWH* 41 (1993), 212.

53. For a full discussion of the 1864 election campaign see pp.220–2 below.

54. Quoted in Michael Fellman, *Citizen Sherman: A Life of William Tecumseh Sherman* (Lawrence, Kan., 1995), p.186.

5

OUR DELIVERANCE IS NIGH: THE QUEST FOR SOUTHERN INDEPENDENCE

Born in the CSA?: The unusual case of southern nationalism

Several weeks after the battle of Antietam in 1862 an English business-man, William C. Corsan, arrived in the new slaveholding republic by boat from Union-occupied New Orleans. His mission was to investigate the prospects for reinvigorating his Sheffield cutlery firm's southern market which, like so many British markets in America, had been devastated by the outbreak of the Civil War. Corsan traveled eastward across the vast expanse of Confederate territory, finally ending his journey in Richmond. In spite of being unimpressed by the deplorable state of southern railway carriages (particularly the copious amounts of tobacco juice on the floor), the Yorkshireman saw and heard enough to convince himself that the Confederacy was a viable entity. When he returned home he published an account of his experiences that seemed to confirm W.E. Gladstone's observa-tion that southerners had made a nation. The inhabitants of the Con-federacy, insisted Corsan, would never return to the Union. Contrary to northern claims, there was no Union sentiment left in the South. The Confederates were now self-sufficient in foodstuffs and were beginning to build up their own manufacturing base in the midst of a confident slaveholding society. '[I] see', he concluded, 'very little chance for the North in the task she has undertaken ... Nations, no matter how small and unmeritorious, *cannot* be annihilated.'[1]

Corsan's remarks are a useful corrective to the views of some scholars that the South's defeat was inevitable. The United States emerged as such a powerful force on the world stage during the twentieth century that the result of the Civil War can easily be seen to have been foreordained. Yet, as Corsan and many of his contemporaries correctly observed, white southerners were engaged in a desperate struggle for nationhood that might well have divided the United States into at least two separate entities. The fact that they were able to resist Yankee domination for four years testifies not only to the depth of their hatred of the invader but also to the mobilizing capacity of the government in Richmond and the closely related development of a separate Confederate identity. Some historians have contended that the Confederacy collapsed as a result of internal weaknesses and divisions.[2] To argue thus is to approach the question of southern defeat from the wrong angle. Domestic problems did undermine the Confederate war effort but they did so primarily because those problems were exacerbated by military pressure exerted by the enemy.[3] In the final analysis the Confederacy perished because it faced an opponent that was its superior in terms of manpower and material resources and at least its equal in terms of will.

The Confederacy poses an obvious problem for any student of nationalism because the South failed in its bid to become a separate nation state. This might well lead one to conclude that from the very outset southern whites lacked the mental and physical wherewithal to strike out on their own. Perhaps, so the argument might run, they failed to make a nation because in reality there was very little to distinguish them from the wider population. Southerners were by birth and training Americans – hence their putative inability to forge a durable separate identity in wartime.

On the face of things this argument has much to recommend it. As we have seen, most whites in the region during the 1840s and 1850s regarded themselves not only as southerners but also as Americans, as loyal citizens of the United States. When the Lincoln administration had announced its determination to contest secession, many whites in the slave states refused to abandon their adherence to the Union. This was particularly true of former Whigs in the border states as well as large numbers (though not a majority) of nonslaveholders. As William W. Freehling has noted, roughly 300,000 white southerners (two-thirds from the border states, the rest from the upper or middle South) actually fought for the Union.[4] Many of these men were upland yeomen and propertyless whites who resented the power of black-belt planters. Maryland, Missouri, and Kentucky; mountainous East Tennessee, western North Carolina, and West Virginia (which broke away from the Confederacy and formed a separate state of the Union in 1863); and the hill country of Alabama all furnished troops for the northern invaders. Added to the lack of enthusiasm for the South displayed by nearly four million black slaves who were at best mainly coopted Confederates (and, as time progressed, open unionists), southern white unionism depleted even further the already limited resource base available to the Rebels.

Further support for the argument that the Confederacy collapsed from within is provided by widespread evidence of class and gender tensions in the Confederate heartland. Nonslaveholding whites, even those living in the plantation districts, grew increasingly discontented as the region's slaveholding elites appeared to bolster their own privileges while simultaneously demanding greater sacrifices from the plain people of the South. White women of all classes, moreover, came to resent the Confederate authorities for sending their menfolk to the grave and for failing to protect females from the hardships of war – hunger, banditry, recalcitrant slaves, and Federal occupation. As the war ground on, southern armies were increasingly weakened as ordinary soldiers (most of whom were nonslaveholding whites) left the front to return home and attend to the wants of the families for whom they had enlisted in the first place.

The notion that the Confederacy collapsed from within has much to recommend it. However, it fails to confront the reality that the majority of southern whites fought doggedly for their liberty (as they saw it) at tremendous cost to themselves. At war's end 258,000 southern men, one quarter of the South's white military-age population in 1860, had given their lives to earn what they regarded as a new birth of freedom. Another 200,000 were wounded in the same process. If the North lost even more men (roughly 360,000 dead), the southern death rate from disease and in battle was significantly higher than that of the Yankees: one in three compared with the Union's one in six. Without a massive effort on the part of its people, such an astonishing level of sacrifice would not have been possible. Whereas the North mobilized roughly 50 percent of its military age population (2.2 million men), the equivalent figure for the Confederacy was 75–85 percent (a total of between 750,000 and 850,000 men).[5]

The commitment and suffering on the home front was scarcely less impressive. Although the war certainly intensified existing fissures within southern society and progressively undermined the existing racial order, backing for the Rebel cause was tenacious in the deep and upper South. Experiences for whites differed widely over gender and class, but women as well as men, slaveholders as well as nonslaveholders, were all touched directly by the conflict and all paid the heavy price of rebellion. Some lost faith in the Confederate experiment as the costs of war increased and the killing grew in intensity. Large numbers adhered to the cause as long as Lee's army remained in the field. While many scholars have contended that the South eventually collapsed from within as a result of doubts over slavery, burgeoning class conflict, and persistent states' rights opposition to centralized power, the available evidence supports Gary Gallagher's view that the primary agents of southern defeat were the armed forces of the United States.[6]

Confederate mobilization and state formation

If the South were to have any chance of defeating the North on the battlefield, it needed firstly to mobilize all its available resources as speedily and effectively as possible and, secondly, to convince the vast majority of its free citizens that it was worth making huge sacrifices for the Confederacy. The efforts to secure these objectives contributed to the interconnected processes of state formation and nation building in the wartime South.

When the Confederate government moved its capital from Montgomery to Richmond in the spring of 1861 it announced its determination to defend the upper as well as lower South from northern aggression. The defense of a frontier stretching 1,500 miles from east to west and 2,500 miles along the coast, however, required more than a simple transfer of bureaucrats from Alabama to Virginia. As soon as it became clear that the North would not be dissuaded easily from coercing the seceded states back into the Union, the Confederate government embarked on a series of pragmatic policy initiatives which quickly began to challenge the antebellum polity grounded in localism. Opposition to the centralizing tendencies of the war grew steadily over time, to such an extent that some historians believe the Confederacy died of a surfeit of states' rights.[7] While there is some truth in this contention – tension between center and periphery was one of the most serious faultlines within the wartime South – it seems more reasonable to suggest that the steady growth of central power was a crucial reason why the South was able to fight a prolonged war against one of the most powerful economies on earth.

As in the North, many of the initial mobilization efforts were undertaken by state governments. The nuclei of the two main Confederate armies, the Army of Northern Virginia and the Army of Tennessee, were provided by existing state militias. State governors such as Joseph E. Brown of Georgia were furnishing arms and men for the Confederacy even before the formal outbreak of war, though Brown was soon complaining about the Confederate Congress's decision to authorize the initial tender of troops directly to President Davis. This move, he averred, was 'a very dangerous infringement of States rights' and he ordered that units resorting to direct tender had to leave their weapons behind when they left the state.[8] In addition to furnishing men for the Confederate armies, state governments joined local authorities in organizing supplies for the troops, alleviating blockade-induced shortages of essential goods such as salt, and providing limited assistance to the growing numbers of indigent whites on the home front.

However, as northern military pressure began to bite by the winter of 1861–62, Confederate leaders sensed that a beleaguered South could not survive without greater centralized direction. The loss of Kentucky, middle Tennessee and northern Virginia not only constituted a major blow to southern morale but also robbed the incipient nation of some of its prime farmland and horse-rearing country. Even more serious was the desperate shortage of manpower when McClellan's move to the Yorktown Peninsula threatened Richmond itself. In the spring of 1862, just weeks after legislators had empowered the president to suspend the writ of habeas corpus and declare martial law in areas considered vulnerable to enemy attack, a relatively compliant Confederate Congress passed the first national conscription act in American history. Enrolling all able-bodied white males between the ages of 18 and 35, the measure ensured that by 1863 the task of augmenting and replenishing the country's military forces would be undertaken by officials employed directly by the national government rather than the individual states.

This radical development did not go uncontested. Governor Brown immediately attacked the act as unconstitutional, a view shared by his fellow Georgian, Confederate Vice President Alexander H. Stephens. Many ordinary southerners were especially outraged by Congress's decision to exempt certain occupations from military service: ministers and doctors, for example, and even more controversially (from October 1862) the owners or overseers of 20 or more slaves. Yet while conscription was frustrated in part by the likes of Governor Brown and undoubtedly helped to fan the flames of class antagonism, it served its primary purpose in stimulating a rash of volunteering at a critical moment in the history of the Confederacy. More than that, it announced that the centralizing tendencies unleashed by the war were beginning to find concrete form. If the

South were to survive as an independent entity, it was clear to many people that the traditional republican values underpinning secession would have to undergo a major transformation.

The trend toward centralization proceeded apace as the North tightened its noose around the Confederacy. Both of the South's major armies implemented rigid discipline to reduce the incidence of desertion and straggling. Citizen-soldiers, notoriously resistant to discipline in all of America's previous wars, were subject to rigorous penalties (including death) if they chose to leave their units without official permission. On the home front, private property was liable to impressment by national officials who purchased goods required by the army at prices set by the government.

Wealthy slaveholders were by no means exempt from these developments, for state and Confederate authorities did not hesitate to use their human chattels for a wide range of defense duties. Government-employed bonded labor played a crucial role in the Rebel war effort. Slaves were used throughout the Confederacy, on plantations, in the construction of fortifications, in niter mines, munitions factories, quartermaster shops, hospitals, and commissary depots. As shortages of essential supplies worsened and the incidence of poverty outstripped the capacity of local authorities to reduce it, Richmond stepped in to fund government manufactories. Supplementing the output of private firms such as Richmond's Tredegar Ironworks, these plants not only provided jobs and wages for indigent white women and children but also supplied the Confederacy with sorely needed food, clothing and *matériel*.

A dramatic increase in the size of the national government bureaucracy accompanied the steady expansion of central-state functions. Crucial to the relative success of the southern war effort was the work of the Confederate War Department, ably administered by the clear-sighted Virginian, James A. Seddon, between November 1862 and January 1865. Unlike his predecessor, George Randolph, Seddon worked well with the notoriously overbearing Davis. The war minister was never given a free rein over the department because Davis normally took crucial military decisions in consultation with his generals in the field. Yet Seddon succeeded in his principal task of making the best of the country's limited demographic and economic resources. Owing in large measure to Seddon's own efforts and those of his subordinates in charge of the war department's key supply bureaus, whole sectors of the Confederacy's wartime economy had been brought almost totally under central direction by the spring of 1863. The Confederacy never came close to matching the North's manufacturing output during the Civil War, but without government subsidy and outright ownership of textile mills and ordnance factories the contest would have been lost long before Appomattox.

Although the antebellum proslavery writer and Mississippi planter, Henry Hughes, regarded statism as essential to the protection of the peculiar institution, Confederate centralism was a product of wartime necessity, not ideology. This fact did not make the trend any more acceptable to old-style republicans (ever watchful for signs of impending tyranny) or those slaveholders who resented government efforts to interfere with private property rights. As mobilization and centralization proceeded in tandem against a backdrop of military defeat in the west and stalemate in the east, criticism of the administration's policies spread, articulated at the top by constitutional conservatives like Stephens who feared the corrosive impact of centralized government on individual liberties and states' rights, and at the grassroots by ordinary men and women disaffected by the prolongation of the war. For the most part, however, elites and plain folk alike remained committed to the goal of southern independence in spite of undergoing some of the most grievous suffering ever seen in North America. Many disaffected whites did lose heart as the enemy closed in, but a surprisingly large number remained defiant to the last. To understand the durability of support for the Confederacy, we must probe the sources of wartime southern nationalism.

Nova ordo servorum

Although Confederate nationalism was a new phenomenon, its origins could be found in the antebellum period when growing numbers of southerners had begun to think of themselves as different from other Americans. The existence of slavery lay at the root of these perceived differences. The peculiar institution provided the foundation for a hybrid society that mixed deference with democracy and paternalism with the most appalling cruelty. The white South's resulting attachment to white supremacy, patriarchy, honor, and republicanism rendered the majority of its inhabitants acutely loyal to the region of their birth and extremely sensitive to external criticism. Antebellum southern sectionalism derived much of its strength from proslavery ideology – a composite intellectual justification for the ownership of one human being by another that had garnered much popular support by the late 1850s. If leading southern ideologues differed in their emphases (Hughes was unique in his interventionist view of the state's role in society), they agreed that slavery was essential to the maintenance of white liberty. In their view the institution promoted an ordered, stable, and cultured society, one that contrasted favorably with the money-grubbing and ethnically heterogeneous North. More than that, they insisted that blacks also benefited from slavery because the institution brought a barbarous people into contact with civilized Christian whites.

For all its trenchant criticisms of northern society, proslavery ideology was profoundly racist in the sense that its practitioners held blacks to be a permanently inferior species. The Virginia seces-sionist, Edmund Ruffin, was one of many antebellum writers who insisted that racial slavery was best for everyone. The white race, he asserted in a pamphlet published in 1858, was 'the most superior race of mankind'. Negroes, in contrast, had been shown to be incap-able of improvement so 'that no unprejudiced mind can now admit the equality of intellect of the two races, or even the capacity of the black race, either to become or remain industrious, civilised, when in a state of freedom and under self-government – or, indeed, in any other condition than when held enslaved and directed by white men'.[9]

For southern whites of all classes racial slavery was central to both their own conception of liberty and their loyalty to section. Regardless of social status, all white southern males could envision themselves as free and independent citizens in stark contrast to the enslaved blacks in their midst. Until slave prices began to rise precipitately in the 1850s, moreover, many nonslaveholders could dream of a day when they too could purchase blacks and enter the ranks of the slaveholding elite. The dependent status of white women also con-tributed toward manly self-respect but in the Old South race trumped gender as a determinant of social status. White women, therefore, also benefited from the psychological and material wage provided by slavery and normally assumed they had as much stake as any male in the perpetuation of the peculiar institution.

What made southern identity such a potent phenomenon in the mid-nineteenth century was the emergence of a powerful external threat in the shape of the Republican party: fear and contempt for the Republicans was enough to convince large numbers of south-erners in 1860–61 that the only way to preserve their unique way of life was to cut themselves off from the North. Yet in order to sustain a long and bloody war against the United States, southern whites needed to transform an amorphous regional loyalty into the kind of relatively coherent national identity that inspired the Italians, Czechs, and Poles in the mid-nineteenth century. While their commitment to white supremacy, republican self-government, family, and community did much to make them Confederates in the first place, the actual strength of their patriotism was generated by several other factors: primarily the Civil War itself but also the actions of leading opinion makers within the South. As Drew Gilpin Faust has observed, the process of building Confederate nationalism was self-conscious and ongoing, molded in part by elites but rendered unusually inclusive because of the socially disruptive effects of the war and the plantocracy's urgent need for grassroots aid.[10]

Predictably, given the speed of events and the imperative to establish some continuity with the past, the Confederacy's first steps into nationhood were highly derivative. The South's first national banner, the red, white, and blue Stars and Bars, was cloned from Old Glory, the flag of the United States. Apart from its prohibition on abolition, the Rebel Constitution closely resembled that of 1787. When Jefferson Davis was inaugurated provisional president of the Confederate States of America in January 1861 the absence of a national anthem necessitated the playing of the *Marseillaise*. For most southerners, however, the French Revolution was much too radical to be regarded as a fit role model for their own bid for liberty. Even before the attack on Fort Sumter far greater stress was placed on the lessons provided by the patriot heroes of the American War of Independence, unsurprisingly so in view of the secessionists' claims that they were acting in the true spirit of the Revolution. George Washington, the Virginia slaveholder who had fathered the United States, featured prominently on the Confederate seal and one of the country's first postage stamps. The writers of popular songs – significant manufacturers of national identity in a region with a lower literacy rate than the North – lauded southern exploits on eighteenth-century battlefields like Cowpens and Yorktown. Attempts to locate the Confederacy firmly in the context of America's republican past were not simply part of a top-down process. Revolutionary symbols were imbued with such power primarily because the common folk of the South had been nurtured on tales of the War of Independence, at home, in church, at the hustings, and in school. White southerners from all social groups believed themselves to be replicating the struggles which their ancestors had waged against the British. Little wonder, therefore, that Confederate opinion makers sought to galvanize and legitimize their cause through heavy use of emotionally charged and quintessentially American historical symbols.

Official and popular emphasis on the Revolutionary past (not to mention states' rights and preservation of the federal Constitution) might well lead one to conclude that the Confederacy did not represent a radical disjuncture in American history. However, in a chilling speech at Savannah on March 21, 1861 Vice President Alexander H. Stephens insisted that the Confederate experiment should be seen as a new departure rather than a continuation of American republican ideals. Antislavery agitation, he said, 'was the immediate cause of the late rupture and present revolution'. Founding Fathers such as Thomas Jefferson, revered southerners though many of them were, had believed mistakenly that slavery was an evil that would pass away and that all men were born equal. 'Our new Government', intoned Stephens,

> is founded upon exactly the opposite ideas; its foundations are laid, its cornerstone rests, upon the great truth that the negro is not equal to the white man; that slavery, subordination to the superior race, is his natural and moral condition. This, our new Government, is the first, in the history of the world, based upon this great physical, philosophical, and moral truth.[11]

For some of its supporters, the Confederacy represented a major break not only with the American past but also with the rational Enlightenment and its allegedly warped ideas about natural rights. The new nation would stand or fall with the institution that provided its fundamental reason for existence.

Onward Christian soldiers

Central to the Confederates' hopes for a successful resolution to their struggle was the people's faith in God. Evangelical Protestantism had been part of the fabric of daily life in the antebellum South and religion was one of the main building blocks in the construction of a separate southern identity. From the outset Confederate leaders tried to emphasize that one of the critical distinctions between North and South was the latter's closeness to the Creator. Another of the few differences between the constitutions of the two warring parties was the Confederate document's explicit invocation of 'the favor and guidance of Almighty God' – a call echoed by the new national motto, 'Deo Vindice' ('God will Avenge').[12] Southern politicians and clergymen argued that the US Constitution had been tainted from the beginning by its deist origins. Atheistic, materialistic Yankees would now be confronted by a truly Christian nation whose inhabitants had humbled themselves before God in order to make themselves the instruments of the Divine plan for the world.

In an effort to strengthen the linkage between ordinary southerners and their Creator, President Jefferson Davis issued ten proclamations for fast days during the Civil War. White southerners, he contended, must submit themselves to God's will if they were to subdue the enemy. State and local authorities followed his lead by issuing their own calls for ritual fasting. Clergymen in cities such as Richmond (where there were 33 churches in 1860) participated enthusiastically in the enterprise by delivering special fast-day sermons. Sometimes printed to reach a wider audience than their immediate congregation, these declamations tended to focus specifically on the present by imploring southerners to cleanse themselves of sin and bend themselves to the will of God.

The jeremiads received powerful backing from the denominational press which played its own unique role in fostering Confederate identity and morale. As well as repeating the clergy's impassioned attacks on sinful behavior such as greed and the mistreatment of slaves, religious newspapers joined other propagators of opinion in defending the South's cause in the long-established Christian tradition of the just war. As part of this defense (which exhibited obvious continuity with antebellum proslavery ideology) southern slavery was regularly depicted as a divinely sanctioned institution central to the notion of the Confederacy as a covenanted nation. Blacks were an inferior heathen race whose only hopes of uplift came via their enslavement at the hands of a Christian people. In the words of Marinda B. Moore, the author of one of the wartime South's best-selling geography primers for young children, black Africans were slothful and vicious, prone to cruelty, and ignorant of the Gospel. By contrast, she wrote, 'the slaves who are found in America are in much better condition. They are better fed, better clothed, and better instructed than in their native country.'[13] Patently, one of God's main purposes for the Confederacy was to lead poor, benighted Negroes to the bright throne of Jesus Christ. If southern whites did this properly and repented of their sins, how could the God of Battles fail to deny them ultimate victory?

Not all white southerners were persuaded by promises of salvation through Christian penitence and suffering. As criticism of the government's conduct of the war grew over time, some newspapers began to lose patience with Jefferson Davis's repeated calls for public fasting and Heavenly aid. His public displays of piety and implicit criticism of popular behavior clashed with the efforts of several editors to raise morale by urging manly, Anglo-Saxon Confederates on to glorious deeds in the field. Shortly after the twin disasters at Vicksburg and Gettysburg in July 1863, the *Richmond Examiner* attacked the president's preoccupation with religion by insisting that 'There is neither Christianity nor religion of any kind in this war. We prosecute it in self-defense, for the preservation of our liberty, our homes and our Negroes.'[14] In another blast at the end of August 1863 the *Examiner's* tone grew more acid. Northerners, observed the editor, 'do not seem now to rely on fast and humiliation. They have recently indulged in thanksgiving for victory, but their panacea for defeat seems to be fresh levies of men, more ironclads and additional fifteen-inch guns.'[15]

In spite of the criticism leveled against efforts to create a civil religion for the Confederacy, deeply religious convictions mediated the wartime experiences of large numbers of southerners. This was especially true of white women who constituted the mainstays of the Confederate home front during the Civil War. Often active participants in the secessionist maneuvers of late 1860 and early 1861, southern white women of all social classes found their lives altered by the ensuing turmoil. Hegemonic patriarchal values, underpinned by evangelical notions of female propriety, ensured that women did not normally volunteer to fight (though some expressed a wish that they could do so and a handful did actually find their way into uniform). However, a combination of patriotism, voluntarism, and, in many cases, economic necessity led them to undertake a variety of labors. At the beginning of the war wealthy planters' wives and urban middle-class women formed organized groups to sew military uniforms and to collect and distribute relief to those who required it in the community. Over a thousand female voluntary organizations were set up in the South between 1861 and 1865.[16] Like their similarly resourceful grandmothers in the Revolutionary War, they toiled willingly for the Confederacy, sure in the knowledge that the Rebel cause was as just as that of the patriots and that their duty as women was to support their menfolk at the front. When the sheer scale of the war rendered their efforts inadequate to the task at hand and as the incidence of poverty increased, the Confederate state stepped in to employ significant numbers of poorer women (and some hard-hit middle-class women) in its textile factories.

Southern patriarchy was challenged but not overturned by the Civil War. There were many strong women in the wartime South – President Davis's wife, Varina, among them – and some were bold enough to become teachers, hospital visitors, and government clerks.

Generally, however, they avoided full engagement in the public sphere, preferring to participate in supportive activities that were essentially extensions of their antebellum domestic role and which consequently would excite minimal opprobrium. The limited nature of southern white women's public involvement was highlighted by the relative paucity of female nurses in the Confederacy. In contrast to the North (where large numbers of white women were employed in army hospitals) the majority of such workers in Dixie were blacks of both sexes.

The experience of white women differed considerably throughout the South. In areas closest to the fighting or in parts of the Confederacy occupied by Federal troops, the main concern of slaveholding families was the tendency of their black laborers to run away to seek employment in cities or with the Union army. 'Refugeeing' – decamping with one's property to more secure regions of Secessia such as Texas – was not an option for everyone, and many planters' wives and daughters found themselves having to undertake such basic tasks as cooking and washing for the first time. In the Confederate heartland of the deep South where substantial numbers of slaves continued to labor on plantations, the main problem for elite women was how to control large numbers of blacks when most of the able-bodied white men in the locality had gone off to fight. Living among a captive race had been stressful enough in the antebellum period, but during the war the strains of everyday life were greatly increased by the reduced level of white male protection. Although some women willingly increased their dependence on favorite slaves, many worried incessantly not only about their inability to impose discipline on their chattels but also the awful possibility, however remote, of midnight murder at the hands of their human property. As one agitated resident of Vicksburg put it bluntly, 'I fear the blacks more than I do the Yankees.'[17]

Notwithstanding such anxieties, Confederate women remained remarkably steadfast in their support for a cause that deprived them of the male protection they had been brought up to expect in a patriarchal system. There were several reasons for this, not least the relief efforts of the Confederate state and the huge sacrifices being made by the men in uniform. But equally important in sustaining morale on the home front were the otherworldly attachments of most southern white women.

When southern clergymen spoke out against sinfulness and corruption, about the pressing need for collective reform and humility, the majority of their listeners in church were women. Evangelical

Protestantism allowed Confederate women to bear many of the enormous burdens imposed by war, in large part because the central
Christian motif of salvation through suffering spoke to them directly
in their capacity as Confederates and women. While devotion to their
families connected them automatically to the national cause and
enabled them to cope with all kinds of daily privations, their ability
to imagine a wider community was enhanced still further by the
jeremiads of the clergy and the collective pain endured by countless
women across the South. For some, though certainly not for all,
the idea of the Confederacy as a redeemer nation, chosen by God to
effect His purposes in the world, was a genuine comfort. So too was
the transcendent example of Christ's own suffering on the Cross
when they were confronted by the ultimate loss: the death of their
menfolk in the service of the state. A Tennesseean, Belle Edmondson,
articulated the close relationship between religion and patriotism
when she noted privately, 'God grant successful may be the termina-
tion of 1864 ... Oh! my savior I have buried the past. Guide and lead
me from temptation. After you God, then I live for my Country. God
bless our leaders in Dixie.'[18]

The Gospels were not the sole source of sustenance for Confederate women. The Old Testament provided them not only with the
example of the suffering Job but also with the encouraging message
that a just and wrathful God would reward His chosen people by
smiting their enemies at some uncertain point in the future. Like
their menfolk, southern women were good haters. Once the Federals
began to make civilians bear the hard hand of war, women were
among the first to suffer. Instead of undermining their opponents'
will to fight, Yankee depredations of all kinds incensed numerous
Confederate women, thereby intensifying their commitment to the
nation's cause. When, in the summer of 1862, General John Pope
announced his determination to subsist off the land and punish
those who supported guerrillas in northern Virginia, female civilians
joined Robert E. Lee in condemning his action as barbarous. When
Union troops began destroying property indiscriminately and running
off slaves, their actions merely confirmed the suspicions of many
southern women that the Yankees were vandals as well as abolitionists.
The devastation wrought by Sherman's men on her family's Georgia
plantation in late 1864 appalled the diarist Catherine Rowland.
'[T]hey are certainly the vilest wretches', she wrote of the marauding
bluecoats, '& must be overtaken in their wickedness.'[19]

The relationship between home front and battle front was a critical
factor in the South's tenacious resistance to northern arms. This

relationship evolved over time as the slaughter grew in scale and the rigors of civilian life became harder to endure. At the beginning of the Civil War large numbers of southern women took positive steps to ensure that the ranks of the Confederate armies were filled. Southern men joined up for many reasons, among the most important being their determination to protect their female dependants from the awful consequences of Republican rule. Consciously or unconsciously, however, Confederate women placed additional pressure on men to enlist. They did so not only by making regimental banners and uniforms but also by reminding men that they were honor-bound to fight for the South.

This initial female enthusiasm waned as the number of casualties rose to heights unanticipated during the heady days of secession. Growing numbers of southern mothers and wives wrote to government officials requesting, even begging, them to allow their menfolk to return home to look after the family homestead. At the same time a collective dialog took shape in the form of mutual correspondence between soldiers in the field and women at home. When their appeals went unheard by the authorities, some southern women added encouragement to desert to their litany of complaints about civilian life and their understandable fears about the safety of their loved ones. A running battle sometimes developed between women and soldiers. Gustave Cooke, an ambitious Texas volunteer, repeatedly strove to bolster his wife's flagging morale. 'You must not write for me to come home', he told her, 'because I ought to know when I can best be spared from the service.' Added Cooke, with an artful domestic twist,

> Let us then be proud that we are able to make a sacrifice to our beloved country which will redound to our credit and its advantage. If God shall guide us safely through the trials and dangers of this great ordeal, through which we are passing, I hope to have laid the foundation for a life of respectability and honor for us and to have placed our little daughters upon a high round in life's social ladder.[20]

Just as it was in the North, the relationship between women and soldiers in the Confederacy was symbiotic: frequent correspondence between these connected spheres of Confederate life ensured that the state of morale at home affected that at the front and vice versa. Until the final stages of the war, patriotic advice flowed in both directions. When one soldier told his mother in April 1864 that he had received a medical furlough, he discovered a rude shock in the mail. 'I am sure the Board was right not to send you back to the field', replied the mother sternly, 'but you are wrong in the idea that their action makes you "a free man". You are bound by the duties of your position, & can only be "free" when you conscientiously perform them ... [Y]our time belongs to your Country & not to your pleasures.'[21] The scale of desertion and straggling in the Confederate forces, checked in part by the injection of greater discipline from the summer of 1862, increased significantly during the last year of the war. Enough women, however, continued to suffer defiantly and bolster their menfolk to ensure that the Confederacy remained a viable entity until the winter of 1864–65.

Notwithstanding the vital importance of the home front, Rebel officials and southern women alike understood fully that military success was the only sure means of gaining independence. The armies themselves thus provided much of the impetus for Confederate nationalism. In part the military's contribution to the southern cause was symbolic. The country's armed forces furnished the Confederacy with a pantheon to rank alongside that of any other self-respecting country. After his accidental death in May 1863, Stonewall Jackson emerged as the preeminent Confederate martyr. While many southerners found his demise hard to explain in the context of their claims to be a chosen people, Jackson – a devout Presbyterian – was an ideal role model for a Christian nation at war: stern, pious, and an effective killer of Yankees. The Virginian's bold exploits in the Shenandoah Valley and at Second Manassas made him a living, breathing hero by the summer of 1862, but leading southern clergymen were quick to develop his posthumous reputation in the wake of his demise after Chancellorsville. In a memorial sermon, the Presbyterian minister, James B. Ramsey, told his grieving congregation that instead of questioning God's judgment they should rejoice that their Creator had given them the 'perfect Christian hero'. 'Who could believe', he asked, that 'God would have given us such a man, and answered in every step his prayers for two eventful years, and blessed him as our defender, if he had not designs of mercy for us, and was not preparing for us a glorious deliverance, and us for it?.' Southerners, concluded Ramsey, had only to seek God's grace, as Jackson himself had done, to secure themselves the ultimate victory.[22]

While Stonewall Jackson was thus assimilated into the clergy's grand strategy to make a Christian nation, the war continued to grind out other Confederate martyrs: the gallant Lewis Armistead, for example, one of George Pickett's brigade commanders who was killed leading the charge at Gettysburg, and the talented cavalry officer, Robert Rodes, who died fighting Sheridan's bluecoats at the battle of Opequon Creek in September 1864. Deceased patriot heroes, however, had their limitations as well as their uses. Dead men could not win a fight to the finish with the United States.

Southern civilians – men, women, and children – hungered for news from the front. They wanted victories and, after McClellan's retreat from the Peninsula in 1862, they expected them. Grounds for optimism were found in the performances of the Army of Northern Virginia, the country's most feared fighting force headed by the man widely regarded as the greatest living exponent of the art of war: General Robert E. Lee.

What gave this shy, retiring man such popular appeal was, first and foremost, his consistent ability to defeat the enemy. White southerners appreciated his dignified bearing and highly developed sense of public service but what they most admired was his boldness. For all his famed gentility and good breeding (he was related to George Washington through his wife, Mary Custis), Lee was one of the most creative and aggressive strategists of his day. Once he had proved his talents in the summer campaigns of 1862, the southern people took him to their hearts. While soaring casualty rates and the defeat at Gettysburg prompted a measure of public criticism, the daring nature of his triumphs thrilled a nation in embryo. In the words of the *Richmond Daily Dispatch*, the battle of Chancellorsville ranked 'amongst the most brilliant in the annals of the Southern Confederacy, already illuminated with triumphs which, for number and magnitude, are not surpassed in history'.[23] Because Lee's successes proved that the Yankees could be whipped, they acted as a reservoir of southern morale later in the war when Confederate victories began to dry up. At a time when public confidence in the Davis administration was declining and the Army of Tennessee was in headlong retreat before Sherman, General Lee and his invincibles steeled large numbers of southerners to keep up the fight.

By the final months of the Civil War the Army of Northern Virginia was the last major bastion of Confederate will. In complete contrast to its western counterpart which, Chickamauga aside, was repeatedly bested by the Federals, the Confederacy's eastern army maintained the upper hand over its opponents until the summer of 1864. Lee himself played a leading role in holding his troops together. A strict disciplinarian who did not hesitate to demand stern measures against deserters and stragglers, he was as devoted to his men as he was to the Rebel cause. The majority of the rank and file appreciated his attention to their wants and amply repaid his faith in battle. Lee was also ably assisted by some of the most talented corps commanders of the war, notably Stonewall Jackson and James Longstreet, whose own achievements and personalities attracted grassroots loyalty on their own merits.

As Richard McMurry has shown, there were several reasons, apart from the quality of Lee's generalship, why the Army of Northern Virginia proved to be so much more effective than the Army of Tennessee.[24] The eastern theater was better equipped in terms of infrastructure. Virginia had the best railway network in the Confederacy, making it easier for Lee to maneuver his troops than was the case for Braxton Bragg and Joseph E. Johnston on the other side of the mountains where the distances were much greater. The fact that the national government was centered in Richmond was also a contributing factor. Jefferson Davis has often been criticized for underestimating the importance of the west. While by no means fair, it is true that the Army of Tennessee suffered from logistical inequality (Georgia, for example, supplied the eastern army with food) and was never given its fair share of the South's limited resources. Yet what really made the difference between the two southern armies was the quality of Lee's officer corps. This applied not only to the corps commanders themselves but also to lower-grade officers, many of whom had been trained at the Virginia Military Institute or the Citadel in South Carolina (Tennessee had no such equivalent) or had received a relatively sound military education in the ranks of Virginia's superior state militia. Good leadership at all levels produced a remarkably well-trained and disciplined army whose catalog of victories bred a level of self-confidence necessary to sustain morale in the face of acute adversity.

Regardless of the theater in which they fought, southern men had a variety of reasons for risking their lives for the Confederacy. Ordinary Rebel soldiers, especially those who had volunteered in the early stages of the war, were motivated not only by their attachment to their leaders but also, and here they were no different from their peers in the Union armies, to those who fought around them. The predominantly volunteer armies of the Civil War were generally organized at the community level. Whole companies were made up of men from the same town or county and then consolidated to form regiments from the same state. Prominent among the Confederate force at Wilson's Creek in 1861, to take one example, was the 3rd Louisiana Infantry, a newly constituted regiment made up of companies from several parishes in the Pelican state. Fighting under a blue silk flag bearing the motto 'Southern Rights Inviolate', these companies had originally born names that reflected their community of origin. The men who enlisted in them continued to think of themselves as the Shreveport Rangers, the Caldwell Guards or the Iberville Grays and were so regarded by the inhabitants of these places who remained at home.[25] Southerners therefore were fighting for their families and localities within an institutional context that encouraged them to work together as a unit. If a soldier shirked his duty he might well be endangering friends from home. Correspondence from the front, moreover, would bring any serious dereliction of duty to the attention of his local community, showering dishonor and shame upon himself and his family.

Yet Rebels fought for more than just themselves, their home towns, and their immediate family, friends, and comrades. They were also fighting an ideological war – a righteous struggle for freedom linked directly to their own search for manly independence, honor, and status in a white, slaveholding republic.

Although a majority of Confederate troops were nonslaveholders, Rebel soldiers of all classes understood that defeat would reduce their own stock of liberty, degrading them to the status of the region's enslaved black population. 'We are expecting a hard fight here soon', reported one of Lee's men in April 1864, 'and I do hope it will end the war and what is left a live can return home to live free from the loud roaring of the enemyes canon which has so long been heard in our land trying to force us to live as the colored race of our land[.]'[26] The fear of ordinary white Confederates that defeat would place southern white men on the same level as the country's black dependants helps to explain their vicious contempt for the Union's 'colored' troops. Several well-documented massacres of black Federals occurred during the Civil War, few worse than the butchery at the battle of the Crater in 1864. Desperate to pierce the Rebel lines at Petersburg, General Ulysses S. Grant sanctioned an ambitious plan to tunnel underneath no-man's land and then explode a huge mine beneath the enemy's trenches. The resulting explosion in the early hours of July 30 opened up a breach in Lee's defenses, but inept leadership on the part of Grant's subordinates allowed the enraged Confederates to regroup and then trap the assaulting Federals in the huge hole left by the detonation of the mine. When black troops at the Crater tried to surrender they were cut down in droves. 'They got no quarter to their hearts sorrow', recorded one Rebel, '600 was killed in the trenches. Glory, glory, enough for a dozen days.'[27] At the battle of Nashville later in the year, a Union soldier noted a similar trend. The outnumbered Confederates went into a 'frenzy' at the sight of black troops and fought 'like demons, slaughtering the poor blacks fearfully'.[28] A common commitment to white supremacy thus did much to sustain the South's will to fight on in the final stages of the war.

Religion was as central as race to the Confederate war effort. The same profound faith in God which enabled so many southern civilians to bear the burdens of war in the expectation of ultimate victory enabled many ordinary Rebel soldiers to do the same. Of course, the war bred cynicism and fostered such iniquities as swearing, drinking, and whoring. Yet the very strength of evangelical Protestantism in the antebellum South meant that southern volunteers often went into the army with a Christian resolve that did much to bolster their morale in the field. Whereas some were inclined to adopt a fatalistic approach to life, the majority of these men drew much-needed succor from faith and prayer. 'I feel truly thankful that God in his mercy has again spared me where so many are falling in every fight', one Confederate soldier told his sister after surviving the Federal assault at Missionary Ridge in November 1863. 'I can not hope to come out safe if we fight again, but we will pray to meet again.'[29] Far from undermining religious faith, the huge strains imposed by direct participation in the bloodiest conflict ever fought on North American soil appears to have strengthened it.

Together with the constant threat of death, sustained missionary efforts by the southern churches broadened the extent of religious enthusiasm within the Rebel armies. Revivals began in the Army of Northern Virginia in the wake of the slaughter at Antietam and were soon reported in the Army of Tennessee. They continued sporadically over the next two years, peaking at times of particular tension, for example in camp at Dalton, Georgia, following Bragg's disastrous defeat outside Chattanooga. As many as 100,000 Confederate soldiers may have undergone a conversion experience at some time during the war.[30] While the highly individualistic nature of southern Protestantism prevented the southern churches from engaging in the type of large-scale, corporate Christian project on which the northern denominations embarked, personal faith in God strengthened the soldiers' attachment to the Confederacy. Southern defeats and growing hardships often cemented that allegiance still further, though normally they were coupled with calls for repentance that closely resembled those of the clergy. 'The father of all will remember his children', Gustave Cooke told his wife while busy harrying Sherman's troops after the surrender of Atlanta:

Whenever we become humble and acknowledge Him our deliverance is nigh. Until we do this and amend our wicked ways we may expect this war to continue and horrors will be added to horrors til the great end is achieved. ... We are a wicked and rebellious people whom he will chastise into submission. But in achieving independence we must not only pray and watch but work. Steady, determined resolution, earnest, untiring labor and unflinching, Spartan bravery can accomplish our independence with Gods blessing.[31]

The most visible symbol of the South's martial Christianity was the Southern Cross (the Confederate battle flag), a reworking of the Cross of St Andrew which was adopted initially by the eastern army at an impressive ceremony in Virginia in the fall of 1861. Thousands of Confederate troops gathered at Centreville to hear the country's adjutant general urge them to drive back the Yankees under its 'untarnished folds ... and find nationality, everlasting immunity from an atrocious despotism, and honor and renown for yourselves – or death.'[32] Rising hatred of the enemy and daily sanctification of the new banner by the blood of patriots soon rendered it a more popular emblem than the derivative Stars and Bars adopted at the start of the conflict. In May 1863 the Confederate Congress responded to military and civilian pressure by officially incorporating the Southern Cross into a new national flag, the so-called 'Stainless Banner'. The proliferation of the battle flag during the course of the Civil War testified to the power of religious symbolism. As Robert E. Bonner has noted, it also underlined the capacity of the Confederacy (from below as well as above) to generate and consolidate a distinctive nationalism under the most straitened conditions.[33]

The death of slavery and the collapse of the Confederacy

One of the many ironies of southern history is that the war to save slavery resulted in the destruction of the peculiar institution. This occurrence was the most dramatic manifestation of the severe stress placed on southern society by the exertion of Federal military pressure. Those historians who have emphasized internal dissension as the main reason for southern defeat may have mistaken consequence for cause, but there is no denying the fact that the war widened existing divisions within local society to the point at which, in the winter of 1864–65, concerns about home were contributing directly to the steady demoralization of troops at the front.

As we have seen, the war exerted great strain on a predominantly agrarian society. Even though the nationalist project was far more successful than some scholars have suggested, it was undermined from the beginning by inherent structural flaws linked directly to the existence of slavery. The latter, as noted above, hindered industrial growth and urbanization. Thus the Confederate war effort was hampered consistently by a lack of essential supplies: not only arms and railroad iron but also, for example, by the absence of a well-developed publishing industry and a lack of paper which made it difficult for elite southern nationalists to communicate with the masses. Class tensions between slaveholders and nonslaveholders, moreover, complicated attempts to define southern whites as a united people, ethnically homogeneous compared with the allegedly 'mongrelized' society of the North. While the Confederate government tried to alleviate some of these tensions by providing centralized relief for the poor and curtailing privileges for the wealthy (especially the deeply unpopular practice of permitting individuals to avoid the draft by providing substitutes), wartime impressment of slaves and foodstuffs, inflation, taxation, and conscription exacerbated political and social friction throughout Secessia. As Yankee pressure increased, first on the geographical peripheries of the South and then on the southern heartland itself, social order in some areas began to break down. Large swathes of Missouri, Tennessee, Virginia, North Carolina, and other states were beset by guerrilla warfare and banditry. Most seriously of all, the peculiar institution itself began to unravel as Federal troops penetrated deep into the Confederacy. By late 1864 northern armies and fleeing slaves had brought the southern nation to the verge of collapse.

Wartime politics reflected the growth of internal divisions inside Dixie. One of President Davis's most serious problems was rampant factionalism. Although the strength of antiparty feeling and the paucity of genuine two-party competition in the antebellum South stifled the development of organized political groupings during wartime, the consensual desire for unity in the face of external aggression did not curb all opposition to the government.

In poor health throughout the war, Jefferson Davis battled against the odds to secure southern independence. No-one could doubt his profound commitment to the cause or his faith in ultimate victory. He was an active, engaged, and aggressive commander-in-chief who accepted the need to fight a defensive war while grasping every opportunity to take the war onto enemy soil. He also understood that he had an important role to play in manufacturing nationalist sentiment and wasted few chances in speeches and proclamations to berate the wickedness of Yankee despotism. As Confederate victories dried up and the hardship of everyday life increased, the president urged his people to make even greater sacrifices. There was, he announced in August 1863, no alternative 'but victory or subjugation, slavery, and the utter ruin of yourselves, your families, and your country'.[34] Like his northern counterpart, Abraham Lincoln, he had his faults. He was a poor administrator, finding it hard to delegate responsibility or make crucial decisions quickly. His failure to halt the debilitating factionalism inside the Army of Tennessee's high command and his lack of interest in financial matters undoubtedly contributed to the South's defeat. For the most part, however, he was popular with ordinary Confederates. His most potent enemies came from the ranks of the country's political elite.

Among Davis's harshest critics was his vice president, Alexander H. Stephens who, bereft of meaningful power, intensified his attacks on conscription and the repeal of habeas corpus as the war progressed. Insistent that the Confederacy stood for nothing if it impinged adversely on the freedoms of individual white men, the embittered patriarch of Liberty Hall launched an outspoken attack on his superior just weeks after passage of the 1864 Conscription Act which drafted all white males between the ages of 17 and 50 and extended the executive branch's power over the labor pool of the South. The president, he contended in an address to the Georgia legislature on March 16, was assuming arbitrary powers that no English parliament would have bestowed on a reigning monarch. Georgians should remonstrate formally against executive usurpation before tyranny and corruption undermined their precious republic completely. Other leading Confederates lacked Stephens's high principles but were similarly critical of Davis. Several of them, like Robert Barnwell Rhett, were original fireeaters who never quite overcame their frustration at being marginalized after the secession crisis. Others, among them the popular Texan Louis T. Wigfall (a close friend of the disgruntled general, Joseph Johnson) and Stephens's fellow Georgian, Robert Toombs (who called Davis a 'stupid, malignant wretch'), were motivated by personal dislike of, as well as ideological opposition to, the president.[35]

Fortunately for Davis, his powerful opponents disagreed among themselves over critical issues. Senator Wigfall was a vociferous supporter of tough war measures in marked contrast to many other opponents of the president who feared the consequences of such actions for southern liberty. Fanatical secessionists like Rhett had little in common with former unionists who wanted the president to seek a negotiated peace. Importantly, moreover, the consensual political culture of the Confederacy prevented any of these potentially dangerous enemies from mobilizing grassroots opposition to the administration. Disillusionment with Confederate policy was certainly intense at various stages of the war (for example, in the spring of 1862 when the Yankee hordes were at the gates of Richmond), but the majority of southern politicians were astute enough to recognize that in a death struggle with the North persistent opposition to the country's legitimate authorities was likely to result in political eclipse. Even though the Confederate Congress became less compliant over time, only in North Carolina did the nucleus of a full-blown anti-administration party evolve.

While government conscription was unpopular throughout the Confederacy, North Carolina differed from most of the other southern states because support for secession had been limited until Lincoln announced his determination to suppress the Rebellion. William W. Holden, an ambitious Raleigh newspaper editor, assumed the leading role in forging a workable coalition between former Whigs and Democrats who had supported a cooperationist stance during the secession crisis. In the state's gubernatorial election of 1862 Holden's Conservative party emerged victorious in the guise of an imposing Confederate colonel, Zebulon B. Vance. But instead of aligning himself with Holden, whose attacks on the Davis administration became increasingly fierce, the new governor maintained his loyalty to the Confederacy while continuing to criticize unpopular measures such as conscription.

Several other southern governors followed suit. In Texas, for example, Pendleton Murrah, widely regarded as the administration candidate in the 1863 gubernatorial race, clashed repeatedly with Confederate authorities over issues such as conscription, impressment, and the regulation of cotton purchases, yet remained a determined supporter of the national cause. With the South in mortal danger, any politician who pressed his criticism of the Davis administration too far ran the risk of being designated a traitor. Even Governor Joseph Brown of Georgia, one of the South's most vigorous defenders of states' rights, was sensitive to charges that he was obstructing the country's war effort and continued to emphasize his commitment to the Confederacy.

Federal military activity raised criticism of the central government to new levels. While this did not result in the replacement of factionalism by organized interparty competition in Congress or the states, it did culminate in attempts during the second half of 1864 by some of Davis's most ardent critics to promote the idea of a negotiated peace through separate state action and/or the holding of an interstate convention that might secure a reconstruction of the Union on a suitably conservative basis. These moves met with little success, in part because Richmond made clear its opposition to peace without independence but also because large numbers of southerners remained committed to the goal of nationhood. In North Carolina the most ardent peace advocate was William Holden. His cause, however, was tainted by his open appeals to the state's disaffected poor as well as his perceived disloyalty to the Confederacy. When he ran for governor against Zebulon Vance in the summer, he lost by a wide margin. Over 77 percent of those participating in the election (including nearly 90 percent of the soldiers who voted) backed Vance and a continuation of the struggle.[36]

The peace movement fared no better further South. More than two months after the fall of Atlanta, Linton Stephens, the vice president's brother and a close ally of Governor Brown, introduced resolutions into the Georgia legislature calling for a ceasefire and a peace settlement on the basis of individual state sovereignty. Commissioners from both sides were to assemble in convention and draw up a peace plan subject to the approval of national and state governments. The measure, which followed President Lincoln's July 1864 offer of peace on the basis of the abolition of slavery and the restoration of the Union, never saw the light of day. Aided by a hostile response from Jefferson Davis and the local press, its opponents easily prevented passage of the resolutions. The Georgia senate went one step further and passed a resolution of its own informing the president of the people's gratitude for his 'able, fearless, and impartial conduct of our Government for the past year' and assuring him that 'our confidence in his wisdom, purity and patriotism is unshaken and without abatement'.[37]

When Davis did allow peace commissioners to meet with Lincoln and Seward at Hampton Roads in early 1865, he did so only on condition, firstly, that they acted as representatives of the national government and, secondly, that they did so on the basis that southern independence was non-negotiable. Lincoln, victorious in the November presidential election and sensing victory in the field, was in no mood to negotiate on these terms. The belated conference ended in predictable failure and the killing continued.

Given the intense suffering caused by the Civil War, what seems most impressive is not the extent of social and political unrest but the relative lack of it. Those who have argued that the Confederacy imploded lay great stress on evidence of popular disorder such as the food riots of 1863 which were sparked off by widespread shortages, high prices, and public antipathy to perceived extortionists. In fact such outbreaks were limited in both intensity and ferocity, and all were dwarfed in scale by the bloody New York draft riots which occurred in the same year. Urban theft and rural banditry increased over time, much to the alarm of the propertied classes. Neither problem, however, was in itself sufficiently serious to endanger the Confederate cause until the closing months of the war, though both sapped morale on the home front and, in conjunction with the arrival of the Yankees themselves, contributed to the rising military desertion rates. By February 1865 only 160,198 out of a total of 355,122 Confederate soldiers were present for duty.[38] Some wealthy southerners actually welcomed the arrival of Federal troops in their community precisely because they expected them to preserve or restore social order in the wake of the Confederacy's collapse. Eventually, even David Schenck, a North Carolina secessionist, was relieved to see the Federals occupy his home town. The neighborhood, he recorded in his diary in the spring of 1865, had been terrorized by armed mobs of deserters and bandits but 'the Yankees put them down where they were', thereby allowing the town's solid citizens to reassert control by arresting the marauders.[39] By this stage Schenck, in common with a number of other disillusioned Confederates, had begun to see the South's mounting social disorder as a result of rampant democracy. If a monarchy was out of the question (and Schenck would have been happy to accept one as the solution to the country's ills) perhaps the all-conquering Yankees would serve almost as well.

In view of the mounting pressure exerted by the Union blockade and troop movements, it is perhaps remarkable that southern white society cohered as strongly as it did. This was testimony not only to the high level of racial unity occasioned by the existence of slavery but also to the strength of incipient Confederate nationalism. By late 1864, however, the southern cause was certainly in desperate trouble. Johnson's western army was in disarray after the defeat at Nashville. Large numbers of troops in the Army of Northern Virginia remained defiant, but Lee was rightly concerned about his inability to staunch the flow of deserters in the ranks and cope adequately with high casualty rates among his highly motivated officer corps. Meanwhile the home front continued to crumble.

It was at this critical stage of their liberation struggle that some Confederates began to consider an unprecedented move. The South could not put enough soldiers into the field. Without more men the dream of independence would be gone inside a matter of months. Therefore what was to be lost by arming the slaves? First injected into public debate in early 1864 by Major General Patrick Cleburne, one of the country's most talented commanders, the controversial proposal found widespread support from leading Confederates during the final winter of the Civil War. This pragmatic *volte face* on the part of those in the vanguard of the fight to found a proslavery republic was a mark of the depths to which the southern cause had sunk. It was also a recognition that the struggle to defy the abolitionist menace had brought the peculiar institution itself to the brink of collapse.

In the early stages of the war, slaveholders had tried to convince themselves that their blacks were loyal and did not pose a threat to the security of the home front while white men were away fighting for kin and country. As long as freedom remained out of their reach, most enslaved blacks did remain outwardly loyal and spent the war working for their owners on farms or, when impressed by the Confederate authorities, on building fortifications. While enslaved blacks made this essential contribution to the southern war effort involuntarily, a tiny minority of them did fire shots in anger for the Confederacy. In the first half of the war especially, favorite slaves were taken as body servants to the front by their masters and some of these were allowed to bear arms. In April 1863 George W. Tillotson, a private in a New York regiment, reported that Union soldiers had captured 'some negro rebel prisoners' while operating in Suffolk County, Virginia.

> One was caught in a tree fireing at our sawmillers, there was a white reb also with him but they killed the white one and captured the black and he ... declared that if he was back there he would fight us just as hard again and also that there was fifteen thousand more out there like him, who was just as stout as he, and they would fight just as well so you can see how much niggers want to fight for their own freedom.[40]

Unfortunately for the southern cause the Confederacy could not rely on its enslaved population to the extent indicated by this unusual Rebel. The Confederate Congress responded to masters' fears about slave unrest by passing legislation designed to guarantee a white male presence on the plantations. Local authorities supplemented these measures (often denounced as class legislation by nonslaveholders) by ensuring that regular patrols continued to sweep the countryside for slaves who had left their place of work without permission from their owner. The upheavals of war, however, progressively weakened the peculiar institution as slaveholding families moved into towns for greater security, as Confederate impressment undermined the complex relationship that bound slaves to masters and, most seriously of all, as the Union army closed in.

From the moment Federal troops first set foot on Confederate soil, slaves ran away to enemy lines. When Confederate authorities in eastern Virginia began to impress able-bodied free blacks and slaves for work on fortifications during the summer of 1861, significant numbers of those targeted made their way to the Union outpost at Fortress Monroe. General Benjamin F. Butler, the local Federal commander, was no abolitionist but he recognized the military import of what was happening. His solution, endorsed by the War Department in Washington, was to define the slaves as confiscated property – as contraband of war – and then employ them in the Union cause. Word soon spread of Butler's policy. By July there were already 900 blacks living at the fort. Although the process of emancipation was constrained initially by Abraham Lincoln's conservative stance on slavery, a growing stream of southern 'contrabands' made their way to Federal lines when they had the opportunity. To a large extent, therefore, congressional legislation supporting military confiscation of slaves and the Emancipation Proclamation (which made a virtue of slave flight in the Confederacy) simply imparted legal substance to a process initiated by blacks themselves. As enemy troops and gunboats pressed ever deeper into Confederate territory, southern slaveholders in the Mississippi Valley and elsewhere found their heavy investments in human property dwindling away. By August 1864 slaveowners in Liberty County, Georgia, reported that they were facing ruin because of 'this now constant drain'. As many as 20,000 slaves worth between 12 and 15 million dollars, they claimed, had run off to join the Yankees, 'to which loss – may be added the insecurity of the property along our borders & the demoralization of the negroes that remain, which increases with the continuance of the evil & may finally result in perfect disorganization and rebellion'.[41] Slaves, in fact, did not rebel *en masse* during the war (an act which would have horrified most Yankees as well as Confederates), but they did persist in undermining the southern cause not only by running away and sometimes inflicting damage on property, but also – and most importantly – by enlisting in the Union armies from the spring of 1863 onward. Edmund Kirby

Smith, commanding Confederate forces in the Trans-Mississippi Department, was one of several officers to highlight the problem posed by the enemy's decision to enlist slaves. 'Our plantations are made his recruiting stations,' wrote Smith eight weeks after the fall of Vicksburg, 'and unless some check can be devised, a strong and powerful force will be formed which will receive large additions as he advances on our territory[.]'[42]

The proposal to arm the slaves grew out of this recognition that slaves would be employed to destroy the Confederacy unless the South belatedly chose to make maximum use of its limited human resources. Many of Davis's noisiest critics, however, were swift to condemn the idea. Louis T. Wigfall, for example, had supported the use of blacks as military laborers but told Congress it was now time to settle the question 'whether this was to be a free negro country or a free white man's country'. Confronted with 'no choice between subjugation and universal emancipation', he would never consent to make 'a Santo Domingo' of the South.[43] 'If slaves will make good soldiers our whole theory of slavery is wrong', said the Georgian, Howell Cobb.[44] Here was the rub. The Confederacy desperately required more soldiers to keep Grant and Sherman at bay, yet Confederate leaders found it difficult to imagine their new nation without slavery. Slavery, in short, was central to the liberty of white republicans. Once it was gone Alexander Stephens's dream of an independent proslavery nation would vanish with it.

The constant loss of white manpower at the front, however, kept the issue on the political agenda throughout the winter of 1864–65. Testing the waters, Jefferson Davis told Congress in November that the government should purchase 40,000 slaves and train them as military laborers with the promise that they would be emancipated after the war. Secretary of State Judah P. Benjamin went one step further in a speech in Richmond on February 9, 1865. He insisted that there was no alternative to arming the slaves and guaranteeing freedom to those conscripted. The critical intervention, however, was probably that of Robert E. Lee. The respected commander was convinced that slavery was doomed and that, with the manpower situation so desperate, it would be better to arm and emancipate slave soldiers than have the enemy use them against the Confederacy. 'I think the measure not only expedient but necessary', he stated in a letter intended for public circulation.[45]

Toward the end of February the Confederate Congress finally bowed to pressure from the government, the military, and the Virginia legislature and passed a bill providing for the conscription of slaves. Even this measure bore the signs of the winter's fierce debate. It limited the president to conscripting not more than a quarter of male slaves aged between 18 and 45 in any state and gave slaveholders and state governments a veto over whether slaves in the armed services could be declared free. Although a subsequent military order did guarantee the freedom of any slaves who fought for the Confederacy, it made no mention of emancipating their families. The move to arm the slaves was thus limited in conception: a product of military necessity, constricted in scope, and intended to control any racial change arising out of the war rather than initiate a new social order. In any event the act had no impact on the outcome of the war. A few companies of blacks working in government installations around Richmond were mustered into the service of the Confederacy, but within days the capital had fallen and Lee's army had surrendered to Union forces.

Many factors led to the demise of the Confederacy. From the outset, owing largely to slavery's impact on industrial growth, the odds were against its survival, for the North possessed crucial advantages in terms of the demographic, technological, and economic resources on which it could draw. If Yankee will was sustained, concerted Union pressure all along the line was likely to tell eventually. So too were deficiencies in Confederate mobilization. Some of these problems were clearly structural. Again because of slavery, the South lacked a mature banking sector and a large urban middle class. Without both of these Richmond was unable to follow the North and finance the war primarily through periodic issues of interest-bearing bonds. Indeed, the abject failure of Confederate monetary policy – by no means entirely the fault of the finance minister, Christopher Memminger – contributed significantly to the deterioration of morale on the home front and in the army. Higher taxation might have alleviated some of the worst effects of galloping inflation which was caused primarily by shortages of essential supplies and an excessive reliance on paper currency. Of course, taxation of any kind was no more popular among ordinary southerners than it was in the North and the country's tax base was limited. Yet there were alternative ways to raise money. Greater efforts might have been made at an earlier stage of the war to export cotton through the northern blockade. Wealthy planters, moreover, could have been required to bear a greater share of the country's financial burden. Their influence, however, was too great at state level to permit any sustained attempt to squeeze the rich.

An obvious disadvantage facing the South was its lack of indigenous raw materials, especially iron which was essential to make repairs to its increasingly ramshackle railway network. Before the war southern train operators had relied heavily on northern and British sources of supply for engines, rolling stock, and track. Largely deprived of those sources after Fort Sumter, the Confederacy was left heavily dependent on local manufacturers. These were never numerous or large enough to meet wartime military demands. Richmond might have acted more energetically to ease the problem. However, Confederate centralization had its limits, and the government made no attempt to impose order and system on the railroads through nationalization or the creation of a public–private body similar to the United States Military Railroads. The relative lack of government activism in the essential sphere of communications also hurt the Confederate war effort. Whereas the United States Military Telegraph, another mixed enterprise, built over 15,000 miles of military telegraph lines in order to connect the War Department in Washington with its armies in the field, Richmond declined to intervene. The South constructed only 500 miles of telegraph line between 1861 and 1865, thereby leaving its generals far more reliant than their opponents on the cavalry for information.[46]

To blame the Confederates for their own defeat, however, is to miss the point. Whatever the rights and wrongs of their cause, white southerners made a strong bid for independence from the United States. Their efforts were hampered by the economically debilitating effects of slavery, by numerous strategic and tactical errors, as well as by rampant factionalism, interstate rivalry, divisions within the ruling elite over the wisdom of centralized government, social tensions, and the progressive destruction of the peculiar institution. But the Rebels fought hard and long for their freedom. Ultimately, only the power and persistence of the enemy brought them to their knees.

Notes

1.   W.C. Corsan, *Two Months in the Confederate States: An Englishman's Travels Through the South* (1863: Baton Rouge, La, 1996), pp.138, 140.

2.   See e.g. Paul D. Escott, *After Secession: Jefferson Davis and the Failure of Confederate Nationalism* (Baton Rouge, La, 1978) and Richard E. Berringer *et al.*, *Why the South Lost the Civil War* (Athens, Ga, 1986).

3.   Gary W. Gallagher, *The Confederate War* (Cambridge, Mass., 1997).

4.   William W. Freehling, *The South vs. The South: How Anti-Confederate Southerners Shaped the Course of the Civil War* (Oxford, 2001), p.61.

5.   Gallagher, *Confederate War*, pp.28–9.

6. *Ibid.*, p.157.

7. The classic statement of this thesis is Frank L. Owsley, *State Rights in the Confederacy* (Chicago, 1925).

8. Quoted in Joseph H. Parks, *Joseph Brown of Georgia* (Baton Rouge, La, 1977), pp.146–7.

9. Edmund Ruffin, *The Political Economy of Slavery or The Institution Considered in Regard to Its Influence on Public Wealth and the General Welfare* (n.p., [1858]), p.15.

10. Drew Gilpin Faust, *The Creation of Confederate Nationalism: Ideology and Identity in the Civil War South* (Baton Rouge, La, 1988), p.7.

11. John L. Wakelyn, ed., *Southern Pamphlets on Secession: November 1860–April 1861* (Chapel Hill, NC, 1996), pp.405–6. (Passage italicized in the original).

12. Harry S. Stout and Charles Grasso, 'Civil War Religion, and Communications: The Case of Richmond' in Randall M. Miller *et al.*, eds, *Religion and the American Civil War* (New York, 1998), p.321.

13. Marinda B. Moore, *The Geographical Reader for the Dixie Children* (Raleigh, NC, 1863), p.10.

14. Quoted in Stout and Grasso, 'Civil War Religion', pp.338–9.

15. Quoted in *ibid.*, p.340.

16. Drew Gilpin Faust, *Mothers of Invention: Women of the Slaveholding South in the American Civil War* (Chapel Hill, NC, 1996), p.24.

17. Mrs A. Ingraham quoted in *ibid.*, p.59.

18. Quoted in Gallagher, *Confederate War*, p.76.

19. Quoted in Lee Ann Whites, *The Civil War as a Crisis in Gender: Augusta, Georgia, 1860–1890* (Athens, Ga, 1995), p.103.

20. Cooke to Lizzie Cooke, Feb. 11, 1862, Gustave Cooke Papers, GLC.

21. Mrs William Mason Smith quoted in Gallagher, *Confederate War*, p.76.

22. Quoted in Daniel W. Stowell, *Rebuilding Zion: The Religious Reconstruction of the South, 1863–1877* (New York, 1998), p.4.

23. Quoted in Stephen W. Sears, *Chancellorsville* (Boston, 1996), p.444.

24. Richard M. McMurry, *Two Great Rebel Armies: An Essay in Confederate Military History* (Chapel Hill, NC, 1989).

25. William Garrett Piston and Richard W. Hatcher III, *Wilson's Creek: The Second Battle of the Civil War and the Men Who Fought It* (Chapel Hill, NC, 2000), p.7.

26. S. Walsh to R.L. Proffit, April 11, 1864, Proffit Family Papers, SHC 3408.

27. [James Oswald] to John G. Scurry, Aug. 2, 1864, John G. Scurry Papers, GLC.

28. Private Smith quoted in Reid Mitchell, *Civil War Soldiers* (New York, 1988), p.174.

29. Edward K. Ward to S.G. Ward, Dec. 8, 1863, Edward K. Ward Papers, GLC.

30. Gardiner H. Shattuck, Jr, *A Shield and Hiding Place: The Religious Life of the Civil War Armies* (Macon, Ga, 1987), p.96.

31. Cooke to Lizzie Cooke, Sept. 16, 1864, GLC.

32. Thomas Jordan, 'Order No.75', 28 Nov. 1861, quoted in Robert E. Bonner, 'Flag Culture and the Consolidation of Confederate Nationalism', *JSH* 68 (2002), 314.

33. *Ibid.*, 322.

34. Quoted in William J. Cooper, Jr, *Jefferson Davis, American* (New York, 2000), p.447.

35. Quoted in *ibid.*, p.444.

36. George C. Rable, *The Confederate Republic: A Revolution Against Politics* (Chapel Hill, NC, 1994), p.270; Cooper, *Davis*, p.477.

37. Quoted in Parks, *Joseph Brown*, p.309.

38. Brian Holden Reid and John White, ' "A Mob of Stragglers and Cowards": Desertion from the Union and Confederate Armies, 1861–65', *Journal of Strategic Studies* 8 (1985), 64.

39. Schenck diary, [April?] 1865, SHC 652.

40. George W. Tillotson to A. Elizabeth Tillotson, April 17, 1863, George W. Tillotson Papers, GLC.

41. Virginia slaveholders to Jefferson Davis, Oct. 13, 1864, in Ira Berlin *et al.*, *Freedom: A Documentary History of Emancipation 1861–1867. Series One, Vol. 1: The Destruction of Slavery* (Cambridge, 1985), p.807.

42. Smith to Sterling Price, Sept. 4, 1863, in *ibid.*, p.772.

43. Quoted in Alvy L. King, *Louis T. Wigfall: Southern Fire-eater* (Baton Rouge, La, 1970), p.207.

44. Quoted in Rable, *Confederate Republic*, p.290.

45. Quoted in Bruce Levine, ' "What Did We Go to War For?": Confederate Emancipation and Its Meaning' in Susan-Mary Grant and Brian Holden Reid, eds, *The American Civil War: Explorations and Reconsiderations* (Harlow, 2000), p.242.

46. Paul A.C. Koistinen, *Beating Ploughshares into Swords: The Political Economy of American Warfare, 1606–1865* (Lawrence, Kan., 1996), pp.232–3.

6

LAST FULL MEASURE OF DEVOTION: THE UNION IN WARTIME

The fact that the North was better equipped than the South to wage a four-year civil war did not mean that its inhabitants would be able to suppress the Rebellion successfully. The pages of history are littered with examples of supposedly weaker peoples defeating economically superior forces – witness, for example, the achievements of the Americans themselves in the eighteenth century and the Italians in the nineteenth, not to mention many of the bitter decolonization struggles of the twentieth. In order to defeat the enemy, northerners had to do two things. Firstly, they had to mobilize their resources effectively. Secondly, they had to go the distance. The United States survived the fiery trial of 1861–65 because a clear majority of northerners (not to mention a sizeable minority of southerners) were ready to undergo enormous privations to deliver the nation from its foes.

To coerce the Rebels back into the Union in the face of prolonged resistance required competent leadership on the part of elites and positive backing for the cause from the great mass of ordinary people. Different individuals and groups, however, often disagreed over what the Union stood for and why the huge sacrifices required to save it were worth making. Just as it did in the Confederacy, the war served some people's aims and thwarted those of others. More importantly, perhaps, it generated new agendas, unanticipated by almost everyone in the 1850s. Resource mobilization combined with the drift toward a hard war policy to foster central-state formation, repression of dissent, and, startlingly, the development of a more inclusive civic nationalism that shook the foundations of the white Republic. If some conservatives were willing to contest the view that the old Union could not be salvaged, rather more northerners made clear their often grudging readiness to accept change as the price of national unity. In that readiness lay the seeds of hope for the black people of America, free and slave.

Multiple agendas

After the humiliating defeat at First Manassas, northerners' initial enthusiasm for suppressing the Rebellion by force soon gave way to a more steely determination to see the job through. The journey from Sumter to Appomattox was a difficult one. Even if Shelby Foote is right to argue that the North fought with one hand tied behind its back, this judgment should not blind us to the very real hardships endured by northerners in the field and on the home front.[1] Three hundred and sixty thousand Union soldiers were dead by the spring of 1865. Another 275,175 had been wounded. War expenditures by federal, state, and local governments ran into billions of dollars at a time when real poverty was a growing menace to large numbers of ordinary Americans. The national debt, normally regarded as a source of dire corruption, stood at a massive $2.8 billion, nearly 50 percent of the country's gross national product.[2] Given such costs and the relative complexity of northern society, it was little wonder that the task of fighting the Confederacy had a profound impact on malleable individual and group identities and on the way northerners related to concrete abstractions like the nation-state.

The vast majority of northerners insisted that the Union had to be preserved. If they had not done so, Lincoln's first call for troops would have been received in relative silence and large numbers of 'War Democrats' would not have agreed to cooperate with the Republicans in contesting secession. Why they determined thus is less easy to assess. Many well-to-do individuals – especially large commercial capitalists in New York City – harbored strong doubts about coercion during the winter of 1860–61, but they generally supported the war once it began because they had a vested economic interest in maintaining the Union. The patriotism of most northerners, however, was rooted primarily in the republican concept of civic duty. The majority of northern men supported the war effort because they believed themselves to be living under the most democratic government the world had ever known. As enfranchised citizens of the American Union, the fount of all their liberties, they held it their duty to protect this government from those slaveholding aristocrats who, they had been assured, were conspiring to destroy the country for their own selfish ends. The thousands of young volunteers who rushed spontaneously to the colors in the spring of 1861 had been reared on nation-building stories of the Revolution. School primers and patriotic orators had underscored the message that the United States was a beacon of freedom and progress. National symbols such as the Constitution and the Star-Spangled Banner were to be revered. Those who sought to tear them up were traitors. Like the Tories of old, disloyal southerners warranted chastisement at the hands of manly patriots acting in the tradition of the minutemen.

To the extent that the Confederates were fighting an ideological war, the same was equally true of the North. Men and women on both sides of the Mason-Dixon Line believed themselves to be struggling for republican liberty against the encroachment of tyranny. But of course northerners were no more and no less idealistic than southerners. They fought or served for reasons of self-interest as well as a strong commitment to the collective good, though the two were often connected. Many European-born soldiers in the Union army enlisted not only because they believed their adopted country was worth fighting for – in many cases the United States had proved a refuge from Old World despotism, prejudice, and poverty – but also because military service paid better than their civilian jobs and seemed likely to hasten their assimilation into American life. This was especially true of the Irish and German soldiers who entered the Union army, either in specifically ethnic regiments such as Michael Corcoran's 69th New York and the 32nd Indiana commanded by the former Prussian army officer, Augustus Willich, or, more commonly, in regiments containing a majority of native-born volunteers. Marcus Spiegel, a Reform Jew who had left Germany with his parents after an upsurge in anti-Semitism in the mid-1840s, was an ambitious colonel in the non-ethnic 67th Ohio. 'I feel as good and as happy as a man can be under the circumstances of being away from those whom he loves dearly', he told his family in March 1862:

My position is respectable and honorable. I have the respect of all who know me, am loved by my Boys and feel as though I had the good wishes of many a friend besides my relatives at home and abroad. The position pays and my chance for promotion with influential Friends here to back me is fair though I will not press it.[3]

In spite of having to retreat with McClellan on the Peninsula, Spiegel was sure 'that we shall come out of the contest victorious, and if anything does happen to me, I am only offering a small sacrifice for my beloved country, which always so generous and kind, has opened her arms to receive the down-trodden of other nations'.[4]

Unlike Spiegel, some of the European-born volunteers enlisted as much to serve the old country as their adopted homeland. Sometimes, for example, the Irish were recruited through explicit appeals to their hatred of the English. A Confederate triumph, recruiting officers averred, would play into the hands of the prosouthern British establishment. Service in the Union army, moreover, would hone the famed fighting skills of the Celts in preparation for the coming liberation of Ireland. When the Irishmen of the 69th New York charged up Henry Hill at First Manassas, one of their officers was heard to shout 'Boys! – look at that flag – remember Ireland and Fontenoy.'[5] While their white skins and Democratic party allegiance had begun the process of assimilation in the antebellum period, European-born volunteers in the North were aware, just as they were in the South, that military service might help to draw the sting of local nativists. That this was not always the case in practice – German regiments in Howard's division, for example, took much of the blame for the Union collapse at Chancellorsville – testified more to the persistence of northern nativism than to the ethnic Americans' lack of fighting ability.

Other groups had their own agendas. Abolitionists who had become increasingly tolerant of violent antislavery methods in the late 1850s generally welcomed the outbreak of war as an opportunity to secure emancipation by force of arms. Even William Lloyd Garrison announced his support for the Lincoln administration, though he struggled to reconcile his pacifism (admittedly on the wane since Harpers Ferry) with his readiness to endorse Federal coercion of the South. Like other abolitionists who previously had been treated as social pariahs for their radical views on human bondage, Garrison soon found that the conflict gave his once unpopular cause an unanticipated legitimacy and greatly expanded the size of the North's antislavery constituency.

Significant numbers of clergymen were swift to link their support for the Union with calls for action against slavery. In a sermon preached a day after the surrender of Fort Sumter, Henry Ward Beecher, one of the North's most prominent ministers, told his Brooklyn congregation that the Union cause was blessed by God. Formerly an advocate of peaceable secession, Beecher, like many other Christian reformers, realized that once the fighting had begun they were no longer under any obligation to favor a moderate approach to the national crisis. 'I hold', said Beecher, 'that it is ten thousand times better to have war than to have slavery.'[6]

During the spring of 1861 Congregationalists and Presbyterians in a number of states voiced similar sentiments. The war, claimed one Congregational gathering in Iowa, was a contest between 'Right' and 'Wrong' which God had permitted in order 'to open the eyes of the Nation and of the world to the inherent wickedness of Slavery; to punish us as a Nation for our collusion with and support of it, and in the end to exterminate it'.[7]

Northern free blacks were sympathetic to such religious readings of the crisis, yet uncertain about what the war meant for themselves. The minority of literate, middle-class blacks debated fiercely how to respond to the dramatic turn of events. Some of them had been willing to support the revival of colonization fever in the 1850s because of the pervasiveness of white racism. However, as astute leaders like Frederick Douglass were aware, the polarization of North–South relations gave blacks the chance to exploit divisions within the ruling race. During the secession crisis Douglass did his utmost to foster coercion sentiment in the North and when war broke out immediately gave fierce rhetorical support to the notion of an antislavery war. The conflict, he told an audience in Rochester, New York, in June 1861, should resemble the 'war in heaven' between the archangel Michael and the dragon. At its close 'not a slave should be left a slave in the returning footprints of the American army gone to put down this slaveholding rebellion'.[8]

Although many blacks shared the belief of some white immigrants that evidence of loyalty to the cause could only redound to their benefit, there were cautionary voices aplenty to be heard in the early months of the war. What, asked one black New Yorker, was the point of rushing to support a government that had never done anything to protect them? 'We of the North must have all rights which white men enjoy; until then we are in no condition to fight under a flag which gives us no protection.'[9] Initially, most of the evidence seemed to support the cynics. President Lincoln's determination to hold the border slave states in line led him to annul Major General John C. Frémont's emancipation edict in Missouri in October 1861. Blacks who volunteered to join the Union army were abruptly turned away on the grounds that black soldiers would dissuade white men from joining up. At the end of the year, notwithstanding congressional legislation to use black 'contrabands' as military labor and the readiness of some Union commanders and ordinary soldiers to interfere with slave property, blacks faced an uphill struggle in their attempts to make the Civil War a war for human freedom.

Efforts by blacks, white abolitionists, and radical Republicans to revolutionize the conflict were anathema to many northerners, especially those attached to the Democratic party. As far as they were concerned the sectional conflict was an unfortunate white man's quarrel, a family dispute that should be settled as quickly as possible with as little damage to the antebellum status quo as possible. Many leading generals in the army adhered to this narrow view of northern war aims, notably General George B. McClellan, the best known War Democrat in the country, whose opposition to extra-legal property seizures and military emancipation reflected the feeling of large numbers of northerners during the first year of hostilities.

Initially, influential moderates and conservatives in the Republican party tolerated such views because Democratic support for the Union cause was essential. It was for this reason that President Lincoln in his first annual address in late 1861 sought to reassure northern Democrats that the conflict should 'not degenerate into a violent and remorseless revolutionary struggle.'[10] The advocates of bipartisan cooperation had numerous critics in both organizations. Many Democrats, particularly those representing border state slaveholders and 'butternut' areas of the lower Midwest settled by disproportionate numbers of southerners, were early critics of Federal coercion and its related evil, centralization (so-called 'consolidation'). Radical antislavery Republicans, on the other hand, feared that attempts to pander to the whim of McClellan and his ilk were bound to result in the demise of the Union. While some of them did acquiesce in moves to form bipartisan Union coalitions, there was no let-up in their calls for tougher military policies.

Not all conservatives were fearful of an alteration in the status quo. A coterie of patrician New Yorkers sensed that the war gave them an ideal opportunity to pursue their antebellum designs of promoting a more ordered and cohesive society in America. Among them were the Reverend Henry W. Bellows, a gifted Unitarian minister; Frederick Law Olmsted, the chief architect of Manhattan's Central Park; and the diarist, George Templeton Strong. Each of these well-connected men was alarmed by the unruly society generated by the growth of industrialism, white male democracy, and the disturbing influx of huge numbers of impoverished foreigners. Correctly perceiving that modern wars could not be fought successfully without a large measure of discipline, structure, and scientific rationalization, their goal was to foster elite participation in a more powerful central state that would be the envy of the Old World. The great problem with America, observed Strong just before the attack on Fort Sumter, was that: 'We have never been a nation, we are only an aggregate of communities, ready to fall apart at the first serious shock & without a centre of vigorous national life to keep us together.'[11] The very act of mobilizing the North's resources seemed sure to promote the growth of an efficiently run unitary republic. Contended Bellows in a sermon preached in early 1861, 'We are not going to war, I trust, to force fifteen states to live under a Government they hate. But we will go to war to save order and civilization, with any faction, conspiracy, rabble, or political party that strives, in illegal and treasonable ways, to break up the Government.'[12]

Northern women were to be the unwitting agents of the New Yorkers' grand design for national uplift. In the spring and early summer of 1861 women's war work helped to equip the first Union volunteers. This massive effort complemented faltering efforts by the individual state governments to fill the vacuum created by the lack of concrete aid from Washington. Northern women were no more expected to bear arms than their southern counterparts but they too were swift to support the national cause. The daughters, wives, and mothers of the American Republic performed numerous patriotic roles in the Civil War – making flags for the local infantry company, sewing bandages, knitting uniforms, serving as hospital visitors, and (here they made a more decisive entrance into the public sphere than their Confederate counterparts) taking up employment as nurses and relatively well-paid government workers.[13] Some of these contributions were undertaken on an organized basis at the community level for the antebellum North had a much stronger tradition of female voluntarism than the Old South. Bellows and his allies saw that by coopting established female relief networks and thereby harnessing what they regarded as women's natural propensity to produce supplies for the Union war effort, they could 'translate provincial charitable efforts into a centralized system of army relief and ... mold organic patriotism into a general devotion to the principles of law, order, and a strong state'.[14]

The New Yorkers' response to what they saw as the chaotic system of supply was to form a private organization, the US Sanitary Commission, designed to bring efficiency to the business of wartime supply at each point of the chain. Special depots were set up to collect goods manufactured in the home by northern women, and well-paid agents were employed to distribute uniforms and other supplies to army field hospitals. Bellows, Olmsted, and Strong occupied the top three positions in the Commission. They hoped that the new organization would instill the right values into the state as well as the people. In June 1861 President Lincoln gave his formal approval to the Commission which proceeded to act as a privately funded adjunct of the War Department, furnishing a welter of advice to government officials (especially those in the Medical Bureau) deemed to be lax in the implementation of modern sanitary methods.

Among the many difficulties confronting the Commission's elite male leaders was the fact that most northern women had somewhat different goals. Their main aim was to help the country's patriotic soldiers in whatever way they could. Even the small band of women's rights activists linked from May 1863 to Elizabeth Cady Stanton and Susan B. Anthony's National Loyal Women's League in New York had little option but to subordinate their desire for suffrage to the immediate aims of winning the war and demolishing slavery. Very few women, regardless of their social status or attitude toward reform, saw their work in the same clinical light as those who headed the Sanitary Commission. The latter's high-handed efforts to muscle in on the traditional female role of local benevolence was bound to create friction, as was the organization's stress on scientific methodology rather than Christian duty. Equally irksome to northern women was the Commission's complacent assumption that their war work was a natural outgrowth of their separate feminine natures. Large numbers of women experienced genuine poverty in the early 1860s and found unpaid war work impossible to do on top of all their other tasks, inside and outside the home. By 1863 there were signs that the Sanitary Commission had begun to alienate the very people on whom it was primarily dependent for supplies. For all its faults, however, the Commission did impart a measure of urgently needed system into the country's ramshackle army medical services. In a war in which bullet wounds caused fearful damage to limbs and vital organs, when antisepsis and antibiotics were unknown, and when most treatments did as much harm to patients as good, this was no small contribution.

Given the multiplicity of different agendas existing at the outset of the American Civil War, it was highly likely that the northern war effort would be beset by serious internal divisions. Two connected developments – the fraught process of military and economic mobilization and the relentless shift toward a hard war policy – produced major social and political friction across the United States. While the North may have been better able than the Confederacy to withstand domestic dissent, this fact should not permit us to underestimate the severity of wartime strife in the Union.

Government initiatives

When Abraham Lincoln called for troops in April 1861 few northerners guessed at the tremendous sacrifices that would be required to crush the Rebellion. At first the people and governments of the individual states took the lead in raising and equipping troops for the country's armed forces. Less than 18,000 strong in peacetime, the army saw its size increase steadily during the war to the point at which, in the spring of 1865, the North had more than 2.2 million men in arms. Governors in the more populous, urbanized, and economically developed northeastern states fared best in their attempts to contribute to the incipient war effort.[15] In addition to possessing a larger pool of manpower than their western peers, energetic executive officers such as Governors John A. Andrew of Massachusetts and Edwin D. Morgan of New York were able to draw on the aid and expertise of wealthy local elites – especially bankers, merchants, and railroad men. In some of the less developed prairie states, local businessmen were unable to provide the level of financial support necessary to meet their allotted troop quotas. As a result the federal government began to take charge of military mobilization in states like Iowa during the early stages of the war.

By the winter of 1861–62 it had become clear that even the more industrialized states were having difficulty meeting the demands of modern warfare. The trend was set. Congress passed a national conscription act in July 1862 and the following spring provided for the creation of enrollment boards in each congressional district. Although the individual states continued to play an important role in the Union war effort throughout the conflict, Washington began to emerge as the dominant partner. Essential tasks such as gathering the huge sums of money necessary to fight the Confederacy, the procurement of military supplies, the transportation of armies, and the implementation of effective supply mechanisms were undertaken by federal officials, often in conjunction with private bodies such as the Sanitary Commission and large commercial banks in New York, Philadelphia, and Boston.

By far the most important of the central government's wartime bureaux was the rapidly expanding War Department run from 1862 onward by Edwin M. Stanton, a machiavellian Ohio politician whose energy, political astuteness, incorruptibility, and ferocious loyalty to the Union made him a significant player in Lincoln's cabinet. Aided by talented colleagues such as Henry Halleck, the president's chief military liaison officer who recognized the significance of modern business techniques for the successful prosecution of an industrial war, and Adjutant General Montgomery Meigs who presided over the vital Quartermaster's Department, Stanton oversaw the enlistment, transfer, and supply of vast numbers of American servicemen over a wide geographical area. One of the most noteworthy results of their efforts was the relative efficiency and abundance with which Federal troops, especially those in the eastern theater, were provisioned. In marked contrast to the Rebels, whose own sources of supply were much more limited than those of the North, Union soldiers in Virginia seldom went without adequate food and clothing. 'Eating is the chief annoyance', reported one hungry Confederate while serving on the Rappahannock front in late 1863: 'The whole country around here is bright with tin cans used by the Yanks for vegetables, condensed milk, lobster, oysters, fruit and everything else.'[16]

The urgent need for more centralized coordination of the war effort combined with suspicion of European-style statism and the strength of private business in the North to ensure that many of the Union's organizational initiatives in the sphere of military mobilization were mixed public–private ones. Although Lincoln asserted government control of American railroads on the grounds of military necessity, he and Stanton agreed not to exercise this control in practice as long as the companies cooperated with Federal officials. The United States Military Railroads, the government agency which coordinated railroad operations under the overall authority of the War Department, employed civilian and military personnel to operate trains, coordinate schedules, and construct (or reconstruct) lines.

With government bureaux also fostering cooperation between private firms and Washington, the relationship between business elites and the central state became progressively close. The Colt, Remington, and Parrott companies, for example, prospered by furnishing large quantities of small arms and artillery to the War Department, while du Pont and other firms worked with the government to develop adequate and effective supplies of gunpowder. In certain areas where the antebellum state had exercised its power, the federal authorities were able to rely on the government's own resources. This was especially true when it came to the manufacture of the rifled musket. Whereas the Confederates were forced to seek foreign supplies of this essential weapon throughout the war, the North ceased doing so in mid-1863, largely owing to massively expanded production at the US Ordnance Department's facility in Springfield, Massachusetts.

While constitutionalism, political pragmatism, and the capitalistic roots of their free-labor ideology imposed limits on central-state activism, most leading figures in the dominant Republican party understood that the Union could not be maintained by a rigid emphasis on antebellum federalism. Ex-Whigs within the organization found it easier to accept the wartime growth of federal power than those who had once belonged to the party of Andrew Jackson. But while former Democrats were often less inclined to contemplate interventionist solutions to the country's ills, many of them soon came to terms with the fact that greater centralization was an essential precondition for national salvation.

The Republican-controlled Congress played a major role in wartime policymaking. In spite of important divisions between easterners and westerners, antislavery radicals and conservatives, rural and urban politicians, and ex-Whigs and Democrats, the Republican party remained remarkably cohesive in the face of its patriotic battle against treasonous slaveholders and the threat from Peace Democrats (or 'Copperheads') at home. The legislative results of this internal unity were unmistakably statist and growth-oriented in complexion. The Morrill Tariff, passed easily in 1861 after the withdrawal of southern congressmen, was a blatantly protectionist measure designed to stimulate the growth of domestic industry. The Republicans' developmental streak was also evident in the party's support for measures designed to promote commercial farming in the West. These included not only homestead and agricultural college acts but also legislation providing 20 million acres of land-grant aid and substantial federal loans to help build a transcontinental railroad – an antebellum project thwarted by sectional divisions over the optimal route to the Pacific. Although the road was to be built primarily by two private companies, the Union Pacific and the Central Pacific, the government was authorized to appoint its own representatives to the board in order to reduce the possibility of corruption. By far the most interventionist action (and no less developmental in its own way), however, was the government's incremental assault on slavery.

The attack on the peculiar institution grew directly out of demands within the Republican party and the North at large for a much harsher policy toward the South. Those demands were a product of public frustration with the failure to defeat the Rebels as rapidly as expected. As the Union body count rose, growing numbers of politicians and ordinary citizens began to ask why slavery, the mainstay of the Confederacy, should remain immune to government action. The very real sacrifices demanded of civilians and soldiers alike seemed to require that the property rights of disloyal slaveholders should cease to act as a drag on Federal policy.

During late 1861 and 1862, abolitionists began to sense for the first time that the tide was beginning to turn in their favor. A majority of northerners appeared ready to set aside their racial prejudices and commitment to constitutional proprieties and at last accept the necessity of emancipation. This radicalizing trend was enhanced by a discernible intensification of religious faith at home and in the army. Bloodshed on an industrial scale in pursuit of national goals stimulated calls for a holy war against the southern traitors. The northern clergy played a central role in this development, insisting that God would hardly grant the people's prayers for victory unless they purged themselves and their country of sin. Greatest among those transgressions, they urged, was a toleration of slavery. 'If by our reverses we shall be made willing to be corrected as Israel was, then shall we yet be victorious over all our enemies', contended one representative minister seeking to find meaning in the unexpected reversal at Second Manassas.[17] Act decisively against slavery and God would surely smite His people's enemies as He did the idolators of the Old Testament.

With President Lincoln convinced that interference with slavery would obstruct his efforts to keep Kentucky and the other border states in the Union, congressional Republicans took the lead in responding to perceived military exigencies and the slaves' evident determination to reach Union lines. Shortly after the debacle at First Manassas they passed the First Confiscation Act. This statute declared that any property (including slaves) used to aid the Confederate war effort could be confiscated and used by the military as General Butler was in the process of doing at Fortress Monroe. Lincoln's repeal of Frémont's extremely popular emancipation edict, however, highlighted the differences between the two branches of government on this issue during the first year of the conflict. It did little to convince Republicans that the administration was ready to fight fire with fire and was widely condemned within the party. In December Congress set up its own Joint Committee on the Conduct of the War to press the administration into a more vigorous suppression of the Rebellion.

During the first half of 1862 military victories brought increasing amounts of southern territory under Union control. The need to determine the legal status of slavery in these areas became more imperative by the day as thousands of ragged 'contrabands' – men, women, and children – made their way toward Federal positions. In May Major General David Hunter, commanding a Union beachhead on the Carolina coast, made another attempt to emancipate the slaves via military edict but his order met the same fate as Frémont's. Republican lawmakers, however, were in no mood to be quiescent. During the spring of 1862 they began in earnest the task of demolishing the old slaveholding Republic. As well as prohibiting Union commanders from returning fugitive slaves to their owners, they provided for emancipation in the District of Columbia and the western territories – areas over which the federal government had relatively clear legal jurisdiction. In July they passed the Second Confiscation Act, a controversial statute that declared all persons engaged in rebellion against the United States liable to fine, imprisonment, and the emancipation of their human property. Confederate officeholders were to have all their real and personal property confiscated immediately and all other Rebels would suffer the same penalty if they continued to support the enemy within 60 days. The president came close to vetoing the measure but signed it in part because forfeitures were not to extend beyond the life of individual offenders.

Notwithstanding his doubts about the merits of the Confiscation Act, Abraham Lincoln had already decided to act decisively against slavery by the summer of 1862. A long-time opponent of the institution, the president had suppressed his personal feelings in order to maintain the loyalty of northern and border slave state conservatives. As he put in a public letter to Horace Greeley on August 22, 1862, his 'paramount object' was to save the Union: 'If I could save the Union without freeing *any* slave I would do it, and if I could save it by freeing *all* the slaves I would do it; and if I could save it by freeing some and leaving others alone I would also do that.'[18] By the time he composed this document, however, he had already decided that the time was ripe for decisive action against the cornerstone of the Confederacy. The military situation demanded it. A clear majority of Republicans and some War Democrats favored it. International opinion was likely to welcome it. As for the border slave states, they were now secure and their resident shareholders remained impervious to Lincoln's strenuous attempts to encourage compensated emancipation linked to voluntary colonization of the freed slaves.

On July 13, four days before passage of the Second Confiscation Act, Lincoln attended the funeral of Edwin Stanton's infant son. Riding back to the White House, he told Secretary of State William Seward and Secretary of the Navy Gideon Welles that he had concluded 'that we must free the slaves or be ourselves subdued'. The country, he thought, 'was prepared for it' and he was satisfied that the war powers of the president provided sufficient legal justification to carry out the measure.[19] When the full cabinet discussed Lincoln's scheme on July 21 it met strong opposition from conservatives Montgomery Blair and Caleb Smith. While the president was determined to go ahead with his plan, he did accept Seward's cautionary advice. The secretary of state argued that with the military situation so gloomy any emancipation proclamation would be dismissed as an act of desperation. Wait, he said, for a military victory in order to obviate this criticism. McClellan's strategic victory at Antietam provided the administration with what it had been waiting for. On September 22 Lincoln issued his preliminary Emancipation Proclamation which promised to declare (on January 1) 'forever free' all slaves in Rebel-held territory unless southern whites resumed their allegiance to the Union.[20] The official Proclamation signed on New Year's Day did more than simply signal the destruction of slavery in the Confederacy. It omitted the proposals for compensation and colonization contained in the preliminary draft and instead authorized Union commanders to enlist black men into the armed forces of the United States. As the Civil War entered a third year, a potent combination of black agency and federal action had brought slavery to the verge of extinction.

Abolition proved to be an untidy process. From May 1863 the War Department's Bureau of Colored Troops played a leading role in the systematic military recruitment of free blacks and slaves, its efforts aided by black leaders like Frederick Douglass and antislavery Republicans such as Governor John A. Andrew of Massachusetts. The Union army now became an army of liberation, attracting thousands of sable recruits and freeing numerous slaves as it moved through the Confederate South. In the border slave states and Union-occupied portions of the Confederacy such as Tennessee the peculiar institution began to wither away as the army offered sanctuary and employment to most fugitives regardless of their owner's allegiance to the Union. Blacks who were unwilling or unable to fight were put to work for wages on abandoned plantations administered or leased by the Treasury Department or housed in large government-supervised contraband camps located around the South. Conditions in the camps were poor, prompting the federal government to announce its interest in the transition from slavery to freedom. In March 1863 Secretary Stanton charged three respected abolitionists (designated the American Freedmen's Inquiry Commission) to investigate the refugee problem and recommend suitable action. After taking testimony from blacks and whites, the commissioners proposed that a Bureau of Emancipation should be set up to exercise federal guardianship of the former slaves. While they suggested that this agency should not be 'a permanent institution', the recommendation was a clear reflection of the war's centralizing tendencies.[21]

In common with the other wartime statist initiatives, the AFIC's proposal for a temporary Emancipation Bureau was entirely consistent with the Republicans' northern vision of America's national destiny. This vision had proved to be a compelling one for a majority of northern voters in 1860 and it came as no surprise that once in power the party attempted to give it concrete form. The Republican blueprint was rooted in free-labor ideology and drew strength from the party's consistent use of the South as a primary source of oppositional identity. That is to say, the Republicans looked ahead to a future in which the society and economy of the United States would be structured wholly along the lines of the North's free-labor system – meritocratic, incentivizing, and productive in contrast to the allegedly barbarous and enervating peculiar institution which enabled southern slaveholders to warp the fabric of the entire nation.

Although the Republicans worked from a discernibly Whiggish agenda, a large proportion of the landmark legislation of the Civil War era was as much pragmatic in nature as it was ideological in conviction. This was true not only in the case of emancipation policy but also, arguably even more so, in that of fiscal policy. From late 1861 senior Republican senators and congressmen worked with Secretary of the Treasury Salmon P. Chase and powerful private bankers in New York City to create a national banking system and a national currency to replace the country's ramshackle antebellum financial structure. Congress also passed a number of other related measures designed to help finance a ruinously expensive war – most notably, perhaps, the United States' first graduated income tax.

Many Republicans, especially those from eastern states with stable banking systems, were unsympathetic to the idea of national banks, yet came to support the reform because of intensive lobbying from westerners and the pressing need to cement ties between financial elites and the government. Because the war was financed primarily through the sale of long-term government bonds bearing interest payable in gold and the printing of a national paper currency ('greenbacks') linked directly to these bonds, both the US Treasury and Congress came to see the creation of a guaranteed market for federal securities (in other words a reliable depository for a large portion of the national debt) as an essential precondition for economic mobilization.

The ad hoc nature of government policy was highlighted by Chase's decision in 1862 to employ a Philadelphia banker, Jay Cooke, as an agent to sell a major tranche of government bonds. Although the decision to allow Cooke a fixed share of the profits proved controversial, Chase's hand was forced by the commercial banks' suspension of specie payments and the mounting day-to-day costs of fighting the Confederacy. Fortunately for Chase and the Union, Cooke was an accomplished salesman. He set up an efficient marketing network which employed hundreds of local agents, mostly bankers themselves, working on commission throughout the northern states. He advertised widely in the secular and religious press, combining appeals to national patriotism and individual self-interest. He also supplied gifts to agents and editors, opened up offices at night to sell bonds to working people, and pressed clergymen to support the sales campaign in their sermons. These innovative techniques enabled Chase to dispose of the majority of the bonds within a matter of months. While the largest portion went to wealthy northerners, less well-to-do citizens bought their fair share of the issues and in so doing made their own contribution to the Union war effort. By purchasing government bonds (and spending the new greenbacks) ordinary Americans could feel yet another tangible link to the national government.[22]

The administration's heavy reliance on bond sales to finance the war solidified the kind of close relationship between the national government and the country's financial elites that Alexander Hamilton had regarded as an essential building block of nation building in the late eighteenth century. This relationship, widely regarded by Jacksonian and Civil War-era Democrats as insidious, was less a result of some deep Republican design to augment the power of the central state than an inevitable product of economic mobilization. Even in those cases where ideology may have constituted the principal dynamic for government action, passage of critical measures was generally aided by the extraordinary political context that the war provided.

Dissent and democracy

The logical result of a war to save American democracy from the destabilizing actions of a treacherous minority was an increase in popular support for the idea of a stronger national government – indeed, for the very notion of government itself. To a large extent the ferocity of the war played into the hands of those patrician conservatives who had founded the US Sanitary Commission. Disciplined action, efficient mobilization of resources, and greater intrusion of the central state into the lives of ordinary people were all regarded by such elites as positive outcomes of the war. While such developments were accepted by large numbers of ordinary people too, a substantial minority of northern citizens proved to be much less enthusiastic. As the war began to bite, internal dissent swelled dramatically across the northern states. By the summer of 1864 Lincoln was facing electoral defeat and Peace Democrats were anticipating a negotiated settlement with the Confederacy.

If the nature and scale of domestic dissent varied over time and place, its fundamental cause was war-born centralization. Like their patriot forebears, most antebellum northerners had learned to be suspicious of central power. 'Consolidation' was the curse of the Old World, the spawn of monarchy, and the midwife of oppression. When the Civil War yielded such expediencies as increased taxation, conscription, and the impairment of loyal slaveholders' property rights, it therefore touched upon some raw nerves, particularly those of many Democrats who had been conditioned to equate Republicanism with such bugbears as old-style Federalism, upper-class Whiggery, and intrusive Yankee moralizing. These demons took on threatening dimensions when set against a background of declining real wages for many industrial workers, mounting bloodshed and stalemate on the battlefield, and faltering attempts to elevate black men to equal citizenship. Opposition to the Lincoln administration and its abolition war emerged as a major factor in northern politics from 1862 onwards, eliciting ill-advised Republican attempts to crack down on alleged traitors. Government repression, limited though it was, simply heightened fears among northern Democrats that fundamental American liberties were under threat.

Evidence of substantial grassroots disaffection with the administration manifested itself in the midterm elections of 1862 when the Democrats capitalized on Lincoln's decision to issue the preliminary Emancipation Proclamation. Initial opposition to the measure was often intense. On the home front many working-class whites responded positively to Democratic claims that they were about to lose their jobs to the masses of freed slaves who allegedly would flood into the North. In the army many soldiers, particularly native-born Democrats and European immigrants, were disgusted by the dramatic shift in government policy. In Wisconsin a number of German and Irish militia companies disbanded in order to avoid fighting for emancipation. One southern Illinois regiment mutinied over the issue. The sense of betrayal was palpable in the blunt comment of one New England soldier that he did not

> want to se enney more fighting dun for the nigger ... I do not want to se enny more young men deceived in this war buy Crokers and officeceekers triing to make young men believe that they are fighting for the union it is as false as hell, it is bull nigger that they are a fighting for, the northern fanaticks do not care a dam for the union or contry if they can best carrey the day and have a shee nigger in, if they had kept that word nigger out of Congress this rebellion would have been settled much sooner.[23]

The Democrats' performance in the 1862 campaign was their best in the North since the turbulent realignment of the mid-1850s. Benefiting from the depressing military situation, popular racism, and fears of creeping despotism occasioned by the administration's decision to countenance the arbitrary arrest of its critics, they gained 35 congressional seats from the Republicans, won statewide races in Illinois, Pennsylvania, and Indiana, and elected their gubernatorial candidates in New Jersey and New York. Some chastened Republicans, Horace Greeley included, began to fear that the Proclamation had been a step too far and that a government which he had chided so recently for being too conservative on the slavery question was now in danger of outpacing the voters.

Lincoln's political instincts proved superior to those of the notoriously inconsistent *Tribune* editor. Union troops were highly literate and heavily politicized. They were already learning from their own experiences that the administration was right: that the Confederacy could not be defeated on the battlefield alone, that the will of the southern people to go on fighting had to be snuffed out. While few northern soldiers were abolitionists by choice, a clear majority of them were willing, by mid-1863, to accept Lincoln's argument that emancipation would strike at the heart of the Rebellion. Some changed their minds because of the assistance they received from slaves while campaigning in the South. Others were genuinely convinced by the arguments of Protestant ministers that emancipation would put their suffering country right with God. But the majority of the North's fighting men were converted to antislavery by the simple realization that it was one more weapon in the fight to maintain the Union. Conditioned in part by the popular minstrel shows of the antebellum period, white soldiers generally regarded ragged southern blacks as figures of amusement, members of a childlike servant class incapable of rising to the heights attained by the white race. (Some blacks in fact were employed as servants by Federal officers.) But by the spring of 1863 most Yankee soldiers had reached the conclusion that southern blacks had one great advantage over their white masters: they were loyal to the Union. What better way to avenge oneself against a determined foe than by undermining the institution on which its precious freedoms were based? As one sharp observer in Grant's western army put it in September 1863:

> The soldiers believe in putting down the Rebellion and they
> argue everything from the Anti-Slavery stand point, not because
> they have any feeling on the moral question of slavery but
> because they think it a good joke on the Rebels to strike
> them through the Institution they cherish most.[24]

The prevalence of such reasoning combined with the determination of the ordinary citizen-soldier (and civilian) to get the job done explain why the government felt confident enough to start arming black troops from the spring of 1863. Those who found the idea of black men carrying guns either ridiculous or alarming could at least find comfort in the presumption that the new recruits would reduce the numbers of white men killed by Rebels.

The discernible radicalization of public opinion, perhaps an inevitable result of the fact that the Civil War was a people's war fought primarily by volunteers rather than conscripts, was not accompanied by any decrease in the ferocity of the antiwar opposition. Just as conscription and impressment increased dissent in the Confederacy during 1863, so did federal interference in everyday life provoke simultaneous disquiet in the United States.

Few northern communities were unaffected by the deepening polarization of local politics. More closures of Democratic newspapers, more attempts by the military to silence critics of the war (most infamously General Burnside's imprisonment of the Ohio Copperhead, Clement L. Vallandigham, in May 1863), and vigorous attempts to enforce a new national conscription act produced violent disturbances across the country. Although the worst of these incidents occurred in the great urban centers of the North, small-town

America was also affected. In Kingston, Ohio, James M. Maitland, a prominent Democratic leader and committed unionist, watched with alarm as the Republicans tarred their critics with the brush of disunion. 'My own opinion now', he reported shortly before the battle of Gettysburg, 'is that we have more to fear from a Military despotism than from the army of Jeff Davis. We certainly are bordering on [it] as fast as ever a nation did: it is becoming now unsafe in many places for people to speak their sentiments in regard to the manner in which our affairs are conducted.'[25]

A few days later Maitland attended the annual Independence Day celebrations in Urbana where he was relieved to see a heavy shower of rain disrupt proceedings just as the main speaker was 'amplifying on the negro and beginning to get into the merits of the sable man'.[26] As elections beckoned, political excitement in the area increased. In the second week of August one of Maitland's neighbors was run out of town for voicing support for Vallandigham. Another Democrat opened fire when 'rioters' threw missiles at his buggy. To make matters worse a man rumored to be a Methodist preacher then arrived in town to abuse the government's opponents as traitors. When a Democrat told the minister to preach religion, not politics, several members of the congregation 'arose to their feet and denounced him as Butternut and Copperhead &c. and were for putting him out of the House'. Had they tried, added Maitland, 'there would have been some bruised noses and faces ... .'[27]

In New York City the violence was on a completely different scale. In July 1863, in three days of the worst rioting ever seen in the United States, laboring men and women (the majority of them hard-pressed Irish Americans from the teeming tenements of lower Manhattan) rampaged through the streets in a frightening display of popular fury sparked by official attempts to enforce the draft. Targeting any symbols of elite Republican power, the mob attacked policemen and soldiers, vandalized the property of the rich, sought in vain to destroy the hated *Times* and *Tribune* buildings on Newspaper Row, and, most disturbingly of all, embarked on the indiscriminate lynching of blacks. Order was only restored when Federal troops, freed from the battlefront by the close of the Gettysburg campaign, arrived in force to subdue the rioters. Official figures put the death toll at 119 but contemporaries estimated that as many as a thousand people might have been killed overall.[28] Draft riots occurred in several other areas, notably in western Pennsylvania where Irish coalminers were at the forefront of draft resistance and in Chicago's heavily immigrant third ward.

These outbreaks of unrest revealed the extent to which wartime dissent was rooted in cultural difference and social inequality. Some Irish-born working people, in particular, sensed that their precarious American identity, closely linked to their color in the mid-nineteenth century, was being eroded by capitalist elites seemingly more attentive to the needs of their pet blacks than those of independent-minded white republicans. The inclusion of a substitution clause in the 1863 Conscription Act (allowing individuals to escape the draft on payment of a 'commutation fee' of $300) merely confirmed their suspicions that this was a rich man's war in which they were mere pawns of an uncaring establishment.

The depth of social divisions in the North, however, should not be exaggerated. The strains of war challenged but ultimately failed to overcome the desire of most northerners to see the war through to a successful conclusion, even during the dark months of late 1863 and the first half of 1864. On the Union home front this long period of military stalemate after the victories at Gettysburg and Chattanooga was characterized by draft evasion, labour unrest, and, perhaps most damagingly of all, apathy. Disillusionment with the administration was so pervasive that many Democrats and Republicans believed that Lincoln could not be reelected in November 1864.

Notwithstanding the elusiveness of a decisive military victory, Father Abraham remained popular with many northerners. The growing furrows etched across his expressive face testified not only to the enormous burdens of high office at a time of national crisis but also to the fact that the Union commander-in-chief was not aloof from the suffering of ordinary citizens. A humane man who understood the power of personal and collective grief as much as any American, Lincoln groped Job-like to find a meaning for the nation's trials, using as his guide a deepening conviction that there was a Divine purpose in the war, a purpose unknowable to ordinary mortals. As the fiercesome bloodletting continued, the president began to use his speeches to articulate the many reasons why the Union had to survive.

In November 1863 Lincoln accepted an invitation to speak at the opening ceremony of one of the new national military cemeteries at Gettysburg. Responsibility for the country's fallen heroes was one more example of the federal government's increasing influence, and the president was determined to use this opportunity to locate meaning in the midst of widespread suffering. Although contemporaries were slow to grasp his achievement, he accomplished everything he set out to do. The Union dead were central to Lincoln's conception of the nation's future purpose, their blood a sacrifice to the goal of a more inclusive polity. 'Four score and seven years ago', he began,

> our fathers brought forth on this continent, a new nation, conceived in Liberty, and dedicated to the proposition that all men are created equal.

> Now we are engaged in a great civil war, testing whether that nation, or any nation so conceived and so dedicated, can long endure.

It was entirely right, said the president, that Americans should gather to honor those who had given their lives on the battlefield. 'But, in a larger sense', he continued,

> we can not dedicate – we can not consecrate – we can not hallow – this ground. The brave men, living and dead, who struggled here, have consecrated it, far above our poor power to add or detract. The world will little note, nor long remember what we say here, but it can never forget what they did here. It is for us the living, rather, to be dedicated here to the unfinished work which they who fought here have thus far so nobly advanced. It is rather for us to be here dedicated to the great task remaining before us – that from these honored dead we take increased devotion to that cause for which they gave the last full measure of devotion – that we here highly resolve that these dead shall not have died in vain – that this nation, under God, shall have a new birth of freedom – and that government of the people, by the people, for the people, shall not perish from the earth.[29]

Lincoln's eloquent attempts – in his Gettysburg Address and in other orations – to ennoble the Union cause by making a civil religion of democracy struck a chord with thousands of northerners desperate to learn that their loved ones had not died in vain and that their own civic efforts were not without transcendent purpose.

In his ability to communicate directly with a broad constituency and to sacralize a brutal civil war, the president far surpassed any of his rivals within the dominant Republican organization. His inability to crush the Rebellion, however, made him vulnerable to political attack. Although he saw off the egotistical Salmon Chase before securing the Republican nomination at Baltimore in early June 1864, he remained less popular within the upper reaches of the Republican party than he did in the country at large. Among the key issues dividing Lincoln from many congressional Republicans was what to do with those areas of the South occupied by Union troops.

Restoring the Union: Phase one

Reconstruction – the process of restoring Rebel states to their proper relationship within the Union – began as early as 1861.[30] As commander-in-chief Lincoln assumed the primary responsibility for the endeavor, fostering unionism in the occupied South as part of his broader goal of winning the war as quickly as possible. Inclined to exaggerate the strength of southern unionism, he welcomed efforts by ostensibly loyal men in Union-occupied parts of the Confederacy to set up rival governments to the secessionists. He was quick to recognize the so-called 'Restored Government' of Virginia formed at Wheeling in June 1861 and applauded Congress's decision to admit its representatives the following month. When Union forces began to penetrate the upper South and Louisiana, he appointed lieutenants to oversee the process of restoration. After Buell took Nashville in March 1862 the president appointed Andrew Johnson, a staunchly loyal War Democrat, to the position of military governor. In North Carolina, where the Federals had established beachheads on the coast, the post went to Edward Stanly, a former Whig who had left the state for California. And in the wake of Farragut's stunning success at New Orleans, Lincoln appointed George Shepley, a Union officer from Maine, as provisional governor of Louisiana.

Friction arose between the White House and congressional Republicans for several reasons. In part the issue was control. As early as July 1861 some Republicans opined that the legislature and not the executive should have principal oversight of the restoration process. Differing constitutional views provided a second source of tension. Lincoln believed that the Rebellion was the work of individuals, not states. As soon as southern unionists were able to reassert themselves they should be allowed to set up new loyal governments and apply to have their delegates readmitted to Congress. Debates in Washington during the spring of 1862 revealed that many Republicans saw matters in a different light. The desire to suppress the Rebellion as forcibly as possible led some senators and congressmen to assert that the southern states had surrendered their rights by seceding from the Union. This meant that they could be reduced to the dependent status of territories and subjected to an undetermined period of military rule. 'The United States', contended Fernando Beaman of Michigan,

> is a nationality, a sovereign Power, with vast territorial possessions ... over which it is entitled to governmental jurisdiction, from which allegiance is due, and to which it owes the obligations of protection and a just administration of law ... It is manifest that the Federal government has sovereign power over all parts of its possessions.[31]

Although legal notions such as state suicide and territorialization won backing from all sides of the Republican party, they found the strongest support from antislavery radicals like James S. Ashley and Owen Lovejoy of Ohio. Both of these congressmen had opposed the conservative Crittenden Resolution of July 1861 which (designed to appeal to the border slave states after the debacle at First Manassas) had declared that the war was not being pursued 'for any purpose of conquest or subjugation, or purpose of overthrowing or interfering with the rights or established institutions of those [Rebel] states'.[32] Although the resolution had passed, a majority of Republicans in Washington agreed by mid-1862 that slavery was the fount of the Rebellion and must be destroyed. Radicals saw territorialization as the ideal means to accomplish this end. For them the abolition of slavery was just one element in a much larger national project: the complete overthrow of the South's political and social structure. Central to their ambitions would be the citizenship rights of the slaves.

No break occurred between Lincoln and his party in 1862. The president's acceptance of the need for military rule and his pro- posals for compensated emancipation ensured continued cooperation between the executive and the legislature. Tensions were evident when Governor Stanly of North Carolina closed a school for black children in New Bern and allowed persons taking an oath of loyalty to the Union to regain possession of their slaves. The Emancipation Proclamation, however (which took Stanly by complete surprise), consolidated party unity. As long as Lincoln evinced a desire to act decisively against the peculiar institution, his copartisans in Washington seemed ready to soft-pedal on their controversial calls for territorialization. But one result of the Emancipation Proclama- tion was to focus attention on those partially occupied states ex- empted from its provisions. In 1864 Louisiana emerged as the main flashpoint for Republican differences over restoration, slavery, and the civil rights of southern blacks. One of the main figures in this development was Lincoln's most radical cabinet member, Salmon P. Chase.

A churchgoing Episcopalian and committed abolitionist, Chase had subordinated the fight against racial prejudice to the broader struggle against the Slave Power. Many contemporaries regarded him as an arrogant figure driven by an overweening ambition for the highest political office. No matter how just the charge, the powerful Secretary of the Treasury possessed a genuine hatred of slavery and a prescient awareness that the fate of American blacks was closely bound up with that of the Republic.

In common with most radicals, Salmon Chase struggled not only with his own racial prejudices but also with the white supremacist assumptions of most northern voters. However, wartime events convinced him that slavery, the engine of the Rebellion, had to be destroyed; that blacks were morally entitled to equal rights under the law; and, crucially, that because slaves were the only substantial loyal population in the South, liberated blacks ought to be enfranchised in order to counter the baleful influence of their former masters. By August 1862 Chase was arguing in cabinet that loyal blacks in the border slave states might be allowed to vote. For him, proven devotion to the Union – not race or color – should be the principal qualification for manhood suffrage. In the same month, sensing that black suffrage held the key to Reconstruction and that male citizenship was closely linked in the public mind to the ballot, he took the first major step toward achieving his aims by soliciting an opinion from US Attorney General Edward Bates on the question of whether black men were American citizens. Pronouncing the *Dred Scott* decision 'dehors the record', Bates ruled decisively that all free persons born in the United States were citizens of the United States.[33]

At a time when only a handful of abolitionists like the black leader, Frederick Douglass, were calling for black suffrage as a concomitant to service in the Union army, Chase was ahead of the game. Seeking to build on Bates's opinion, he took every opportunity during 1863 to disseminate his belief that blacks were fellow human beings worthy of respect. Rightly conscious of the way in which language was used to dehumanize the mass of black slaves encountered by the Union armies, he insisted that federal officials abandon the popular label of 'contraband' in favour of 'freedmen, Afric-Americans, blacks, negroes, [or] colored citizens'.[34] More significant, perhaps, were his efforts to speed the transition from slave labor to free labor and to enshrine black suffrage as a central feature of government Reconstruction policy in the troubled state of Louisiana.

Wartime taxation and confiscation placed Chase's Treasury Department in control of vast amounts of land in the occupied South. Although most of this land fell into the hands of speculators, many of them northerners eager to make money out of cotton cultivation, Chase encouraged philanthropic attempts by a group of New England capitalists to put blacks to work on eleven plantations in the occupied Port Royal district of South Carolina. Although the businessmen wanted a profit from their investment, one of their central aims was to show the country that blacks would work for wages and without coercion. The experiment was not an unalloyed success (the 'freedmen' seemed keener to work their own land than labor for money), but the profits were large enough to undermine white assumptions about the innate laziness of blacks.

The Port Royal experiment was far from typical. In late January 1863 Major General Nathaniel P. Banks, the Federal commander in the Gulf theater who did not share Chase's optimism about blacks' capacity to work without supervision, laid the foundations for a controversial labor system designed to keep Louisiana's slaves toiling on the sugar plantations. Slave-born blacks who did not enlist in the Union army were required to perform paid work in the fields at wage rates determined by the government. While the new system attracted criticism from radicals for allegedly bolstering a status quo based on coercion, President Lincoln deemed it an acceptable form of apprenticeship and pressed on with his own policy of restoration. Wary of imposed solutions and desirous of encouraging self-reconstruction by southern whites, Lincoln told Banks in August 1863 to make haste in creating a free-state government in New Orleans. While he expressed a desire that local blacks should be liberated and educated by the new regime, the president's missive made no mention of black suffrage – at this stage a nonissue as far as most northerners were concerned.

White Louisiana unionists did not share Chase's determination to make equal rights the cornerstone of federal Reconstruction policy, but his commitment to franchise extension gelled neatly with the vociferous demand of local free blacks for the vote. Uniquely (because of its former status as a French and Spanish port in the eighteenth century), New Orleans possessed a population of around 11,000 free blacks. These were mainly wealthy mixed-race 'mulattos' who had smartly transferred their allegiance from the Confederacy to the United States after the city fell into Federal hands in April 1862. When preparations finally began in late 1863 for the election of delegates to a new constitutional convention, the *gens de couleur* agreed to petition the local military commander for the vote and, if unsuccessful, to take their case to Washington. Shortly afterwards Chase wrote to the president of the Free State Committee in New Orleans, Thomas J. Durant, making known his wish that 'colored citizens' should be registered to vote in the forthcoming elections. This policy, he said, was in line with the attorney general's opinion on black citizenship and was required on the grounds of justice and the security of the Union.[35]

In spite of being a former slaveholder, Durant understood the political advantages of acting in conformity with a powerful patron in Washington and ingratiating himself with the assertive creole population of New Orleans. Consequently, when he responded to Chase on December 4, he said that he favoured enfranchising free-born blacks as 'an act well founded in justice'.[36]

As Durant's letter made its way to Washington President Lincoln delivered a Proclamation of Amnesty and Reconstruction designed not only to speed up restoration and emancipation in the occupied South but also to secure executive control over these interconnected processes. Whenever 10 percent of southern whites in a Rebel state had taken an oath of future loyalty to the Union, they were invited to form a free state government that would abolish slavery and send delegates to Congress. In spite of the fact that Lincoln made no provision for black rights beyond liberation, congressional Republicans initially found little to criticize in the document. Yet signs of future discord could be discerned. The abolitionist Wendell Phillips denounced the Proclamation on the grounds that it 'frees the slave and ignores the negro'.[37] In the House of Representatives Chase's radical ally, James Ashley, introduced a Reconstruction bill incorporating the president's Ten Percent plan but ordering the enrollment of all loyal adult male citizens in elections to the conventions that would draw up new constitutions for the reconstructed states.

Chase himself redoubled his efforts to enshrine black suffrage as an integral element of Reconstruction. He used Durant's involuntary support for franchise extension to elicit what appears to have been the first endorsement of this policy from the White House. As Chase explained events to Durant at the end of 1863, the secretary told the president of Durant's views whereupon he (Lincoln) 'said he could see no objection to the registering of such citizens [the *gens de couleur*], or to their exercise of the right of suffrage'.[38] This was clever work on Chase's part – prodding one of the South's leading unionists to endorse at least limited suffrage for blacks and then using that endorsement to secure Lincoln's acquiescence in franchise extension in Louisiana. The secretary's efforts to promote reform, however, did not stop here, for his design was to extend the suffrage to as many blacks as possible. At the close of his communication with Durant, he ventured the hope that the forthcoming Louisiana constitutional convention would go beyond limited suffrage and adopt the principle of 'universal suffrage of all men, unconvicted of crime, who can read and write, and have a fair knowledge of the Constitution of the State and of the United States'.[39] Here was a bold declaration in favor of impartial suffrage for all races, one that embraced not only the *gens de couleur* but also the freedmen who would be liberated by the new constitution.[40]

At this stage Chase's views ran ahead of those held by Durant and his free black allies in New Orleans. Few white Louisiana unionists or *gens de couleur* were enthusiastic about admitting tens of thousands of newly liberated bondsmen to the body politic. His views were certainly anathema to the sugar planters of southern Louisiana whose opinions exerted a disproportionate influence on the military government. As a result the Banks regime, lacking any instructions to the contrary from Lincoln, failed to register any blacks during the winter of 1863–64 and began to throw its weight behind the moderate unionist faction headed by Durant's rival, Michael Hahn. Outraged, the mulattos dispatched two of their number to Washington with a petition praying for the enfranchisement of free blacks in Louisiana.

By the time Arnold Bertonneau and Jean Baptiste Roudanez arrived at the capital in March they discovered that congressional radicals had begun to fret about the apparent conservatism of Lincoln's Ten Percent plan. The latter, it was alleged, made it too easy for Rebels to regain power and offered no security for loyal citizens, including the former slaves. Ashley's effort to enroll blacks had failed, but it was nonetheless an important statement that some radicals did not see white-only suffrage as an adequate solution to the problem of reestablishing southern loyalty to the Union. Determined to make black suffrage a fundamental element of Reconstruction, Senator Charles Sumner, another Chase ally, persuaded the two creoles to adapt their petition to suit the broader national goals of the radical Republicans. Whereas the original document had called for the enfranchisement of 'colored' men who were free before the Civil War (in other words, the *gens de couleur*), the revised petition requested the suffrage for all Louisiana black males 'whether born slave or free, especially those who have vindicated their right to vote by bearing arms'.[41]

On March 12 Bertonneau and Roudanez were granted an audience at the White House. As Chase's meeting with the president in December had already revealed, Lincoln was now personally in favor of limited suffrage (doubtless because he sensed that support for reform was gaining momentum within the Republican party and recognized that blacks should be rewarded for enlisting in the Union army). The following day he tried to spur suffrage reform in Louisiana by writing to the state's new unionist governor, Michael Hahn, who had been elected on February 22 against the opposition of Durant and his pro-Chase ally in the New Orleans customs house, Benjamin Flanders. The Flanders camp (which had been outraged by General Banks's insistence that elections should be held under the unreformed antebellum constitution) had downplayed the issue of black suffrage during the campaign, whereas Hahn's supporters had capitalized on Durant's alliance with the *gens de couleur* to appeal to the racism of local white unionists. In his letter to the governor Lincoln asked if the forthcoming constitutional convention might not provide for partial suffrage extension to blacks. 'I barely suggest for your private consideration', he wrote,

> whether some of the colored people may not be let in – as, for instance, the very intelligent, and especially those who have fought gallantly in our ranks. They would probably help, in some trying time to come, to keep the jewel of liberty within the family of freedom. But this is only a suggestion, not to the public, but to you alone.[42]

Although LaWanda Cox has asserted that this letter reveals the gap between the radicals and Lincoln on black rights to have been smaller than often supposed, it is clear that, unlike the radicals, the president was not prepared to impose black suffrage of any description as a fundamental condition of Reconstruction. Initially, his views had minimal impact on events in Louisiana.[43] The Banks–Hahn administration did attempt to enroll mulattos for the constitutional convention elections, but legal restrictions, the extent of white supremacist feeling, and the tentative wording of Lincoln's letter curtailed the effort. When the lilywhite convention met during the spring and summer of 1864 the delegates took care to meet Lincoln's non-negotiable demand for emancipation. However, the furthest they were prepared to move on suffrage (and Lincoln's wishes were made known to leading members of the convention) was to make provision for the state legislature to enfranchise blacks at some point in the future.

The ongoing struggle between president and Congress to control the process of Reconstruction, inseparable from persistent concerns about Lincoln's capabilities as a war leader and the upcoming general election, came to a head in the summer of 1864. The Wade–Davis bill passed on July 2 anticipated another sweeping Republican extension of federal power. It required emancipation as a precondition for the reorganization of any state government; demanded that 50 percent, not 10 percent, of the 1860 electorate had to vote in the constitutional convention elections intended to inaugurate loyal state governments; and required voters to take an 'ironclad' oath that they had not voluntarily aided the Rebellion. The absence of black suffrage and stress on civil rather than military government showed that this was not primarily a radical statute. However, even though Democratic opposition to a Thirteenth Amendment abolishing slavery meant that this was the only antislavery measure pending in Congress, Lincoln refused to sign it. He sensed correctly that the bill was motivated in part by animus toward his recent renomination. But more than that he denied that Congress alone had any constitutional right to abolish slavery in the states and was not prepared to see his wartime Reconstruction efforts in Louisiana and neighboring Arkansas (where a unionist government had also been set up under the Ten Percent plan) come to nought.

The president's pocket veto was the source of much anger in Congress. A good deal of the ill will felt toward Lincoln found its way into the Manifesto written by the architects of the defeated bill, Senator Benjamin F. Wade of Ohio and Representative Henry Winter Davis of Maryland. Released as part of an ongoing effort to derail Lincoln's presidential candidacy at one of the bleakest stages of the northern cause, this document excoriated the president for allegedly obstructing the will of Congress on a range of issues and derided the Ten Percent governments in New Orleans and Little Rock as entirely lacking in popular legitimacy. The heated language, however, masked an underlying unity within the Republican party. The organization had come too far to place the fate of the Union in the hands of the Democrats.

Victory!

The outcome of the war, not Reconstruction, was the major issue in the 1864 election campaign. The Republicans (reconstituted temporarily as the Union party) went to the country promising a military victory over the Confederacy and passage of the Thirteenth Amendment to rid the country of the scourge of slavery. The opposition was split. A breakaway coalition of mainly German Republicans and radical abolitionists met in Cleveland to nominate John C. Frémont for president. Their convention cheered a letter from Wendell Phillips calling for land and the ballot to be given to southern loyalists. It also adopted a platform advocating congressional control of Reconstruction and a constitutional amendment to 'secure to all men absolute equality before the law'.[44] Far more threatening to Lincoln were the attempts of elite eastern Democrats, including the New York financier, August Belmont, to elevate the former Union commander George McClellan to the presidency. Over 50,000 northern soldiers had been killed or wounded in Virginia during May and early June with nothing to show for it apart from a stalemate outside Petersburg. If the war continued to go badly for the administration, McClellan would be a hard man to beat.

At their national convention in Chicago, Peace Democrats and regular Democrats ratified a platform denouncing the war as a 'failure' and calling for a cessation of hostilities 'with a view of an ultimate convention of the States, or other peaceable means, to the end that, at the earliest practicable moment, peace may be restored on the basis of the Federal Union of the States'.[45] No mention was made of abolishing slavery, in part because, as the Democrats knew well, there was little likelihood of the Confederates entering into negotiations if emancipation was made a precondition for talks. Some observers – the Confederate vice president, Alexander H. Stephens, among them – sensed that a Democratic victory in the election might pave the way for a recognition of Confederate independence. And so it might have proved if Sherman had not taken Atlanta on September 2.

Along with what the Republicans deemed the Copperheads' submissionist platform, Sherman's stunning victory placed the Democrats on the defensive. No-one understood this better than McClellan himself. On September 8 the general publicly accepted the Democratic presidential nomination with the statement that: 'The reestablishment of the Union in all its integrity is, and must be, the indispensable condition in any settlement'.[46] Although McClellan said nothing about slavery in this letter, his overriding emphasis on maintaining the existing Union made it likely that the war would continue regardless of the outcome of the presidential election. Committed as he was to southern independence, Jefferson Davis would certainly not negotiate on such a basis.

During the election campaign the Democrats strove to regain the initiative by attacking the opposition at its most vulnerable points.[47] Party propaganda scored the Republicans' alleged monomania on black rights and supposed fondness for race-mixing (or 'miscegenation' as one of their pamphleteers dubbed it). The Republicans, however, dodged such attacks with relative ease, playing down the slavery issue and confidently linking their opponents' peace platform to treason and disunion.

The Democrats also lambasted Lincoln's allegedly tyrannical disregard for constitutional freedoms. Here too they made only limited headway. It is true that by the close of the war the government had eroded civil liberties by its sporadic suspensions of habeas corpus and the arbitrary arrest of at least 15,000 people. However, the vast majority of those imprisoned without trial were not political prisoners – disaffected Democrats critical of the administration – but residents of those border slave states prone to Confederate guerrilla action.[48]

The real problem for the Democrats was that after the Union victories at Atlanta, at Mobile, and in the Shenandoah Valley, it was clear that the war would be won. Only a minority of northerners were willing to switch horses in midstream. Lincoln and his running mate, Andrew Johnson, secured a hard-earned victory at the polls, the Union ticket receiving 2.2 million votes to McClellan's 1.8 million. Only three Union states – Kentucky, Delaware, and New Jersey – found their way into the Democratic column. The Republicans also registered hefty majorities in the House and Senate and overturned most of the Democratic gains of 1862. Soldiers voted 116,887 to 33,748 in favor of their hero, Father Abraham – a telling figure in view of the support that McClellan had once enjoyed among the ranks of the Army of the Potomac. 'I cant fite for the Union and vote against it', confided one artilleryman from New York.[49]

Congress reconvened in early December. While the public fixed its gaze on military events in Virginia and the Carolinas, the politicians in Washington returned to the debate over Reconstruction. Notwithstanding the friction caused by the Wade–Davis bill, President Lincoln and his party were agreed on many fundamentals. Both rejoiced in the House of Representatives' belated approval of the Thirteenth Amendment (which now went to the states for ratification) and Lincoln supported Congress's decision in March 1865 to create the Bureau of Freedmen, Refugees, and Abandoned Lands. A direct response to the report of the AFIC, the Freedmen's Bureau was set up as a temporary federal office inside the War Department. Its main task was to impart greater efficiency to the process of emancipation and to exercise paternal oversight over the freed slaves. While Republicans (and blacks) differed over the extent to which the government should intervene in the southern labor market, there was fairly general agreement on the part of the president and congressional Republicans that the liberated slaves should be protected from exploitation. Rather less intraparty unity was evident on other Reconstruction issues. Divisions over the place of black suffrage, the extent of federal power, and control over the process remained.

Buoyed by his reelection Lincoln aimed to push ahead with his lenient plan of Reconstruction, ideally with the support of the majority of Republicans in Congress. The request of senators and representatives from Louisiana to be seated was bound to prove a major test for executive policy, not least because the New Orleans legislature had declined to mandate any form of black suffrage during the fall, thereby infuriating local blacks (both *gens de couleur* and freedmen) and the radical Republican and abolitionist critics of the Hahn–Banks administration. Knowing the president's personal wish for limited black suffrage, Governor Hahn had urged franchise extension but to no avail. In common with Hahn, both Lincoln and General Banks (whom the president ordered to Washington to lobby for the admission of Louisiana) were prepared to endorse suffrage for intelligent blacks and those who had fought for the Union. But crucially none of them were willing to tolerate the *imposition* of such a measure on any state. The Constitution appeared not to allow it. Moreover, any attempt to force the measure on southern whites might damage the prospects for a speedy end to the war and endanger the Union party coalition in the North. Large numbers of Republicans in Washington, moderates as well as radicals, thought such conservatism was likely to threaten the security of the Union in the long run. They agreed that traitors must be punished; that loyal southerners (black and white) should be allowed to protect themselves through the ballot box; and that Congress was empowered under the Constitution to guarantee a republican form of government to every state in the Union.

Against a background of strident black and abolitionist calls for suffrage reform during early 1865, Congress debated a new Reconstruction bill that radicals hoped would inject some much-needed steel into the government's southern policy. At first it seemed that an intraparty compromise between the president and the radicals might be possible. The original version of James Ashley's Reconstruction bill proposed to recognize the unionist government of Louisiana while enfranchising blacks in other southern states.

Lincoln liked much of what he saw in the bill but thought one or two sections 'rather calculated to conceal a feature which might be objectionable to some'. Among these was the provision for black voting and jury service. According to the president's secretary, John Hay, Banks agreed. 'What you refer to', the general told Lincoln, 'would be a fatal objection to the Bill. It would simply throw the Government into the hands of the blacks, as the white people under that arrangement would refuse to vote.'[50]

The administration's reluctance to impose even limited franchise extension on southern whites combined with the radicals' enthusiasm for reform to destroy any prospect of compromise. Ashley's bill eventually died in the House and a radical filibuster in the Senate led by Charles Sumner prevented the recognition of Louisiana. By the spring of 1865, the Republican party still lacked a coherent plan of Reconstruction.

For all that, the war had been won. If the North's victory was not inevitable, there can be no denying that northerners possessed many advantages over the Confederates in their struggle to define their national identity. The United States did not require legitimization in the same way that the embryonic southern nation did. It was accepted as an established nation-state by the great European powers. Its government and people did not have to confront the immediate problem of having to generate new symbols of nationhood. Its institutions were diverse and, in the main, solid. Its citizens were relatively literate. They could be reached by the country's abundant print media: the partisan and denominational presses, books from the northeastern publishing houses, and patriotic pamphlets issued by the Loyal Publication Society (an initiative of the New York Union League which was itself an outgrowth of the patricians' Sanitary Commission). Importantly, the northern home front remained largely free from southern invasion. Ordinary noncombatants felt the severe strains of war but they possessed greater material resources than southern whites. Crucial in this respect was the North's most defining feature – free-labor capitalism – which proved equal to the task of supplying the Union cause with the volume of manufactures necessary to wage a prolonged war against a predominantly agrarian foe. Along with the northern people's gritty determination to save the Union, the iron goods of an industrializing society made the difference between defeat and victory.

Perhaps it would be unwise to push the contrast between northern and southern nation-building too far. As the heated debates over wartime Reconstruction revealed, the very act of fighting a bloody civil war led many northerners to question what their country stood for. If we accept that the construction of national identity is an ongoing process, then it becomes clear that the United States itself underwent a degree of redefinition between 1861 and 1865. The war did not issue in the millennium as some radical evangelicals had hoped it would. As George M. Fredrickson has observed, the conflict represented a triumph for conservative nationalism, not the abolitionists' utopian blueprint for American society.[51] Nevertheless we should be careful not to use too much hindsight when evaluating the Civil War's impact on the United States. In the spring of 1865 many Americans had good cause to anticipate the future with hope. Prominent among them were the people Salmon Chase wanted to call 'Afric-Americans'. If only, Charles Douglass told his father, Frederick, the latter could have been present in Washington after news of the passage of the Thirteenth Amendment had been received on January 31:

> such rejoicing I never before witnessed[:] cannons firing[–] people hugging and shaking hands[–] white people I mean[–] flags flying all over the city. I tell you things are progressing finely and if they will only give us the elective franchise and shoulder straps (which is only simple justice) that will be all I ask, every thing else which is right will surely follow ... .[52]

Abraham Lincoln, the supreme embodiment of the northern cause, did not live to oversee future events, but judged solely in terms of national development his achievement had been immense. This most unassuming of presidents had single-mindedly (though not single-handedly) sustained the momentum of a fratricidal war that portended disaster for the Union. It is Lincoln who must be credited with supplying both the practical and the visionary leadership that kept the ship of state afloat amid the storm of proslavery rebellion. His political skills, well honed in antebellum Illinois, enabled him to hold together, against great odds, an unstable antisouthern coalition that included conservative War Democrats as well as radical antislavery Republicans. A pragmatist with a keen moral sense, he never deviated from his original insistence that the Union must be saved. He had a sound grasp of the public pulse, proving to be an expert reader of grassroots opinion and a sound judge of when changing political conditions allowed him to pursue new agendas. He used his patronage power adeptly to maintain support for the administration and, possessing a relatively sound grasp of military strategy, eventually located the generals who would crush the Confederacy on the battlefield. Using all available tools to connect with the people (most notably setpiece public addresses and carefully crafted private communications), he held out the alluring prospect of a better Union and thereby imparted meaning to what many participants regarded as a meaningless slaughter. Modern scholars rightly contest Thomas Carlyle's hoary contention that history is the preserve of Great Men. But no-one seeking a full understanding of the North's victory in the Civil War can attain that end without a proper appreciation of Abraham Lincoln's contribution to the preservation of the United States.

Notes

1. Geoffrey C. Ward *et al.*, *The Civil War: An Illustrated History* (New York, 1990), p.272.

2. Paul A.C. Koistinen, *Beating Ploughshares into Swords: The Political Economy of American Warfare, 1606–1865* (Lawrence, Kan., 1996), p.186.

3. Frank L. Byrne and Jean Powers Soman, eds, *Your True Marcus: The Civil War Letters of a Jewish Colonel* (Kent, Ohio, 1985), p.81.

4. *Ibid.*, p.147.

5. Thomas Meagher quoted in JoAnna M. McDonald, *We Shall Meet Again: The First Battle of Manassas (Bull Run) July 18–21, 1861* (Oxford, 1999), p.148. Irishmen fought in the French army against the British at the battle of Fontenoy in May 1745.

6. Beecher, sermon in David B. Chesebrough, ed., *'God Ordained This War': Sermons on the Sectional Crisis, 1830–1865* (Columbia, SC, 1991), p.84.

7. Quoted in Robert Cook, *Baptism of Fire: The Republican Party in Iowa, 1838–1878* (Ames, Ia, 1994), p.137.

8. Quoted in William S. McFeely, *Frederick Douglass* (New York, 1992), p.212.

9. Henry Ford Douglass quoted in James M. McPherson, ed., *The Negro's Civil War: How American Blacks Felt and Acted During the War for the Union* (New York, 1991), p.34.

10. *CWL*, 5, p.49.

11. Jeanie Attie, *Patriotic Toil: Northern Women and the American Civil War* (Ithaca, NY, 1998), p.65.

12. Bellows, sermon in Chesebrough, ed., *'God Ordained'*, pp.84–5.

13. In spite of widespread male resistance around 20,000 northern women were employed in nursing and other medical support services during the

Civil War – over 3,000 of them as army workers under the authority of Dorothea Dix, the well-known reformer who served as the government's Superintendent of Women Nurses. Elizabeth D. Leonard, *Yankee Women: Gender Battles in the Civil War* (New York, 1994), p.xix.

14. Attie, *Patriotic Toil*, p.76.

15. Koistinen, *Beating Ploughshares*, pp.102–30.

16. Quoted in Daniel E. Sutherland, *Seasons of War: The Ordeal of a Confederate Community, 1861–1865* (New York, 1995), p.296.

17. James D. Liggett, sermon in Chesebrough, ed., *'God Ordained'*, p.97.

18. *CWL*, 5, p.388.

19. Gideon Welles quoted in Allen C. Guelzo, *Abraham Lincoln: Redeemer President* (Grand Rapids, Mich., 1999), p.338.

20. *CWL*, 5, p.434.

21. Quoted in Eric Foner, *Reconstruction: America's Unfinished Revolution 1863–1877* (New York, 1988), p.69.

22. Phillip S. Paludan, *'A People's Contest': The Union and Civil War, 1861–1865* (New York, 1988), pp.116–17.

23. George O. Bartlett to Ira Andrews, Jan. 4, 1863, George O. Bartlett Papers, GLC.

24. Cyrus C. Carpenter to R.E. Carpenter, Sept. 13, 1863, Cyrus C. Carpenter Papers, State Historical Society of Iowa, Des Moines.

25. Maitland to Joseph M. Maitland, June 29, 1863, Joseph M. Maitland Papers, GLC.

26. Maitland to G.M. Mast, July 5, 1863, Maitland Papers, GLC.

27. Maitland to Joseph M. Maitland, Aug. 16, 1863, Maitland Papers, GLC.

28. Edwin G. Burrows and Mike Wallace, *Gotham: A History of New York City to 1898* (New York, 1999), p.895.

29. *CWL*, 7, p.23.

30. On the tortuous progress of wartime Reconstruction see esp. Foner, *Reconstruction*, pp.1–76, and William C. Harris, *With Charity for All: Lincoln and the Restoration of the Union* (Lexington, Ky, 1997).

31. Quoted in Herman Belz, *Reconstructing the Union: Theory and Policy during the Civil War* (Ithaca, NY, 1969), p.52.

32. Quoted in *ibid.*, p.25.

33. Bates to Chase, Nov. 29, 1862, in James M. McClure *et al.*, eds, 'Circumventing the Dred Scott Decision: Edward Bates, Salmon P. Chase, and the Citizenship of African-Americans', *CWH* 43 (1997), 309.

34. Chase to James M. McKaye, July 25, 1863, Chase Papers (UPA mic.), reel 28.

35. Chase to Durant, Nov. 19, 1863, Chase Papers, reel 29.

36. Durant to Chase, Dec. 4, 1863, Chase Papers, reel 30.

37. Quoted in Belz, *Reconstructing the Union*, p.188.

38. Chase to Durant, Dec. 28, 1863, Chase Papers, reel 30.

39. Chase to Durant, Dec. 28, 1863, Chase Papers, reel 30.

40. Wartime supporters of black suffrage considered several forms of franchise reform. At the conservative end of the spectrum *partial suffrage* involved the exclusive imposition of certain tests on potential black voters (e.g. literacy tests, military service, payment of taxes). *Impartial* (or *equal*) *suffrage* required such tests to be applied to blacks and whites alike. The most radical reformers favored *universal suffrage* which would confer the ballot on all naturalized adult males regardless of color.

41. Ted Tunnell, *Crucible of Reconstruction: War, Radicalism and Race in Louisiana 1862–1877* (Baton Rouge, La, 1984), p.78.

42. *CWL*, 7, p.243.

43. LaWanda Cox, *Lincoln and Black Freedom: A Study in Presidential Leadership* (Columbia, SC, 1981), pp.94–7.

44. Quoted in James M. McPherson, *The Struggle for Equality: Abolitionists and the Negro in the Civil War and Reconstruction* (Princeton, NJ, 1964), p.270.

45. Quoted in David E. Long, *The Jewel of Liberty: Abraham Lincoln's Re-Election and the End of Slavery* (Mechanicsburg, Pa, 1994), p.283.

46. Quoted in *ibid.*, p.276.

47. On the 1864 election campaign see not only *ibid.* but also James M. McPherson, *Battle Cry of Freedom: The Civil War Era* (New York, 1988), pp.774–806.

48. Mark E. Neely, *The Fate of Liberty: Abraham Lincoln and Civil Liberties* (New York, 1992).

49. Leander Davis quoted in William C. Davis, *Lincoln's Men: How President Lincoln Became Father to an Army and a Nation* (New York, 1999), p.210.

50. Tyler Dennett, *Lincoln and the Civil War in the Diaries and Letters of John Hay* (New York, 1988), pp.244–5.

51. George M. Fredrickson, *The Inner Civil War: Northern Intellectuals and the Crisis of the Union* (New York, 1968), p.188.

52. Charles R. Douglass to Frederick Douglass, Feb. 9, 1865, Frederick Douglass Papers, LC (mic.), reel 2.

7

WAR BY ANY OTHER NAME: THE STRUGGLE OVER RECONSTRUCTION, 1865–76

The welcome return of peace in the spring of 1865 witnessed a continuation of the wartime Reconstruction process that would resolve as yet unanswered questions about the relationships pertaining between state and federal governments, North and South, and blacks and whites. More specifically, it brought into sharper focus a problem that had bedeviled all postemancipation societies in the western hemisphere: how to effect a smooth transition between slavery and freedom. Because this problem was intertwined with the task of promoting national reconciliation and the struggle to order power relations in the newly restored Union, the fraught politics of Reconstruction dominated American life in the decade after the Civil War.

Lincoln's successor in the White House, Andrew Johnson, undertook to restore the late Rebel states to their proper constitutional place inside the Union. His mistake was to underestimate the impact that the Civil War had had on the people of both sections. When it seemed apparent that Johnson's lenient policies were allowing ex-Confederates to obstruct federal policy and regain their former influence through the ballot box, congressional Republicans attempted to promote at least a modicum of reform in the conquered South. Black suffrage made possible the sudden entry of black Americans into southern political life, a development that was contested fiercely by their former masters. Only as war memories began to fade and new issues began to preoccupy the country did Reconstruction come to an end.

The aftermath of war

In his brief second inaugural address delivered on March 4, 1865 President Abraham Lincoln, chastened by God's evident determination to punish Americans for the sin of slavery, announced that having fought a hard war, he would seek a generous peace. As his rousing peroration made clear, his overriding goal was national reconciliation:

> With malice toward none; with charity for all; with firmness in the right, as God gives us to see the right, let us strive on to finish the work we are in; to bind up the nation's wounds; to care for him who shall have borne the battle, and for his widow, and his orphan – to do all which may achieve and cherish a just, and a lasting peace, among ourselves, and with all nations.[1]

Lincoln's yearning for reunion did not signify that he was ready to embrace the South on any terms. The death of slavery was not negotiable and he was personally in favor of limited black voting in the interests of justice. Precisely what these racial concerns would have meant in terms of postwar Reconstruction policy we shall never know. On the murky evening of April 14 John Wilkes Booth, a strikingly handsome Shakespearean actor and southern sympathizer consumed with hatred for the tyrant he held responsible for destroying the Confederacy, approached the president's box while Lincoln was attending a play at Ford's Theater in Washington. Born in a proslavery district of Maryland, Booth may have been pushed over the edge by the president's recent endorsement of black suffrage. 'This means nigger citizenship', he is alleged to have muttered, before vowing to ensure that no more such speeches were ever made.[2] Gaining easy access to the box, Booth leveled a loaded derringer at the back of Lincoln's head. He fired once from close range, leapt clumsily onto the stage and then made what proved to be a temporary escape at the back of the theater.[3] The president died in a boardinghouse across the street at 7.22 am the next morning, the most illustrious victim of a conflict that, even at this late stage, was continuing to claim hundreds of American lives.

With a new Congress not scheduled to meet until December 1865, the man presented with the difficult task of formulating Reconstruction policy in the postbellum era was Vice President Andrew Johnson. As wartime governor of Union-occupied Tennessee, Johnson had endorsed emancipation and was renowned for his aversion to the South's disloyal planter class. Because his power base lay among the white yeomen and common whites of mountainous East Tennessee, a population that had suffered grievously at the hands of Confederate irregulars during the war, hopes were high among radical Republicans that the new president would take a much tougher line than Lincoln on treason – perhaps even go one step further and mandate black suffrage as a precondition for readmitting the late Rebel states to Congress. Conservatives, in contrast, hoped that as a former Democrat, Johnson would accomplish the task of restoration without major changes to the federal polity, thereby forestalling any ill-considered attempts to reorder southern society and elevate black men to the level of whites.

On May 29, 1865, having garnered a variety of firsthand accounts of southern feeling, the president issued two proclamations in which he finally announced his intentions. The first of these maintained Lincoln's policy of pardoning the majority of ordinary Confederates providing they took an oath pledging support for emancipation and future allegiance to the United States. But in addition to repeating his predecessor's requirement that elite Confederates must petition for presidential pardons, he excluded from the general embrace of pardon and amnesty any Rebel who owned more than $20,000 of taxable property.

Radical Republicans who believed that this new class of exemptions might pave the way for the destruction of the disloyal plantocracy were less impressed with the second edict. The North Carolina proclamation provided a model by which those southern states without loyal governments could be restored to the Union. Johnson appointed a provisional governor, the wartime peace advocate William Holden, who was required to call elections for a constitutional convention that would establish a 'republican form of government'. While this presumably meant that the convention would negate the original act of secession and endorse the abolition of slavery, the absence of any mention of black suffrage meant that the election would be racially exclusive. Johnson had decided that the lilywhite electorate in place at the outbreak of war would devise the framework for state government in the postbellum era.

Other gubernatorial appointments followed. Apart from the elevation of Holden and Andrew J. Hamilton of Texas, Johnson's choices were relatively conservative. Opting for a combination of upcountry men and solid Whiggish planters who had either sat out the war or operated as internal critics of the Confederate war effort, he seemed eager to appeal to moderate southern whites. Neither black suffrage nor wholesale confiscation of Rebel estates was likely to figure prominently on their agenda.

The president's apparent decision to prioritize restoration over Reconstruction was seen at the time (and has been judged many times since) as a missed opportunity to build a more equal society in the American South.[4] White southerners, according to this argument, were so demoralized in the spring of 1865 that they would have accepted any terms dictated by the victors. Johnson's policy allegedly caused them to believe that Washington would impose only limited terms and that concerted opposition to the radicals' objectives would win a sympathetic hearing in the North.

In fact, as the wide range of reports reaching Johnson during the late spring of 1865 clearly revealed, opinion within the South varied tremendously. While a minority of ex-Rebels remained defiant, the majority of local whites conceded that the dream of a southern nation was over. The whole fabric of southern life had been undermined by the destructive power of war. Roughly one in three Confederate soldiers was dead, a death rate twice as high as that of the North. Put another way, over a quarter of the region's draft-age male population had left to fight the Yankees and never returned.[5] Although portions of the South such as the interior of Texas remained physically unscathed, the material damage in many areas was huge. Southern railroads were in a chaotic state. Large sections of major cities such as Atlanta, Richmond, and Columbia had been reduced to rubble by fire and artillery bombardment. Whole farming regions such as the Shenandoah Valley and those parts of Georgia and the Carolinas visited by Sherman's bluecoats had been rendered temporarily unproductive. Most significantly of all slavery, the cornerstone of antebellum southern life, was dead. It was a devastating loss to those who had invested heavily in human property and one that has been valued financially at $2.7 billion.[6] But more than that, its demise undermined the very stability of a society whose racial and class distinctions had depended entirely on the existence of human bondage.

Lost manpower, a general dearth of credit, and widespread property damage affected important social and economic institutions as well as ordinary families. Church property, for example, had been vandalized by Union troops or appropriated for military use. The once flourishing denominational publishing houses had ceased to operate and many clergymen and lay officials had perished in the war. One Baptist college in Mississippi had lost nearly all of its 104 faculty members and students who had volunteered to serve in the Confederate army.[7]

An even more serious outcome of the war was that the temporary destruction of the cotton nexus had destroyed the region's banking system. The resulting paucity of currency and credit meant that the Republicans' goal of creating a vibrant free-labor economy throughout the postbellum South was stillborn. Determined to spread the risk of cotton cultivation, hard-up planters began to work their farms with the labor of sharecroppers. The latter (who were disproportionately black) were furnished with seed, tools, and fertilizer and generally received one-third of the crop at the end of the year. While the system gave the freed slaves a measure of autonomy, it condemned the majority of them to a life of poverty. Whites also were deeply affected by the ruined economy. Some planters were forced to sell up completely, and growing numbers of upcountry yeomen farmers saw no option but to shift from corn to cotton cultivation in their urgent search for liquid cash. Thus did a war for southern independence hasten the region's dependence on the uncertain world market for cotton.[8]

Yet despite the profound traumas of defeat and poverty, most white southerners were neither repentant nor excessively compliant. Northern politicians, clergymen, and voters cast around eagerly for signs that the former Confederates would become loyal Americans and that they accepted responsibility for the carnage of the previous four years. Had God not decided the issue in favor of the North, they reasoned? Was slaveholding not an abomination in the eyes of the Lord? Had not southern whites instigated the war by rebelling against the best government on earth? Such questions often led to calls for vengeance in the shape of wholesale confiscation of landed property and capital punishment for southern war criminals – especially the arch traitor Jefferson Davis who, after being captured ignominiously in southern Georgia at the end of the war, was languishing without trial in Fortress Monroe.

Southerners were incensed by what they regarded as evidence of northern vindictiveness and hypocrisy. Four years of bloodletting had left a deep legacy of bitterness on both sides. Relatively few of the defeated Confederates were prepared to accept the northern view that slavery had been the cause of their downfall. Even though the shock of final defeat temporarily unnerved many evangelicals in the region, southern clergymen rejected attempts by northern churchmen to brand southerners as sinners. Instead they built on wartime exegesis to argue that the Lord had decided to chastise His people for their lack of humility and faith. True Christians were perfected by suffering, ran the argument, not by the kind of self-serving triumphalism practiced by the Yankees.

Entrenched doubts about the ability of blacks to survive outside slavery bolstered the general lack of contrition over the peculiar institution. Could it be, asked one white Baptist, that it was God's intention to destroy a divinely ordained institution that had been meant to protect blacks? Such an idea was ludicrous, he answered, because God could not possibly have allowed such suffering 'that an inferior race might be released from nominal bondage and endowed with a freedom which, to them, is but another name for licentiousness, and which must end in complete extermination, so far as human foresight can judge'.[9]

If there ever was a time when the South lay prostrate at the feet of the conqueror, it was only for a fleeting moment. Even after their comprehensive military defeat, most southern whites had no conception of slavery as sin. This did not mean that they all regretted the passing of the peculiar institution. Some forward-looking individuals believed that slavery had retarded regional economic development and saw emancipation as an opportunity to diversify, even into the realm of manufacturing. However, this standpoint was seldom accompanied by any sense of war guilt. Still less did it embrace the idea that the 'freedmen' should be permitted to take their place as equals in postwar southern society. 'Both History and Experience', wrote one Confederate veteran in typical vein in June 1865, 'prove that free negroes are the worst members of society[,] & being by nature an indolent theiving & filthy race when left to shift for themselves [(]being inferior intellectually to the whites[)]] they will either degenerate into barbarism or gradually evaporate as the Indians have done.'[10] Even those who understood that economic recovery could not take place without black labor were hostile to any suggestion that their former charges should be granted much more than the right to work for white employers. As a southerner and former slaveholder himself, President Johnson had a shrewd understanding of what whites in the region would tolerate in the sensitive area of race relations. Confederates had fought to preserve their racial order. At the close of a vicious civil war when local white men were in danger of being emasculated by emancipation and military defeat, it was unlikely that those same men would welcome the prospect of sharing power with a race they regarded as innately inferior.

Not until the summer and fall of 1865 did northerners begin to realize the yawning gap that existed between Yankee and southern interpretations of the war's outcome. Black suffrage was still the coming question but at this juncture Republicans remained divided over the wisdom of mandating it as a condition of the South's readmission to Congress. While some Republican party activists wanted to begin by enfranchising black men in the northern states because of the colored race's wartime service to the Union, nonradicals feared that any endorsement of black suffrage would make them vulnerable to racist assaults from the Democratic opposition. Even though strong backing from grassroots Republicans was clearly evident, conservatives' insistence that the issue did not have majority support among the electorate at large seemed to be confirmed by the defeat of black suffrage in state-ordered referenda in Connecticut, Minnesota, and Wisconsin.

No-one understood the divisive impact of this issue more than the president himself. On August 15 Johnson sent instructions to William L. Sharkey, Mississippi's new provisional governor, ahead of the first meeting of the state constitutional convention. As well as indicating his desire that the convention should ratify the Thirteenth Amendment abolishing slavery, he added his own suggestion that the Mississippians might enfranchise literate and property-owning blacks. Unlike Lincoln (who had recommended partial black suffrage in 1864 as a move to extend American democracy), Johnson's express aim was to 'disarm the adversary'. By introducing this cautious reform, he told Sharkey, 'the Radicals, who are wild upon negro franchise, will be completely foiled in their attempts to keep the Southern States from renewing their relations to the Union by not accepting their Senators and Representatives'.[11] Even at this early stage of his presidency, Johnson appears to have mapped out his grand political strategy: isolate those he designated extremists on both sides of the Mason-Dixon Line and construct a conservative cross-sectional coalition that would advance the cause of national reconciliation and progress.

The president's determination to restore the Union on a relatively conservative basis had grievous consequences for blacks who had begun to farm on land seized from Rebels during the war. In August and September he ordered the Freedmen's Bureau, in control of 850,000 acres of confiscated and abandoned southern land at the end of the war, to return the property of ex-Confederates who were petitioning for executive pardon. He also curtailed the seizure of property of wealthy Confederates and ended the Bureau's ongoing policy of setting aside 40 acre plots for the freedpeople.

Much of the land nominally belonging to blacks lay within a huge strip of land in coastal Georgia, South Carolina, and Florida set

aside for ex-slaves by General William T. Sherman in his Special
Field Orders Number 15. Sherman, well known for his hostile attitude
toward black refugees, had issued the directive in January 1865 to
prevent fugitive slaves encumbering the movement of his troops.
The *New York Tribune* had criticized what it saw as the separatist
impulse behind Sherman's move. The Orders, it noted, assumed
'that the negro is a race apart and different from the white, and, if
intrusted with freedom, must be isolated and left entirely to itself'.[12]
However, even though Sherman's directive sprang largely from
prejudice against blacks, its effect was to settle 40,000 freedmen on
land taken from the region's planter class.

The task of telling these people that the land was to revert to
their former masters fell upon General Oliver O. Howard, the pious
head of the Freedmen's Bureau. In October Howard arrived at a
church on Edisto Island, South Carolina, to importune a large group
of former slaves to become reconciled to local whites. He then
appointed a committee of freedmen to investigate the best mode
of transferring the land. The committee's response articulated the
collective sense of betrayal. Avowedly loyal blacks, they insisted, were
promised homesteads by the federal government:

> If it does not carry out the promises its agents made to us,
> if the government haveing concluded to befriend its late
> enemies and to neglect to observe the principles of common
> faith between its self and us its allies in the war you said was
> over, now takes away from them all right to the soil they stand
> upon save such as they can get by working for *your* late and
> their *all time* enemies ... we are left in a more unpleasant
> condition than our former ... You will see that this is not the
> condition of really freemen.[13]

All seemed to be going according to plan for Andrew Johnson
until southern whites unintentionally handed the initiative to the
president's Republican critics. In the absence of a clear lead from
the White House, the southern constitutional conventions failed to
indicate regrets about past behavior, for example by repealing their
secession ordinances *ab initio*. They also balked at a forthright declaration of emancipation and a number of them refused to repudiate
putatively illegal wartime debts incurred by Confederate state governments. Concerned northerners then witnessed the first postwar
southern legislatures enact 'black codes' designed to reimpose a
measure of control over the former slaves.

The codes were a product of white concerns about the alleged shiftlessness, criminality, and unreliability of local blacks. Whereas the latter were determined to test the boundaries of freedom, for example by traveling miles to locate kinfolk separated by the inter-state slave trade, whites found signs of black mobility unsettling. David Schenck, an unrepentant North Carolina secessionist and former slaveholder, noted in his diary on June 7, 1865 that his cook, Harriet, was on the point of leaving his employ. It would be difficult, he mused, to replace her 'while the whole system of labor is in a perfect chaos. Every fool negro thinks freedom consists in leaving his master and being idle as long as possible.'[14] The black codes sought to ease fears of a postemancipation descent into chaos by introducing stringent penalties for vagrancy and breaking contracts. Even though they went far beyond existing antebellum law in pro-tecting some of the freedpeople's most basic civil rights, the new laws left the door open for the continued disbarring of blacks from testifying in court and serving on juries. They also hindered the efforts of black men to control their own households (an essential precondition for full male equality in the patriarchal South) by providing for the apprenticeship of children.

By the late fall of 1865 growing numbers of Republicans were beginning to sense that President Johnson's policy threatened to restore defeated Confederates to power. Southern whites did little to alleviate this concern by electing Alexander H. Stephens, vice president of the Confederacy, and a number of Rebel generals to Congress. The fact that these delegates were mainly former Whig cooperationists with only limited initial enthusiasm for secession had little bearing on the northern response. Southern whites, on the other hand, did their cause few favors by levying heavy poll taxes on the freedmen and, even more seriously, using state-sanctioned and extra-legal methods, violence included, against recalcitrant blacks who refused to accept the constricted version of freedom now on offer.

These developments boded ill for Andrew Johnson. Most northerners would not betray the Union dead and surrender the fruits of war to unrepentant traitors. Up to a point Johnson under-stood this and in late 1865 urged southerners to take more account of northern views, for example by not sending Stephens to Washington. He also pressurized southern legislators to ratify the Thirteenth Amendment abolishing slavery. Although his efforts did not fall entirely on deaf ears (Georgia's ratification on December 6 allowed Secretary of State William Seward to declare the amendment adopted), disquiet across the North had intensified. By the time a new Congress assembled in December it was clear he would have to either find common ground with worried Republican leaders or forge a new coalition of northern conservatives and southern whites.

Congressional Reconstruction

Congressional Republicans quickly announced their determination to contest the executive branch's dictation of southern policy. A Joint Committee on Reconstruction, co-chaired by Senator William Pitt Fessenden of Maine and Congressman Thaddeus Stevens of Pennsylvania, was formed to ensure legislative input into policy-making, and the admission of southern representatives was delayed to await the findings of this new body. At this early stage of the session only a minority of Republicans in Washington sought a quarrel with the president. Most of these were radicals who insisted that the southern states should be governed as territories or that the Constitution empowered Congress to provide every state with a republican form of government. Hoping to continue the trend of wartime state building in order to extend federal protection to the freedpeople, Thaddeus Stevens contended that congressmen were 'making a nation' and demanded military rule, black suffrage, and land redistribution to guarantee racial equality.[15]

Moderate Republican leaders, however, such as Fessenden, John Sherman, and Lyman Trumbull in the Senate, and John A. Bingham in the House, rejected what they regarded as excessive meddling with the rights of the individual states. They did so for several reasons. All of them believed that further alterations in the relationship between center and periphery might result in irretrievable damage to the existing polity and were predisposed to interpret the Constitution more narrowly than they had done during the Civil War. As Fessenden averred, 'I upheld many things then that perhaps I would not uphold now because they are not necessary.'[16] Few moderates thought that enfranchising large numbers of illiterate ex-slaves would promote the public welfare and all knew that a majority of northern voters (as distinct from Republicans) were unenthusiastic about black suffrage. Some of them, moreover, had returned from visits to the White House convinced that Johnson would allow Congress to advance temperate Reconstruction measures. They certainly had no wish to initiate a disastrous split between party and president – an event that could only redound to the benefit of the Democrats who, in their eyes, had sought to damage the Union cause during the war. Personal rivalries also prevented moderates from making common cause with radicals in Washington. The loquacious Charles Sumner, for example, was held in growing contempt by centrists for what they deemed his impractical crusade for black equality.

While the Joint Committee heard damning testimony from blacks and whites on the extent of antiunionist violence in the southern states, two important measures were brought to the floor from Trumbull's Senate judiciary committee. The first of these, the Freedmen's Bureau bill, reflected Commissioner Howard's desire to bolster the Bureau as an important weapon in the Republicans' ongoing project to build a free labor society in the postwar South. Trumbull's measure extended the life of the Bureau, provided for direct federal funding, and authorized its officers to assume jurisdiction of equal rights cases involving blacks. Modest provisions were included to boost the freedmen's access to land ownership.

The second and more far-reaching of the two measures was a civil rights bill, envisioned primarily as a means of enforcing the Thirteenth Amendment and as a tool to nullify the black codes. In conformity with Edward Bates's 1862 ruling on citizenship, this measure declared all persons born in the United States to be American citizens, though an exception was made for untaxed Indians. All citizens were guaranteed basic civil rights: for example, the right to testify in court and make contracts. Justice was to be administered equally by the states and federal officials were authorized to act promptly if those operating under state law failed to secure the equal rights of all citizens. Passed with nearly unanimous Republican support, neither of these acts was regarded by moderates as particularly controversial. While representing a continuation of the wartime trend toward central government activism, the fundamental aim (as evidenced by the failure to provide for a national police force or to touch private infringements of civil rights) was to protect the emancipated slaves without doing irreparable damage to the Constitution.

In February and March 1866 Johnson surprised almost everyone by vetoing both bills. His forthright veto messages made clear his opposition to making wards of the freedpeople as well as his preference for white supremacy over racial equality. Although the president had profound ideological and constitutional objections to these measures, his chief political aim was to marginalize the radicals. On Washington's Birthday he delivered an intemperate public address in which he equated leading radicals like Stevens and Sumner with southern traitors for opposing 'the fundamental principles of this Government'.[17]

Johnson failed to achieve his goal. Determined to protect loyal unionists against what they saw as a Confederate revival in the South, the moderates eventually joined forces with radicals to override the two vetoes with the required two-thirds majority in both houses. Personally they were furious with Johnson. Fessenden, for example, privately denounced the president's 'exhibition of folly and wickedness ... He has broken his faith, betrayed his trust, and must sink from detestation into contempt.'[18]

The urgent task of formulating a constructive alternative to the mild restoration policy of the executive branch fell to the Joint Committee on Reconstruction, the most important special congressional committee created during the nineteenth century. The result was a proposed constitutional amendment representing a compromise between radical and moderate Republicans on terms distinctly favorable to the latter. Reflecting the radicals' demand for black equality as the baseline for Reconstruction and the moderates' wish to protect southern unionists without undermining the fabric of American government, the amendment contained several provisions. Among the most important were, firstly, an inclusive declaration of national citizenship which negated the 1857 *Dred Scott* ruling that blacks were not citizens of the United States and, secondly, a landmark prohibition on any attempts by the individual states to 'abridge the privileges or immunities of citizens of the United States', to deprive 'any person of life, liberty, or property, without due process of law', or to deny anyone 'the equal protection of the laws'. Also included was a prohibition on Confederates holding federal office – a move designed to stifle the political effects of President Johnson's wholesale pardoning of ex-Rebels. A deliberately convoluted section reduced the congressional representation of any state which denied the vote to its adult male citizens on the grounds of race. Northern states could thus continue to withhold the vote from women, unnaturalized foreigners, and illiterates, while those in the South could choose between enfranchising blacks or accepting a diminished national role.

Even though the radicals had wanted much more than this – notably a positive extension of the franchise to blacks and the disfranchisement of former Confederates – the amendment bore witness to the Civil War's expansive impact on American nationalism and government. For the first time a national responsibility to protect the civil rights of all citizens was enshrined in the Constitution along with a path-breaking transformation of vague natural rights into concrete legal ones. Although Charles Sumner chose to condemn the measure on the lofty grounds that 'a moral principle cannot be compromised', more pragmatic radicals chose to support the measure because they lived, as Thaddeus Stevens put it, 'among men and not among angels'.[19]

Having formulated their response to the president's policy, the Republicans prepared to take their cause to the northern electorate. Fessenden's skillful Report of the Joint Committee on Reconstruction, widely disseminated as a campaign document in the 1866 congressional elections, was a critical contribution to the ongoing 'national dialog' over federal policy.[20] To claim that the defeated southern states could simply resume their former status, contended the Report, was absurd:

> If this is indeed true, then is the government of the United
> States powerless for its own protection, and flagrant rebellion,
> carried to the extreme of civil war, is a pastime which any
> State may play at, not only certain that it can lose nothing
> in any event, but may be the gainer by defeat.

In its hearings the Joint Committee had found 'decisive' proof that 'intense hostility to the federal Union' still existed in the southern states. Therefore, concluded the Report, the late insurrectionary states should be excluded from representation in Congress until 'adequate safeguards for the future' (in the shape of the Fourteenth Amendment) had been implemented.[21]

When Johnson encouraged the former Rebel states to reject the amendment and set in motion plans to form a National Union movement incorporating northern Democrats, conservative Republicans, and southern whites, battle was joined. Further evidence of white supremacist violence provided by well-documented massacres of loyal blacks in Memphis and New Orleans during the summer of 1866 gave the Republicans the upper hand. So did Johnson's autumnal 'swing around the circle', a whistle-stop tour of the North in which the president, consumed with self-pity, delivered a series of embarrassing harangues against his radical enemies. Notwithstanding the White House's belated patronage offensive against federal office-holders known to oppose presidential policy, the Republicans triumphed easily in the elections, often playing down the divisive issue of black suffrage in order to avoid alienating conservatives. But this apparent mandate for congressional Reconstruction did not solve their problems. Between October 1866 and January 1867 ten southern legislatures rejected the Fourteenth Amendment. A hostile president and minimal southern support for congressional policy made it unlikely that, as matters stood, the measure would ever secure the necessary three-quarters majority of states for ratification. The Republican-dominated Congress was therefore left with the difficult task of devising a new plan of Reconstruction.

White southerners' refusal to ratify the Amendment ended attempts at self-reconstruction in the region and brought renewed calls from radical Republicans for a root-and-branch reform of southern society. White unionists in the region did not generally share the enthusiasm of some radicals for land redistribution, but in the wake of racial violence and defeat at the recent polls, they were now prepared to support the ultras' demands for black suffrage. Moderate Republicans, by contrast, were now on the defensive. They remained unenthusiastic about universal suffrage (though many would have accepted limited or impartial suffrage) and did not want to break up the cotton plantations they deemed critical to the South's economic recovery. However, unless they moved beyond the Fourteenth Amendment it was likely they would be squeezed between Johnson and the radicals.

The result, after extended and sometimes bitter debate, was another internal Republican compromise, this one marginally more to the radicals' taste. Combining two complementary bills, one relating to affairs in Louisiana and the other extending the powers of the army in the South, the Reconstruction Act of March 1867 placed Johnson's provisional governments under direct military supervision. US army commanders in five military districts covering every ex-Rebel state except Tennessee (which had ratified the Fourteenth Amendment and been restored to its normal relations within the Union in 1866) were empowered to protect life and property when civil authorities failed to do so. This remarkable statute also disfranchised large numbers of former Confederate officeholders and explicitly required southern states to enfranchise blacks and whites on an impartial basis. Although a Senate committee had provided for black suffrage in the constitutional convention elections, it had not mandated its incorporation into the new constitutions themselves. The intervention of Charles Sumner in a Republican caucus on February 14, however, had enshrined this provision into the bill by a margin of just two votes.

When the Reconstruction Act came to a vote in the Senate, moderate leaders gave it their reluctant assent, notwithstanding grave disquiet and growing impatience with what they saw as the radicals' enthusiasm for central power and impractical obsession with equal rights. Why did the moderate Republicans support a measure that would admit tens of thousands of recently freed and mainly illiterate slaves into southern political life? The answer lies partly in their desire to stave off the lengthy period of military occupation desired by radicals like Stevens. If southern blacks were given the privilege of voting, they reasoned, they could be left to control their own destiny without the aid of federal protection which was expensive, corrosive of good government, and a barrier to sectional reconciliation. For moderates, the clinching argument in favor of the Reconstruction Act was its incorporation of a provision first introduced by Congressman John A. Bingham, a centrist Republican from Ohio. This clause made it clear that once the southern states had complied with the conditions laid down by Congress (most notably ratification of the Fourteenth Amendment) normal political life would resume. The South would regain its seats in Congress and federal commanders would cease to interfere in the region's internal affairs. While the enfranchisement of southern blacks represented a major gain for the radicals, the latter failed to secure the demolition of Johnson's provisional governments or wholesale land confiscation and redistribution. The Reconstruction Act therefore pointed the way toward a more inclusive democracy while at the same time emphasizing the limits of Republican statism.

The moderates' fears were also assuaged by the fact that the black suffrage clause of the act was confined to the emancipated slaves. Although large numbers of northern Republicans were as ready to endorse or at least accept the idea of black suffrage as they had been in the second half of 1865, centrist leaders knew that their political base at home was still vulnerable to Democratic race-baiting. Under the Reconstruction Act the majority of northern states that had not enfranchised their black male citizens could continue to disfranchise blacks with impunity.

Nevertheless, bolstered by several supplemental measures, the Reconstruction Act gave wide powers to US commanders in the South. Although Ulysses S. Grant, the general in chief, was in an unenviable position trapped between the president and Congress, he proceeded to oversee the Reconstruction process in a manner reasonably satisfactory to Republican leaders – a fact of no small importance when the Republicans came to deliberate upon their presidential nominee. When President Johnson tried to obstruct congressional policy with legal pronouncements and outright dismissal of military personnel, he succeeded only in prompting the radicals to remove him from office.

The president survived one impeachment attempt in late 1867 but then wantonly reignited political passions by dismissing Edwin Stanton, a strong supporter of congressional policy, from his post as Secretary of War. Stanton had been lawfully suspended from office during the summer of 1867, a period of congressional recess not covered by the new Tenure of Office Act, a measure designed to constrain Johnson's ability to remove federal officeholders opposed to his policy. The secretary's outright dismissal in February 1868 seemed to breach the Act, although some doubt attached to this presumption because his appointment (in the first instance to Lincoln's cabinet) predated passage of the law. In fact Stanton had no intention of obeying Johnson's order and helped precipitate a crisis by barricading himself in his office with a group of Republican senators. With the president scratching around for allies in the army high command and the US Supreme Court under Chief Justice Salmon P. Chase reluctant to strike down congressional legislation, the radicals' impeachment drive gained momentum. They made Johnson's alleged breach of the Tenure of Office Act the centerpiece of their indictment.

On May 26, at the close of a five-week Senate trial during which opinion in the country at large became dangerously polarized, the president was acquitted by one vote. While Johnson helped his cause by remaining unusually silent throughout the proceedings, the key to his salvation was held by seven moderate Republican senators who provided him with his margin of victory. The course of men like Fessenden and Trumbull was determined by a variety of factors, not least their fears about the impact that impeachment would have on a balanced constitution. Hardly less significant was their determination to prevent power falling into the hands of Benjamin F. Wade of Ohio, a leading radical. As president *pro tem* of the Senate, Wade would replace Johnson if impeachment succeeded. The moderates regarded themselves as guardians of the Constitution against irresponsible ultras whose support for currency inflation and sectional vengeance would bring ruin to country and party. Their controversial votes ended Wade's chances of securing the Republican presidential nomination at the party's national convention. That honor went to the popular Union hero, General Grant, whose candidacy received powerful backing from New York City's commercial elite, eager to promote stability and profit by drawing a line under Reconstruction.

The ensuing campaign was one of the most unpleasant in American political history.[22] Grant's Democratic opponent was the former New York governor, Horatio Seymour. A conservative on major economic issues, Seymour was an uninspiring candidate. He left his copartisans (many of whom favored paying off the enormous Union debt in depreciated greenbacks rather than specie) with little alternative but to rail against the racial peril unleashed by congressional Reconstruction. His running mate, Frank Blair, Jr, made no secret of his contempt for federal policy by insisting that the radicals had placed southern whites under the domination of 'a semi-barbarous race of blacks' who yearned to 'subject the white women to their unbridled lust'.[23] Rather than confronting such charges directly, Republicans retaliated by linking the Democrats to wartime treason and postwar instability. 'Let Us Have Peace' was Grant's campaign slogan, but there was little sign during the summer and fall of 1868 that either party was ready to stop the mudslinging. Although white supremacist violence prevented blacks from voting in parts of the deep South, Grant emerged victorious from the contest with a large majority in the electoral college and the Republicans secured control of both the House and the Senate.

The election's principal significance lay in the fact that it ensured there would be no rollback of the Republicans' southern policy. Southern states that had not yet ratified the Fourteenth Amendment would have to do so in order to be readmitted to Congress. As a popular referendum on Reconstruction, however, the election gave little hope to the radicals. Voters in Iowa and Minnesota chose narrowly to enfranchise blacks in their home states, but more whites in the country as a whole voted for Seymour than for Grant. Many Americans clearly assumed that Reconstruction was virtually over. The political violence in states like Louisiana and Georgia, however, suggested otherwise.

Black life in the postwar South

Although the congressional legislation of 1866–67 was intended to impose a degree of uniform policy across the South, Reconstruction proved to be a diverse and uneven process. Some areas, notably those in which the black population was negligible, were scarcely touched by it at all. Others, particularly the plantation areas of the deep South, experienced widespread political upheaval as local blacks became actively involved in civic affairs for the first time. The direct application of federal power by army commanders and Freedmen's Bureau officers (as well as the unofficial activities of northern benevolent organizations) expanded the freedmen's opportunities in several fields, especially politics and education. But while federal intervention constituted a significant complement to southern blacks' impressive capacity to organize their own lives and helped produce important gains, the empowerment of blacks touched raw nerves among most former Confederates who had gone to war, at least in part, to preserve white supremacy. Racist violence directed against the new Republican governments spawned by congressional legislation contributed significantly to the demise of Reconstruction by the mid- to late 1870s.

Having played a positive role in their own liberation, the emancipated slaves were in no mood to wait passively for federal aid. It is true that as evangelical Christians they regarded the North as the agent of God's deliverance. But it did not follow that they simply expected the conqueror to provide for all their wants after the complex web of master–slave relations had been broken. Even before the war was over, southern black men had begun to press their interconnected claims for manhood, autonomy, and equality. While some did harbor early hopes that they might receive 40 acres and a mule from Washington, those hopes were soon dashed by Andrew Johnson's decision to return confiscated land to its original owners. As it became clear that only a few radical Republicans were willing to contest the president's move, blacks increasingly confined their efforts to more attainable objectives. Resolutions passed by numerous local meetings and conventions after Appomattox indicated their desire to secure the electoral franchise and a decent education, two essential corollaries of full citizenship which, as the black codes clearly revealed, most former Confederates were determined to deny them.

Lacking a strong economic base in the late 1860s, the freedpeople had recourse to several forms of aid in their quest for equality. The family – in many instances the reconstituted family – remained at the heart of rural black community life as it had done under slavery. It was greatly strengthened, however, by the ending of the domestic slave trade and altered, too, by the initial withdrawal of black female and child labor from the fields. So widespread was this latter trend that it led to a decrease in agricultural productivity after the war. One estimate suggests that the number of 'man-hours' per capita may have dropped by at least a third of the amount of labor extracted through coercion under slavery.[24] Nonetheless, there were severe limits on the ability of black men to set themselves up as conventionally respectable heads of household. Most black women simply could not afford to take the bourgeois route to domestic happiness. Large numbers helped to swell the urban growth of the late 1860s by finding jobs as domestic servants and washerwomen. The black population of Atlanta, for example, increased from 1,900 to 10,000 between 1860 and 1870, much of this growth due to the influx of freedwomen.[25] Of the majority who remained in the rural areas, relatively few were able to stay out of the fields on a permanent basis.

The other key institution in black life was the church, one of the principal sources of community building in the Reconstruction era. Like the family, the church underwent significant change as a result of wartime upheavals. Emancipation allowed many blacks to withdraw from the white Presbyterian, Methodist, and Baptist churches in which they had been enrolled under slavery. In no mood to be segregated as second-class Christians in white churches and eager to assume more control over their own religious lives, blacks across the South formed their own congregations during the late 1860s and 1870s. While many of these churches initially remained affiliated with the major southern white denominations, most had joined separate black connections by the end of Reconstruction.

Among the most influential of these connections were the northern-based African Methodist Episcopal Church and the African Methodist Episcopal Church Zion, both of which joined northern white benevolent organizations such as the American Missionary Association (AMA) in proselytizing actively among the ex-slaves. Black organizers such as James Walker Hood, a Zionist emissary whose separatist efforts were encouraged by federal military authorities in coastal North Carolina, enjoyed great success in their attempts to assimilate old congregations and develop new ones.[26]

The black churches served what Eric Foner calls 'multiple functions'.[27] They provided blacks with a range of valuable resources in the fight for equality: buildings in which the freedpeople could meet beyond the gaze of southern whites; pooled finances that could be put to educational and political uses; communal spaces in which blacks could develop essential leadership and organizing skills. The church was thus a major source of the surge in black political organizing which took place after the Civil War. Men, women, and even children entered the public sphere for the first time by attending political meetings from the summer of 1865 onward, many of these events held in churches such as Richmond's First African Baptist. They also participated actively in the proceedings of the new state constitutional conventions, their sporadic comments from the gallery and enthusiastic participation in hastily convened mass meetings outside evoking the inclusive, demonstrative style of black church services.[28] During 1867 black ministers were in the vanguard of the Union League movement which presented large numbers of freedmen with their entrance into Republican party politics. Many local League meetings, moreover, were held in churches with a Bible placed prominently on a table at the front of the house.

As well as loci for political education, black churches were, of course, centers for religious teaching. Here southern blacks of all ages imbibed the lessons of evangelical Christianity, especially the need for personal responsibility and the biblical message that salvation could only come through faith, suffering, and struggle. The gospel of self-help, so potent a factor in the development of southern black communities in the late nineteenth and early twentieth centuries, was rooted in the Reconstruction church.

Few sympathetic white observers of the freedpeople failed to comment on their thirst for education. For obvious reasons most slaveholders had endeavored to keep their human chattels in a state of ignorance. Once free, southern blacks wanted the same standard of education as whites. Here again their churches played an important role, furnishing teachers not only for Sunday Schools but also for rudimentary day schools which were themselves often housed in modest church buildings. Educating a race, however, was an enormous task and one that was well beyond the capacity of blacks to accomplish through self-help alone. It was in this sphere that white allies provided significant aid to the emancipated slaves. White benevolence came in private and public forms. Northern Christians provided much of the funding and personnel for the diverse outreach programs of the mainstream denominations. Freedmen's aid societies, often extensions of female antislavery and wartime networks, raised money for charitable endeavors in the South – largely on the back of widespread sympathy for the Confederacy's most demonstrably loyal population. The federal government also played a critical role in trying to alleviate the worst shocks of emancipation by providing Freedmen's Bureau schools for blacks.

Although much of this assistance was invaluable to impoverished and illiterate southern blacks, it was not without its negative side. The generosity of many northern Christians, black as well as white, was often matched by their paternalistic attitudes toward the former slaves who were generally deemed to be emerging from the barbaric sink of southern slavery. Few of the 4,000 white female teachers who taught in the Freedmen's Bureau schools were willing to allow that there might be something to admire about African-American culture as they encountered it in places like the Sea Islands of Georgia and South Carolina where local blacks spoke Gullah and practiced a highly demonstrative form of religion heavily imbued with African cultural survivals. Well-meaning schoolteachers often deemed traits such as laziness, irresponsibility, and criminality to be as much a product of race as of slavery. In their eyes their mission was a civilizing one – a potentially inclusive one perhaps but one that, in the short term, precluded the development of equal relationships between blacks and whites.

The Freedmen's Bureau itself has often been criticized for its treatment of the emancipated slaves.[29] Staffed by US military officials who liaised directly with local Union commanders, the Bureau was the Republicans' chief vehicle for fashioning a beneficent free-labor society in the late Rebel states. Bureau officers were empowered to oversee the drawing up of contracts between white employers and black laborers, to set up special courts when state and local governments failed to protect the freedpeople's basic rights, and to furnish federally funded education to blacks in their allotted district. While the determination of some Bureau commissioners such as Davis Tillson in Georgia and Wager Swayne in Alabama to cooperate with local whites did more to serve the interests of planters than those of blacks, the majority of officers tried to prevent ex-Confederates from using coercive methods of labor control. Even Tillson insisted that the freedpeople were 'under the guardianship of the Nation'.[30] The real problem besetting the Bureau was not its alleged favoritism toward the old plantocracy but its paucity of funding and employees. Equally seriously, the rapid demobilization of the Union army during 1865–66 and subsequent military focus on the subjugation of the Plains Indians meant that the Bureau (wound up by Congress in 1869) was heavily reliant for enforcement of its decisions on a tiny occupation force spread over a vast slice of territory. Agents often found the task of shielding blacks from white violence intensely frustrating. 'Nothing but troops can prevent abuse of freemen', commented one Bureau officer in central Texas in July 1867.[31] Because troops were always hard to come by in the Reconstruction South, many of these hard-pressed federal agents actively encouraged blacks to form Union Leagues and Republican party organizations. Indeed, it was primarily as Republicans that black men would pursue their struggle to achieve equality.

The passage of the Reconstruction Act in March 1867 heralded the advent of a potentially revolutionary era in southern history.

Freedmen across the South voted in large numbers for new constitutional conventions that would enshrine their main objectives into law. Although blacks were generally underrepresented in these bodies, they constituted a majority in the South Carolina and Louisiana conventions and at least one-fifth of the members in five others.[32]

White conservatives in the region were appalled by what they saw as the Yankees' imposition of Negro rule, the nightmare that Calhoun had foreseen in the late 1840s. In a representative fit of outrage, one white Tennesseean denounced the North for imposing a despotism from which even the Russians had shrunk in Poland. 'There is', he wrote,

> a refinement of vengeance[,] tyranny, and cruelty, in depriving
> the intelligent, the cultivated, the white of that section [the
> South] of all political power and vesting it in the ignorant,
> the brutal, the black[,] the former slave of the white, and
> stimulating him to use such power in every possible way
> to ruin, oppress[,] degrade and insult his former master.[33]

Virulently racist attacks on the conventions ensued. In North Carolina, for example, where P.T. Barnum's circus was touring, white newspapers lampooned the local political gathering as the 'Gorilla Convention', the 'Menagerie' and the 'Congo-Kangaroo Konvenshun', this in spite of the fact that only a tenth of the delegates were black.[34] Deeply rooted fears about the consequences that black empowerment might have for the future of white male republicanism produced not only racial slurs and conventional predictions about imminent race mixing but also further instances of sporadic violence. For the most part, however, lower South conservatives initially advised inaction at the polls as the most effective response to the new constitutions. They expected that if these objectionable documents failed to receive majority backing from local whites, radicals in Congress would have to impose even more extreme policies, thereby driving an even deeper wedge into northern public opinion. Such hopes were soon extinguished. In no mood to hand back the initiative to unrepentant traitors, Republicans in Washington passed a supplementary Reconstruction Act allowing ratification of state constitutions on the basis of a simple majority of the votes cast in the election. Conservatives were left to ponder their next move.

The constitutional conventions of 1867–68 produced a set of progressive documents that generally mandated equal rights, black suffrage, and state-supported public schools and provided a fertile environment for economic development. These accomplishments were not the result of total unity within the Republican coalitions that dominated most of the states in the wake of the First Reconstruction Act. Even in states like Mississippi, where blacks were numerically dominant partners in the coalition, they had little choice but to cooperate with a disproportionately influential minority of white Republicans. Tensions existed between all the main elements of the coalition. Former slaves did not always see eye to eye with educated northern blacks, though black delegates at the conventions tended to speak with a more united voice than whites whose principal faultline lay between northern 'carpetbaggers' who had settled in the South at the end of the war and so-called 'scalawags', white southerners who had chosen to support the Republican party.

The scalawags themselves were a diverse group. Many of them were wartime unionists from the southern hill country. Some were prominent ex-Confederates, among them Georgia's wartime Confederate governor Joe Brown, his close ally, Rufus Bullock (the peach state's first Republican governor), and, perhaps most astonishingly of all, General James Longstreet of Virginia. As the convention debates indicated, the two main groups of white Republicans often had very different priorities. Scalawags like Brown and Bullock did not wish to promote racial equality. They became Republicans primarily because they were attracted by the party's capacity for promoting much-needed economic growth, but also because they sensed (as a result of persistent class tensions between upcountry folk and black-belt elites) that they could attract 'common whites' into a winning Republican coalition if the right policies were pursued. White northern carpetbaggers were a mixed bunch. Some like Adelbert Ames, a Union general from Maine with a distinguished service record, exhibited a genuine commitment to a more just society. Others, like George Spencer, a midwestern veteran of Sherman's army who was elected to the US Senate from Alabama, entered local Republican politics in search of wealth and power.

The differing aims and constituencies of these factions resulted in disagreement over a number of important issues. The black desire for the franchise and legal equality was generally accepted by scalawags but the latter, well aware of grassroots antipathy to racemixing, favored explicit endorsement of segregation in the new constitutions. While blacks' desire for autonomy meant that they were often prepared to accept separate facilities in some areas of everyday life (especially schools), they were wary of legislation that stigmatized them as inferior. Without a significant constituency of their own, white carpetbaggers tended to side with blacks in the constitutional conventions and the new state legislatures. However, one of their main goals was to promote greater investment in the southern economy – hence their enthusiasm for providing state subsidies for railroad development, an enterprise that initially garnered a good deal of cross-class support in the wartorn South. Scalawags and blacks were hardly less supportive of developmental policies in the conventions, but they often parted company over the freed slaves' readiness to fund state government initiatives such as schools, mental asylums, and hospitals through increased taxes on land.

Another prominent source of internal friction, especially in states where whites were in a majority, was the determination of unionist scalawags to disfranchise large numbers of ex-Confederates in order to bolster their tenuous hold on power. During the winter of 1868–69 this issue was partly responsible for a serious split between centrist and radical Republicans in the second session of Texas's constitutional convention. Moderates cooperated with conservative Democrats in Austin to defeat an attempt by radicals to deprive former Rebels of the vote. Even if the process of drawing up new constitutions highlighted the unifying impact of Democratic hostility on southern Republicans, it was evident from the start that the party would find it difficult to cohere on a permanent basis.

Reconstruction had its greatest impact on areas in which blacks were in a majority. In many counties where plantation agriculture had thrived before the war, the combination of demographic strength, manhood suffrage, and a high-profile federal military presence gave blacks the opportunity to continue the process of community building. This was especially true in urban places where US troops and sympathetic army commanders were based, but even in the countryside African-Americans were able to reinforce their newly won freedom by sending children to school, participating in Republican meetings, going to the polls as first-class citizens, and serving on juries and as elected local officers.

It was in the political sphere that the effects of Reconstruction were most visible. Roughly 80 percent of southern Republican voters were black in the late 1860s and early 1870s.[35] If whites secured the lion's share of public office in this period, sheer weight of numbers combined with a growing mood of assertiveness to ensure that African-Americans would begin to challenge that stranglehold. The extent of this political upheaval should not be exaggerated. No black governor was elected in any state and only in South Carolina did blacks come close to gaining their fair share of local offices. No more than 20 percent of public posts in the South were occupied by African-Americans at the height of Reconstruction. Few of these positions were at the federal level: only 6 percent of southern congressmen elected between 1868 and 1877 were black. More than 80 percent of these state and national officeholders were literate men. A disproportionate number of them were light-skinned and professional. More than a quarter had been free before the war, many of these being northern black carpetbaggers. Yet the very fact that significant numbers of blacks were being elected to offices ranging from parish juries to the US Senate bore testimony to the dramatic change wrought by federal policy in large parts of the postwar South. Previously blacks had never come close to exercising political power on this scale. Once the embers of Reconstruction had cooled, however, the majority of African-Americans in the South would not be free to vote or hold office again until the 1960s.

In addition to a measure of political power, Reconstruction gave the freed slaves greater access to education, thereby sustaining the multifaceted ideology of racial uplift that would find its most potent form in the career of Booker T. Washington at the turn of the century. Notwithstanding fierce southern white opposition to integrated public schools (and often to the very notion of black education), the tenacious efforts of blacks and their white allies bore fruit in the steady growth of black literacy during the final decades of the nineteenth century. By 1876 nearly 40 percent of black children were enrolled in school, over three times the figure for 1870 when the black illiteracy rate was over 80 percent. By 1900 the rate was down to 45 percent. There were several reasons for this swift improvement. Freedmen's Bureau schools played their part. There were more than 4,300 of them by 1870 accommodating over 250,000 students (mostly in or near urban areas).[36] The effort made by black teachers, parents, and children was equally significant. So was the action of paternalistic northern whites such as the wealthy Bostonian George Peabody whose charitable foundation not only provided financial support for racially separate southern public school systems but also helped to persuade a minority of local whites that public education for both races fostered social cohesion.

Outside assistance was especially important when it came to fostering the first black colleges in the South. Northern Protestant organizations such as the AMA provided the impetus for institutions such as Fisk in Nashville, Tennessee, and Tougaloo in Mississippi. Booker T. Washington's *alma mater*, the Hampton Normal and Agricultural Institute in Virginia, was the brainchild of a former commander of black troops and Freedmen's Bureau officer, General Samuel C. Armstrong. A zealous proponent of evangelical values such as individualism, self-discipline, and hard work, Armstrong thought black people 'in the early stages of civilization', lower on the evolutionary scale than the Polynesian islanders of his native Hawaii, yet backward because of slavery rather than as a consequence of their race.[37] With the financial support of the Freedmen's Bureau, the AMA and some wealthy northerners, he made Hampton into a tightly run vocational school designed to instill his favorite Christian virtues into black students. Students were required to perform two days of manual work per week and contribute a percentage of their earnings toward their schooling. Washington (who entered the school in 1872) learned the central message well: if blacks were going to succeed in southern life, they had to learn to walk before they could run.

This was not the only lesson the renowned black leader claimed to have imbibed at Hampton. As southern blacks discovered in the aftermath of their reenfranchisement during the mid-1960s, political power does not translate automatically into economic gain. As long as whites monopolized ownership of land and credit, they were well positioned to limit any benefits that blacks might secure through their involvement in Republican party affairs. One of Booker T. Washington's chief aims after leaving Hampton was to nurture a culture of black enterprise that would provide a springboard for the race's equal participation in American society. Amid the 'Christian influences' at Hampton, Washington wrote later, 'I was surrounded by an atmosphere of business, and a spirit of self-help that seemed to awaken every faculty in me and cause me for the first time to realize what it means to be a man instead of a piece of property.'[38]

The moral discipline and manual training provided by the new black colleges was a critical factor in the development of the bourgeois ideology of racial uplift that Washington came to personify. Often misunderstood solely as a prop of conservative accommodationism, uplift ideology represented the black quest for a positive identity in a postemancipation society that was both capitalist and racist. During Reconstruction what can loosely be described as the black elite played their own role in developing and sustaining small businesses across the South. Their grocery stores, barber shops, and saloons were grossly undercapitalized and always vulnerable to economic collapse. Nonetheless, these businesses functioned as important institutions in the evolution of self-sustaining, semi-autonomous black communities. They also laid the foundations for the development of the modern black middle class.

While the freed slaves' embrace of evangelical Christianity made some blacks receptive to the racially transcendent values of bourgeois capitalism, only a minority of them were in a position to benefit from the limited economic space provided by Reconstruction. Republican free-labor ideology held out the promise that those who worked hard would reap the material rewards from their labor. For the mass of former slaves tied to the plantations, that promise was never realized. Life as a sharecropper or share-tenant, entailing as it did residence and labor on a portion of a white-owned plantation, may have brought blacks a degree of freedom from white interference but it did not normally provide an escape route from poverty. Yet there were ways in which blacks were able to begin acquiring land during Reconstruction. Four thousand families had purchased land under George W. Julian's Southern Homestead Act by 1869.[39] Unfortunately much of the public acreage reserved for settlement under this measure was marginal, the best southern land being owned already by planters. South Carolina's Republican government created a land commission which, in spite of its well-earned reputation for corruption, placed around 44,000 acres in the hands of blacks by the time the books were closed in 1890. Depressed economic conditions in the postwar South also facilitated the purchase of farms by blacks in areas like the Mississippi Delta. The result of these developments was the emergence of a fragile class of black yeomen. Within 15 years of the formal abolition of slavery in the United States, roughly 20 percent of black farm operators owned their own land.

The South redeemed

Instead of guaranteeing the 'just and lasting peace' that Lincoln had called for at the end of the Civil War, Reconstruction was followed in the 1890s by the era of *de jure* segregation in which the emancipated slaves – poor, disfranchised, and harassed – were reduced to second-class citizens in the land of their birth. Numerous explanations have been advanced for what blacks understandably saw as their betrayal. Some of these focus on developments in the North where continued public support was essential if radical Republican hopes for equality were to be fulfilled. The primary reason, however, for the ultimate demise of Reconstruction as a political process was that southern whites were determined to prevent blacks from enjoying the equal protection of the laws.

Although a federal military presence was maintained in parts of the South until 1877, Reconstruction came to an end in most states before this date. The decision to link ratification of the Fourteenth Amendment with readmission of individual southern states to Congress virtually guaranteed a swift return to civil government in the defeated Confederacy. The problem facing southern Republicans was that once federal protection had been withdrawn, they had to compete for office with rival Democrats. Historically southern Democrats had been staunch supporters of slavery, secession, and white supremacy. Notwithstanding defeat in the Civil War, a majority of them remained as vigorously opposed to 'Negro rule' as they always had been. Various groups aligned to the region's Democratic party waged campaigns of political terror against their opponents. The aim was simple: to sap local Republican morale by murdering and intimidating black unionists and their white allies. Foremost among the clandestine counter-revolutionary groups was the Ku Klux Klan, the brainchild of General Nathan Bedford Forrest, one of the Confederacy's most feared cavalry leaders notorious for his role in a massacre of black soldiers at Fort Pillow in April 1864. By the time of the Grant–Seymour campaign, the Klan had transcended its origins as a social organization for Confederate veterans in Tennessee to become the paramilitary arm of the Democratic party in the South and the spearhead of local white resistance to Reconstruction. Several black politicians were murdered by Klansmen in the months preceding the 1868 presidential election. They included an Arkansas congressman, three Republicans in the South Carolina legislature, and several members of the constitutional conventions. The results in some areas were devastating for southern Republicans. In Louisiana and Georgia they ceased campaigning entirely. In many parts of these and other states the black vote in the election collapsed dramatically as the freedmen's concern for security overrode their eagerness to participate in politics.

Grant's election victory caused some southern Democrats to rethink their support for violence and join several leading northern Democrats in endorsing a 'New Departure' for the party.[40] This policy envisioned a grudging embrace of the recent constitutional amendments that would allow the treason-tainted Democrats to put the past behind them and reach out to moderates on both sides of the Mason-Dixon Line. Any hopes, however, that the two major parties could start fighting new battles over important grassroots concerns pertaining to the economy and education were soon thwarted. Democrats in Tennessee, Mississippi, Texas, and Virginia did evince a willingness to endorse the New Departure strategy. But when the Grant administration tried to reach out to centrist Democrats in Virginia by offering to avoid a substantial proscription of ex-Confederates in return for explicit guarantees of black suffrage in the state constitution, it succeeded only in paving the way for the defeat of the regular Republican candidate for governor in 1869. The new president wanted peace but not at the expense of the Democrats' return to power.

Several factors stymied the administration's efforts to bring stability to the postwar South. Party factionalism was a major obstacle.[41] Moderate white Republicans in most southern states appealed directly to former Whigs whose support was regarded as essential for electoral success. They did so primarily by advocating an amnesty for all former Confederates and by looking to economic growth as the panacea for the region's backward condition. Republican regimes in the deep South placed great faith in state aid for railroads – a policy designed to attract forward-looking whites to their uneasy coalition. In the lower South, however, they found their goals imperiled by the growing mood of black assertiveness. James Lusk Alcorn, for example, was elected governor of Mississippi in late 1869. Alcorn, a wealthy white ex-Whig from the black belt, had urged his fellow planters to follow him into the Republican party in order to control Reconstruction. His attempts to woo former Confederates into the modernizers' fold through the use of executive patronage merely alienated blacks who then began to transfer their support to the white carpetbagger, Adelbert Ames. Similar factionalism bedeviled the Republicans elsewhere, making it difficult for Grant to know which group of his ostensible allies he should support.

Southern Democrats meanwhile were increasingly divided between unreconstructed conservatives and those who wished to adopt the New Departure approach to politics. While the latter were bidding for support from the same centrist group of whites as the moderate Republicans, conservatives rejected talk of accommodation with blacks and Yankees. Large numbers of ex-Confederates remained unable to accept black suffrage as a permanent feature of the political landscape. The strength of white unity on this issue ensured that the majority of local Democrats remained aloof from any New Departure-style initiatives.

During the late 1860s and early 1870s a combination of Republican weakness and Democratic political terrorism allowed these conservatives to 'redeem' the majority of southern states from what was widely perceived to be barbarian rule. The vulnerability of the southern Republican regimes was evident from the outset. Given the strength of Civil War memories, it was hardly surprising that these regimes were regarded by most southern whites as illegitimate – as manifestations of the North's vindictive desire for revenge over the brave but vanquished South. The fact that they were so closely linked to the former slaves greatly exacerbated the hostility to Republican governance and increased whites' determination to regain power at home.

Not all of the votes cast against the Republicans during Reconstruction stemmed from white supremacist urges. The Republican agenda of state aid for railroads and public schools required higher taxes on land at a time when most southern whites had barely begun to recover from the ravages of war. These same policies also provided a fertile breeding ground for corruption. Black and white politicians were susceptible to the inducements provided by railroad lobbyists and an inflated public trough. Several Republican regimes were notoriously venal, especially those in South Carolina and Louisiana. While corruption was certainly endemic throughout Civil War-era America – among Democrats as well as Republicans, North as well as South – its grip on some southern Republicans gave substance to the conservative Democrats' calls for retrenchment.

The Republicans' limited constituency further sapped the party's ability to withstand the Democratic revival in the South. Perhaps more might have been done to attract lower-class whites into the coalition, for example by promoting policies designed to relieve the plight of impoverished debtors. Yet such moves normally found little support among blacks (who saw the mounting pile of white indebtedness as a means to secure land) and ran counter to the Republicans' desire to attract the votes of well-to-do ex-Whigs, most of whom turned out to be as opposed to Reconstruction as any former Democrat. Clearly class divisions did exist among southern whites during this period, just as they had done during the Civil War. Relatively few non-elite whites, however, proved willing to put aside their traditional attachment to white supremacy in order to make common cause with (mainly black) Republicans. Indeed, large numbers of them could be found among the ranks of the Klan.

By 1870 conservative governments were back in power in Tennessee, Virginia, Georgia, and, after Governor William Holden's controversial use of black militiamen to suppress terrorism, in North Carolina. The new regimes often shared the Republicans' enthusiasm for railroads but they moved quickly to constrain the rights of plantation laborers and to limit black suffrage by requiring payment of poll taxes as a precondition for voting. In many areas where blacks constituted a majority or a near majority, 'white-line' Democrats had gained power largely by using violence against their opponents. The Ku Klux Klan and other white supremacist organizations linked to the Democratic party were active in several states during the election campaigns of 1870, notably in Georgia and South Carolina. Confronted with the prospect of Democrats regaining power throughout the South just five years after Appomattox, Republicans in Washington strove once again to protect the gains won at such cost with the blood of the Union dead.

In the spring of 1870 Republican-controlled states in New England, the Midwest, and the South provided the votes necessary for ratification of the Fifteenth Amendment. This measure prohibited the federal government and the individual states from denying the right of American citizens to vote 'on account of race, color, or previous condition of servitude'. Sometimes interpreted as a cynical attempt by beleaguered Republicans to secure the vote of northern blacks, it sprang directly from the party's longstanding, if by no means consistent, determination to guarantee equal rights for loyal blacks.[42] The measure was certainly controversial. A majority of white voters in populous states such as New York and Ohio had again registered their opposition to local black suffrage in 1868. Some western congressmen were concerned that the amendment might force them to acquiesce in the enfranchisement of thousands of Chinese immigrants who had come to America to find work on the Pacific coast. Support for the amendment, however, from black leaders and white radicals was intense. Few Republicans could deny that black men had fought loyally for the Union, that their security was still threatened in the South, and that the continued disfranchisement of many northern blacks was an embarrassing incubus when it came to making southern policy. While moderate Republicans in Congress harbored doubts about the amendment's impact on federal–state relations, they had good pragmatic and intellectual reasons for endorsing it.

Enforcing the constitutional rights of citizens was no easy task. In spite of being an antebellum Douglas Democrat, Grant was supportive not only of the Fourteenth and Fifteenth Amendments but also of Republican attempts to give those measures real teeth. Between May 1870 and June 1872 Congress passed five statutes designed to sustain the federal government's ability to enforce national laws in the former Confederacy. The most significant of these, the First Enforcement Act, provided punishments for state officials who tried to prevent enfranchised citizens from voting, outlawed conspiracies by two or more individuals to prevent citizens from exercising their rights under federal law, and directed US officials to prosecute violations of the Fifteenth Amendment. The other four measures were essentially supplements to this statute, the most important of them being the so-called Ku Klux Force Act, passed in April 1871 in the wake of well-documented reports of widespread Klan violence in South Carolina. This act increased the president's power to use federal military force to suppress domestic disturbances and allowed him to suspend the writ of habeas corpus in areas where terrorist groups were active. When Grant used his powers under this measure against the Klan during the final stages of his first term, it proved to be remarkably effective in quelling Klan activity in Mississippi, Florida, and especially South Carolina.

The political will to enforce these measures remained strong through the 1872 election campaign. Signs of internal Republican opposition, however, began to emerge before that contest as self-confessed 'liberals' within the organization announced their opposition to the Grant administration. In part the Republicans were undergoing a crisis of identity. With slavery abolished, the South defeated, and black suffrage implemented, some northerners sensed that the party had fulfilled its mission. But there was more to the Liberal Republican revolt of 1871–72 than this.[43] Elite reformers such as E.L. Godkin, editor of *The Nation*, were prominent among those seriously disappointed with Grant for failing to curtail what they regarded as the malign influence of the spoils system on American government. Serious evidence of corruption within the administration had already begun to emerge and calls for a meritocratic civil service had failed to elicit concrete results. Importantly, so far as the future of Reconstruction was concerned, the reformers were also at odds with the president's efforts to enforce the constitutional amendments with the use of troops. In their view the continued use of federal force in the South undermined fundamental individual liberties and thwarted the critical goal of sectional reconciliation. While not oblivious to the plight of southern blacks, many Liberals were unconvinced that the freed slaves were sufficiently removed from bondage to cast their votes in the unfettered manner demanded of independent-minded citizens. In their view education rather than political strife was the best solution to the problems besetting the freedpeople.

The Liberals' open hostility to federal power in general and to Reconstruction in particular paved the way for an unhappy marriage of convenience with the Democratic party. At their convention in Cincinnati in May 1872 they nominated for president Horace Greeley, the veteran editor of the *New York Tribune* whose backing for a general amnesty for Confederates allowed freetraders to overlook his longstanding commitment to protective tariffs. New Departure Democrats, in the ascendancy within their own organization, then endorsed their old foe, hopeful that his strong record on slavery and the Rebellion would give them the ammunition they needed to defeat the country's supreme war hero.

Although pro-Grant 'stalwarts' in Congress undercut the Liberals' platform by passing an Amnesty act, bitter disputes over foreign policy provided the opposition with a major ally in the ample shape of Senator Charles Sumner. Sumner, the staunchest congressional supporter of black rights in the wake of Thaddeus Stevens's death in 1869, was at odds with the administration on two major external issues. The first of these, the extent of American claims for damages inflicted by the British-built Confederate raider, the *Alabama*, during the Civil War, was finally settled by arbitration and Senate ratification in 1871–72. Grant and his patrician secretary of state, Hamilton Fish, had accepted the arbitration award of $15.5 million as the basis for a final settlement of the controversy. In doing so they acted in the uneasy spirit of Anglo-American amity which had also seen the federal authorities crack down on Fenian (Irish nationalist) incursions into Canada from the United States in the late 1860s. Sumner, once a pronounced Anglophile, had opposed what he regarded as such lenient action, publicly calling for the cession of Canada to the United States as well as the establishment of permanent principles for the settling of international maritime disputes. Even more damaging to relations between the powerful senator and the administration was the latter's policy in the Caribbean.

As the fierce national debate over Reconstruction showed signs of cooling, domestic support for overseas expansion began to grow. Congress, for example, displayed highly visible support for Cuban insurrectionaries in 1869 and would probably have granted them belligerency had it not been for the cautious stance of Hamilton Fish. The secretary showed little more enthusiasm for another Caribbean venture, the proposed annexation of the Dominican Republic. This scheme, however, had the full backing of President Grant's private aide, Orville E. Babcock, who was conspiring with American investors and Buenaventura Báez, the local dictator, to secure US control over this small yet fertile nation. Grant sent the annexation treaty to the Senate in 1870 partly because of his friendship with Babcock, partly because of the strategic and commercial benefits for the United States, and partly, so he claimed, because annexation would give southern blacks leverage in their ongoing struggle against the former Confederates. Sumner, a fierce opponent of proslavery expansion in the Caribbean basin as well as anything that smacked of black colonization, led the opposition to the Treaty which was lost in the Senate on June 30. When Grant tried to revive it the following winter, Sumner attacked the president as a bully and again helped to defeat the measure. For his pains he was removed from his influential position as chairman of the Senate committee on foreign relations. In view of these events it was hardly surprising that Sumner finally emerged as an open supporter of the Liberal revolt in July 1872.

While President Grant was damaged by these tussles with the Massachusetts senator, his opponents found themselves unable to overcome their own substantial problems in the November election. Many leading Liberals were vulnerable to Republican charges that they were 'soreheads' acting out of pique at being passed over for office. Significantly more Democrats, especially in the South, were unable to stomach the idea of voting for Greeley, an eccentric reformer who had made a career out of lambasting the Slave Power. Even more importantly, the Republicans were able to expand their core constituency in the North by alleging that a vote for the opposition amounted to a betrayal of the Union cause. Greeley proved to be reasonably competitive but Liberal strength was confined mainly to Sumner's New England. Narrow successes in the Republican-controlled states of the South helped Grant win an overwhelming victory in the electoral college and a comfortable popular majority of 55 percent.[44]

From this point onward Reconstruction began to crumble. Further revelations about the extent of graft within the Grant administration increased the public's suspicion that political life was intolerably corrupt – a sense that was heightened when congressmen unwisely voted themselves a substantial pay rise (or 'salary grab' as it was widely dubbed by the press). Americans' sensitivity to charges of malpractice leveled against Republican governments in the South was correspondingly increased, as was Grant's reluctance to provide federal aid to his embattled copartisans below the Mason-Dixon Line.

The northern will to support Reconstruction was further eroded by the onset of a major economic depression in the summer of 1873. Southern policy, previously seen as a critical political issue in the North, was increasingly relegated to a subordinate position in the public mind as voters began to fret about their own welfare and worrying evidence of social unrest (manifested in strikes and demonstrations) at home. Growing economic stringency also placed added pressure on southern Republicans who were forced to cut back even further on expensive programs of state-funded education and who saw their hopes of economic expansion destroyed in the wake of the Panic. In some states internal disputes over control of patronage made life even harder for local Republicans. This was the case not only in Louisiana where the supporters of William Pitt Kellogg sought to impeach Henry Clay Warmoth, a rival Republican candidate for governor, but also in Arkansas where disaffected Republicans participated in a *coup d'état* against their own party's regime in 1874.

Initially, President Grant responded to events by renewing his efforts to conciliate southern whites in the hope that a softer line on Reconstruction would win converts to Republicanism. Acquiescing in the Democratic seizure of power in Texas produced no concrete gains. The new conservative administration in Austin simply dismantled Republican programs including the state's embryonic system of free public schools. Elsewhere white-line Democrats read Greeley's electoral defeat as proof that the New Departure had failed and resorted once again to violence. Made aware that con-ciliating southern whites meant abandoning the freedpeople to their fate, Grant combined calls for intraparty reform with the dispatch of federal troops to areas where Republicans were under threat from renewed outbreaks of Klan-style terrorism. In September 1874 the president reluctantly sanctioned military aid for Governor Kellogg in Louisiana where at least 100 blacks had been murdered in the Colfax 'riot' the previous year and where subsequently the paramilit-ary White League had launched a systematic campaign of assassina-tion against Republican officeholders. Such high-profile intervention found little favor with an electorate that was becoming bored with Reconstruction and inclined to blame the Republicans for the country's economic woes. In the midterm elections of late 1874 the Democrats won control of the lower house of Congress for the first time in nearly twenty years. They also gained ten new Senate seats and won gubernatorial races in several southern states where whites outnumbered blacks. The results were a devastating blow to the party in power and to the faltering cause of racial equality.

During the campaign Democrats capitalized not only on the depression but also on Charles Sumner's attempts to pass a wide-ranging Civil Rights bill designed to outlaw segregation in public places and provide for integrated public schools. Racial integration, especially of schools, was regarded as the most pernicious form of race mixing by virtually all southern whites and large numbers of northerners. In fact even southern blacks had declined to press for integrated schools, partly because of the trend toward autonomy but also because of the issue's effect on whites. (Only in cosmopolitan New Orleans had southern Republicans undertaken positive steps to integrate the public schools.) Sumner's moral absolutism, however, led him to press his radical measure in Congress with the support of some assertive southern black Republicans who had begun to embrace the schools issue as a means of ridding their party of white moderates. The Massachusetts senator died shortly after the congressional elections, widely mourned by blacks as one of the era's pioneering white crusaders for equal rights. As a testament to his memory (and a final swipe at incoming Democrats) Republican congressmen voted to pass the Civil Rights Act in the final days of the session. But before doing so they made sure to excise the provision for integrated schools. With a presidential election only two years away they had no reason to alienate more white voters than they needed to.

Lingering hopes that the 1875 Civil Rights Act and a reinvigorated enforcement policy on the part of the executive would breathe new life into Reconstruction were raised briefly by Grant's decision to bolster again the beleaguered Kellogg regime in Louisiana with military force. 'I have deplored the necessity which seemed to make it my duty under the Constitution and laws to direct such interference', he told the Senate in an unusually angry message on January 13, but 'neither Kuklux Klans, White Leagues, nor any other association using arms and violence to execute their unlawful purposes can be permitted in that way to govern any part of this country.'[45] However, when cautious Republicans in the upper chamber blocked another enforcement bill the writing was on the wall. White-line Democrats in Mississippi took the occasion to rid themselves of 'Negro rule' through the wholesale intimidation of black Republicans prior to the state election of 1875. The carpetbag governor, Adelbert Ames, wired desperately for troops but was rebuffed by Attorney General Edwards Pierrepont, a former Democrat who told Ames frostily that northerners were tired of hearing about southern outrages and that Washington would not help until the state had done all it could to suppress the violence. Although the disbandment of the state's active black militia companies did prompt a lull in terrorism, local Democrats stepped up their intimidation again shortly before the election. The result was a massive downturn in the Republican vote in many black-belt counties. Mississippi, the home of Jefferson Davis, was redeemed at last.

Pressured by terrorism, economic misery, and mounting charges of corruption, the president toned down his comments on Reconstruction, opting instead to stir up public sentiment against Catholic efforts to fund denominational schools at government expense. Even though Grant had not abandoned southern Republicans entirely, his attempts to enforce the recent constitutional amendments were undermined by prominent jurists intent on preventing further erosion of the federal polity after the Civil War. In the *Slaughterhouse Cases* of 1873 the US Supreme Court had decided by a margin of 5–4 that the 'privileges and immunities' clause of the Fourteenth Amendment did not extend to economic rights.[46] In his verdict upholding the regulatory powers of the state of Louisiana, Justice Samuel Miller, a moderate Republican who feared that radical policies portended 'the eventual destruction of some of the best principles of our existing Constitution', drew on Chief Justice Taney's reasoning in the *Dred Scott* case to posit a critical distinction between state and national citizenship.[47] His list of rights protected by the federal government included few of any great concern to blacks whose most fundamental rights, according to the majority of the Court, remained under the primary protection of the states. Even though the judges had not questioned the essential validity of the Fourteenth Amendment, the black leader Frederick Douglass had no doubt that Miller's notion of dual citizenship played into the hands of white supremacists. 'Two citizenships', he told the former abolitionist Gerrit Smith, 'mean no citizenship. The one destroy[s] the other. ... The nation affirms, the State denies, and there is no progress. The true doctrine is one nation, one country, one citizenship, and one law for all the people.'[48]

Douglass's fears were confirmed in March 1876 when the Republican-dominated Supreme Court drew on *Slaughterhouse* to strike down essential sections of congressional enforcement legislation. In *US V Cruikshank* and *US V Reese* a majority of justices again articulated their conviction that the protection of individual rights was the duty of the state and not the federal government. Only when it could be proven that state officials discriminated on grounds of race was the United States constitutionally empowered to intervene. Remnants of the Enforcement Acts remained on the statute books well into the twentieth century, as did the constitutional amendments of the Reconstruction era. But the Court rulings of the 1870s and a subsequent decision in the *Civil Rights Cases* (1884) which invalidated the 1875 Civil Rights Act laid the legal foundations for the long years of Jim Crow segregation.

Reconstruction was not quite over by the time of the 1876 presidential election. Federal troops continued to bolster Republican regimes in South Carolina, Louisiana, and Florida. In most parts of the South, however, the Reconstruction experiment had ended by the close of Grant's disastrous second term. While the achievements of the Republicans' southern policy in the fields of education, law, politics, and community building were far from negligible (no less so than the achievements of the emancipated slaves themselves), Reconstruction had demonstrably failed to provide security and justice for the freedpeople. Southern whites in general and the Democratic party in particular bore primary responsibility for this failure, but secondary blame could justifiably be attached to Republican politicians and ordinary northern voters. If the planter class had not succeeded in its principal aim of independence, it had at least guaranteed the survival of white supremacy for the foreseeable future.

Notes

1. *CWL*, 8, p.333.

2. Quoted in David H. Donald, *Lincoln* (London, 1995), p.588.

3. Booth was cornered and killed by Federal troops in northern Virginia on April 26. Four of his co-conspirators were executed on July 7. Although Booth had been in contact with the Confederate secret service, there is no evidence that high-ranking southern leaders like Jefferson Davis knew of any plot to murder President Lincoln.

4. See e.g. Eric L. McKitrick, *Andrew Johnson and Reconstruction* (Chicago, 1960), pp.154–8 and *passim*.

5. Gary W. Gallagher, *The Confederate War* (Cambridge, Mass., 1997), pp. 30–1.

6. Figure cited in Patrick O'Brien, *The Economic Effects of the American Civil War* (Basingstoke, 1988), p.13.

7. Daniel W. Stowell, *Rebuilding Zion: The Religious Reconstruction of the South, 1863–1877* (New York, 1998), pp.15–21.

8. Steven Hahn, *The Roots of Southern Populism: Yeoman Farmers and the Transformation of the Georgia Upcountry 1850–1890* (New York, 1983), pp.137–203.

9. John Leland quoted in Stowell, *Religious Reconstruction*, p.43.

10. E.M. McCaleb to T.P. Chandler, June 6, 1865, GLC 1594.

11. Johnson to Sharkey, Aug. 15, 1865, in Paul H. Bergeron, ed., *The Papers of Andrew Johnson: Vol. 8, May–August 1865* (Knoxville, Tenn., 1989), p.600.

12. *New York Daily Tribune,* Jan. 30, 1865.

13. Quoted in Eric Foner, *Reconstruction: America's Unfinished Revolution 1863–1877* (New York, 1988), p.160.

14. Schenck Diary, June 7, 1865, SHC 652.

15. Quoted in Eric Foner, *A Short History of Reconstruction* (New York, 1990), p.105.

16. *Congressional Globe,* 39 Cong., 1 sess., p.27.

17. Quoted in Foner, *Reconstruction,* p.249.

18. Fessenden to Elizabeth C. Warriner, Feb. 25, 1866, William Pitt Fessenden Papers, Bowdoin College.

19. *Congressional Globe,* 39 Cong., 1 sess., p.3149.

20. Bruce Ackerman, *We The People: Vol. 2, Transformations* (Cambridge, Mass., 1998), p.161.

21. *Report of the Joint Committee on Reconstruction at the First Session Thirty-Ninth Congress* (1866: repr. Freeport, NY, 1971), pp.xi, xvii, xxi.

22. Detailed accounts of the 1868 election campaign include John Hope Franklin, 'Election of 1868' in Arthur Schlesinger, Jr, ed., *History of American Presidential Elections 1789–1968,* 9 vols (New York, 1985), 3, 1247–66, and Foner, *Reconstruction,* pp.337–45.

23. Quoted in *ibid.,* p.340.

24. Roger L. Ransom and Richard Sutch, *One Kind of Freedom: The Economic Consequences of Emancipation* (Cambridge, 1977), p.46.

25. Tera W. Hunter, *To 'Joy My Freedom: Southern Black Women's Lives and Labors after the Civil War* (Cambridge, Mass., 1997), p.21.

26. Sandy Dwayne Martin, *For God and Race: The Religious and Political Leadership of AMEZ Bishop James Walker Hood* (Columbia, SC, 1999), pp.51–8.

27. Foner, *Reconstruction,* p.92.

28. Elsa Barkley Brown, 'Negotiating and Transforming the Public Sphere: African American Political Life in the Transition from Slavery to Freedom' in Jane Dailey *et al., Jumpin' Jim Crow: Southern Politics from Civil War to Civil Rights* (Princeton, NJ, 2000), pp.28–66.

29. See e.g. William S. McFeely, *Yankee Stepfather: General O.O. Howard and the Freedmen's Bureau* (New Haven, Conn., 1968), pp. 3, 7, 328, and Leon F. Litwack, *Been in the Storm So Long: The Aftermath of Slavery* (New York, 1979), pp.382–3, 386.

30. Quoted in Paul A. Cimbala, 'Reconstruction's Allies: The Relationship of the Freedmen's Bureau and the Georgia Freedmen' in *idem* and Randall

M. Miller, eds, *The Freedmen's Bureau and Reconstruction: Reconsiderations* (New York, 1999), p.320.

31. James J. Emerson quoted in Randolph B. Campbell, *Grass-Roots Reconstruction in Texas, 1865–1870* (Baton Rouge, La, 1997), p.172.

32. Foner, *Reconstruction*, p.318 and note.

33. Henry J. Hunt to Henry K. Craig, Oct. 4, 1867, GLC 2382.035

34. Quoted in Karen L. Zipf, '"The Whites Shall Rule the Land or Die": Gender, Race, and Class in North Carolina Reconstruction Politics', *JSH* 65 (1999), 514–15.

35. This statistic and those that follow are taken from James M. McPherson, *Ordeal By Fire: The Civil War and Reconstruction* (New York, 1982), pp.555–7.

36. Randall M. Miller, 'Introduction' in Cimbala and *idem*, eds, *Freedmen's Bureau*, p.xxviii.

37. Quoted in Louis R. Harlan, *Booker T. Washington: The Making of a Black Leader* (New York, 1972), p.61.

38. Quoted in *ibid.*, p.72.

39. Foner, *Reconstruction*, p.246.

40. *Ibid.*, pp.412–25.

41. The fissiparity of southern Republicanism is the central theme of Michael Perman, *The Road to Redemption: Southern Politics, 1869–1879* (Chapel Hill, NC, 1984).

42. For a negative assessment of Republican motivation see William C. Gillette, *The Right to Vote: Politics and the Passage of the Fifteenth Amendment* (Baltimore, 1965).

43. On the Liberal Republicans see Patrick W. Riddleberger, 'The Break in the Radical Ranks: Liberals vs. Stalwarts in the Election of 1872', *Journal of Negro History* 44 (1959), 136–57, Richard Allan Gerber, 'The Liberal Republicans of 1872 in Historiographical Perspective', *JAH* 62 (1975), 40–73, John G. Sproat, *'The Best Men': Liberal Reformers in the Gilded Age* (New York, 1968), pp.12–110, and Foner, *Reconstruction*, pp.488–99.

44. Extended accounts of the 1872 election include William C. Gillette, 'Election of 1872' in Schlesinger, ed., *History of American Presidential Elections*, 4, pp.1303–30, and Foner, *Reconstruction*, pp.499–511.

45. Quoted in Brooks D. Simpson, *The Reconstruction Presidents* (Lawrence, Kan., 1998), p.179.

46. Foner, *Reconstruction*, pp.529–31.

47. Quoted in Charles Fairman, *Mr. Justice Miller and the Supreme Court, 1862–1890* (Cambridge, Mass., 1939), p.191.

48. Quoted in Xi Wang, *The Trial of Democracy: Black Suffrage and Northern Republicans, 1860–1910* (Athens, Ga, 1997), p.124.

8

LAND OF GOLD: THE FAR WEST IN THE MID-NINETEENTH CENTURY

If postbellum dreams of a united, prosperous nation were stymied by persistent sectional divisions over Reconstruction, they gained sustenance from developments in the Far West. This was hardly surprising. Frederick Jackson Turner's famously influential, though far from uncontested, invocation of the West as the crucible of American national identity was delivered in 1893 but it drew on a wealth of political and social experience, cultural transactions, and economic boosterism in the middle decades of the nineteenth century.[1] The relative paucity of the region's population belied the importance of the trans-Missouri region as a factor in the emergence of the United States as a modern nation.

The West's significance, in the decades before Turner looked at the census statistics of 1890 and pronounced the frontier closed, was partly a product of one of the most potent images in the country's history. Deeply rooted notions of an American Eden achieved their most powerful cultural resonance in the era bounded by the California gold rush and the final defeat of the Lakota (Sioux) Indians in 1876. It was during this period that thousands of settlers from all parts of the globe flocked to the region in pursuit of wealth, opportunity, and independence. At a time when these ideals seemed to be endangered by the sectional conflict, the West encapsulated the American conception of Manifest Destiny.

Artists did as much as anyone to convey these deeply felt yearnings. In 1861 Emmanuel Leutze was employed by the federal government to decorate the Capitol building in Washington – a commission that resulted in his justly renowned 'Westward the Course of Empire' (1862), a pean to the unstoppable and, by extension, unifying momentum of frontier settlement. Specifically biblical allusions were probably most evident in the sweeping canvasses of Albert Bierstadt whose popular, heavily romanticized western landscapes illustrate the validity of Mark David Spence's judgment that the region's physical aspect 'provided the basic elements of a scenic anthem that praised the grandeur and power of the United States'.[2] Such grandiose productions, however, were not to everyone's taste.

In the early spring of 1861 Samuel Langhorne Clemens, a restless Missourian who would prove to be a caustic critic of Bierstadt, accompanied his brother on the long journey to Nevada. Orion Clemens's reward for supporting Abraham Lincoln in the recent presidential election had been an appointment as secretary of the new territory, a remote and arid land brought suddenly to the forefront of the American imagination by the discovery in June 1859 of the 'Comstock Lode', an area of rich silver deposits on the eastern side of the Sierra Nevada. A decade later Sam Clemens, writing under the riverine pseudonym of Mark Twain, would consolidate his growing literary reputation by gently satirizing his western experiences in the pages of his second major work, *Roughing It*. 'I was young and ignorant', Twain recalled, 'and I envied my brother':

> Pretty soon he would be hundreds and hundreds of miles away on the great plains and deserts, and among the mountains of the far West, and would see buffaloes and Indians, and prairie dogs, and antelopes, and have all kinds of adventures, and may get hanged or scalped, and have ever such a fine time, and write home and tell us all about it, and be a hero. And he would see the gold mines and the silver mines, and maybe go about of an afternoon when his work was done, and pick up two or three pailfuls of shining slugs, and nuggets of gold and silver on the hillside. And by and by he would become very rich, and return home by sea, and be able to talk as calmly about San Francisco and the ocean, and 'the isthmus' as if it was nothing of any consequence to have seen those marvels face to face.[3]

Although the tarnished West that emerged from Twain's semi-autobiographical account was scarcely more credible than the image created by visual publicists like Leutze and Bierstadt, his comic creation did at least impart a sense that the region was a real place and that genuine hardships there were not unknown. Easily forgotten amid the torrent of landscape paintings and promotional literature accompanying the frontier movement was the fact that the West was indeed a real geographical space. Hundreds of thousands of men, women, and children – by no means all of them white Euroamericans – shared Twain's youthful vision of a more exciting and prosperous life in the trans-Missouri West. Collectively they formed one of the great migratory streams in the history of the United States and in the process they transformed or destroyed existing human and eco-logical communities. Although a substantial number of them did advance their material status as a result of their decision to move, many found that the region was not the Eldorado or the Garden of Eden they had been led to believe. By the end of the 1870s the settler's goal of a producer paradise was rapidly being undermined by the same social and economic forces that were turning the wider nation into the most dynamic capitalist society on earth. Nowhere in the postwar era were the tensions inherent in the republican vision more plainly visible than the great American West.

The mining frontier

Diplomacy and war rendered Thomas Jefferson's vision of a con-tinental empire a reality. The Oregon Treaty of 1846 with Britain stabilized the country's northwestern border with Canada along the 49th parallel, paving the way for the penetration of United States influence into the Pacific Northwest, one of the most fertile regions of North America. The Treaty of Guadalupe Hidalgo which ended the war with Mexico two years later gave the 'yanquis' access to what had once been the borderlands of New Spain. Subsequent diplomatic negotiations, commercial pressure, and military activity further expanded the national domain. The Gadsden Purchase in 1853, bought with a view to promoting the goal of a southerly railroad route to the Pacific, added another 30,000 square miles of Mexican territory. American merchants and missionaries strengthened the processes that rendered the Hawaiian (or Sandwich) Islands, over 2,000 miles off the Pacific coast, a satellite of the United States long before formal annexation in 1898.

Spearheading American expansion after the Civil War was Secret-ary of State William H. Seward. In 1867 he took advantage of good relations between the Union and Tsarist Russia to purchase the nominally Russian territory of Alaska for $7.2 million. Dismissed as a frozen wasteland by many critics of the treaty, 'Seward's Folly' (3.6 million square miles in area) was actually rich in minerals as well as fur and fish, though the bulk of its subterranean resources would not begin to be tapped until the Alaska gold rush at the end of the century. Seward had other grandiose plans, most of which went unfulfilled in part because of widespread personal antipathy toward him among congressional Republicans. The Senate, for example, blocked his efforts to give federal aid to New York businessmen trying to build an isthmian canal in Central America and rejected a trade reciprocity treaty with the Sandwich Islands that would have bound them closer to the United States by opening up the American market to Hawaiian sugar. Seward's attempts to promote trade with Asia were also thwarted. A US warship did participate in a European-led action to open up Japan to foreign trade and Christian missions, but the secretary's desire to exert a similar influence on Korea and China never matched the constrained nature of American power in the immediate aftermath of the Republic's recent bloodletting.

If Seward's schemes for informal overseas empire offered a glimpse of the future, America's expansionist energies in the postwar era were directed much more effectively to its own contiguous territory. During the middle decades of the nineteenth century the federal government pursued a ruthless policy of extinguishing Indian titles to land that had supposedly been guaranteed to the indigenous inhabitants of the continent by treaties ratified in the US Senate. If land availability had been the key to the growth of a genuinely meritocratic society, the Far West seemed ideally suited to bring the hopes of free-soil expansionists to successful fruition.

Settlement of the Pacific slope began in earnest with the California gold rush of 1849, the event which precipitated the deep political crisis over slavery culminating in the Compromise of 1850. An eccentric carpenter, James Marshall, had located gold in John Sutter's millrace on January 24, 1848, just nine days before California was ceded formally to the United States. There was no immediate dash to the area. It took time for word of the discovery to reach the more settled portions of the country and initially the eastern press was skeptical about the scale and value of the findings. By the summer a degree of momentum had begun to build. Confirmatory letters appeared in the newspapers. The new American territorial governor dispatched a sample of gold to Washington that arrived shortly after the 1848 presidential election. James K. Polk exhibited fourteen pounds of the precious metal in the course of his outgoing message to Congress in December. The difficult question of whether the allure of untold riches justified the social cost of westward migration then began to exercise families and whole communities across the nation. Would-be migrants, mostly men, wrestled with their consciences, endeavoring to square their desire to get rich with their family commitments.

The decision to go was seldom easy. Even if the trip was eventually sanctioned by kinfolk, there were other factors to consider, not least the high cost of travel to California by sea (via the isthmus of Panama or Cape Horn) or the arduous nature of the cheaper overland journey. By late 1848, however, growing numbers of Americans had decided to migrate. Eighty thousand of them left for the California goldfields during the following year, swamping the small resident population of Mexicans, Indians, and whites. By 1854 around 300,000 migrants had arrived in the state.[4] Although a majority of the newcomers were native-born whites (with northerners predominating over southerners), sizeable numbers of Irish, Britons, Frenchmen, Australians, Mexicans, Chileans, Peruvians, Chinese, and free blacks were also drawn to the goldfields.

The initial camps in the Sierra Nevada mountains were centers of egalitarianism in a country where republican simplicity was fast being eroded by the modernizing trends of the age. Placer mining (the sifting of gold dust from streams with the use of a pan) required minimal outlays of capital and even less technical skill. Theoretically it was therefore open to anyone who could make the journey to the Pacific slope. The Forty-Niners grouped together to protect their claim sites and, in the absence of civil justice, set up their own courts to administer their laws. Work in the mountains was hard and the climate, especially in the winter, offered little consolation. For some observers, including the Brooklyn journalist Walt Whitman, the enthusiasm for California embodied the best of America's dynamic, democratic spirit. For others, notably the pioneer environmentalist Henry David Thoreau, it represented the worst. 'The recent rush to California', he wrote in his journal on February 1, 1852,

> & the attitude of the world, even of its philosophers and prophets, in relation to it appears to me to reflect the greatest disgrace on mankind. That so many are ready to get their living by the lottery of gold-digging without contributing any value to society, and that the great majority who stay at home justify them in this both by precept and example! ... If I could command the wealth of all the worlds by lifting my finger, I would not pay such a price for it. It makes God to be a moneyed gentleman who scatters a handful of pennies in order to see mankind scramble for them. Going to California. It is only three thousand miles nearer to hell.[5]

The prospect of untold riches for the many ended in the space of a few years. The first to lose out were Hispanics who were swiftly expelled from the mining camps by whites who had no intention of sharing the anticipated bounty with those they held to be of inferior racial stock. US military officials and the new California legislature aided the process of expulsion with nativist orders and legislation, but the white 'Argonauts' themselves were soon casualties of basic geological conditions and economic trends. Most of the gold lay beneath the surface of the earth. To reach it required the sinking of shafts, the use of environmentally destructive hydraulic mining, and the crushing and processing of vast quantities of rock quartz. To do this required skill, technology, and capital – assets which the average miner simply did not possess. As early as the mid-1850s California mining had become a sophisticated industry – the prosaic preserve of urban banks, mining companies, and wage laborers rather than a mecca for the independent citizen of the Republic.

Although the majority of white miners did not attain their goals in the high Sierras, they fared better as a group than the existing inhabitants of California whom they helped to displace. The old Mexican elite, large 'rancheros' in the main, made some initial gains by furnishing beef to the Argonauts. However, the failure of the Treaty of Guadalupe Hidalgo to guarantee their property rights resulted in an expensive litigation process that left most of them greatly reduced in land and status. Even harder hit were the local Indians, particularly in the northern part of the state where they were hunted down systematically by white settlers. In combination with pandemic Eurasian diseases, the genocidal activity of professional Indian killers like Hi Good and Robert Anderson reduced a native population of roughly 150,000 in 1848 to just 30,000 in 1870.[6]

From the perspective of regional and national development, the dark side of the California gold rush evinced by these figures was counterbalanced by the event's contribution to American economic growth. During the early 1850s the United States contributed 45 percent of the total world production of gold. Notwithstanding the onset of economic recession in the middle of the decade, California boomed as interior towns such as Stockton and Sacramento grew up to service the local mining economy and as commercial agriculture spread into the fertile Central Valley (see Map 7). High British demand for American grain after the repeal of the Corn Laws made wheat cultivation one of the most profitable occupations in the state, contributing significantly to the diversification and sophistication of the economy.

The new towns spawned ambitious business elites. The most famous of these was a group of Sacramento merchants who had prospered as a result of the gold rush. In November 1860 the so-called 'Big Four' – Collis P. Huntington, Mark Hopkins, Leland Stanford, and Charles Crocker – provided the initial capital for a visionary, yet decidedly risky transportation venture. Their Central Pacific Railway Company quickly began work on the daunting western leg of the projected transcontinental railroad. After the receipt of federal largesse during the Civil War, the project would bring these investors riches beyond their wildest imagination.

The most striking product of California's urban growth, however, was San Francisco, the premier port on the west coast and within twenty years the tenth largest city in the United States with a population of 150,000. Rivaling New York in its ethnic and racial diversity, the Bay City established itself as the economic powerhouse of the Far West. As well as being the principal point of entry for migrants, it was the chief entrepôt for western metal and grain exports. The business district centered around California Street was the locus for many of the major commercial houses which oiled the region's nascent development. In an area in which capital shortages were endemic, funding from gold-rush fortunes as well as eastern and overseas investors spurred the rapid growth of urbanization, infrastructure, large-scale commercial farming, and technologically advanced extractive industries such as mining and logging.

Two local institutions, both founded during the Civil War, played a particularly important role in promoting capitalism on the West Coast: the San Francisco Stock and Exchange Board and William Chapman Ralston's Bank of California. Ralston, a pioneer capitalist, had taken charge of the Exchange by 1868 and channeled vast amounts of speculative mining capital into regional business ventures. By far the most productive of these enterprises were the newly discovered Comstock silver mines of Nevada's Washoe country. Admitted to the Union in 1864, Nevada was little more than 'an economic satrapy of San Francisco's capitalists' at this juncture of its history.[7] Ralston and his associates masterminded what was essentially a colonial capitalist enterprise, forging a virtual monopoly on the Comstock, and plowing the profits into a wide portfolio of investments that included telegraph lines, canals, insurance, and, of course, more mines. Thus did San Francisco's buccaneering speculators contribute to the rapid economic development and diversification of the Far West in addition to the swelling of their own fortunes and those of the Bay City itself.

San Francisco's position as the New York of the Pacific coast was exemplified by its social as well as its economic dynamism. After an initial phase of lawlessness caused by growing hostility to the rule of the local Democratic party (heavily Irish in complexion and pro-southern in orientation), the city's politics stabilized rapidly to provide a solid framework for the growth of voluntary associations (many of them, like the Hibernian Society or the black San Francisco Atheneum, ethnic or racial in origin) and prominent civic institutions.[8] As was the case in the eastern states, urban social development owed a good deal to elite civic activism. Wealthy businessmen, many of them domiciled on Nob Hill, helped to improve the local environment not only by funding the creation of public parks and libraries but also by providing patronage for artists and writers. It was William Ralston, for example, who commissioned Frederick Law Olmsted, the architect of Manhattan's Central Park, to design a pleasure garden for the Bay City – a project that eventually resulted in the construction of Golden Gate Park. Elite patronage, moreover, made San Francisco one of America's leading artistic centers by the early 1870s, its place confirmed by the founding of a design school in 1874.[9]

The opening up of the Pacific slope mines and the fertile agricultural land of California and Oregon paved the way for American settlement of the West coast, but what of the vast acreage (part Louisiana Purchase, part Mexican Cession) which lay between the Sierra Nevada mountain range and the boundaries of settlement in the Mississippi Valley? Migrants from the eastern states who made their way to the Pacific on the overland trails were crossing a huge swathe of the national domain that retained its hold on the popular imagination as 'the Great American Desert'. Artists and writers might credibly depict California as a Land of Canaan, but for those travelers who journeyed across the high plains in the 1850s the vast interior across the Missouri River carried more than a measure of genuine threat.[10]

At the time of the Civil War the frontiers of Victorian civilization had pushed well beyond the Mississippi into southern Minnesota, western Iowa, the Missouri–Kansas border, and eastern Texas but railroad construction had not yet caught up with the advance of white settlement from the east. Traversing the Mississippi in the 1850s the tracks reached only as far as Saint Joseph, Missouri, by 1860. Ahead of the westbound migrants lay a daunting journey, by wagon train or stage coach, of at least three weeks. The country lying before them was a relatively arid yet diverse region of grasslands and semi-desert sliced vertically down the center by the towering snow-capped peaks of the Rocky Mountains. The main thoroughfares through this vast land – the California, Oregon, and Santa Fe Trails – had been established by 1850 and the routes themselves were protected by a network of US military forts. Beyond the trails, however, lay lands which, even after assorted military expeditions and Pacific railroad surveys, remained only partially charted by the federal authorities. Uncharted or semi-charted did not mean uninhabited. More than 30 tribes of nomadic and sedentary Indians numbering around 75,000 people in 1860 dwelt on the great plains which were also home to two dwindling concentrations of bison: the northern and southern herds.[11] Before the Colorado and Nevada mineral rushes of the late 1850s, there was, aside from the relatively small numbers of federal troops and traders, only one significant community of whites in the interior: the persecuted band of Latter Day Saints who had trekked west to the Great Basin of what became Utah Territory in 1850.

Like the Indians, the Mormons aroused feelings of deep antipathy among a majority of Americans. In part this was a consequence of the Mormons' clannishness which derived from their attachment to the scriptural revelations of their martyred founder, Joseph Smith. Like most religious sects the Mormons regarded themselves as God's chosen people. Under the leadership of Smith's fellow prophet Brigham Young, a former carpenter who proved to be one of the most practical and successful empire-builders of his generation, they strove to develop a genuinely communitarian society far from the gaze of hostile 'gentiles' who, predictably, regarded the Mormons' theocratic ways, rejection of the Trinity, and attachment to polygamy (the West's own 'peculiar institution') as an even greater threat to the nation's welfare than Catholicism. Indeed, during the mid-1850s, Republican politicians had twinned polygamy with slavery as part of their ongoing attempt to locate their new party in the vanguard of progress. Their chief opponent, President James Buchanan, had no more time for Mormons than they did. Frustrated by Young's apparent attempts to foster an autonomous state centered on the town of Salt Lake City, Buchanan dispatched federal troops to restore the government's hold on the territory. Young agreed to meet Washington's terms before the army moved in, but simmering Mormon–gentile tensions resulted in a bloody assault on a wagon train of southern settlers in August 1857 by a combined militia group of Saints and Paiute Indians. The Mountain Meadows Massacre in southwestern Utah (which left 120 dead) was a serious embarrassment for Mormon leaders and did little to convince westbound settlers that Utah was anything more than a sink of iniquity. Mark Twain, impressed though he was by the order and cleanliness of Salt

Lake City, claimed (perhaps only half in jest) that he had arrived in the territory convinced that the Mormons employed 'Destroying Angels' set apart by the Church for the purpose of conducting 'permanent disappearances of obnoxious citizens'.[12]

Mormon hopes of founding a utopia ('Deseret') remote from the corrupting influences of gentile society were undermined not only by the exertion of federal authority but also by the commercial growth of Salt Lake City as a transit point on the emigrant trail. Crucial in this latter regard was the discovery of gold in the front range of the Rockies in July 1858. Pike's Peak hysteria stimulated the second major pulse of westward migration before the Civil War. Indeed, more than twice the number of people participated in the Colorado gold rush than its California predecessor.[13] The effects were similar. New 'instant cities', of which Denver rapidly emerged as the most significant, sprang up overnight and the high plains region was integrated at speed into the nation's market economy.[14] As had been the case in California, the native inhabitants of the land bore the brunt of the American invasion. Two decades of squalid Indian wars were the immediate result.

The subjugation of the Plains Indians

It is easy to romanticize the Plains Indians of the mid-nineteenth century. They can seem to the modern reader (as they did to a few contemporary whites) enviably free spirits, at one with themselves and their environment – innocent victims of an aggressive and technologically superior foe. There is some truth to this compelling image. The unique folkways of tribes like the Lakotas, the Cheyennes, and the Apaches were largely or entirely destroyed by the remorseless advance of white settler society. The horse nomads of the western high plains (in contradistinction to the horticultural tribes of the Missouri River Valley and Indian Territory) organized their material and spiritual lives around the bison hunt, the vast and dramatic landscapes over which they roamed, and the seemingly limitless skies under which they encamped. Until market penetration occurred and whites demanded leaders with whom to treat, internal hierarchies were relatively undeveloped. Women played an integral role in the activities of the nuclear and extended family which constituted the essential building blocks of Indian societies. As well as taking charge of domestic affairs in the tipi, sowing and harvesting corn, and making clothes, they sometimes participated in tribal councils, playing a dominant role when the men were away. Religion was central to everyday experience. Rites such as the Sun Dance imparted a profound sense of interdependence, not only collectively within the group, but also universally between individuals and the natural environment and between the living and the dead. Possessing an essentially holistic cosmology, the Plains Indians saw the world as Mother Earth. They had no concept of private ownership and no fear of death (which was, to them, a mere extension of life).

Such views help to explain the modern fascination with Indian lore and culture but fall short of providing a total picture of Native American society. The Plains Indians had not been entirely isolated from whites during the first half of the nineteenth century. In fact the reverse was true. Commerce, though at times controversial among the tribes, had occurred on an extensive basis ever since the arrival of the Spanish and French on the southern plains in the eighteenth century. Horses, firearms, and other European goods, traded for Indian products such as furs and bison robes, had been altering local Indian societies for decades before the mineral discoveries opened the floodgates of white settlement. The Cheyennes and neighboring tribes owed their legendary mobility to their willingness to adapt to changed circumstances, particularly their acquisition of fleet-footed ponies for use in the chase. Indians, moreover, acquired horses and guns to kill not only the bison but also each other.

Intertribal warfare was endemic on the high plains during the early 1800s. Even if it is true that such conflicts were fought primarily to satisfy honor or vengeance rather than to secure profit or territorial gain, it is likely that more Indians died in internecine strife before 1850 than in battles with the US army thereafter. The expansion of powerful warrior societies such as the Lakotas in the north and the Apaches in the south ensured a ready supply of Indian clients for the United States government. Many tribes or factions of tribes sought survival through accommodation rather than conflict. Some, like the slaveholding Cherokees of Indian Territory who fought in vain for the Confederacy, went as far as any people could to adopt the ways of the white man.

While it may be a disservice to history to view the Indians as entirely innocent victims of American empire building, the fact remains that the period between 1850 and 1876 witnessed the destruction of a unique way of life. Given that they were regarded in law as 'domestic dependent nations', why was it that the tribes of the high plains were allowed to be crushed so decisively by the government and people of the United States? There are several answers to this question. The most obvious one is that the Indians were obstacles to the onward march of progress. Most Americans championed individual property ownership, land improvement, and the production of commodifiable surpluses. If they possessed a modicum of romantic or Christian sympathy for Native Americans, they had little understanding of, let alone respect for, the Indians' communitarian and naturalistic traditions. But perhaps even this is too charitable an explanation for what was essentially a ruthless, imperialistic process of conquest. White settlers wanted the land on which the Indians hunted or farmed and, as since the dawn of the Republic, they were none too fastidious about how they procured it. Written and pictorial claims that the Indians would inevitably be swept aside by the juggernaut of progress were, in reality, mere justifications for naked greed.

Escalating white settlement of the Far West occasioned by the mineral strikes and the relentless desire for farmland and timber had a devastating effect on the Indians' natural environment. Although the tribes themselves had caused a measure of environmental destruction through their deliberate burning of grassland to improve forage, the hunting of bison, and the excessive grazing of large herds of horses, the ecological transformation wrought by white settlement was on a much greater scale. The new arrivals destroyed delicate ecosystems by diverting and polluting watercourses, cutting down trees by their thousands, and slaughtering bison (the Indians' main source of food) for fun. Their fear of Indian raids and reprisals resulted in military action which closed off traditional hunting grounds for good. Worse still, white encroachment brought new diseases against which the Indians had little immunity. The familiar pattern of widespread Indian deaths from smallpox, measles, and other airborne scourges that had characterized the history of New World indigenes from their earliest contact with Europeans persisted into the middle decades of the nineteenth century, carving swathes through whole tribes and sapping the collective will to resist. In 1849 a cholera epidemic carried onto the plains by California-bound Argonauts killed about 1,200 Pawnees. At least 1,000 Piegan Blackfeet perished in the deadly smallpox epidemic of 1869–70.[15]

Had Washington sought to protect its wards against the depredations of western settlers, it is possible that the fate of the Plains Indians might have been a happier one. The federal government, however, made only faltering attempts to interpose itself between the settlers and the Native Americans. This was partly a result of limited resources. The number of federal troops in the Far West was never large. In the 1850s 90 percent of the army was stationed at 79 posts strung out along the main emigrant routes to the Pacific. This force numbered little more than 7,000 men, a tiny number in view of the huge distances involved. Their main task was to protect American citizens, not the Indians. Western settlers were notoriously vocal in demanding their perceived rights and few congressmen (certainly not those from the states of the Mississippi Valley) were willing to defy them. Even if some bureaucrats in the notoriously corrupt Department of the Interior may have harbored genuine concern for the indigenes, all branches of the federal government adhered to developmental objectives which the settlers were bound to further.

The best that Washington could offer the Indians in the 1850s was a continuation of the treaty system – the ultimate aim being to concentrate them in designated areas with a view to ultimate pacification and the prevention of expensive race wars. A series of treaties (documents agreed by federal negotiators and Indian headmen and ratified by the US Senate) were drawn up in the wake of the Indian Appropriation Act of 1851 which embodied the principle of concentration. None of them were worth the paper on which they were written. The main problem was that white settlers did not believe the Indian had any legitimate claim to the soil for which they hungered and therefore ignored the provisions of these treaties. The result was ever-increasing encroachment on tribal lands. Under enormous social strain some Indian bands accepted what they saw as the inevitable and acquiesced in containment in return for gifts, bounties, and promises of federal annuities. Others rejected the idea of surrender at the outset or soon left the reservations as the deleterious consequences of accommodation became apparent.

The small tribes of the Pacific coast region had no chance of resisting effectively the sometimes genocidal actions of the settlers, but their more mobile peers on the high plains possessed the will and the resources at least to contest the American conquest of their domain. Sporadic warfare broke out across the plains in the 1850s and intensified in the next two decades. Until the 1870s the army's ability to achieve a complete pacification was hindered, firstly, by the limited reach of the antebellum central state and then, subsequently, by the Civil War which virtually emptied the region of regular troops. While the residents of Indian Territory were torn apart by the Civil War (Cherokees, for example, furnished men for both the Union as well as the Confederacy), the tribes of the high plains and northern prairies seized the opportunity provided by the absence of federal soldiers.

In the summer of 1862, a familiar mix of bureaucratic chaos and callousness deprived the eastern (Santee) Sioux of essential government rations. In the ensuing uprising, the deadliest in American history, hungry Indian braves slaughtered more than 400 whites in southwestern Minnesota. Preoccupied though he was by Lee's invasion of Maryland, President Lincoln was forced to dispatch Union troops to the area under the command of the ill-starred General John Pope. In common with most army commanders, Pope had little time for Indians and proclaimed that his intention was 'utterly to exterminate the Sioux if I have the power to do so ... They are to be treated as maniacs or wild beasts.'[16]

Pope proved to be a more effective foe of Indians than he was of Confederates. The revolt was suppressed by October and the Minnesotans looked forward keenly to a rash of military executions. Lincoln resisted the calls for vengeance. Even though he had once served in the Illinois militia against the Sauk and Fox, he listened sympathetically to the cautionary advice of Minnesota's Episcopalian bishop, Henry B. Whipple, and his own commissioner of Indian affairs, William P. Dole. After studying each case personally, he reduced a list of 303 Sioux men scheduled for execution to 39 (of whom one was pardoned at the last minute). The Minnesotans were outraged but manifestly the incident revealed Abraham Lincoln in his most humane light.

Rather less mercy was in evidence on the central plains during the latter stages of the Civil War. White settlement occasioned by the Colorado gold rush polarized the local tribes. While some chiefs like the inveterate trader, Black Kettle, counseled peace and signed treaties, radicalized military societies such as the Cheyenne Dog Soldiers confronted the invaders with force. In the spring of 1864 simmering tension between settlers and off-reservation Indians erupted into open warfare after white troops killed a moderate Cheyenne leader, Starring Bear. Raiding on settlements and migrants along the Platte River produced more than a score of white deaths, provoking near hysteria in Denver. When Indians turned a deaf ear to a proclamation issued by John Evans, the Republican governor of Colorado, a second edict ensued authorizing whites to kill on sight all so-called 'hostiles' who had failed to turn themselves in for 'protection'. The result was one of the worst atrocities perpetrated on the American frontier.

On November 29 Colonel John Chivington, an ordained minister in the Methodist Church, led two regiments of largely untrained state troops to a camp of peaceable Cheyennes and Arapahos wintering on the banks of Sand Creek. Urging his men to 'remember the murdered women and children on the Platte', Chivington unleashed a brutal attack on the unsuspecting Indians.[17] At least 150 natives, two-thirds of them women and children, perished in the resulting massacre. The militiamen vented their wrath by scalping their victims, mutilating the corpses, and carrying away female genitalia as trophies and decorations. Cheyenne and Arapaho braves responded with more ferocious raiding in alliance with the Lakota chief, Spotted Tail. Public opinion in the East was critical of Chivington, and the federal government did at least condemn the incident and offer compensation. Some tribal leaders signed a peace agreement accepting a reservation in Indian Territory. The Dog Soldiers, however, remained aloof and continued to harry settlers in the remote Smoky Hill region of Kansas in the years following the Civil War. With Comanche raids a simultaneous and constant threat further south in Texas, it was apparent that, notwithstanding a set of treaties signed with all the warring tribes in the fall of 1865, the army's job was far from over.

The Great Sioux War of 1866–68 helped precipitate a major shift in federal policy. The conflict itself was a product of further white penetration into traditional hunting grounds as well as the relative weakness of the United States Army in the immediate aftermath of the Civil War. Angered by the government's decision to construct forts along the Bozeman Trail (the main emigrant route from Nebraska's Platte River to new gold strikes in Montana Territory), Red Cloud, the leader of the militant Lakota company of Oglala warriors, organized resistance to settler encroachment in collaboration with Arapaho and Cheyenne radicals. In December 1866 a detachment of 79 US soldiers under Captain William J. Fetterman was sent to relieve the pressure on whites in the Powder River area and wiped out by hostile Indians. Although the sensational 'Fetterman massacre' increased exterminationist sentiment among the settlers and prompted the army to redouble its efforts to punish the enemy during 'Hancock's War', Washington chose to consider abandonment of the forts in pursuit of a less confrontational policy toward the Plains Indians. In July 1867, just weeks before at least 60 Indians were killed in the Wagon Box Fight at Fort Phil Kearny, Congress authorized a peace commission to negotiate the removal of the indigenes onto two huge reservations (one north of Nebraska, the other south of Kansas) on which the only whites allowed would be government agents. Red Cloud held out against an agreement for over a year but the majority of Indians – Comanches and Kiowas in the south, Cheyennes and Arapahos on the central plains, and the Lakotas in the north – had agreed reluctantly to go onto the reservations (where they became the responsibility of the Interior Department) by the beginning of 1869. Although off-reservation hunting rights were incorporated into the treaties, these rights were recognized primarily to secure Indian compliance and would only be guaranteed as long as there were enough bison to kill.

The Indians who signed the Treaties of Medicine Lodge Creek and Fort Laramie in October 1867 and April 1868 respectively were neither naive nor cowed. As the Crow chief, Blackfoot, asserted to federal peace commissioners at Fort Laramie, his people would renew hostilities if the United States continued to hem them in. How could they maintain peaceful relations with whites, he said, 'when you take our lands, promising in return so many things which you never give us?'. Indians, he continued, were not 'slaves' or 'dogs': 'We want to live as we have been raised, hunting the animals of the prairie. Do not speak of shutting us up on reservations.'[18]

Tribal bands who refused to treat with the authorities remained the responsibility of the US military. Lieutenant General William T. Sherman, Commander of the vast Department of the Missouri, wrestled with numerous problems, not least the fact that the postwar army was too small to deal effectively with its tasks in the Far West and the Reconstruction South.[19] Although fully aware that white settlers, railroads, and telegraph lines doomed the Indian to near extinction, he was confronted by the short-term need to limit the havoc caused by an elusive and determined foe possessed of a close familiarity with the harsh western terrain. The fruit of limited resources and unattainable goals, Sherman's twin strategy of dispersion for defense and temporary concentration for punitive attack depended heavily for success on the deployment of converging columns to corral and chastise renegade Indians.[20] Because the columns lacked maneuverability, surprise was essential – hence the decision of the army high command to campaign into the winter when Indian food supplies were low and the enemy was preoccupied with survival.

The strategy spawned a not untypical tragedy at the so-called battle of the Washita. On November 27, 1868 Lieutenant Colonel George Armstrong Custer and his 7th Cavalry, aided by Osage scouts, tracked a group of Southern Cheyennes under Black Kettle inside snowbound Indian Territory. As Custer, a flamboyant, overbearing commander described by one of his own officers as 'the most complete example of a petty tyrant that I have ever seen', put it: 'the Indians were caught napping'.[21] Black Kettle, a peace chief who had been present at the Sand Creek massacre, was one of up to 100

Indians butchered in another bloody day's work on the frontier. The following summer witnessed the final rout of the most militant Cheyenne grouping, the Dog Soldiers, at Summit Springs in eastern Colorado. Many of the defeated were killed and then scalped by Pawnees who had played a leading role in locating the camp for Major Eugene Carr's 5th Cavalry.

By the time the American public read of these latest triumphs, former abolitionists like Wendell Phillips and Lydia Maria Child had joined forces with other reformers, including Bishop Whipple, to demand a change in policy. Pointing out the reality of ballooning expenditure, widespread evidence of corruption involving Indian agents and contractors, and the persistent failure to subdue the Indians, the humanitarian lobby found many eastern politicians willing to listen to them. As early as January 1868, a congressional investigating committee produced a landmark report largely in tune with the reformers' demands. Although the document repeated the familiar refrain that civilization should 'not be arrested in its progress by a handful of savages', it went on to recommend the assimilation rather than the destruction of the Indians.[22] The missionary bodies of the country's churches, it argued, should devote increased time and money to proselytizing among the Indians and teaching them English and the value of farming. Just over a year later, in April 1869, Congress built on these findings by establishing the Board of Indian Commissioners. The 'peace policy' of the Grant administration was underway.

Unhappily for the objects of their sympathy, neither Congress nor the Christian reformers had any more time for the lifestyle and value systems of the Indians than the army high command. Personally, Sherman was skeptical that pacified Indians could be assimilated into American society and seemed content that they should be shunted aside in the pursuit of progress. 'Indians are funny things to do business with', he wrote privately in September 1867, 'and the more I see of them the more satisfied I am that no amount of sentimentality will save them from the doom in store for them.'[23] Reformers were heavily critical of the army's no-nonsense (and in some instances blatantly exterminationist) attitude to the Indians. However, their own proposals anticipated the complete destruction of Indian culture for in their view this was the only way to save childlike barbarians from extinction. In November 1869 the Board of Indian Commissioners, a body composed of laymen from all the mainline Protestant denominations, released its first report. The Board made several important recommendations: the concentration of Indians on small reservations, the division of tribal land into privately held plots ('allotment in severalty'), the discouragement of tribal relations, citizenship for members of the so-called Civilized Tribes in Indian Territory, the abandonment of financial annuities on the grounds that they created dependency and corruption, an end to treaty making, the appointment of government teachers for each tribe, and the encouragement of Christian missions.

Although this call for separation, education, and assimilation provided the blueprint for future US Indian policy, the immediate goals of the reformers in the 1870s were hampered by several obstacles. Notwithstanding the abolition of the treaty system in 1871 and the initial appointment of Indian agents nominated by the churches, the peace policy was eroded from all sides. Corruption continued to pervade the Indian service. Whites refused to respect existing treaties. Significant numbers of Indians refused to be boxed in on reservations. And all the time the US military, with the approval of President Grant, undermined the spirit of the new policy by redoubling its efforts to find and destroy any Indians deemed to be uncooperative. Warfare, therefore, continued on the Great Plains into the 1870s. In the south Apache raiding persisted for another decade, but Cheyenne and Comanche resistance was finally subdued in the Red River War of 1874–75. The northern tribes, however, continued to hold out, aided in part by the remoteness of their last hunting grounds in Dakota and Montana Territory. In June 1876, on the eve of the centenary of the American Revolution, they inflicted a sensational military defeat on the United States.

The humiliation of Custer's 7th Cavalry at the Little Bighorn had its origins in renewed white encroachment on the final refuges of the Lakotas. In 1872 and 1873 preliminary surveys began along the Yellowstone River in Montana for construction of a northern railroad route to the Pacific. In the summer of 1874 Custer was ordered to explore routes through the Black Hills, a region sacred to the Lakotas inside the extensive Great Sioux Reservation (roughly equivalent to modern South Dakota west of the Missouri) created by the Treaty of Fort Laramie. Two mineral prospectors accompanying the expedition found traces of gold in the region. Coming as they did in the midst of a serious postwar economic depression, press reports of the discovery induced a new surge of gold fever. Miners began to enter the Black Hills with the connivance of the federal government, thereby placing severe pressure on the peace policy.

With Grant himself a lukewarm peace advocate and the likes of Sherman and Sheridan backing the efforts of railroad men and settlers to open up the northern plains, there was no doubting the result. In May 1875 a delegation of Sioux chiefs including Red Cloud visited the White House where they were informed by the president that as he could do nothing to stem the tide of white invaders they would have to make further land concessions. Perhaps, he thought, they might even consider removing to Indian Territory.

With the hawkish new secretary of the interior, Zachariah Chandler, and his commissioner of Indian affairs, Edward P. Smith, firmly committed to military coercion, the army high command moved to destroy what it regarded as the last major obstacle to progress and civilization in the Far West – the roughly 3,400 Teton Sioux (including Crazy Horse's Oglalas and Sitting Bull's Hunkpapas) and Northern Cheyenne warriors who remained not only wedded to their traditional lifestyle away from the reservations but also determined to prevent the advance of the Northern Pacific Railroad. In the late spring of 1876 the army dispatched three bluecoated columns into Montana's Powder River region – a remote area that lay at the heart of the hostile Indians' summer hunting grounds. Although the northbound column was intercepted and forced to turn back by an Indian war party led by Crazy Horse, the other two met at the confluence of the Yellowstone and Rosebud Rivers on June 21. The commander of the expedition, Brigadier General Alfred H. Terry, then prepared plans for a two-pronged search-and-destroy strike against his recalcitrant foe. While Terry would accompany Colonel John Gibbon's force west and south along the Yellowstone and Bighorn streams, Custer was detailed to lead his 600 cavalrymen and 25 Indian scouts in a southwesterly direction up the Rosebud. Terry's intention seems to have been for Custer to locate the main Indian village and then drive its residents into the embrace of his own column. He had, he told Custer, every confidence in his 'zeal, energy, and ability' and left plenty of leeway in his orders for the experienced cavalry commander to act on his own initiative when battle commenced.[24]

With the help of his Crow scouts Custer found the enemy's village on the banks of the Little Bighorn River on the morning of June 25. Expecting the Indians to take flight and ignorant of the fact that there were at least 2,000 warriors in camp, the overconfident commander divided his force on approach. It was a fatal mistake. Captain Frederick Benteen's troopers went missing on reconnaissance. Major Marcus Reno's companies were thrown back after they forded the river to attack. And Custer and the other 209 men who accompanied him were outgunned, outnumbered, and slaughtered as they tried to move on the encampment downstream. Only the approach of the Terry/Gibson column the next day saved Reno's embattled command from a similar fate.

Arising as it did at the beginning of the 1876 presidential election campaign, news of the disaster was readily assimilated by both political parties. Democrats were swift to blame the debacle on Grant's peace policy and the corruption which they held to be endemic in the Indian service and the administration in general. The southern press lost no opportunity to draw links between this national humiliation and Reconstruction. In a move suggestive of the positive effect that the Indian Wars may have had on sectional reconciliation, papers like the *Mobile Register* and *New Orleans Picayune* urged the government to take federal troops from 'their political services at the South and send them where the honor of the flag ... may be redeemed'.[25] The president and his Republican allies, in contrast, tried to attach the blame onto Custer, a controversial figure at the best of times who had already earned the president's enmity for endorsing charges of fraud leveled against key figures in the administration.

The battle of the Little Bighorn was no more than a pyrrhic victory for the Indians. The army continued its pursuit of the renegades and effectively brought the war to an anticlimactic end with routine victories in late 1876 and early 1877. Sitting Bull and his followers sought sanctuary in Canada, and Crazy Horse was killed while in custody in May 1877. Forced cession of the Black Hills followed, and the Lakotas confronted a dismal future confined on a much smaller reservation than the one granted to them in 1869. The culturally and psychologically destructive process of assimilation and allotment was about to begin in earnest.'

Toward a modern West

The federal government's role in developing the Far West was primarily facilitative. As well as acquiring the region, surveying it, and corralling Indians onto reservations, Washington used its enormous influence as the largest landowner in the region to stimulate economic growth. The marginalization of the native inhabitants of the soil was not, in fact, simply the result of military action but also the inevitable product of communications advances and white settlement encouraged by the central state.

Especially significant in this respect were congressional efforts to promote the construction of western railroads. Politicians assumed that such heroic projects would advance the cause of national unity by connecting the Pacific coast settlements to the East and fostering American occupation of the trans-Missouri interior. Realizing that capitalists would not assume all the risks attached to building railroads across such a vast, thinly populated space, the Republican-dominated Congresses of the immediate postwar era donated huge portions of the national domain to fulfill the long-held dream of transcontinental railroad communications. Burgeoning public revulsion at the accompanying corruption terminated the land grant policy in 1871, but in the space of a decade Washington donated more than 125 million acres to assist the construction of railroads.

The two companies that benefited most from these generous initiatives (as well as federal loans ranging from $16,000 to $48,000 per mile) spent the postwar years building track eastward across the Sierras and westward across the Great Plains. Although charges of graft were already threatening to swamp several leading directors, the Central Pacific and Union Pacific finally united their rails in a grand ceremony at Promontory Point, Utah, on May 10, 1869. The photographer, Captain Andrew J. Russell, captured for posterity the moment when the continent was joined from coast to coast by an iron band. His carefully posed photograph of the final handshake between the two chief engineers omitted the Chinese workers who had labored so effectively to help make this event possible, but it provided contemporaries with fitting confirmation of the (relative) speed at which the Republic was hurtling toward its destiny. Riding the rails at 30 miles an hour, Americans could now cross the continent in less than a week.

Wedded to the goals of promoting widespread farm ownership and rapid economic growth, Washington applied its policy of land disposal to individual settlers as well as railroad companies and local governments. In fact the 1862 Homestead Act never fulfilled its primary purpose of settling small farmers on western land, largely because much of the land set aside for homesteading was too arid to support family farming. The majority of settlers who purchased land did so from the railroads or large speculators rather than the federal government. This fact should caution us not to place too much emphasis on Washington's direct role in western settlement. Even in the territories, where the writ of the central state ran largest, political life was dominated by courthouse rings made up mostly of lawyers, merchants, and newspaper editors. Normally their developmental goals gelled neatly with the broader economic objectives of the national government and the business concerns of the railroad companies whose powerful lobbies were increasingly resented by local people.

Notwithstanding a severe economic depression, development in the Far West proceeded apace during the 1870s. Population nearly doubled from 968,504 in 1869 to 1,789,703 in 1879 and in the same decade more than 16,000 miles of railroad track were laid.[26] The shape of the modern western economy was already clear: heavy dependency on outside investment capital (domestic and foreign), leading extractive sectors such as mining, timber, and, to an extent, agriculture generated by an abundance of natural resources, and a relatively cheap labor force of mostly nonwhites employed by the large railroad, logging, and mining companies. The population of this rapidly evolving region was extremely mobile and highly urban – indeed, the Far West was the most heavily urbanized region of the United States.

Western society was ethnically and racially plural but short on tolerance, equality, and stability. While it was dominated politically by whites, significant populations of Hispanics in the Southwest, Chinese in California, blacks in Texas, and Native Americans through-out the region had a lasting impact on the local culture. There was often little love lost between these groups. Indeed, much of the lawlessness associated with the West had its origins in simmering ethnic and racial tension. Euroamericans had no compunction stereotyping nonwhites as dirty, lazy, and criminal and, on occasion, they used lethal force to confirm their domination. Many of the vigilante movements that sprang up during this formative period of western history were rooted in ethnic conflict. The Irish (no better than half-white as far as many Anglos were concerned) provided the main target for the San Francisco Vigilance Committee during the 1850s. In Los Angeles the principal victims of lynchings were Hispanics. Extra-legal violence often mirrored official repression, for neither the courts nor the state and territorial enforcement agencies were inclined to protect the lives of minorities. One of the main purposes of the Texas Rangers, for example, was to combat Indians and Hispanics – a task that further exacerbated interethnic strife along the Mexican border.

Racial hatred was not the only reason why many white Americans were so hostile to minority groups. Some of them, like Hinton Rowan Helper, feared the effect that the immigrants' clannishness and alleged refusal to contribute to the wider society would have on the welfare of the Republic. Helper, the controversial author of *The Impending Crisis* in 1857, wrote an earlier book containing impressions gleaned from a visit to gold-rush California. He took offense in *The Land of Gold* (1855) at Chinese immigrants not simply because

he regarded them as inferior but also because of their incompre-
hensible language, their fondness for pigtails, chopsticks, and wooden
shoes, and their unmistakable 'coolie' hats. These Asian immigrants,
he wrote, 'are more objectionable than other foreigners, because
they refuse to have dealing or intercourse with us'. 'They are', he
insisted, 'ready to take all they can get from us, but are not willing
to give anything in return.'[27]

Helper's observations on the cultural cohesion of the Chinese
were not without substance but he was wrong in his charge that they
were mere sojourners and opportunists. Herein (just to prove that
the immigrants could not win either way) lay another cause of
xenophobia. By 1880 there were over 75,000 Chinese immigrants
in California, the majority of them peasants from Guangdong
(Canton) Province drawn to *Gum Sham*, the 'Mountain of Gold', by
the lure of regular paid employment, first in the mines, then as
members of Central Pacific construction crews, and increasingly in
urban enterprises ranging from prostitution to restaurant ownership,
factory work, and laundering. Local whites, particularly working men
who were competing with the Chinese for jobs, became increasingly
resentful of the Asians' presence. The growth of so-called 'anti-coolie
clubs' after the Civil War fueled anti-Chinese sentiment in the state
(a feeling made clear by western politicians during the congressional
debates over the Fourteenth and Fifteenth Amendments). In San
Francisco a young newspaperman named Henry George, soon to
become a well-known campaigner on behalf of America's producing
classes, wrote influential articles repeating Helper's complaints about
the unassimilability of the Chinese and the negative impact of
Chinese migrants on wage rates. When the two major parties failed
to curb Asiatic immigration at the height of the depression, workers
formed their own organization in the Bay City. One of the
Workingmen's party's most strident demands was for an end to the
employment of Chinese labor.

If the plural West was no multicultural utopia, it was at least
becoming a more stable society by the close of the 1870s. Frontier
vigilantism persisted but the proliferation and maturation of urban
places acted as a broadly civilizing force (at least in the sense that
whites understood the term 'civilization'). Civic boosters were
influential in this respect, for endemic social conflict was hardly
fertile soil for capitalist development. But women too played a
crucial role in domesticating western society. Although the mineral
discoveries in California, Colorado, Nevada, and other areas sparked
migration surges that were primarily male, the settlements that

followed in their wake evinced a healthier gender balance. Church women replicated their role in the East, participating in organized crusades against such manifestations of immorality as prostitution and drunkenness. It was not simply a question of coercive do-gooding. Western women acted to protect not only the home and family, but also – sometimes – the bodies of the most vulnerable females in society. In San Francisco, for example, where large numbers of Chinese girls scraped a wretched living as prostitutes, the Presbyterian Mission Home founded in 1874 provided an outlet for the benevolent impulses of middle-class white women. With the aid of the local police, the reformers rescued the girls from squalid Chinatown brothels and furnished them with a safe haven (run on orthodox domestic lines) at the Mission Home. In the countryside, where female organizations such as this were nonexistent, the Indians and bison gave way prosaically to family farms and large cattle ranches employing a new breed of worker that would soon be mythologized as the cowboy.

Order and stability came at a high price. One of the main costs of *laissez-faire* capitalism in the Far West was environmental destruction on an industrial scale. The mining industry alone, for example, was responsible for the complete deforestation of the Lake Tahoe region and the pollution of California's rivers. But perhaps the most startling environmental catastrophe was the demise of the buffalo. The southern herd of bison, numbering perhaps 15 million in 1870, was reduced to a few hundred by the end of the decade.[28] Disease (spread by the rapid expansion of cattle ranching) and hunting by Indians played a part in this sudden decline, but the main cause was the tanning industry's insatiable demand for hides. Civilian hunters armed with the latest repeating rifles slaughtered the bison *en masse*. Some of the hunters became renowned for their activities, none more so than William F. Cody, a former Union scout during the Civil War whose bovine killing sprees furnished plentiful supplies of meat for railroad construction crews. Cody's exploits were brought to the attention of the American public in the popular dime novels of Edward Z.C. Judson ('Ned Buntline'), and by the mid-1870s Cody, better known as 'Buffalo Bill', was making a fortune in Manhattan with his own series of western dramas.

Not everyone was happy to get rich from, or was oblivious to, the fate of the bison. A small but growing movement opposed to cruelty against animals joined with a portion of the Indian reform lobby to produce significant pressure for curbs on bison hunting. Regulatory bills were debated in Congress in 1874 and 1876, but ultimately moral and humanitarian concerns were trumped by the majority view that rendering the bison extinct would facilitate subjugation of the Plains Indians.

The very fact that Congress was willing to discuss the fate of the bison signaled the dawn of a new phase in the history of the West. Educated and perceptive Americans were beginning to realize, firstly, that western resources were finite and, secondly, that if those resources were to benefit the Republic in the long term, they had to be managed more efficiently. In *Man and Nature* (1864), one of the first of a long line of influential American conservation tracts, the New Englander, George Perkins Marsh, warned that the Republic's advance toward national greatness was grounded in 'wasteful processes' that might one day bring about its downfall.[29]

The embryonic conservation movement was manifested in early efforts to set up parks in areas of outstanding natural beauty. Frederick Law Olmsted arrived on the Pacific coast in 1863 having agreed to give up his position with the US Sanitary Commission in order to become manager for the giant Mariposa Estate in California. The patrician New Yorker was convinced that nature could have a recuperative effect on those living in an expanding industrial society. After Congress ceded the Yosemite Valley and the Mariposa Big Tree Grove to California for recreational purposes, Olmsted headed a commission to formulate the state's response to the grant. In his 1864 report he insisted that Yosemite should be protected from all private development and, as the United States was a democracy, be made accessible to as many people as possible. He recommended construction of a scenic road with frequent viewpoints as well as a small number of holiday cabins. 'Before many years', he observed prophetically, 'if proper facilities are offered, these hundreds will become thousands and in a century the whole number will be counted a million.'[30]

Although the report was shelved on the grounds of cost, it provided a blueprint for what would eventually become America's national park system. The first of these reserves, Yellowstone, was created in March 1872, partly as a result of awe-inspiring images of the Yellowstone country produced by the photographer, William H. Jackson, and the landscape painter, Thomas Moran. There was, of course, a downside to these well-meaning initiatives. Tourists (already in evidence by the 1870s) would have their own negative effect on the local environment. Moreover, creating parkland out of the wilderness required conscious acts of removal and reconceptualization on the part of the conquerors. Yellowstone soon became one of postbellum America's favorite vacation spots, but the government's reluctance to offend the delicate sensibilities of visitors resulted in the expulsion of the local Indians in 1879.[31]

Whereas before the Civil War most Americans had tended to see the West in religious terms – as evidence of God's bounty and as a land to be exploited by those willing to use their talents – the years after Appomattox witnessed a growing realization that the region's long-term future depended on the proper application of scientific methods. Among the most influential of this new breed of westerners was John Wesley Powell. Powell, the son of abolitionist parents, had lost an arm in the carnage at Shiloh and, after mustering out, was appointed curator of the Illinois Natural History Museum. In the spring of 1869, at almost precisely the same moment that the golden spike ceremony was taking place at Promontory, Utah, he embarked on the last of the great western exploratory expeditions. Funded primarily by private money (though his team was permitted to draw free army rations), the Powell expedition traversed the headwaters of the Colorado River and the magnificent, largely uncharted, canyonlands of southern Utah and Arizona. Fêted as a hero on his return, Powell received congressional backing to undertake several government surveys of the high plateaux and at the end of the decade was appointed to head the new US Geological Survey.

As Donald Worster suggests, the survey must be seen not only as 'a project characteristic of a modern nation-state steeped in the perspective of science' but also as a 'more thoroughgoing way of taking possession, of establishing empire'.[32] While Powell was, in this respect, an agent of American imperialism, his sensitive approach to the landscape and peoples of the West set him apart from those who sought simply to exploit the land for personal gain. With his belief in evolutionary science strengthened by his observations of the rocks and rivers of the canyonlands, Powell was no dreamer. As well as being a staunch nationalist, he held that economic develop-ment, properly controlled, was beneficial to human progress and that the eclipse of the Indian was inevitable. On the other hand his numerous direct encounters with the region's native inhabitants contributed to his understanding of the Indians' terror of white settle-ment and skeptical assessment of white claims to racial superiority. His receptivity to alternative ways of life enabled him to learn not only from the Indian but also from the Mormons. The Saints' cooperative ethos and pioneering efforts in the field of hydraulic agriculture provided him with answers to one of the West's most pressing problems. In 1874 he warned a congressional committee that far from being a land of plenty the West was an extremely arid region. Only innovative methods of irrigation, he insisted, could enable parts of the region to sustain commercial agriculture. While this was a message that few Americans wanted to hear at this juncture in time, Powell's bureaucratic and scientific approaches to western problems would begin to bear fruit in the following decade.

The tribulations of Henry Eno

The incorporation of the West into the national and international economy had a mixed impact on the region's potent image as a land of opportunity. The image, however, proved durable enough to sustain many migrants, even those who found little but hardship across the Missouri. Although some of these settlers, especially the Euroamericans among them, succeeded in bettering themselves in the relatively fluid society of the West, the frontier experience could prove a sobering one even for the most resourceful and literate members of the Republic's privileged racial caste. Henry Eno was unusual in that he had turned 50 by the time he decided to migrate to the Pacific coast. Yet his career mirrored that of many Americans who went west in a bid to improve their quality of life and was, in many ways, more typical of the white encounter with the region than was that of John Wesley Powell.

Henry Eno was born in 1798, the eldest son of a prosperous Federalist lawyer in the New York community of Pine Plains. After a rudimentary schooling, he took up the law. A five-year struggle against alcoholism threatened to blight his life but by 1836 he was confident enough to join the mass migration of New Englanders and New Yorkers into the rapidly growing region of the upper Mississippi River Valley. Settling in Fort Madison, a small yet characteristically ambitious town in what was, from July 1838, Iowa Territory, Eno soon discovered that there were already too many lawyers to go around. The news that gold had been located in far-off California seemed to present this rather 'retiring and austere' figure with the chance he had been looking for.[33] In common with most migrants, he had mixed motives for wanting to leave 'the States' behind. His wife, Elizabeth, was in failing health and could only benefit from a change of climate. As a lawyer he anticipated having a role in the framing of a constitution for the new state of California, securing an office as a local judge, and capitalizing on the abundance of legal business likely to accrue from the settlement of Mexican land claims. And on top of all this was the prospect of great mineral wealth. 'If there is any gold there', he told his brother, 'I want that & intend to have it ... .'[34]

By 1852 the Enos were ensconced in the remote, ramshackle mining settlement of Mokelumne Hill, high up in the California Sierras. They lived in a one-and-a-half-storey dwelling with a canvas roof and kept their heads above water with the help of Eno's law practice and some paying guests at their 'Temperance House'. He then invested the money from his law business into the Mokelumne Canal Company, a typically speculative western venture designed to channel river water to the mines for hydraulic purposes. 'I have all I am worth invested', he wrote home in October 1853, 'If I succeed according to my hopes I shall pay the East a visit next year. If not of course stay here, or if the Sandwich Islands are annexed go a little farther west. The best you know is always west of where we are.'[35] This last, telling comment hinted at the fact that the Enos' fortunes were on a knife edge. In the mid-1850s the canal project was caught up in California's economic downturn of 1854–55 and the couple soon found their debts piling up. The absence of ready cash meant that there was no prospect of returning home immediately. 'My lot is cast in California', wrote Eno stoically, '[W]hether for good or evil I cannot say but whatever it is I must be content.'[36]

During the mid-1850s Eno made several business trips to San Francisco. He bemoaned the high level of corruption and welcomed the drastic efforts of the city's extra-legal Vigilance Committee to restore order and justice to a community hitherto powerless to resist the machinations of unelected politicians, 'New York shoulder stickers' (Irish hoodlums), and 'bowie knife Chivalry' (southerners).[37] Although a supporter of the Know-Nothings in the presidential contest of 1856, he began to side increasingly with the Republicans – a clear indication of the reach of antebellum sectionalism. Sadly his private affairs continued to deteriorate. '[I]t is rather mortifying to look back', he confessed, 'and find that altho I have struggled hard to obtain a competence still I have failed where many others have suceeded.'[38]

The end of the Civil War found Henry Eno an impoverished, white-haired widower still living in the high Sierras but now contributing copy to the local newspaper for a mere pittance. In common with many of the early western pioneers, his spirit remained undaunted. Perfectly aware of the precarious nature of his situation, he was refreshingly honest and still convinced that the bustling and youthful society of the Far West had something to offer him. 'This is a good country for a man who has his pockets well lined', he mused in June 1865, 'but it taxes the ingenuity of the poor devil to the utmost to get what bread and meat demands & what clothes comfort & decency requires.'[39]

Matters seemed to take a turn for the better when he was elected county judge and moved to Silver Mountain, a mining settlement that constituted the county seat of Alpine County, one of the poorest districts in the state. 'Laid out for a big town but is a small one', he noted in the spring of 1866, 'about 350 inhabitants all told, from every country under heaven, with a *small sprinkling* of Yankees and Norwegians.' Far from the main centers of habitation, living costs were high. Game was scarce too, though there were some 'silver fox skins worth from $40 to $70 a piece'.[40] As county judge Eno did what he could to spur the growth of the mining industry. He lived frugally, keeping himself healthy (or so he believed) by starving himself when ill and oiling his body twice a week in the manner of the ancients to ward off rheumatism and consumption.

Within a year, however, the restless judge was considering a new venture – this time in Arizona Territory. As usual his problems were mainly financial. The government of California could not afford to pay his modest salary and he was unable to take advantage of the mineral speculations on offer. In April 1867 he was lodging with the superintendent of the IXL mine. The official had assured him that the mine was rich in silver ore but Eno had no savings to invest. 'I see the road to fortune', he told his brother wistfully, 'but cant travel it because I cant pay the tolls.'[41] By the beginning of 1869 the judge was having to walk long distances on business because he was too poor to afford a horse. The only remedy was another move, this time to a new mining region opening up in the wasteland of central Nevada, due east of the one-time boomtowns on the Comstock. 'I know I am not as young as I was twenty years ago', he wrote on leaving California, 'but all the iron in my composition is not yet smelted out.'[42]

March 1869 found Henry Eno in Carson City, the capital of Nevada Territory en route for the White Pine Mining District. There he learned from the Republican governor Henry Goode Blasdell that his destination was a veritable Eldorado. Blasdell, he reported, 'has invested all his means there, has an interest in the mines & is engaged in creating a quartz mill'. The governor had made $100,000 on the Comstock 'but got rid of two thirds of it & confidently expects to recover all losses & make the hundred thousand a million'.[43] From this point the judge's life unraveled. Arriving at White Pine in July 1869 he found what he described as 'the richest silver mining district since Columbus discovered America'. Yet even at this early stage he sensed the likelihood of failure: 'This is the very paradise for speculators & adventurers, men who have some money & some sagacity. But rich as the Country is there will be many more failures than fortunes made here. All the capital I have is brains & they have not been worth much heretofore.'[44] It was a melancholy observation. In August Eno went out on a prospecting trip but, lacking money to invest, came back more buoyed by the thought that he might be able to make money as a paid lecturer back east than by the prospect of mining silver: 'If I can but put my foot on the lower round of fortunes ladder & grasp with my hand another I have faith to believe I can yet climb it.'[45]

Thanksgiving Day 1869 yielded some poignant reflections. 'The record on a retrospect, shows badly', he wrote, 'misspent time, opportunities neglected, and talents such as they are wasted. If my accounts were this day balanced I fear it would show against me. But if it should, & there is a future left me I must strive to get as much setoffs as possible, by untiring industry redeem past time, neglect no opportunity of doing good & exert my best abilities to prove that my life has not been altogether in vain.'[46]

One last adventure beckoned. Eno decided to return to Alpine County, pick up his salary warrants (worth, he thought, no more than 50 cents on the dollar) and then make his way to a mining area on the western edge of California's Death Valley. He spent Christmas in Los Angeles, a town of fewer than 10,000 people which he had not visited since his early days in the state. Time, he thought, had Americanized the physical aspect of the place but the population was still largely foreign – plenty of French, Italians, and German Jews. He considered the residents 'intolerably lazy', even the Yankees who, he said, had imbibed 'all the bad qualities of the Mexicans and none of the good ones'. While still hopeful of success in Death Valley, he was prepared to make the best of it should fortune elude him once again. 'I hold', he wrote, 'that failures when they do not crush or dishearten a man lead to fortune & that obstacles to the resolute are only avenues to success.'[47]

The mines of Death Valley were not paved with gold. Eno made his way back to San Francisco and contracted dysentery. A mugging and the doctors' fees dispossessed him of what few means he had left. For the first time in his life despair began to undermine his resolve. 'The darkest time it is said is just before the day, so I still have hope', he told his brother. 'However I confess that I have been nearer discouraged than I ever was before.'[48] Somehow Henry Eno survived these darkest of days. But the price of failure and old age was dependency. He spent the last eleven years of his life on the New York farm owned by his son-in-law – an ignominious end, at least by the terms under which Eno had lived much of his life, to the career of one dogged pioneer. It was a career that testified not only to the power of the human spirit but also to the chimerical quality of America's western myth.

Notes

1. Frederick Jackson Turner, 'The Significance of the Frontier' (1893) in *idem, The Frontier in American History* (New York, 1962), pp.1–38.

2. Mark David Spence, *Dispossessing the Wilderness: Indian Removal and the Making of the National Parks* (New York, 1999), p.4.

3. Mark Twain, *Roughing It* (1872: repr. Harmondsworth, 1981), pp.49–50.

4. Malcolm J. Rohrbough, *Days of Gold: The California Gold Rush and the American Nation* (Berkeley, Cal., 1997), p.1.

5. Quoted in William E. Cain, ed., *A Historical Guide to Henry David Thoreau* (Oxford, 2000), p.33.

6. Richard White, *'It's Your Misfortune and None of My Own': A New History of the American West* (Norman, Okla., 1991), pp.338–40.

7. Gray Brechin, *Imperial San Francisco: Urban Power, Earthly Ruin* (Berkeley, Cal., 1999), p.79.

8. On the Hibernian Society and the black Atheneum see R.A. Burchell, *The San Francisco Irish 1848–1880* (Manchester, 1979), p.96, and Quintard Taylor, *In Search of the Racial Frontier: African Americans in the American West 1528–1990* (New York, 1998), p.88.

9. Anthony Kirk, ' "As Jolly as a Clam at High Water": The Rise of Art in Gold Rush California' in Kevin Starr and Richard J. Orsi, eds, *Rooted in Barbarous Soil: People, Culture, and Community in Gold Rush California* (Berkeley, Cal., 2000), pp.193–8.

10. For pictorial representations of the Far West in the nineteenth century see esp. William H. Truettner, *The West as America: Reinterpreting Images of the Frontier, 1820–1920* (Washington, DC, 1991).

11. White, *'It's Your Misfortune'*, p.216; Paul H. Carlson, *The Plains Indians* (College Station, Tex., 1998), p.142.

12. Twain, *Roughing It*, p.128.

13. Elliott West, *The Contested Plains: Indians, Goldseekers and the Rush to Colorado* (Lawrence, Kan., 1998), p.xv.

14. Gunther Barth, *Instant Cities: Urbanization and the Rise of San Francisco and Denver* (New York, 1975).

15. Carlson, *Plains Indians*, p.79.

16. Quoted in David H. Donald, *Lincoln* (London, 1995), p.393.

17. West, *Contested Plains*, p.304.

18. Quoted in Spence, *Dispossessing*, p.31.

19. The US army totaled 56,813 in September 1867 falling to just over 27,000 in the mid-1870s. Roughly half of all regular recruits during this period were foreign-born and desertion rates were high. Robert M. Utley, *Frontier Regulars: The United States Army and the Indian, 1866–1891* (New York, 1973), pp.12, 15, 23.

20. Ibid., p.47.

21. Albert Barnitz to Jennie Barnitz, May 15, 1867, in Robert M. Utley, ed., *Life in Custer's Cavalry: Diaries and Letters of Albert and Jennie Barnitz 1867–1868* (New Haven, Conn., 1977), p.50; George A. Custer, *My Life on the Plains* (1874: repr. London, 1982), p.158.

22. Quoted in Francis Paul Prucha, *American Indian Policy in Crisis: Christian Reformers and the Indian, 1865–1900* (Norman, Okla, 1976), p.21.

23. Quoted in Michael Fellman, *Citizen Sherman: A Life of William Tecumseh Sherman* (Lawrence, Kan., 1995), p.267.

24. John S. Gray, *Centennial Campaign: The Sioux War of 1876* (1976: repr. Norman, Okla, 1988), pp.147–8.

25. Quoted in Robert M. Utley, *Custer and the Great Controversy: The Origin and Development of a Legend* (1962: repr. Lincoln, Neb., 1998), p.40.

26. John E. Stover, *The Routledge Atlas of American Railroads* (New York, 1999), p.38.

27. Quoted in David Brown, 'Hinton Rowan Helper's *The Land of Gold* and the Evolution of Race Relations in California', *American Nineteenth Century History*, 1 (2000), p.37.

28. Andrew C. Isenberg, *The Destruction of the Bison* (Cambridge, 2000), pp.138–9.

29. Quoted in Spence, *Dispossessing*, p.36.

30. Quoted in Witold Rybcynski, *A Clearing in the Distance: Frederick Law Olmsted and America in the 19th Century* (New York, 1999), p.258.

31. Spence, *Dispossessing*, pp.58–60.

32. Donald Worster, *A River Running West: The Life of John Wesley Powell* (New York, 2001), p.203.

33. Edward H. Stiles, *Recollections and Sketches of Notable Lawyers and Public Men of Early Iowa* (Des Moines, Ia, 1916), p.324.

34. W. Turrentine Jackson, ed., *Twenty Years on the Pacific Slope: Letters of Henry Eno from California and Nevada, 1848–1871* (New Haven, Conn., 1965), p.103.

35. *Ibid.*, p.110.

36. *Ibid.*, p.120.

37. *Ibid.*, p.125.

38. *Ibid.*, p.129.

39. *Ibid.*, pp.135–6.

40. *Ibid.*, p.143.

41. *Ibid.*, p.163.

42. *Ibid.*, p.173.

43. *Ibid.*, p.177.

44. *Ibid.*, pp.180–1.

45. *Ibid.*, pp.188–9.

46. *Ibid.*, p.192.

47. *Ibid.*, pp.198–9.

48. *Ibid.*, p.206.

9

REFORM, REACTION AND REUNION AT THE DAWN OF THE GILDED AGE

The North's military victory over the South ensured the survival of the American Republic but, as persistent sectional bitterness over Reconstruction indicated, it hardly guaranteed the existence of a strong and healthy nation. The evolving process of nation building begun during the Revolution was not over yet. Indeed, it would not reach a point of maturity until the turn of the century. However, the eventful twelve years spanning the death of Abraham Lincoln and the inauguration of President Rutherford B. Hayes in 1877 laid the groundwork for future greatness.

Reconstruction and the conquest of the West were just two of the most important strands of national development after Appomattox. Others included the seemingly inexorable growth of American capitalism – an uneven process that fueled the concomitant rise of an increasingly modern, dynamic, and self-confident society; the burgeoning involvement of government, business corporations, and voluntary associations in the everyday lives of ordinary people; nascent federal efforts to assimilate European immigrants into American life; and the first genuine signs of reconciliation between white northerners and southerners. Political reunion was finally confirmed by the white South's peaceable acquiescence to Hayes's controversial election victory. While the 'Compromise of 1877' boded well for the cause of national unity, the prospects for racial equality in the new America were poor. Ultimately, neither politicians nor people proved up to the task, begun by the martyred Lincoln, of combining healing with justice.[1]

The economy and society of postwar America

Historians have seldom agreed on the impact of the Civil War on the United States. Judged in terms of its sheer destructive power, its confirmation of the indivisibility of the Union, and its extirpation of slavery from the national domain, it was clearly the great watershed of American history. When viewed against long-term trends such as the growth of the economy or the development of a modern society, however, the war has often seemed less of a cataclysm.

Some scholars have depicted the war as a decisive event in the progress of domestic industrialization and class formation. In 1927 Charles and Mary Beard described the Civil War as 'a social war' in which the capitalist bourgeoisie of the Northeast aligned themselves with the commercial farmers of the Midwest to remove the slaveholding planter aristocracy from power.[2] This result, they contended, paved the way for the country's surging industrial growth in the late nineteenth and twentieth century. Within forty years this orthodoxy had been undermined by scholars working on the politics and economy of the Civil War era. The business elite of the day, it was suggested, was not a monolithic group – industrial and financial capitalists had very different ideas about important issues such as federal monetary policy and the tariff. Economic historians questioned the Beards' notion that the war had been a boon to industrialization by observing that important sectors of the economy had been adversely affected by the shift to a war footing. Walt Rostow, one of the most influential econometricians of the 1950s and 1960s, drove in the knife by positing that the US economy had reached industrial 'take off' in the late antebellum period.[3]

Although the Beards clearly exaggerated the economic significance of the Civil War, their interpretation of the conflict continues to resonate in the writings of modern leftwing scholars who depict the Republican party as the principal agent of modern capitalism in America.[4] It was, after all, the Republicans who oversaw the triumph of 'free labor' and who laid the groundwork for future industrial development with a rash of wartime economic legislation. That they did so as much for patriotic as for selfish material reasons does not mean that they were entirely unwitting creators of the corporate economy that dominates the United States today.

The Civil War did not alter the underlying trends in American economic development.[5] Even if the war had not taken place or if the North had failed to subdue the South, capitalist enterprise would have continued to transform the social and physical landscape of

North America. The American economy grew consistently and at a steady pace throughout the nineteenth century. The war provided a boost for the producers of certain essential commodities such as iron, shoes, and woolens, but US growth actually slowed from an impressive 4.1 percent per annum in the 1850s to 2.9 percent in the 1860s (in large part because of the war's devastating effects on the South and the country's cotton textile sector).[6] No major new technological innovations resulted from the war. Even the Bessemer process that opened the way for the commercial production of steel failed to undermine the paramount status of iron. The most salient economic trends of the postwar era – sustained growth, urbanization, integration of the national market, regional economic specialization, changes in the nature and scale of production and distribution, the proliferation of wage labor, the declining status of agriculture *vis-à-vis* manufacturing and services, and monetary deflation – would all have continued to occur, certainly across the North, if the war had never happened.

At first sight the war's impact on state formation appears to have been greater. Federal power increased as a necessary outgrowth of wartime resource mobilization. An important legacy of central government activism ensued: an interest-bearing United States debt of $2.3 billion in 1866 compared with just $65 million in 1860; a national banking system; government-supported paper money ('greenbacks'); federal welfare payments for disabled Union veterans of $25 to $30 million a year by the late 1860s and 1870s; a system of government-owned soldiers' homes; and massive land subsidies to promote railroad development and education.[7] If we add to these developments the Freedmen's Bureau and the three constitutional amendments of the Reconstruction period, we can be in little doubt that the Civil War had a broadly consolidating effect on the system of American federalism.

Any thoughts that the war spawned a permanent 'Yankee leviathan', however, should be dispelled.[8] The centralizing developments noted above were either temporary or limited in scale. The bonded national debt, a major issue in postbellum politics, had been scaled down to $585 million by 1892.[9] The system of welfare payments for disabled soldiers was not liberalized to embrace all Union veterans until the onset of a concerted campaign by the veterans themselves in the 1880s. Congress ended the distribution of large land grants for railroads in 1871. The Freedmen's Bureau was wound up two years earlier. The radical nationalizing effects of the Reconstruction amendments were partially eroded by the actions of the US Supreme

Court and the obstructive tactics of southern whites. Permanent developments did take place in the sphere of central–state power. Federal agencies such as the US Department of Agriculture (another wartime Republican initiative), the Bureau of Education, and the Bureau of the Census made strides in the scientific collection of data and in the assimilation and defusion of the results – the start of an extended process that would reach maturity during the Progressive era. But such modest bureaucratic innovations would have occurred without the war. The real beginnings of a significant and permanent leap in the administrative and regulatory functions of the federal government lay later in the century.

American society in the immediate postwar years, however, evinced signs of the complexity that would eventually demand substantial increases in central power. Some of those signs were apparently healthy. Between 1865 and 1877 the population rose from nearly 36 to 47 million. A product of natural increase and high levels of immigration from Great Britain, Ireland, Germany, and Scandinavia, this rapid demographic growth acted as a powerful economic stimulus and confirmed the United States as an ethnically plural nation. By no means everyone welcomed this latter development. Nativism manifested itself in numerous forms during this period: in the Republicans' nationalizing campaign for culturally homogenized public schools, in the related calls for an end to public funding for Catholic education, and in a revitalized temperance crusade. But while hostility toward the Irish in particular continued, there was no revival of the Know-Nothing phenomenon after the Civil War. Republican ethnocentrism, the immigrants' whiteness, their loyalty (in the main) toward the Union, and their voting strength all militated against the emergence of another separate party devoted primarily to nativism.

Social health was also promoted by what Albro Martin has termed the 'nervous prosperity' experienced during the immediate postwar years by all regions of the country, rural and urban, outside the defeated South.[10] Some midwestern farmers were initially hit by a drop in foreign demand for American grain, but by the mid-1870s American exports of wheat and wheat flour had overtaken the unprecedented levels of the Civil War. On the prairies the commercial farmers of Iowa and Illinois benefited hugely from the development of the modern corn and hog economy. An increase in railroad construction, financed primarily by northeastern elites and foreign investors, rendered great swathes of the Midwest the agricultural hinterland of rising cities like Chicago and of more established ones like New York. Those cities, in turn, furnished the pork-packing plants and grain mills necessary to process the products of the farm, supplied increasing quantities of manufactured goods for the domestic market, and played host to the plethora of investment banks, commercial lawyers, and insurance companies that greased the wheels of the postbellum economy.

All classes, it seemed, were set fair to benefit from the integration and expansion of the national market. Having prospered during the war, urban elites expected to (and often did) make large profits from investing in railroads, real estate, and western mining operations. Some individuals displayed more overtly predatory instincts than others. In New York Jim Fisk and his ally Jay Gould earned well-deserved notoriety not only as corporate raiders but also as manipulators of the stock market. Their destabilizing activities appalled avowedly more responsible businessmen like the young investment banker J. Pierpont Morgan whose endeavors were better suited to the development of a less anarchic (and therefore more stable and profitable) form of capitalism. Millionaire entrepreneurs like these were relatively scarce before the Civil War but their numbers grew apace in the 1860s. New York City, its position confirmed as the nation's leading financial and commercial center, had several hundred of them as early as 1865. Conspicuous consumption was one of the Manhattan elite's most distinguishing characteristics. They aped the manners of the European upper classes, purchasing huge mansions on fashionable streets such as Fifth Avenue, dressing in the latest French fashions, and hosting exclusive balls.[11]

Money, of course, was at the root of the wealthy's interest in economic development. They financed the postwar urban housing boom, local transportation initiatives such as streetcar lines, and the exploitation of natural resources such as precious metals, coal, and oil because they sought to profit from their risk taking. There were other motives for elite investment. Civic duty, the desire to promote a more ordered and cultured social environment, and a yearning for popular acclaim were important factors in the building of urban amenities. Few cities in the country could afford an institution like New York's prestigious Metropolitan Museum of Art (founded in 1870 as an initiative of the Art Committee of the local Union League Club), but even smaller towns in the Midwest harbored upper-class boosters who sought to improve the local environment by building public libraries and parks. Yet no matter how altruistic such cultural projects may have been in conception, they were fundamentally political in content. By subliminally linking art to wealth or providing social spaces nominally free of class conflict, elites were using culture to legitimize the emerging socio-economic system and thereby disarm potential opposition both to it and to themselves.[12]

While the super-rich were often far from idle, their fondness for display was hardly consistent with the puritanical ideals of American republicanism. There were many signs during the late 1860s and 1870s that the power of this once dominant political ideology had begun to wane under the pressure of economic change. The expansion of an aggressive market-driven and highly commercialized society helped to consolidate new and hegemonic liberal values. Instead of being regarded as synonymous with luxury and corruption, the consumption of material goods (the mainstay of any healthy capitalist society) was increasingly seen as natural and beneficial. Cementing the triumph of commercialism was the country's rapidly proliferating bourgeoisie.

Hard evidence for the continuing rise of the American middle classes, fueled in part by a discernible drift from the countryside to the towns, was provided by new and more highly delineated classifications in the federal censuses of 1870 and 1880. Occupational statistics collected by the enumerators revealed that there were 25,000 clerks and copyists in the United States in 1879 compared with around 6,000 at the beginning of the decade. The number of bookkeepers, office workers in insurance companies, and salesmen and saleswomen had roughly doubled during the same period, and the figure for commercial travelers nearly quadrupled (to 28,000). The number of store clerks, the largest category of nonmanual workers in the census, had grown from 222,000 to 353,000.[13]

The drive and self-possession of the middle classes made up for any weaknesses they may have had in the realm of class consciousness. Such a vast and amorphous social category strengthened, and in large measure spawned, by the changing economy would have been hard pressed to act as a unified entity. Salaried white-collar clerks and shop assistants did not automatically have anything in common with factory managers or railroad company officers, let alone commercial farmers or professionals like doctors, lawyers, and clergymen. Yet even if they did not perceive themselves as a united social grouping, the transforming American bourgeoisie was the most revolutionary class of the era. For it was this diverse group of Americans that bought most heavily into the spreading consumerism and entrepreneurial ethos of what Mark Twain and Charles Dudley Warner dubbed 'the Gilded Age'.[14]

There are several reasons why this was the case. The most obvious one is that the middle classes profited materially from the era's business expansion. But a perception of status, too, was critical. By the late 1860s a clerk in a Manhattan department store was probably earning $10 per week. While this was hardly a king's ransom (only just, perhaps, a republican competence) the individual concerned did at least have the satisfaction of working in a relatively salubrious environment and with a reasonable prospect of occupational advancement. This could not be said of the average longshoreman, sweatshop employee, or packinghouse worker whose experience of the free-labor economy was a very different one. Whatever guilt may have arisen as a result of the relatively comfortable middle-class lifestyle was assuaged by a readiness on the part of opinion makers to accommodate themselves to changing economic realities. Populist evangelical ministers such as Henry Ward Beecher outdid didactic editors like Horace Greeley in their efforts to flatter their own middle-class constituency and diffuse the quintessentially bourgeois values of thrift, hard work, and respectability as widely as possible.

Even though middle-class Americans did not necessarily think of themselves as a coherent entity, their day-to-day social experience set them increasingly apart from proletarians. Not only did they work in better conditions and, on the whole, for higher wages but they also began to live in separate sections of the nation's cities. In Boston, for example, white-collar workers began to gravitate toward the emerging suburbs of Roxbury, West Roxbury, and Dorchester. In Manhattan, they shunned the fetid industrial zones adjacent to the wharves in favour of their own enclaves in the West Village, in Chelsea, Harlem, and the Upper East Side (an area undergoing rapid development in the 1870s). High prices represented a substantial barrier to home ownership, but the sudden popularity of European-style apartment buildings (so-called 'French Flats') began to erode the number of white-collar boarders in the city. Once ensconced in their own space, reasonably prosperous middle-class families could mimic their betters by employing a servant, and decorating their homes with the latest mass-produced furnishings and art. Some of them devoted a portion of their newfound wealth and leisure time to spectator sports. Among the most prominent of these was baseball, already a growing business in some of the North's major cities. Ordered, disciplined, and faster-paced than its floundering competitor, cricket, baseball was ideally suited as the game of preference for the urban middle classes after the Civil War.[15]

In the eighteenth and early nineteenth centuries skilled manual work had been a badge of pride for many Americans. Indeed, artisans were the mainstays of American republicanism. Their ongoing decline resulted partly from the eclipse of skilled labor brought about by mechanization and large-scale industrialization. What Marxists refer to as proletarianization – the relentless deskilling of craftworkers – continued apace during the Civil War era. While the process did not at any stage produce a genuinely radical or united social class in the United States, there were signs in the immediate postwar era of a return to Jacksonian-style class consciousness on the part of America's industrial workers.

What can loosely be described as the American working class was no less diverse than the intermediate class from which it was increasingly separated. In fact in ethnic and racial terms it was far more plural, fragmented as it was between an upper segment of embattled and predominantly native-born skilled workers and a mass of unskilled laborers, male and female, in which European immigrants, African-Americans, and (on the West Coast) Chinese were especially prominent. While friction often characterized relations between the skilled and the unskilled, black and white, men and women, laboring people found themselves living alongside one another in the most squalid industrial zones of the big cities. Even though real wages increased in the second half of the 1860s, few of them could afford a house in the embryonic suburbs and the weekly costs of commuting into the core financial and commercial districts. Of course, this does not mean that they could not live meaningful lives. Even the most impoverished Irish or African-American neighborhood had its fair share of churches, fraternal clubs, and saloons as well as its brothels and gambling dens. However, crime in these areas was often high (juvenile delinquency was a serious problem in the urban North), law enforcement was weak, sanitary conditions were poor, and social cohesion was persistently undermined by alcoholism and disease.

For all their problems and divisions, American workers did not accept their lot passively. As befitted citizens of the most advanced capitalist democracy in the world they sought to better themselves through a combination of individual self-help and collective action. Evangelical Protestantism was central to the lives of numerous native-born workers just as it was for many middle-class Americans. The supposedly bourgeois virtues associated with it – education, individual responsibility, thrift, hard work, sobriety, and respectability – were adhered to avidly by large numbers of skilled workers, most of whom regarded such values as the means to social advancement as well as salvation. Collectively, native-born and ethnic workers attempted to better themselves by forming unions. Organization held not only the key to their hopes for a better life but also to the general spread of reformist zeal in America after Appomattox.

Organizing for reform

What concerned reformers at the dawn of the Gilded Age were the negative consequences of American industrialization. Although they did not always articulate their views in such terms, there was a widespread sense of unease that structural economic change had unbalanced power relations within society and that existing institutions were poorly fitted to deal with the results. For progressive nationalists the Civil War had been a triumph in terms of its eventual result but patently it had not ushered in a truly democratic society, still less the millennial republic foreseen by the Protestant clergy. Prominent ex-abolitionists, elite social reformers, industrial workers, women, and even midwestern farmers all joined the chorus of reform. Although the process was stalled by persistent localism, limited conceptions of government's role in society, ethnic and racial prejudice, and economic depression in the mid-1870s, the achievements of the immediate postwar era provided essential preparation for the much more sustained surge of progressive social activism that occurred at the turn of the century.

For reformers and ordinary citizens alike, the problems confronting the United States were encapsulated in the word 'corruption'. Old-style republicanism was not so outmoded that American citizens were incapable of detecting signs of canker inside the body politic. The Buchanan administration had foundered partly on public concerns about graft in high places in the late 1850s. The Civil War generated numerous avenues for venality, especially the illegal and highly lucrative trade in southern cotton that had enriched thousands of Union army officers, US treasury agents, and politicians. Public concern over corruption intensified after Appomattox. Renewed urban growth, lax regulation of the financial markets, railroad expansion, and Indian removals provided individuals with abundant opportunities for speculation. Apart from the impoverished proletariat, everyone was involved in taking risks for profit. Midwestern farmers bought land for development and formed claim clubs to protect their investments. The urban middle classes purchased stocks and shares in the corporations that were beginning to dominate America's economic landscape. Far more worrying to public commentators than speculation *per se* were the manipulative activities of reckless venture capitalists and a growing realization of the ease with which business corrupted politics.[16] Several high-profile incidents and revelations brought these two trends to the public's attention.

In 1869 Jim Fisk and Jay Gould hit upon the idea of getting even richer by cornering the nation's gold supply. Having convinced President Grant that their scheme would promote the material welfare of the country, they began purchasing gold on credit and driving up the price. So successful were they that financiers and merchants were soon crying foul. The US Treasury was eventually forced to intervene by dumping gold on the market. The price plummeted (though not before Gould had made a fortune) and on September 24 – 'Black Friday' – the market collapsed, prompting a serious financial panic which ruined hundreds of speculators. A full-scale depression was averted but in the aftermath large numbers of businesses folded and thousands of workers were laid off.[17]

While rampant speculation at the expense of the public welfare was more likely to elicit criticism of individual greed than prompt hostility to the capitalist system, consistent revelations about the venal activities of public servants caused even graver public concern and provided a major impetus for reform. Graft was rife throughout Gilded Age America. Machine politicians in the cities, for example, were notoriously venal. Manhattan's Democratic 'boss' William M. Tweed, an ally of Fisk and Gould, used his position as commissioner of public works to secure kickbacks on construction contracts. The depredations of the Tweed Ring cost municipal taxpayers millions of dollars and dwarfed the criminal activities of some southern Republicans that had such a damaging impact on Reconstruction. It was the large railroad companies, however, that did most to exacerbate concerns about political corruption.

As well as pioneering modern forms of business practices, the railroads of this period proved adept at influencing political life. During the antebellum period most Americans had hailed this new form of transport as the great wonder of the age, understandably so in view of its beneficial effect on traveling times, freight rates, and the solidity of the Union. By the early 1870s, however, the initial enthusiasm in the more settled areas of the country had begun to wane. Railroads were increasingly resented by farmers for their impact on local taxation, their tendency to cause fires and kill livestock, and their readiness to impose discriminatory rates on short-haul traffic. Urban residents objected to the encroachment of the railroads onto the streets and to the filth and noise which came along with them. There were few who did not worry about the industry's high accident rate. In 1868, in New York state alone, 150 people were killed and 86 injured in train accidents.[18]

The companies' influence on political life was hardly less disturbing. In order to secure the passage of favorable legislation, railroad officials paid bribes (in the form of stock and cash) and distributed free passes. Numerous governors, state legislators, and congressmen were in the pay of the railroads and some state and territorial legislatures were virtual extensions of the railroad lobby. The companies' power to subvert the democratic process was sensationally revealed by the Crédit Mobilier scandal which broke in September 1872. An *exposé* run by Charles Dana's liberal *New York Sun* announced the discovery of 'the most damaging exhibition of official and private villainy and corruption ever laid bare to the gaze of the world'.[19] It showed how an inner circle of Union Pacific stockholders had formed a dummy finance company – the Crédit Mobilier – so that they could award lucrative construction contracts to themselves and then bribed influential congressmen to keep the deal secret. A congressional investigation ensued, resulting in the expulsion of two members and tarnished reputations for several leading politicians, including Grant's vice president, Schuyler Colfax.

Colfax's embroilment in this scandal highlighted the extent to which the tentacles of corruption had reached into the highest echelons of power. The president himself was, by the standards of the age, a man of some integrity, but out of uniform he proved himself a poor judge of human beings. During the course of his two terms in office several of his closest kinfolk, friends, and advisers were implicated in fraudulent dealings. The worst of these were brought to light by his ambitious secretary of the treasury, Benjamin Bristow, who saw it as his job to rid the president of the corruptionists around him. In 1874 Bristow's zealous efforts uncovered the Whiskey Ring, a network of distillers and distributors whose illegal tax-dodging efforts were abetted by federal officials. Among those implicated were Grant's private secretary Orville E. Babcock and his personal friend General John McDonald. So convinced was Grant that these revelations were part of a grand conspiracy to destroy him that he did not dispense with Babcock's services until March 1876. Such misplaced loyalty on the part of the nation's highest officer merely confirmed the view of Grant's detractors that corruption was corroding the fabric of the Republic.

By no means all reform sentiment focused on corruption, though it is certainly true that this issue generated the most excitement among the public at large. A variety of interest groups, however, regarded it as just one symptom of a deeper malaise: a growing imbalance between classes and sections inside the United States.

Disagreement existed over the source of this imbalance. Middle-class reformers, farmers, and many native-born workers tended to adhere to antebellum notions of equality of opportunity and Whiggish ideas about the existence of a harmony of interests between economic classes in America. While they knew things were wrong they were seldom inclined to blame them on the capitalist system. Instead of questioning the actual basis of social and economic life in the United States, they tended to seek ways in which perceived flaws in the system could be corrected. With proslavery ideology utterly discredited by Confederate defeat, the only coherent critique of North American capitalism was provided by socialists. As these were predominantly German immigrants active in the east coast labor movement, it is not surprising that there was little enthusiasm for the revolutionary 1871 Paris Commune in the United States.

There was nothing new about the notion of reform in the United States. Antislavery, Sabbatarianism, public schools, public health, working conditions, dietary concerns, women's rights, and temperance had exercised numerous antebellum minds. Many of the reform initiatives of the late 1860s and 1870s exhibited a strong degree of continuity with earlier ones. This was true, for example, of the prohibition movement: middle-class evangelicals and native-born working men redoubled their efforts to secure passage of legislation that would severely curtail alcohol consumption. The abolitionists secured their main objective with ratification of the Thirteenth Amendment in 1865 but, although some of their leading figures (Garrison among them) regarded this as reason enough to end the crusade, other antislavery activists insisted that the fight for universal justice should continue. Garrison's chief lieutenant, Wendell Phillips, forged a new career for himself after the war as a tireless campaigner for the rights of blacks, industrial workers, Indians, and women.

The diversity of reform aims prompted a variety of proffered solutions. Labour leaders and their allies sought to improve the lives of ordinary working people by campaigning for an eight-hour day, prohibition, and a government-backed paper currency that would curb the worst effects of postwar deflation. The more radical women's rights activists such as Susan B. Anthony and Elizabeth Cady Stanton strove to promote women's rights in general and female suffrage in particular to secure their ultimate aim of gender equality. In addition to expanding and protecting the rights of black people, radical Republicans tried to stimulate government social initiatives at the state level. Middle-class professionals advocated better in-house training to improve standards, augment their own financial rewards, and exclude incompetent individuals likely to bring the group into disrepute. Elite Liberal reformers threw themselves headlong into the campaign for a meritocratic civil service. Evangelicals focused their attention on what they saw as the rapid advance of moral turpitude: not only liquor drinking but also the spread of pornography among young men. White southern Democrats (who certainly regarded themselves as reformers) aimed to rid themselves of carpetbag rule which was linked closely in their own minds with feeding at the public trough. Many midwestern farmers wanted to curb the arrogance of the railroad companies that were coming to play such a dominant role in their lives. And, as noted above, church leaders concerned about the welfare of the Indians sought to interpose their own influence between that of the army and the victim.

Given the plethora of ends, the persistence of wartime and partisan loyalties, and the unerring capacity of race, religion, ethnicity, class, and gender to divide Americans, it is hardly surprising that the various interest groups found it difficult to agree over means or to join forces with one another. True, they shared a preference for organization and often regarded coalition building as the likeliest avenue for success in an increasingly plural and complex society. Professional organizations proliferated in the late 1860s and early 1870s, as did labor unions, women's groups, and fraternal bodies like the Masons and the principal Union veterans' organization, the Grand Army of the Republic. However, there was only limited agreement about the relationship of reform to government and politics. Groups such as the radical Republicans and the trade unions often looked to government activism as the solution to the nation's ills. Others, liberals and conservatives – many of them enamored with pseudo-Darwinian explanations for social formation – saw government as part of the problem and favored *laissez-faire* approaches to the problems confronting an industrializing society.

Responses to mainstream party politics were closely linked to views about the connection between government and reform. Popular interest and participation in politics remained high after the war. Turnout in the presidential elections of 1868, 1872, and 1876 was, respectively, 78.1, 71.3, and 81.8 percent.[20] Regional, ethnocultural, and class loyalties to the major parties persisted and many American voters continued to cast their ballots in the same direction they had shot in the Civil War – integral reasons for the Republicans' continued political domination of the Northeast and Midwest and their inability to construct durable coalitions in the South. Well-to-do postbellum reformers, however, often regarded the existing political system as the main obstacle to progress. The United States, wrote the Boston lawyer Brooks Adams in 1874, was in the process of being turned from 'a Federal Republic' into 'a consolidated empire with a strong central government, with the states for provinces':

> That this result may be in the end inevitable is nothing to the purpose. It does not seem to me that we are ready yet. The means used to attain this end of subjugating the states are two: 1st, an army of log-rollers pressed on the civil service, 2nd, the party system founded on the caucus which renders all organizations easy victims of the aforesaid log rollers.[21]

At the national level attention was focused particularly on the dominant Republican party which, by the early 1870s, had begun to lose some of its moral luster. This was due not only to a perception that the party had become sullied by corruption (a perception that grew sharper with the scandals of Grant's second term) but also to a related sense that Republicanism now stood for nothing more than a desire to keep its practitioners in power. This latter view gained credence among some of the party's most respected figures. Many of Greeley's elite Liberal supporters in 1872 (not to mention Greeley himself) had played formative roles in the party from the very beginning. While their revolt against the Republican establishment was largely 'a movement of politicians denied place and power', it was by no means devoid of ideological content.[22] Many Liberals genuinely believed that Republicans had squandered their right to govern by dint of their pandering to popular whims and a resolute attachment to the spoils system.

While the Liberals' plans foundered because of an expedient coalition with the Democrats and the strength of entrenched vested interests, other groups found their aims stymied by a lack of genuine commitment from one or other of the two major parties, an inability to forge effective interorganizational alliances, and a surfeit of internal divisions. This was particularly true of the labor and women's movements in the late 1860s and 1870s.

Industrial workers and women had undergone much suffering during the Civil War and emerged from the conflict with an enhanced sense not only of grievance but also of their own capacity to advance their cause. Labor remained divided along ethnic and skill lines with native-born, German, and Irish-American workers forming their own unions. Nominally, the locus of power within the movement lay with the Manhattan-based National Labor Union (NLU), a federation of native-born craft unions established in 1866. The women's movement was small, predominantly middle class, and native born.

The staunchly reformist and lilywhite NLU initially placed its faith in a combination of strike action and political cooperation with sympathetic radical Republicans and Democrats. While the strikes brought higher wages, the radicals in particular temporized over labor's chief demand for an eight-hour day. Wedded to the Republican party's meritocratic free-labor ideology, they were mainly bourgeois politicians whose commitment to the nationalist project made them suspicious of 'class' legislation that might be seen to favor one group over another. On the other hand they were generally supportive of progressive state government initiatives in areas such as fire protection, public health, improved housing, and educational betterment and were aware that Democrats would appeal for working men's votes on the eight-hour issue. A majority of them did support state and federal eight-hour day legislation in the late 1860s but the ensuing statutes were relatively toothless and easily evaded by employers.[23]

The radicals' ambivalent attitude to labor mirrored their stance on women's rights. During the Civil War established feminist leaders such as Stanton, Anthony, and Lucy Stone had subordinated their cause to those of the Union and antislavery. Once emancipation had been achieved and the Republican party was debating an expansion of black rights during Reconstruction, they began to push for the incorporation of female suffrage into the Fourteenth Amendment. The reception from their likeliest allies, the radicals, was disappointingly cool. Adding unnecessary baggage to the amendment, argued one-time abolitionists like Frederick Douglass and Wendell Phillips, would make it even harder to secure ratification. Stanton and Anthony organized an impressive petition campaign to Congress in the winter of 1865–66, but in a representative comment Charles Sumner, the most progressive radical in the US Senate, declared it 'most inopportune'.[24] In May 1866 feminists set up their own organization, the American Equal Rights Association, to lobby and petition for the removal of racial and sexual restrictions in state constitutions. The Association's efforts culminated the following year when the Republican-dominated legislature of Kansas grudgingly provided for separate popular referenda on local women's and black male suffrage.

The 1867 Kansas campaign split the women's movement in two. With local and national Republicans declining to endorse female suffrage (because it was simply ridiculous, hopelessly unpopular with the voters, or damaging to the paramount aim of black enfranchise-ment), Stanton and Anthony arrived on the prairies in September seeking to give the campaign a much-needed fillip. In an ill-judged move that smacked of desperation, they accepted an offer of support from George Train. An impressive speaker, Train was a New York millionaire keen to mobilize women and workers under the Demo-crats' traditional banner of white supremacy. During the final two and a half weeks of the campaign he toured Kansas delivering harangues against the freedmen and holding up the enfranchise-ment of white women as the antidote to black barbarism. Both reform proposals were defeated on November 5 with women's suffrage receiving most backing from counties that also supported the enfranchisement of blacks.

The failure of powerful eastern Republicans to aid the women's campaign infuriated Susan B. Anthony. On her way back from Kansas she delivered a scathing attack on fairweather friends like Horace Greeley and Henry Ward Beecher at the Mercantile Hall in St Louis, Missouri. Responding to claims that her activities had actually defeated black suffrage, she insisted that 'it was not the woman suffrage question that killed the negro question; it was the Republican leaders – the Republican party leaders, who killed negro suffrage, and woman suffrage too'. Frustration was particularly evident in her observations that Missouri had guaranteed equal civil rights to black men under a new constitution in 1865. How much longer, she asked the audience, could local women remain disfranchised –

> in that political degradation – below even slaves – those men who but five years ago were slaves working on the farms and plantations in this state. When you propose to elevate the lowest and most degraded classes of men to an even platform with white men – with the cultivated, educated, wealthy white men of the State – it is certainly time for you to begin to think at least whether it might not be proper to lift the wives and daughters and mothers of your State to an even pedestal.[25]

Along with Train's involvement and the feminists' deep sense of betrayal, such racially charged remarks left a legacy of bitterness. Lucy Stone and other supporters of women's rights (both male and female) accused Stanton and Anthony of treachery to the cause of Republicanism and progress. Stanton and Anthony retorted that the Republican party was 'a sinking ship' that women should abandon.[26] Back in New York they proved as good as their word. Train provided them with the finances for a newspaper, the *Revolution*, which they envisioned as the mouthpiece of an autonomous feminist movement.

What female reformers desperately needed at this moment was allies. Unfortunately, even heavy doses of pragmatic racism failed to secure feminist leaders a hearing at the 1868 Democratic national convention. The incipient labor movement, however, seemed a more likely source of support, particularly as the NLU's founders had expressed themselves in favor of a broad coalition to counter the power of employers. The first signs of an alliance came in September 1868 when four women, Stanton and Anthony among them, were admitted as delegates to the NLU's third annual congress. The meeting failed to endorse women's suffrage, but hopes of a coalition between women and labor seemed to be enhanced by the feminist leaders' decision to support organizing by women typesetters in New York. The alliance never materialized. The male craftworkers who dominated the labor movement in the Northeast proved hostile to the entrance of women into their trades, and Anthony was unseated as a delegate at the 1869 National Labor Congress because of her support for the use of female strike breakers.

The last hopes of a coalition disappeared in the early 1870s. Victoria Woodhull, the potential linchpin of a union between the feminists and labor, was a maverick women's rights activist with close links to the minority socialist wing of the east coast labor movement. In May 1870 Woodhull and her sister launched a radical weekly newspaper in New York with the financial support of the wealthy entrepreneur, Commodore Cornelius Vanderbilt, who was drawn to the two women through a mutual interest in spiritualism. *Woodhull and Claflin's Weekly* carried the first US printing of Marx and Engels' *Communist Manifesto* and supported a wide range of gender-related reforms. The paper's backing for more liberal divorce laws and birth control, criticism of marriage as sexual slavery, and insistence that women were entitled to the vote as citizens of the United States produced a sympathetic response from the readers of the *Revolution* – mostly professional women in the New York City area. But hopes that Woodhull's leftist connections might foster cooperation between the male-dominated labor movement and Stanton and Anthony's newly established National Woman's Suffrage Association (NWSA) were ended by a disastrous turn of events.

Starting in the spring of 1871 Woodhull's reputation was tarnished by newspaper revelations that she was living in the same home as her first and second husbands.[27] Harriet Beecher Stowe, who shared the view of many middle-class women that Woodhull's attacks on marriage were doing more harm than good to the cause of female progress, compounded the wounded reformer's woes by satirizing her as 'Miss Audacia Dangyereyes' in her novel *My Wife and I* (1870–71).[28] This literary assault, serialized in a new religious newspaper, *The Christian Union* (edited by her brother, Henry Ward Beecher), merely intensified the free-lovers' conviction that the destruction of 'Beecherism' was a necessary precondition for women's liberation. Woodhull took the offensive. Firstly, she threatened to expose Rev. Beecher as a hypocrite by publicizing the minister's affair with the wife of a rival Protestant editor, Theodore Tilton. Then she took to the lecture circuit commending the virtues of 'free love' and expressing her conviction that a more liberated attitude to sexuality would help to promote women's rights. The lectures brought her infamy, leading a concerned Commodore Vanderbilt to withdraw his support for the *Weekly*. Worse still, they attracted attention from a young moral reformer, Anthony Comstock, who had been waging war against the sale of sexually explicit material on the streets of Manhattan. Comstock, who was backed by the respectable middle-class officers of New York City's Young Men's Christian Association (YMCA), not only regarded Woodhull (who had now publicized Beecher's hypocrisy) as the epitome of immorality but also saw her celebrity status as a means of promoting his own career. In late 1872 he secured her arrest under a federal statute banning the dispatch of obscene materials in the mails.

After a sensational trial Woodhull was found not guilty on a technicality. Critically, however, she had been deserted by most of her allies who either disliked her manipulation of the Beecher scandal or were concerned that 'free love' was a hindrance to the women's rights movement. With her influence inside the New York City establishment shattered, Woodhull eventually left the United States and ended her days on a country estate in England. She left behind a women's movement that remained active but seriously riven between the Boston-based American Woman's Suffrage Association (which continued to press for change within the traditional confines of the Republican party), the more independent-minded and radical NWSA (which spent much of the decade trying in vain to have female suffrage declared constitutional by the courts), and the mushrooming National Woman's Christian Temperance Union founded by, among others, Frances Willard in November 1874. The real beneficiary from Woodhull's fall was the cause of morality – as defined by the culturally dominant evangelical ethos of the era. Responding to heavy pressure from Anthony Comstock and the

YMCA, Congress passed a stronger federal statute to suppress obscene publications in 1873. It also made Comstock a special agent in the US Post Office, empowering him to confiscate illicit material sent through the mails and to arrest the perpetrators. Washington had got the right man for the job. Comstock used his powers zealously and was still in post at the time of the World War One.

Although female suffrage was not achieved in the United States until 1920, upper- and middle-class American women were beneficiaries of several important and continuing trends during the postwar period. Among them was a decline in the birthrate (a result partly of a conscious decision by thousands of economy conscious, mainly middle-class, wives and husbands to limit the size of their family), the increasing enrollment of females in public and private education, the entry of limited numbers of women into certain professions such as teaching and medicine, and the growth of urban women's clubs which offered valuable opportunities for mutual support and intellectual debate. While the clubs may have built on antebellum and wartime traditions of female voluntarism, their emphasis on intellectual topics and gender issues was new. Even though the Ladies' Social Science Association, founded in 1873, was barely a convincing attempt to establish a national network of women's groups, the rapid growth of organizations like Sorosis in New York City and the Chicago Women's Club laid the groundwork for a powerful reform nexus later in the century.

American workers who could only have benefited from closer links with the women's rights movement (25 percent of nonagricultural workers were female by 1870) made few gains in the 1870s.[29] Socialism was further marginalized by the country's predominantly negative reaction to the bloody Paris Commune. The native-born craftworkers who dominated the labor movement at this stage of its history were as suspicious of the two major political parties as they had been during the Jacksonian period, but they eschewed leftwing politics in favor of supporting the independent Greenback party whose inflationary policies appealed to many ordinary Americans struggling to cope with low wages and expensive credit. The opposition, however, was too powerful. Eastern financial elites and leading Republican and Democratic politicians insisted on the need to contract the currency in order to undo the damage caused by wartime inflation. In fact they held that a resumption of specie payments and a swift return to the gold standard were not only economic imperatives but also moral ones. The cause of hard money was advocated with religious zeal by many Americans who associated gold with real value and respectability. Morality was especially central to the issue of whether or not the Union debt should be paid in gold or in depreciated paper currency. Even though a large proportion of the debt was held by wealthy individuals and institutions, the argument that loyal bondholders must be paid in full was a powerful one. In 1869 the Republican-controlled Congress passed the Public Credit Act committing the nation to repayment of the interest on the Union debt in gold. Contraction of the currency was one of the principal aims of the Grant administration and it would remain so in spite of one of the most serious economic crises of the nineteenth century.

On September 18, 1873 the banking house of Jay Cooke, the Philadelphia financier whose bond sales had bolstered the Union war effort, collapsed. Like most financial disasters this event had more than one cause. Cooke's bank had played a leading role in securing investment funds to aid construction of western railroads. Unfortunately the most important of these roads, the Northern Pacific, found that its income was limited by the paucity of settlement on the northern plains. The value of its securities, too, was undermined by the federal government's deflationary policies. Unable to find a market for millions of dollars of railroad bonds, Cooke's respected banking house folded under the strain. With the bubble of speculation also bursting in Europe and midwestern demand for eastern funds always high at harvest time, the ensuing panic quickly spread to the New York banks and stock market. Although a total collapse of the banking system had been avoided by the end of the year, the country entered upon a six-year economic slump.

The depression of the 1870s (part of a much larger and longer lasting crisis in global capitalism) did not have a uniformly negative impact on the United States. Population growth continued at a healthy rate, agricultural exports were buoyant, and manufacturing output was maintained and even raised in some industries, notably steel. Some sectors of the economy, however, were badly hit. Railroad construction ground to an almost total halt. Two-fifths of southern railroads were in default or receivership. Elsewhere a quarter of railroads defaulted on their debts. Thousands of workers – on the railroads and in certain manufacturing industries such as textiles – were either laid off or suffered a renewed fall in real wages. Bouts of industrial action followed but with the NLU defunct by the mid-1870s and the more proletarian Knights of Labor not yet a national force, the fractured labor movement was poorly placed to resist the combined efforts of the government and employers to suppress strikes and demonstrations with force. Symptomatic of the Grant administration's lack of sympathy with those it saw as radicals was the president's decision to veto a moderately inflationary statute in 1874. Three years later Grant's successor, Rutherford B. Hayes, sanctioned the use of federal troops against railroad workers participating in strikes across the country.

Hardly a revolutionary class, American farmers proved more successful than workers in perfecting the art of organizing and pressurizing government in the 1870s. The secret of their relative success was their membership of the Patrons of Husbandry (more commonly known as the Grange). Founded in 1869 as a social organization intended to overcome the isolation of farm life, the Grange spread rapidly across the Midwest and South. With farmers in both regions confronting major obstacles to their wellbeing, it became increasingly politicized. Although 'middlemen' such as bankers and grain merchants incurred the wrath of northern and southern Grangers alike, the two groups were divided by sectional differences. Whereas the latter played their part in Redemption, assailing freedmen's rights and demanding the abolition of Republican initiatives such as the public schools, their northern peers tried to utilize the power of state governments to counteract what they regarded as the monopolistic power of the railroad companies. Particularly incensed by the railroads' application of discriminatory freight rates to short-haul shipments, they aligned with smaller merchants in the river towns of the upper Mississippi Valley to pressure local politicians into regulating freight rates.[30] Grange-sponsored legislation incorporating the setting up of a state commission with statutory rate-fixing powers was passed in four midwestern states in the 1870s. Such blatant encumbrances on private property were anathema to many Americans in the 1870s (and rendered less than effective by the influence of the railroad corporations). However, they were upheld by the US Supreme Court in *Munn v. Illinois* (1877) as a lawful application of the police powers of the state and prefigured the passage of federal interstate commerce regulation later in the century.

In the final analysis the dominant mood of American elites, institutions, and people in the 1870s was not conducive to radical reform. This was evident from the growing use of anti-Catholicism made by northern Republicans during this period, a trend that resulted partly from their attempts to use the public school as an agent of nationalism. Nearly three million European immigrants entered the country in the 1870s, reviving evangelical fears of a Catholic takeover. Federally supported public schooling along

Protestant lines was regarded by many Republicans as the best means of solidifying the gains secured by Union victory in the Civil War. Creating a homogeneous national culture would thwart the fissiparous designs of both Catholics and southern whites and contribute toward the growth of a more united and better educated people capable of competing with the likes of Britain and Prussia in the struggle for global influence. The Catholic commentator, Orestes Brownson, railed against what he saw as the trend toward a bland Protestant majoritarianism designed to 'overpower and trample on all minorities' and had his prayers answered by the defeat of federal school-aid measures in Congess.[31] However, the onset of the depression (which generated a climate hostile to large-scale government spending) also fueled the growth of nativist rhetoric among Republican politicians. The latter seized on anti-Catholicism not only as the language of patriotism but also as a means of retaining the allegiance of northern evangelicals at a time when the rejuvenated Democrats were making political capital out of economic issues and white racism. In September 1875 President Grant made a high-profile speech in Des Moines, Iowa, in which he raised the alarm against Catholic attempts to undermine public education and called on Americans to preserve a system 'unmixed with sectarian, pagan or atheistical dogmas'.[32] Two months later Rutherford B. Hayes was elected Republican governor of Ohio after an unpleasant campaign in which he had accused Catholics (and by extension Democrats) of trying to destroy the state's public education system by seeking a division of funds to support their own denominational schools.

Persistent ethnocultural prejudice, currency contraction, retrenchment, the ending of Reconstruction, and widespread public applause for the crushing of strikes and demonstrations were sure signs that the depression had ushered in a mood of public conservatism. Nevertheless, the organizing and reform-oriented drive after Appomattox left lasting results in the broad sphere of national improvement: not only the Fourteenth and Fifteenth Amendments and the Ku Klux Acts at the federal level but also judicial support for government regulation of railroad rates, a plethora of new private bodies, numerous state-level agencies and civic institutions, perhaps even the first signs of a decline in mortality rates which probably had more to do with public health initiatives (cleaner water and sewers) than advances in medical research.[33] What none of these achievements could deliver, however, was an end to the lingering sectional rancor left by the Civil War. Only by reducing this could Americans build a truly unified nation.

Faltering steps to reconciliation

Southern whites nursed strong grievances against the Yankee oppressor after 1865. As many as 10,000 disaffected Rebels may have left the country after the war. While most returned from their self-imposed exile, a few unrepentant 'Confederados' preferred to start new lives in Latin America rather than confront the awful reality of defeat. Unhappily, personal and collective grief were not the only stumbling blocks to national unity. Intelligent ex-Confederates like Robert E. Lee made it clear during the Reconstruction years that they accepted the verdict of the battlefield (and with it the destruction of slavery) but their commitment to white supremacy was non-negotiable. If reconciliation were to occur, northern whites would have to abandon any insistence on black equality under the law.

After Appomattox, General Lee had escaped conviction for treason and accepted the post of president of Washington College in Lexington, Virginia. There, seemingly out of the public limelight, he devoted himself to the education of a new generation of young southern men – a generation that, he hoped, could be equipped with the Christian and masculine values necessary to lead the South into a brighter future. Well into late middle age, Lee avoided formal political involvement. However, he could not avoid the issues generated by the debates swirling over Reconstruction. Because of his status as the Confederacy's greatest living hero, his every word on the events of the day was monitored and disseminated by Virginia conservatives seeking to overturn the biracial order imposed on them by Republicans.

Lee made no secret of his belief in black inferiority. 'Wherever you find the Negro', he told one fellow Confederate in June 1865, 'everything is going down around him, and wherever you find the white man, you see everything around him improving.'[34] Virginians, he urged, should start replacing black labor with white immigrants from Europe. When invited to testify before the Joint Committee on Reconstruction at the beginning of 1866, Lee advanced the opinion that former secessionists 'entirely acquiesce in the government of the United States' and were in favor of cooperating with President Johnson's policy of Reconstruction. Northern generosity, he considered, was the surest and speediest means of securing southern loyalty. As befitted a paternalistic ex-slaveholder, Lee tried to be generous toward the freedmen. They were, he averred, 'an amiable, social race. They like their ease and comfort, and, I think, look more to their present than to their future condition.' Virginia, he thought nonetheless, would be better off without them. And how, asked one senator, would southern whites feel if blacks were enfranchised by a new constitutional amendment? 'I think', replied Lee, 'it would excite unfriendly feelings between the two races.'[35]

When sporadic anti-black violence broke out in Lexington, President Lee did what he could to restrain his students from participating. In January 1867 he dismissed or reprimanded several boys accused of burning down a Freedmen's Bureau school in the town. Congressional policy angered a great many elite Confederates but the general urged them to tone down their fiery rhetoric. As wily a political strategist as he was a military one, Lee believed the South could best obtain what it wanted – home rule – not by antagonizing the Republicans but by entering into reasoned debate over the merits of Reconstruction policy.

During the 1868 presidential election campaign Lee participated in an event that highlighted the close connection between reunion and reaction. Forced onto the defensive by Republicans eager to procure votes by sustaining wartime prejudices, northern Democrats sought to prove that the late Rebels were no longer a threat to the country. As part of this effort the former Union commander, William S. Rosecrans, met with Lee and 30 other ex-Confederates at the resort town of White Sulphur Springs, West Virginia, in August. In a carefully staged dialog Rosecrans argued that southern white control of the emancipated slaves was a necessary precondition for a return to peace and prosperity. Lee then joined Alexander Stephens and the other southern notables in signing a public letter acknowledging that secession and emancipation had been decided by the war and stating that without the imposition of radical misrule 'the wounds inflicted by the war would have been in great measure healed'. Blacks, continued the letter, played a critical role in the southern economy, and once home rule were restored '[race] relations ... would soon adjust themselves on a basis of mutual kindness and advantage'.[36]

The Democrats reaped no immediate reward from this heartwarming display of sectional amity. It came too soon after the war's end. Even though Grant was elected on a slogan of 'Let Us Have Peace', the Democrats remained burdened with the taint of treason and the voters handed them a crushing defeat at the polls. The recipe for sectional reconciliation, however, was clear. Southern leaders of General Lee's caliber would happily embrace their former enemies – just as long as they were left in peace to determine their own social order.

Republican victories at the polls in the late 1860s revealed that in the immediate aftermath of the Civil War a majority of northerners were not prepared to betray the Union dead. It is true that there was much talk of rebirth during this period. Walt Whitman continued with his lifelong project of writing the nation. Having spent much of the war nursing Federal and Confederate soldiers in the military hospitals of Washington, Whitman – a committed nationalist of the Jacksonian school – was ideally suited for the task. His powerful 1866 poem 'Reconciliation' constituted what the twentieth-century critic, Edmund Wilson, called a highly charged 'epitaph which would obliterate partisan hatred':

> Word over all, beautiful as the sky,
> Beautiful that war and all its deeds of carnage must in time be
>   utterly lost,
> That the hands of the sisters Death and Night incessantly softly
>   wash again, and ever again, this soil'd world;
> For my enemy is dead, a man as divine as myself is dead,
> I look where he lies white-faced and still in the coffin – I draw
>   near,
> Bend down and touch lightly with my lips the white face in the
>   coffin.[37]

As his preoccupation with color in the last lines reveal, Whitman found it difficult to incorporate the altered position of blacks in American life. The reunited nation that he anticipated may have been ethnically polyglot but it also verged on the racially exclusive.

Although neither Walt Whitman nor Robert E. Lee found four years of internecine killing an insuperable barrier to reconciliation between white Americans, the road to reunion was far from smooth. Reconceptualizing the enemy dead as compatriots, as Whitman managed to do, was not an easy task for everyone. However, in this difficult process of reconceptualization lay the key to postbellum nationhood.

Mourning was pervasive in America during the late 1860s and 1870s. Tens of thousands of corpses were reburied after the return of peace. While southerners were left to take care of their own dead, the federal government took primary responsibility for the interment of those who had given their lives for the Union. Within a decade nearly 300,000 soldiers had been buried in new federally owned national cemeteries such as Gettysburg and Arlington (the latter built in the grounds of Robert E. Lee's colonnaded home overlooking the Potomac).[38] Union and Confederate war graves rapidly became the focus for emotional springtime ceremonies in which local people gathered to pay their respect to those who had made the ultimate sacrifice. Women and children were conspicuous on these occasions, decorating the individual plots with garlands of May flowers. What was soon formalized on both sides of the Mason-Dixon Line as Decoration Day or Memorial Day thus emerged as an important outlet for popular grief in the postwar years.

The accompanying speeches, usually delivered by former veterans or civic leaders, were not necessarily geared toward the development of reconciliatory feeling. Southerners made no attempt to accommodate northern calls for repentance. Confederates had fought courageously for a just cause, they insisted, and Yankees should respect this fact. Whereas northern orators generally mixed unionism with the language of Christian sacrifice, southern speakers – their grief intensified by the fact that they were mourning sectional defeat as well as the Confederate dead – interspersed praise for the noble self-sacrifice of the latter with barbed comments about the evils of Reconstruction. By the 1870s, however, many Memorial Day speeches contained nods toward the goal of sectional reconciliation and, tellingly, northerners and southerners began to attend the same ceremonies. In 1874–75 Union and Confederate veterans could be found mingling at some Memorial Day events, the first concrete sign that grassroots sentiment was starting to change in earnest. The intellectual meeting point for the minority of veterans willing to bury the hatchet so soon after the war was mutual recognition of their opponents' masculine courage. By the late 1880s and 1890s this gendered sense of a shared past would place the veterans themselves at the center of what was, by then, an unstoppable drift toward reunion.

The strength of reconciliationist fervor in the 1870s should not be exaggerated. In 1872 Horace Greeley campaigned for reunion and an end to the disfranchisement of ex-Confederates. Faced with a barrage of Republican propaganda linking him to supposedly disloyal Democrats, he suffered an ignominious defeat. Influential figures in both sections often paid little heed to their late foes as they generated a torrent of war-related opinion, public and private. Many defeated Confederates wasted no time in seeking to justify what most northerners still regarded as treachery. Even after Greeley had helped to secure his release from federal prison, former Confederate president Jefferson Davis indicated that he had no regrets. The first Confederation Congress, he told one correspondent in August 1867, had made clear that a citizen's 'paramount allegiance' was to his state. 'The departure from that creed', he added, 'has been the source of all our ills'.[39] His deputy Alexander Stephens pursued a similar line when he published an account of the late conflict in 1870. Curiously forgetful of his 'cornerstone' address in 1861, he insisted that the South had seceded to preserve its constitutional rights under the original 'compact' and that the war 'was not a contest between the advocates or opponents' of slavery.[40] Perplexing though this claim might seem, it was central to a rapidly developing southern amnesia which, by the turn of the century, had afflicted many northerners too.

Some former Confederate military officers evinced a determination to promote the myth of the Lost Cause. Foremost among them was Jubal A. Early, hardly the ablest of Lee's subordinates but without doubt one of the Confederacy's most vociferous defenders after its fall. Along with other irreconcilables, Early took every opportunity to justify the southern war for independence and to foster popular interest in their particular version of the Confederate past. As well as dominating a revived Southern Historical Society (whose influential series of *Papers* provided a forum for Confederate officers to recon-struct their memories of battle), his clique of Yankee-hating Virginians supported the raising of monuments to the South's fallen heroes. In 1875 their efforts to commemorate Stonewall Jackson's devotion to the Confederacy bore fruit with the unveiling of a statue of the fallen hero in Richmond's Capitol Square.

Notwithstanding the activities of Lost Cause adherents in the 1870s, few white southerners wanted to fight another civil war. Public displays of mourning for the Confederate dead were less manifesta-tions of reactionary politics than understandable instances of the normal grieving process – a process in which individuals and whole communities sought to come to terms with their loss in order to face the future. Decoration Day ceremonies and the unveiling of monu-ments, in the words of historian Gaines Foster, 'thereby helped the South assimilate the fact of defeat without repudiating the defeated'.[41] By the 1870s Jubal Early's defiant brand of Lost Cause nationalism had little to recommend it to the majority of southern whites who wished to move on. They had no desire to renounce their past but nor had they any wish to live in it. The readiness with which former Confederates accepted pardons from Andrew Johnson, the enthu-siasm with which Conservative regimes supported railroad construc-tion, and the pragmatic quality of much southern political rhetoric all portended the rise of New South boosterism in the last two decades of the century.

Along with General James Longstreet (whose political perfidy became inseparable in the view of Early's faction from his alleged blunders at Gettysburg), the former guerrilla fighter John S. Mosby was one of the few leading ex-Confederates to endorse Republicanism in the pursuit of southern progress. Atypical though it was, Mosby's appeal to 'a former Confederate comrade' during the presidential election campaign of 1876 had something in common with Robert E. Lee's eminently practical opposition to the irreconcilables in the late 1860s. Issued as a Republican pamphlet, Mosby's letter mixed reconcilationist sentiment with sound strategic advice. 'I thought you knew that I ceased to be a Confederate soldier about eleven years ago', wrote Mosby, 'and became a citizen of the United States.' The Democratic candidates, Tilden and Hendricks, could not be elected, he insisted, because they were seen to be the candidates of the South:

> In attempting to grasp too much the South will lose everything.
> The sectional unity of the Southern people has been the
> governing idea and base of their politics. So far from its being
> the remedy for anything, it has been the cause of most of the
> evils they have suffered. So long as it continues, the war will
> be a controlling element of politics; for any cry in the South
> that unites the confederates re-echoes through the North,
> and rekindles the war fires there ... To insist on keeping up
> this sectional fight may be very heroic – so was the charge at
> Balaklava – but, in my opinion, is just as reckless and just as
> unwise.

Since the Democrats had now accepted the Reconstruction amendments, averred Mosby (and overturned most of the radical regimes, he might have added), what was the point of squabbling about racial equality? 'You speak of the bitter hostility of the North toward the South', he continued,

> Well, four years of hard fighting is not calculated to make
> men love each other; neither is an everlasting rehearsal of the
> wrongs which each side imagines it has suffered going to bring
> us any nearer to a better understanding. Peace can only come
> with oblivion of the past.[42]

Although Mosby's Republicanism was too much for most white southerners to stomach, his hardnosed view of reality was rooted in local soil. Just how strongly was about to become apparent.

The electoral crisis of 1876–77

In its early stages the 1876 presidential election campaign appeared
to confirm that the major parties had lost interest in sectional strife.
Cognizant that eight years of Grant had tarred the party with the
brush of corruption and determined to ignore the troubled question
of Reconstruction, the Republican convention at Cincinnati in June
passed over tainted leading lights such as James G. Blaine and Roscoe
Conkling and nominated for president Governor Rutherford B. Hayes
of Ohio. Hayes was not in the vanguard of reform but he possessed
a respectable war record, had supported the Reconstruction measures
during his two terms in Congress, and was known to favor honest
government and a meritocratic civil service. Samuel J. Tilden, the
Democratic nominee, personified the fight to purge American politics
of graft, having played a key role in overthrowing the notorious
Tweed Ring in New York City. Participants and observers alike
assumed that the chief issue of the campaign would be reform.

Very quickly, however, the election turned nasty. In the
unredeemed states of South Carolina, Louisiana, and Florida the
campaign centered on the continuing efforts of local white Democrats
to supplant Republican rule. Political violence was endemic in each
of these states during the summer and fall of 1876. The most serious
incident occurred in the Savannah River town of Hamburg, one of
the main black Republican strongholds in South Carolina. On
Independence Day the son and son-in-law of a local white farmer
were allegedly obstructed by a parade of black militiamen led by
Dock Adams, a Union veteran and refugee from neighboring
Georgia. When the white farmer pressed his case before the local
black judge, Adams apparently criticized the judge for entertaining
the complaint and found himself charged with contempt of court.
Tensions rapidly increased. On July 8, the day of Adams's court
appearance, his militiamen were confronted by angry whites. When
the blacks refused to give up their guns, the whites secured arms
and reinforcements from across the river in Augusta. Their opponents tried to flee but at least six of them were gunned down in cold
blood. The Democrats followed up the massacre with a systematic
campaign of intimidation in which their gubernatorial candidate,
ex-Confederate cavalry officer Wade Hampton, criss-crossed the state
with his Red Shirt militia.[43]

Events such as this brought Reconstruction issues center stage.
Sensing that northern voters were growing anxious at the prospect
of Rebels regaining national power on Tilden's coat-tails, Republican

spokesmen were quick to wave the bloody shirt. A vote for Hayes, they claimed, was the only way to prevent a Confederate revival. As was the custom Hayes took no public part in the campaign. However, in private communications he made every effort to encourage his copartisans to attack the Democrats on familiar ground. After the Republicans won narrowly in Maine in September, he told Senator James G. Blaine that 'our strong ground is the dread of a solid south, rebel rule, etc. I hope you will make these topics prominent in your speeches.'[44] In giving such advice, Hayes did not reject outright an alternative strategy outlined by Charles Nordhoff, the influential editor of the *New York Herald.* Nordhoff thought that the Republicans' best hope of winning a close election was to conciliate former southern Whigs and thereby detach them from the Democratic fold. Even while fanning fears of a Rebel revival, Hayes stressed that southern compliance with the Reconstruction laws could be rewarded with home rule.

When the first election results began to filter through to Republican National Headquarters, it seemed that the party's worst fears had been realized. Tilden had carried the crucial northern states of New York, New Jersey, Connecticut, and Indiana and, with Democratic victories likely on the West Coast and in the South, looked certain to enter the White House. Quick-witted Republican strategists William E. Chandler and Daniel Sickles, however, realized that Hayes could still win if he secured the electoral college votes of the three remaining Republican-controlled states in the South. Accordingly they wired party leaders in those states to hold firm and then, at the behest of President Grant, journeyed into Dixie to supervise affairs.

Within days a full-blown electoral crisis beckoned. The Republican-controlled returning boards in South Carolina, Louisiana, and Florida used abundant evidence of fraud and intimidation to throw out sufficient Democratic votes to secure those states for Hayes. Incensed Democrats in Columbia and New Orleans quickly formed rival state governments. On December 6 Republican and Democratic electors in the three southern states formally cast their votes for Hayes and Tilden respectively. On the basis of official state returns, Tilden looked to be a narrow winner in the electoral college. Sensing that the opposition was about to steal the contest, however, hotheads on both sides in Congress cried foul. With the Senate in the hands of the Republicans and the House controlled by the Democrats, the threat of renewed domestic violence was tangible. If Hayes had a majority of one, wrote one alarmed midwestern Republican, after 'the Confederates' carried several of the southern states by fraud and intimidation,

> we ought to put him in the White House if we have to fight through another four year war. I am prepared to shoulder my musket tomorrow, if it should be necessary to meet these men with force. It is humiliating to me to reflect that after all the sacrifices that have been made, these corrupt men can ride rough shod back into power again.[45]

Among those seeking to prevent another descent into anarchy was the incumbent president. Not for the first time (though arguably for the first time since his days as a Civil War commander) Ulysses S. Grant applied impressive leadership qualities in the quest for national salvation. Astutely balancing a commitment to the Republican party as the premier agent of national unity with an awareness of the imperative need to prevent civil strife, Grant used his executive powers to prepare the ground for a solution to the electoral crisis. His first move was to ensure that the relatively few remaining federal troops in the South were deployed to prevent the overthrow of the embattled Republican regimes in South Carolina and Louisiana. Having experienced so much white terrorism during his two terms in office, he knew that a Republican victory was the only hope of protecting southern unionists, black or white. He also understood that Hayes could not win the election without the electoral votes of these states but that domestic peace required Hayes to be seen to have won the presidency legitimately (or at least as legitimately as possible under the circumstances). He therefore made no move to break up the rival Democratic governments by using federal troops – an act that would have done untold damage to Hayes's cause in the court of northern public opinion.[46]

Because the Constitution was silent on the precise mode of counting contested electoral college votes, the president's second decisive intervention came with his backing for an electoral commission to determine the result. This solution carried with it the risk that the Democrats might carry the day, but it was a gamble worth taking because it offered the hope of a peaceful solution to the crisis. If both sides agreed to a commission, they could hardly complain about the final outcome. In the event Republican and Democratic majorities in Congress did support such a measure because they each believed they could emerge triumphant from the process. The commission of 15 was to be composed of five senators (three Republican, two Democrat), five representatives (three Demo-crat, two Republican), and five Supreme Court justices (two Repub-lican, two Democrat, with the fifth judge to be chosen by the other four). Clearly the votes of the fifth judge would be crucial. It was generally believed that these would be cast by David Davis, Lincoln's former campaign manager who was thought to have independent political views. Davis, however, declined to serve and was replaced by a Republican justice, Joseph P. Bradley. In a series of 8–7 votes the commission awarded the disputed electors to Hayes who now emerged as the likely victor.

The crisis was not over yet. Congressional Democrats were still threatening to obstruct the final counting of the votes through the use of filibustering tactics. Unbeknown to the public, shadowy negotiations had been taking place in Washington between influential southern Democrats, some of Hayes's Republican friends from Ohio, and lobbyists working for Tom Scott's powerful Texas & Pacific Railroad. The bottom line in these negotiations was that certain advantages might accrue to the South if it acquiesced in Hayes's election. Among the concessions on offer was the critical one of a restoration of home rule in the unredeemed states as well as the possibility of a southern cabinet minister and federal subsidies for construction of the southern trunk line, the Texas & Pacific. On February 26, 1877 (before the electoral commission had voted on South Carolina) a group of nine Ohio Republicans and southern Democrats met at the Wormley House Hotel in Washington. There it was agreed that Hayes would recognize the Democratic governor of Louisiana, Francis T. Nicholls, as the legitimate claimant and pursue a policy of federal non-intervention in local affairs. Nicholl's representative, Edward A. Burke, promised to safeguard the constitu-tional rights of local blacks. Although President Grant took no part in the meeting, his willingness to accept home rule was made known to the participants by Colonel Burke and undoubtedly helped smooth the path to an agreement.

The significance of these behind-the-scenes negotiations should not be exaggerated. Neither northern nor southern Democrats wanted to incur public opprobrium (still less to spark off another civil war) by delaying the count in Congress beyond the inauguration date of March 4. By this late stage of the crisis their main objective seems to have been to obtain as many concessions from the Repub-licans as they could get. Nevertheless the Wormley House agreement provided the blueprint for mutual acceptance of Hayes's victory. On March 1 with the filibusters showing no signs of tiring, Louisiana's

Democratic congressmen urged Grant to withdraw federal troops from their positions outside the state house in New Orleans. Convinced that it was pointless trying to prop up discredited Republican regimes in the South, the president responded by approving a draft telegram informing Stephen B. Packard, the incumbent carpetbag governor of Louisiana, that Americans no longer approved of military support for his administration. He told Colonel Burke that the message would be sent if the count were finished that evening. In fact the strength of the filibuster meant that the count was not finally completed until the early hours of the following morning. When the result was announced, it transpired that Hayes had beaten Tilden by 185 to 184 votes.

In his inaugural address three days later Rutherford B. Hayes signaled an end to Reconstruction. As long as southern state governments were willing to protect 'the interests of both races carefully and equally', he would pledge 'to put forth my best efforts in behalf of a civil policy which will forever wipe out in our political affairs the color line, and the distinction between North and South, to the end that we have not merely a united North or a united South, but a united country'.[47]

Hayes was as good as his word. Within weeks the withdrawal of federal protection prompted the collapse of the carpetbag regimes in South Carolina and Louisiana. He also appointed a Tennesseean to his cabinet. Southern whites did not live up to their side of the bargain. Although their pragmatic acquiescence in Hayes's triumph ended the danger of renewed civil strife, it was not accompanied by a readiness to protect the rights of the freedpeople. By the end of the century southern blacks were being deprived of the vote, subjected to the indignities of segregation, and cowed into at least partial submission by the proliferation of lynch law.

Hayes's policy did not go uncontested. While some of those northern whites who attacked the president did so because they were genuinely outraged at the perceived betrayal of the former slaves, the strongest and most poignant criticism came from blacks themselves. Initially, Frederick Douglass, the leading black spokesman of his generation, was willing to give the new policy a chance. But once it became evident that the White House had unwittingly delivered southern blacks into the hands of their white supremacist foes, he spoke out. Northerners, he told a Memorial Day crowd in New York City in May 1878, had 'always been ready to meet rebels more than half way and to hail them as fellow-citizens, countrymen, clansmen, and brothers'. But white southerners had not reciprocated.

The Civil War, he reminded his listeners, had a right side and a wrong side:

> It was a war of ideas, a battle of principles and ideas which united one section and divided the other; a war between the old and new, slavery and freedom, barbarism and civilization; between a government based upon the broadest and grandest declaration of human rights the world heard or read, and another pretended government, based upon an open, bold, and shocking denial of all rights, except the right of the strongest.

'Yes, let us have peace', intoned Douglass, mimicking the famous plea of President Grant, 'but let us have liberty, law, and justice first.'[48]

The Centennial election crisis had imparted further momentum into the ongoing process of sectional reconciliation between North and South. Even though the national project was not yet complete, and in spite of the decade's serious economic and social problems, the material future for the Republic was clearly bright. Whether the prospects for equal justice under the law for all Americans were as hopeful in 1877 as they had been in 1865 was less certain. Activists like Frederick Douglass had spent decades pursuing the dream of a racially inclusive America. Only time, the slayer of false hopes and promises, would tell whether the elusive vision would become a reality.

Notes

1. David W. Blight, *Race and Reunion: The Civil War in American Memory* (Cambridge, Mass., 2001), p.3.

2. Charles A. and Mary R. Beard, *The Rise of American Civilization*, 2 vols (London, 1927), 2, p.53.

3. Harry N. Scheiber, 'Economic Change in the Civil War Era: An Analysis of Recent Studies', *CWH* 11 (1965), 396–411.

4. See e.g. John Ashworth, 'Free Labor, Wage Labor, and the Slave Power: Republicanism and the Republican Party in the 1850s' in Melvyn Stokes and Stephen Conway, eds, *The Market Revolution in America: Social, Political, and Religious Expressions, 1800–1880* (Charlottesville, Va, 1996), pp.128–46.

5. On the economic consequences of the Civil War see Ralph Andreano, ed., *The Economic Impact of the American Civil War* (Cambridge, 1962), Scheiber,

'Economic Change', Patrick O'Brien, *The Economic Effects of the American Civil War* (Basingstoke, 1988).

6. Robert E. Gallman, 'Economic Growth and Structural Change in the Long Nineteenth Century' in *CEHUS*, p.7.

7. Richard Sylla, 'Experimental Federalism: The Economics of American Government, 1789–1914' in *ibid.*, pp.530, 534.

8. The phrase originates with Richard F. Bensel. See his *Yankee Leviathan: The Origins of Central State Authority in America* (Cambridge, 1990).

9. Sylla, 'Experimental Federalism', p.530.

10. Albro Martin, 'Economy from Reconstruction to 1914' in Glenn Porter, ed., *Encyclopedia of American Economic History: Studies of the Principal Movements and Ideas*, 3 vols (New York, 1980), 1, p.91.

11. Edwin G. Burrows and Mike Wallace, eds, *Gotham: A History of New York City to 1898* (New York, 1999), pp.951–65.

12. Alan Trachtenberg, *The Incorporation of America: Culture and Society in the Gilded Age* (New York, 1983), pp.144, 147.

13. Stuart M. Blumin, *The Emergence of the Middle Class: Social Experience in the American City, 1760–1900* (Cambridge, 1979), p.267.

14. Twain and Warner, *The Gilded Age: A Tale of Today* (Hartford, Conn., 1875).

15. Blumin, *Emergence*, p.275; Burrows and Wallace, eds, *Gotham*, pp.966–85.

16. This theme is an important one in the historiography of the Progressive era. See Richard L. McCormick, 'The Discovery that Business Corrupts Politics: A Reappraisal of the Origins of Progressivism', *American Historical Review* 86 (1981), 247–74.

17. Burrows and Wallace, *Gotham*, pp.914–15.

18. David O. Stowell, *Streets, Railroads, and the Great Strike of 1877* (Chicago, 1999), p.26. These figures do not include company employees or railroad passengers.

19. *New York Sun* quoted in David Haward Bain, *Empire Express: Building the First Continental Railroad* (New York, 1999), p.677.

20. US Bureau of the Census, *Historical Statistics of the United States: Colonial Times to 1970*, 2 vols (Washington, DC, 1975), 2, p.1072.

21. Quoted in Geoffrey Blodgett, 'A New Look at the Gilded Age: Politics in a Cultural Context' in Daniel Walker Howe, ed., *Victorian America* (University, Pa, 1976), p.106.

22. Michael E. McGerr, 'The Meaning of Liberal Republicanism: The Case of Ohio', *CWH* 28 (1982), 311.

23. On the achievements and limitations of postwar radical Republicanism in the area of social reform and industrial labor relations see David

Montgomery, *Beyond Equality: Labor and the Radical Republicans 1862–187* (New York, 1967) and James C. Mohr, ed., *Radical Republicans in the North: State Politics during Reconstruction* (Baltimore, 1976).

24. Quoted in Ellen Carol Du Bois, *Feminism and Suffrage: The Emergence of an Independent Women's Movement in America* (Ithaca, NY, 1978), p.62.

25. Anthony, speech of Nov. 25, 1867, in Ann D. Gordon, ed., *The Selected Papers of Elizabeth Cady Stanton and Susan B. Anthony: Vol. 2, Against an Aristocracy of Sex 1866 to 1873* (New Brunswick, NJ, 2000), p.110.

26. Du Bois, *Feminism*, p.101.

27. The following account owes a debt to Helen Lefkowitz Horowitz, 'Victoria Woodhull, Anthony Comstock and Conflict over Sex in the United States in the 1870s', *JAH* 87 (2000), 403–34.

28. Joan D. Hedrick, *Harriet Beecher Stowe: A Life* (New York, 1994), p.374.

29. Du Bois, *Feminism and Suffrage*, p.128.

30. George H. Miller, *Railroads and the Granger Laws* (Madison, Wis., 1971).

31. Quoted in Ward M. McAfee, *Religion, Race, and Reconstruction: The Public School in the Politics of the 1870s* (Albany, NY, 1998), p.66.

32. Quoted in *ibid.*, p.192.

33. Michael R. Haines, 'The Population of the United States, 1790–1920' in *CEHUS*, pp.173–5.

34. Quoted in Michael Fellman, *The Making of Robert E. Lee* (New York, 2000), p.27.

35. US Congress, 39 Cong., 1 Sess., *Report of the Joint Committee on Reconstruction* (1866: repr. Freeport, NY, 1971), pp.129–36 (quotations on pp.129, 132, 134).

36. Quoted in Blight, *Race and Reunion*, p.104.

37. Edmund Wilson, *Patriotic Gore: Studies in the Literature of the American Civil War* (New York, 1962), p.484. See also Blight, *Race and Reunion*, p.23.

38. Gary Laderman, *The Sacred Remains: American Attitudes Toward Death, 1799–1883* (New Haven, Conn., 1996), p.120.

39. Jefferson Davis to Frank H. Alfriend, Aug. 17, 1867, GLC 5344.01.

40. Quoted in Kenneth M. Stampp, *The Imperiled Union* (New York, 1980), p.268.

41. Gaines M. Foster, *Ghosts of the Confederacy: Defeat, The Lost Cause, and the Emergence of the New South* (New York, 1987), p.45.

42. John S. Mosby to 'A Former Confederate Comrade', Aug. 6, 1876, Republican campaign pamphlet reprinted from *New York Herald*, Aug. 12, 1876, GLC 6076.

43. Eric Foner, *Reconstruction: America's Unfinished Revolution, 1863–1877* (New York, 1988), pp.570–1.

44. Quoted in Ari Hoogenboom, *Rutherford B. Hayes: Warrior and President* (Lawrence, Kan., 1995), p.269.

45. R.E. Carpenter to Cyrus C. Carpenter, Dec. 10, 1876, Cyrus C. Carpenter Papers, State Historical Society of Iowa, Iowa City.

46. My understanding of Grant's actions during the electoral crisis has been informed by the interpretation provided by Brooks D. Simpson, *The Reconstruction Presidents* (Lawrence, Kan., 1998), pp.191–6. Other historians, notably Eric Foner, have been more critical of the president's allegedly passive actions, *idem, Reconstruction*, p.579. The events that led to Hayes's eventual triumph have proved fertile ground for historians. The main contours of the debate can be followed by consulting C. Vann Woodward, *Reunion and Reaction: The Compromise of 1877 and the End of Reconstruction* (1951: repr. Boston, 1966), Allan Peskin, 'Was There a Compromise of 1877?', *JAH* 60 (1973), 63–75, Michael Les Benedict, 'Southern Democrats in the Crisis of 1876–1877: A Reconsideration of Reunion and Reaction', *JSH* 46 (1980), 489–524.

47. Quoted in Simpson, *Reconstruction Presidents*, pp.207–208.

48. Frederick Douglass, 'There Was a Right Side in the Late War: An Address Delivered in New York, New York, on 30 May 1878', in John W. Blassingame and John R. McKivigan, eds, *The Frederick Douglass Papers. Series One: Speeches, Debates and Interviews. Vol. 4: 1864–80* (New Haven, Conn., 1991), pp.485, 489, 490.

CONCLUSION

THE PROVING TIME: THE UNITED STATES IN THE ERA OF CIVIL WAR

The Civil War, said the poet Walt Whitman, 'proved Humanity, and proved America'.[1] Whitman was no starry-eyed romantic. He had encountered the results of the conflict at first hand in the army hospitals of Washington and was familiar with the human suffering it had wrought. Of course, this was the whole point of his remark. His beloved American democracy had been tested by the great southern rebellion and emerged in some ways the better for it. The 'fearful trip' (as he dubbed it in one of his most popular, though least favorite, poems) was done.[2]

Although the war had much to do with differing conceptions, North and South, about the meaning of the American experiment, the rights of the states and the interpretation of the federal Constitution, the overriding cause of the conflict was the existence of slavery in one part of the Union. In the antebellum period only a tiny minority of northerners was willing to act on its belief that slavery was a moral evil and a ghastly stain on the Republic. Many more, Abraham Lincoln among them, recognized it as a grievous wrong but loved the Union far too much and black people far too little to endanger it by embracing abolition.

Only when southern whites, mobilized by a rational fear that their power was waning, began to defend the South's racial order in the shrillest of terms did northerners begin to comprehend the danger that slavery posed to their own liberties, power, and national vision. By late 1860, in the wake of a string of grave political crises (each of them in some way related to attempts to defend, expand, or contain slavery), North and South could recite a long litany of complaints against their respective foe – just as their forefathers had done against the British during the War of Independence. Men and women on both sides of the Mason-Dixon Line genuinely believed that the 'other' Americans (Southrons or Yankees) constituted an immediate and potent threat to their way of life. The critical event in the coming of the Civil War was the triumph of the Republican party in the presidential election of 1860. As the primary vehicle for northern political power, this new organization struck even patriotic southerners like Jefferson Davis as a negation of everything the Founding Fathers had stood for. The South's response was secession, the creation of the Confederacy, and the fateful decision to attack Fort Sumter. These events in turn produced a decisive counter-response from fervently pro-Union northerners that led directly to the fratricidal strife of 1861–65.

As William W. Freehling has observed, slavery was 'the taproot' not only of internecine strife but also of Confederate defeat. Its existence was the reason why the South was so much less industrialized than its enemy – a fact of enormous importance as the war developed into a struggle of societies as well as armies.[3] Almost as significantly it meant that a fifth column of black slaves constituted a vital potential resource for the Yankee invaders. For the first half of the war this population was largely a wasted resource. For reasons both strategic and political, President Lincoln was preoccupied with keeping the border slave states in the Union and conciliating racist northern War Democrats. But as the contest entered a third year, he accepted the reality that black agency itself had already begun to undermine slavery and, confronted with serious manpower problems, began enlisting tens of thousands of 'Afric Americans' into the armed forces of the United States. White Confederates, who fought tenaciously for their independence, were finally ground down by Grant and Sherman. Both of these Union generals possessed not only the numerical and technological superiority essential for final victory but also the inner self-confidence to outwit the enemy through boldness of thought as well as doggedness of action.

As Walt Whitman understood as well as anyone, Abraham Lincoln personified the Union cause. If Whitman wrote the nation, President Lincoln spoke it. 'The last best hope of earth', the president called the United States in December 1862.[4] He meant it. A southern victory would, he believed, represent a victory for the forces of anti-democracy in the world. What sort of model would the Republic present for humankind if a minority of disaffected slaveholders was allowed to reject the result of a democratic election or (and this was a conclusion he groped toward under the press of wartime events) if brave black men were not liberated and endowed with equal citizenship rights as a result of their loyalty to the national cause?

Lincoln did not survive to see the aftermath of Union victory, but there was plenty of evidence after 1865 to justify his profound faith in the notion of government by the people. During Reconstruction Republican politicians broke with President Andrew Johnson, their party leader, to resist attempts by southern whites to keep blacks in a condition of neoservitude. Their two chief legacies, the Fourteenth and Fifteenth Amendments, contained obvious flaws. Yet in providing a legal framework for an inclusive civic nationalism they furnished incontestable proof that, under certain historical circumstances, a resilient liberal democracy could protect the rights of an oppressed minority – a lesson that would not be lost on twentieth-century civil rights activists. The system generated other signs of what many modern-day observers would regard as health: women and workers of both sexes organizing to expand their liberties, rising government activism to deal with the problems of an increasingly complex society, high rates of European immigration, even the development of an embryonic conservation movement.

Of course, as Barrington Moore, Jr has observed, it was not just democracy that triumphed in the Civil War – it was *capitalist* democracy.[5] Many things were proven – demonstrated – in the war: not merely the strength of the North's plural system over that of the South's slave society or the courage and stoicism of the nineteenth century's 'greatest generation', but also the rich potential of commercial and industrial capitalism to generate the material resources necessary to win a modern war.[6] Slavery may not have been the obstacle to capitalism that some historians have suggested, let alone the insuperable barrier to national economic prosperity that most antebellum northerners assumed. However, it was demonstrably not up to the task of producing the amount of *matériel* required to defeat the North (or at least to fight it to a draw). Lincoln did not deny that the North's democracy was grounded in 'free-labor' capitalism. On the contrary, he regarded this system as the main source of the North's moral and material superiority over the slave South. Whereas northern society was allegedly fluid and meritocratic, its southern counterpart was deemed to be static and nurturing of aristocracy. We can perhaps agree with the emancipated slaves themselves that free labor (even as its *alter ego*, wage labor) was superior in virtually every respect to its bonded counterpart. But for all its capacity to promote steady economic growth, social mobility, and individual rights, American capitalism had its darker side which politicians and people alike were often hesitant to recognize. The near destruction of the Plains Indians and the environmental rape of the Far West were direct results of unfettered capitalist development – what contemporaries usually labeled 'progress' – in the mid-nineteenth century. The same was true of the miserable slums and sweat-shops of America's great cities, the endemic corruption of political life, and the poverty that afflicted blacks and ordinary whites in the postwar South.

The United States was certainly proven in wartime (much as it was in an even more destructive war 80 years later) and had been 'saved' from the egregious sin of slavery. However, it was far from being the born-again nation that northern evangelicals had hoped it might become. Perhaps this would have been asking too much of any country. What was clear by the end of our period was that the potent combination of northern victory and economic dynamism had placed the United States on the cusp of global hegemony. For good or ill, Great Power status was just a generation away.

Notes

1. Roy Morris, Jr, *The Better Angel: Walt Whitman and the Civil War* (New York, 2001), p.244.

2. *Ibid.*, p.243.

3. William W. Freehling, *The South vs. The South: How Anti-Confederate Southerners Shaped the Course of the Civil War* (Oxford, 2001), p.203.

4. *CWL*, 5, p.537.

5. Barrington Moore, Jr, *Social Origins of Dictatorship and Democracy: Lord and Peasant in the Making of the Modern World* (London, 1967), pp.111–55.

6. With acknowledgments to Tom Brokaw, *The Greatest Generation* (New York, 1998).

SELECT BIBLIOGRAPHY

With the exception of a few particularly influential works, this listing includes only secondary books published after 1980. References to older books, scholarly articles, and a number of other more recent works consulted can be found in the endnotes.

Abzug, Robert H., and Maizlish, Stephen E., eds, *New Perspectives on Race and Slavery in America: Essays in Honor of Kenneth M. Stampp* (Lexington, Ky: University of Kentucky Press, 1986).

Ackerman, Bruce, *We The People: Vol. 2, Transformations* (Cambridge, Mass: Belknap Press of Harvard University Press, 1998).

Altschuler, Glenn C., and Blumin, Stuart M., *Rude Republic: Americans and Their Politics in the Nineteenth Century* (Princeton, NJ: Princeton University Press, 2000).

Anbinder, Tyler, *Nativism and Slavery: The Know Nothings and the Politics of the 1850s* (New York: Oxford University Press, 1992).

Ashworth, John, *Slavery, Capitalism, and Politics in the Antebellum Republic: Vol. 1, Commerce and Compromise, 1820–1850* (Cambridge: Cambridge University Press, 1995).

Atack, Jeremy, and Bateman, Fred, *To Their Own Soil: Agriculture in the Antebellum North* (Ames, Ia: Iowa State University Press, 1987).

Attie, Jeanie, *Patriotic Toil: Northern Women and the American Civil War* (Ithaca, NY: Cornell University Press, 1998).

Bain, David Haward, *Empire Express: Building the First Transcontinental Railroad* (New York: Viking Penguin, 1999).

Baker, Jean H., *Affairs of Party: The Political Culture of Northern Democrats in the Mid-Nineteenth Century* (Ithaca, NY: Cornell University Press, 1983).

Bartlett, Irving H., *John C. Calhoun: A Biography* (New York: Norton, 1993).

Benedict, Michael Les, *A Compromise of Principle: Congressional Republicans and Reconstruction, 1863–1869* (New York: Norton, 1974).

Bensel, Richard F., *Yankee Leviathan: The Origins of Central State Authority in America 1859–1877* (Cambridge: Cambridge University Press, 1990).

Blair, William, *Virginia's Private War: Feeding Body and Soul in the Confederacy, 1861–1865* (New York: Oxford University Press, 1998).

Blight, David W., *Frederick Douglass' Civil War: Keeping Faith in Jubilee* (Baton Rouge, La: Louisiana State University Press, 1989).

Blight, David W., *Race and Reunion: The Civil War in American Memory* (Cambridge, Mass: Belknap Press of Harvard University Press, 2001).

Blue, Frederick J., *Salmon P. Chase: A Life in Politics* (Kent, Ohio: Kent State University Press, 1987).

Blumin, Stuart M., *The Emergence of the Middle Class: Social Experience in the American City, 1760–1900* (Cambridge: Cambridge University Press, 1989).

Borritt, Gabor S., ed., *Why the Confederacy Lost* (New York: Oxford University Press, 1992).

Borritt, Gabor S., ed., *Lincoln's Generals* (New York: Oxford University Press, 1995).

Borritt, Gabor S., ed., *Why the Civil War Came* (New York: Oxford University Press, 1996).

Brechin, Gray, *Imperial San Francisco: Urban Power, Earthly Ruin* (Berkeley, Cal: University of California Press, 1999).

Brown, John K., *The Baldwin Locomotive Works 1831–1915* (Baltimore: Johns Hopkins University Press, 1995).

Brown, Richard D., *Modernization: The Transformation of American Life 1600–1865* (New York: Hill and Wang, 1976).

Burrows, Edwin G., and Wallace, Mike, *Gotham: A History of New York City to 1898* (New York: Oxford University Press, 1999).

Burton, William L., *Melting Pot Soldiers: The Union's Ethnic Regiments* (Ames, Ia: Iowa State University Press, 1988).

Carlson, Paul H., *The Plains Indians* (College Station, Tex: Texas A&M Press, 1998).

Carter, Dan T., *When the War Was Over: The Failure of Self-Reconstruction in the South, 1865–1867* (Baton Rouge, La: Louisiana State University Press, 1985).

Carwardine, Richard J., *Evangelicals and Politics in Antebellum America* (New Haven, Conn: Yale University Press, 1993).

Clinton, Catherine, *The Other Civil War: American Women in the Nineteenth Century* (New York: Hilland Wang, 1984).

Collins, Bruce, *The Origins of America's Civil War* (London: Arnold, 1981).

Collins, Bruce, *White Society in the Antebellum South* (London: Longman, 1985).

Cook, Robert, *Baptism of Fire: The Republican Party in Iowa 1838–1878* (Ames, Ia: Iowa State University Press, 1994).

Cooper, William J., Jr, *The South and the Politics of Slavery 1828–1856* (Baton Rouge, La, 1978).

Cooper, William J., Jr, *Liberty and Slavery: Southern Politics to 1860* (New York: Knopf, 1983).

Cooper, William J., Jr, *Jefferson Davis: American* (New York: Knopf, 2000).

Cox, LaWanda, *Lincoln and Black Freedom: A Study in Presidential Leadership* (Columbia, SC: University of South Carolina Press, 1981).

Crawford, Martin, *Ashe County's Civil War: Community and Society in the Appalachian South* (Charlottesville, Va: University of Virginia Press, 2001).

Dailey, Jane, Gilmore, Glenda Elizabeth, and Simon, Bryant, eds, *Jumpin' Jim Crow: Southern Politics from Civil War to Civil Rights* (Princeton, NJ: Princeton University Press, 2000).

Davis, William C., *Jefferson Davis: The Man and His Hour* (New York: Harper Collins, 1991).

Davis, William C., *Lincoln's Men: How President Lincoln Became Father to an Army and a Nation* (New York: Simon and Schuster, 1999).

Dew, Charles, *Apostles of Disunion: Southern Secession Commissioners and the Causes of the Civil War* (Charlottesville, Va: University Press of Virginia, 2001).

Donald, David H., *Lincoln* (London: Jonathan Cape, 1995).

DuBois, Ellen Carol, *Feminism and Suffrage: The Emergence of an Independent Women's Movement in America 1848–1869* (Ithaca, NY: Cornell University Press, 1978).

Dusinberre, William, *Them Dark Days: Slavery in the American Rice Swamps* (New York: Oxford University Press, 1996).

Edwards, Laura F., *Gendered Strife and Confusion: The Political Culture of Reconstruction* (Urbana, Ill: Illinois University Press, 1997).

Engerman, Stanley L., and Gallman, Robert E., eds, *The Cambridge Economic History of the United States: Vol. 2, The Long Nineteenth Century* (Cambridge: Cambridge University Press, 2000).

Escott, Paul D., *Many Excellent People: Power and Privilege in North Carolina 1850–1900* (Chapel Hill, NC: University of North Carolina Press, 1985).

Faust, Drew Gilpin, *The Creation of Confederate Nationalism: Ideology and Identity in the Civil War South* (Baton Rouge, La: Louisiana State University Press, 1988).

Faust, Drew Gilpin, *Mothers of Invention: Women of the Slaveholding South in the American Civil War* (Chapel Hill, NC: University of North Carolina Press, 1996).

Fellman, Michael, *Citizen Sherman: A Life of William Tecumseh Sherman* (Lawrence, Kan: University Press of Kansas, 1995).

Fellman, Michael, *The Making of Robert E. Lee* (New York: Random House, 2000).

Finkelman, Paul, ed., *His Soul Goes Marching On: Responses to John Brown and the Harpers Ferry Raid* (Charlottesville, Va: University Press of Virginia, 1995).

Fogel, Robert William, *Without Consent or Contract: The Rise and Fall of American Slavery* (New York: Norton, 1989).

Foner, Eric, *Free Soil, Free Labor, Free Men: The Ideology of the Republican Party Before the Civil War* (New York: Oxford University Press, 1970).

Foner, Eric, *Reconstruction: America's Unfinished Revolution 1863–1877* (New York: Harper and Row, 1988).

Ford, Lacey K., Jr, *Origins of Southern Radicalism: The Southern Upcountry, 1800–1860* (New York: Oxford University Press, 1988).

Foster, Gaines M., *Ghosts of the Confederacy: Defeat, the Lost Cause, and the Emergence of the New South* (New York: Oxford University Press, 1987).

Fox-Genovese, Elizabeth, *Within the Plantation Household: Black and White Women of the Old South* (Chapel Hill, NC: University of North Carolina Press, 1988).

Frank, Joseph Allan, *With Ballot and Bayonet: The Political Socialization of American Civil War Soldiers* (Athens, Ga: University of Georgia Press, 1998).

Freehling, William W., *The South vs. The South: How Anti-Confederate Southerners Shaped the Course of the Civil War* (New York: Oxford University Press, 2001).

Gallagher, Gary W., *The Confederate War* (Cambridge, Mass: Harvard University Press, 1997).

Gara, Larry, *The Presidency of Franklin Pierce* (Lawrence, Kan: University of Kansas Press, 1991).

Genovese, Eugene D., *Roll, Jordan, Roll: The World the Slaves Made* (New York: Pantheon, 1974).

Genovese, Eugene D., *A Consuming Fire: The Fall of the Confederacy in the Mind of the White Christian South* (Athens, Ga: University of Georgia Press, 1998).

Gienapp, William E., *The Origins of the Republican Party 1852–1856* (New York: Oxford University Press, 1987).

Grant, Susan-Mary, *North Over South: Northern Nationalism and American Identity in the Antebellum Era* (Lawrence, Kan: University Press of Kansas, 2000).

Grant, Susan-Mary, and Reid, Brian Holden, eds, *The American Civil War: Explorations and Reconsiderations* (Harlow: Pearson Education, 2000).

Gray, John S., *Centennial Campaign: The Sioux War of 1876* (1976: repr. Norman, Okla: University of Oklahoma Press, 1988).

Griffith, Paddy, *Rally Once Again: Battle Tactics of the American Civil War* (Marlborough: Crowood Press, 1987).

Grimsley, Mark, *The Hard Hand of War: Union Military Policy Toward Southern Civilians, 1861–1865* (Cambridge: Cambridge University Press, 1995).

Grimsted, David, *American Mobbing, 1828–1861: Toward Civil War* (New York: Oxford University Press, 1998).

Guelzo, Allen C., *Abraham Lincoln: Redeemer President* (Grand Rapids, Mich: Eerdmans, 1999).

Harris, William C., *With Charity for All: Lincoln and the Restoration of the Union* (Lexington, Ky: University of Kentucky Press, 1997).

Harsh, Joseph L., *Confederate Tide Rising: Robert E. Lee and the Making of Southern Strategy, 1861–1862* (Kent, Ohio: Kent State University Press, 1998).

Hedrick, Joan, *Harriet Beecher Stowe: A Life* (New York: Oxford University Press, 1994).

Holt, Michael F., *The Political Crisis of the 1850s* (New York: John Wiley, 1978).

Holt, Michael F., *Political Parties and American Political Development from the Age of Jackson to the Age of Lincoln* (Baton Rouge, La: Louisiana State University Press, 1992).

Holt, Michael F., *The Rise and Fall of the American Whig Party: Jacksonian Politics and the Onset of the Civil War* (New York: Oxford University Press, 1999).

Hoogenboom, Ari, *Rutherford B. Hayes: Warrior and President* (Lawrence, Kan: University of Kansas Press, 1995).

Howe, Daniel Walker, *The Political Culture of the American Whigs* (Chicago: University of Chicago Press, 1979).

Hunter, Tera W., *To 'Joy My Freedom: Southern Black Women's Lives and Labors After the Civil War* (Cambridge, Mass: Harvard University Press, 1997).

Hurst, James Willard, *Law and the Conditions of Freedom in the Nineteenth-Century United States* (Madison: University of Wisconsin Press, 1956).

Ignatiev, Noel, *How the Irish Became White* (New York: Routledge, 1995).

Isenberg, Andrew C., *The Destruction of the Bison* (Cambridge: Cambridge University Press, 2000).

Jacobson, Matthew Frye, *Whiteness of a Different Color: European Immigrants and the Alchemy of Race* (Cambridge, Mass: Harvard University Press, 1998).

Johannsen, Robert W., *To the Halls of the Montezumas: The Mexican War in the American Imagination* (Oxford: Oxford University Press, 1985).

Keller, Morton, *Affairs of State: Public Life in Late Nineteenth Century America* (Cambridge, Mass: Belknap Press of Harvard University Press, 1977).

Kelly, Patrick J., *Creating a National Home: Building the Veterans' Welfare State 1860–1900* (Cambridge, Mass: Harvard University Press, 1997).

Klein, Maury, *Days of Defiance: Sumter, Secession, and the Coming of the Civil War* (New York: Knopf, 1997).

Koistinen, Paul A.C., *Beating Ploughshares into Swords: The Political Economy of American Warfare, 1606–1865* (Lawrence, Kan: University of Kansas Press, 1996).

Kolchin, Peter, *American Slavery 1619–1877* (New York: Hill and Wang, 1993).

Laderman, Gary, *The Sacred Remains: American Attitudes Toward Death, 1799–1883* (New Haven, Conn: Yale University Press, 1996).

LaFeber, Walter, *The Cambridge History of American Foreign Relations: Vol. 2, The American Search for Opportunity, 1865–1913* (Cambridge: Cambridge University Press, 1993).

Laurie, Bruce, *Working People of Philadelphia, 1800–1850* (Philadelphia: Temple University Press, 1980).

Levine, Bruce, *Half Slave and Half Free: The Roots of Civil War* (New York: Hill and Wang, 1992).

Limerick, Patricia Nelson, *The Legacy of Conquest: The Unbroken Past of the American West* (New York: Norton, 1987).

Litwack, Leon F., *Been in the Storm So Long: The Aftermath of Slavery* (New York: Knopf, 1979).

McAfee, Ward M., *Religion, Race, and Reconstruction: The Public School in the Politics of the 1870s* (Albany, NY: State University of New York Press, 1998).

McCardell, John, *The Idea of a Southern Nation: Southern Nationalists and Southern Nationalism, 1830–1860* (New York: Norton, 1979).

McCormick, Richard L., *The Party Period and Public Policy: American Politics from the Age of Jackson to the Progressive Era* (Oxford: Oxford University Press, 1986).

McDonald, JoAnna M., *We Shall Meet Again: The First Battle of Manassas (Bull Run) July 18–21, 1861* (1999: repr. New York: Oxford University Press, 2000)

McFeely, William S., *Grant: A Biography* (New York: Norton, 1981).

McMurry, Richard M., *Two Great Rebel Armies: An Essay in Confederate Military History* (Chapel Hill, NC: University of North Carolina Press, 1989).

McMurry, Richard M., *Atlanta 1864: Last Chance for the Confederacy* (Lincoln, Neb: University of Nebraska Press, 2000).

McPherson, James M., *Battle Cry of Freedom: The Civil War Era* (New York: Oxford University Press, 1988).

McPherson, James M., *For Cause and Comrades: Why Men Fought in the Civil War* (New York: Oxford University Press, 1997).

Miller, Randall M., Stout, Harry S., and Wilson, Charles Reagan, eds, *Religion and the American Civil War* (New York: Oxford University Press, 1998).

Mitchell, Reid, *Civil War Soldiers* (New York: Viking Penguin, 1988).

Mitchell, Reid, *The Vacant Chair: The Northern Soldier Leaves Home* (New York: Oxford University Press, 1993).

Mohr, James C., ed., *Radical Republicans in the North: State Politics during Reconstruction* (Baltimore: Johns Hopkins University Press, 1976).

Montgomery, David, *Beyond Equality: Labor and the Radical Republicans, 1862–1872* (New York: Knopf, 1967).

Moore, Barrington, Jr, *Social Origins of Dictatorship and Democracy: Lord and Peasant in the Making of the Modern World* (Boston: Beacon Press, 1966).

Morris, Roy, Jr, *The Better Angel: Walt Whitman in the Civil War* (New York: Oxford University Press, 2000).

Morrison, Michael A., *Slavery and the American West: The Eclipse of Manifest Destiny and the Coming of the Civil War* (Chapel Hill, NC: University of North Carolina Press, 1997).

Neely, Mark E., Jr, *The Fate of Liberty: Abraham Lincoln and Civil Liberties* (New York: Oxford University Press, 1992).

Neely, Mark E., Jr, *The Last Best Hope of Earth: Abraham Lincoln and the Promise of America* (Cambridge, Mass: Harvard University Press, 1993).

Newman, Louise Michelle, *White Women's Rights: the Racial Origins of Feminism in the United States* (Oxford: Oxford University Press, 1999).

Nolan, Alan T., *Lee Considered: General Robert E. Lee and Civil War History* (Chapel Hill, NC: University of North Carolina Press, 1991).

O'Brien, Michael, *Rethinking the South: Essays in Intellectual History* (Baltimore: Johns Hopkins University Press, 1988).

O'Brien, Patrick, *The Economic Effects of the American Civil War* (Basingstoke: Macmillan, 1988).

O'Leary, Cecilia Elizabeth, *To Die For: The Paradox of American Patriotism* (Princeton, NJ: Princeton University Press, 1999).

Paludan, Philip Shaw, *'A People's Contest': The Union and the Civil War 1861–1865* (New York: Harper, 1988).

Paludan, Philip Shaw, *The Presidency of Abraham Lincoln* (Lawrence, Kan: University Press of Kansas, 1994).

Parish, Peter J., *Slavery: History and Historians* (New York: Harper, 1989).

Perkins, Bradford, *The Cambridge History of American Foreign Relations: Vol. 1, The Creation of a Republican Empire, 1776–1865* (Cambridge: Cambridge University Press, 1993).

Perman, Michael, ed., *Major Problems in the Civil War and Reconstruction* (Boston: Houghton Mifflin, 1998).

Piston, William Garrett, and Hatcher, Richard W., III, *Wilson's Creek: The Second Battle of the Civil War and the Men Who Fought It* (Chapel Hill, NC: University of North Carolina Press, 2000).

Potter, David M., *The Impending Crisis 1848–1861* (New York: Harper and Row, 1976).

Power, J. Tracy, *Lee's Miserables: Life in the Army of Northern Virginia from the Wilderness to Appomattox* (Chapel Hill, NC: University of North Carolina Press, 1998).

Prucha, Francis Paul, *American Indian Policy in Crisis: Christian Reformers and the Indian, 1865–1900* (Norman, Okla: University of Oklahoma Press, 1976).

Rable, George C., *Civil Wars: Women and the Crisis of Southern Nationalism* (Urbana, Ill: University of Illinois Press, 1989).

Rable, George C., *The Confederate Republic: A Revolution Against Politics* (Chapel Hill, NC: University of North Carolina Press, 1994).

Reardon, Carol, *Pickett's Charge in History and Memory* (Chapel Hill, NC: University of North Carolina Press, 1997).

Reid, Brian Holden, *The Origins of the American Civil War* (London: Longman, 1996).

Remini, Robert V., *Henry Clay. Statesman for the Union* (New York. Norton, 1991).

Renda, Lex, *Running on the Record: Civil War-Era Politics in New Hampshire* (Charlottesville, Va: University of Virginia Press, 1997).

Richards, Leonard L., *The Slave Power: The Free North and Southern Domination 1780–1860* (Baton Rouge, La: Louisiana State University Press, 2000).

Richardson, Heather Cox, *The Greatest Nation of the Earth: Republican Economic Policies During the Civil War* (Cambridge, Mass: Harvard University Press, 1997).

Richardson, Robert D., Jr, *Emerson: The Mind on Fire* (Berkeley, Cal: University of California Press, 1995).

Roediger, David R., *The Wages of Whiteness: Race and the Making of the American Working Class* (London: Verso, 1991).

Rohrbough, Malcolm J., *Days of Gold: The California Gold Rush and the American Nation* (Berkeley, Cal: University of California Press, 1997).

Ruffner, Kevin Conley, *Maryland's Blue & Gray: A Border State's Union and Confederate Junior Officer Corps* (Baton Rouge, La: Louisiana State University Press, 1997).

Ryan, Mary P., *Women in Public: Between Banners and Ballots, 1825–1880* (Baltimore: Johns Hopkins University Press, 1990).

Rybczynski, Witold, *A Clearing in the Distance: Frederick Law Olmsted and America in the 19th Century* (New York: Simon and Schuster, 1999).

Salvatore, Nick, *We All Got History: The Memory Books of Amos Webber* (New York: Random House, 1996).

Savage, Kirk, *Standing Soldiers, Kneeling Slaves: Race, War, and Monument in Nineteenth-Century America* (Princeton, NJ: Princeton University Press, 1997).

Saxton, Alexander, *The Rise and Fall of the White Republic: Class Politics and Mass Culture in Nineteenth-Century America* (London: Verso, 1990).

Sears, Stephen W., *George B. McClellan: The Young Napoleon* (Boston: Ticknor and Fields, 1988).

Sears, Stephen W., *Chancellorsville* (Boston: Houghton Mifflin, 1996).

Shattuck, Gardiner H., *A Shield and Hiding Place: The Religious Life of the Civil War Armies* (Macon, Ga: Mercer University Press, 1987).

Silber, Nina, *The Romance of Reunion: Northerners and the South 1865–1900* (Chapel Hill, NC: University of North Carolina Press, 1993).

Silbey, Joel H., *The Partisan Imperative: The Dynamics of American Politics Before the Civil War* (New York: Oxford University Press, 1985).

Simpson, Brooks D., *Let Us Have Peace: Ulysses S. Grant and the Politics of War and Reconstruction, 1861–1868* (Chapel Hill, NC: University of North Carolina Press, 1991).

Simpson, Brooks D., *The Reconstruction Presidents* (Lawrence, Kan: University of Kansas Press, 1998).

Smith, Elbert B., *The Presidencies of Zachary Taylor and Millard Fillmore* (Lawrence, Kan: University of Kansas Press, 1988).

Spence, Mark David, *Dispossessing the Wilderness: Indian Removal and the Making of the National Parks* (New York: Oxford University Press, 1999).

Starr, Kevin, and Orsi, Richard J., eds, *Rooted in Barbarous Soil: People, Culture, and Community in Gold Rush California* (Berkeley, Cal: University of California Press, 2000).

Stokes, Melvyn, and Conway, Stephen, *The Market Revolution in America: Social, Political, and Religious Expressions, 1800–1880* (Charlottesville, Va: University of Virginia Press, 1996).

Stowell, Daniel W., *Rebuilding Zion: The Religious Reconstruction of the South, 1863–1877* (New York: Oxford University Press, 1998).

Thomas, Emory M., *The Confederate Nation 1861–1865* (New York: Harper and Row, 1979).

Thomas, Emory M., *Robert E. Lee: A Biography* (New York: Norton, 1995).

Trachtenberg, Alan, *The Incorporation of America: Culture and Society in the Gilded Age* (New York: Hill and Wang, 1983).

Truettner, William H., ed., *The West as America: Reinterpreting Images of the Frontier, 1820–1920* (Washington, DC: Smithsonian Institution Press, 1991).

Tunnell, Ted, *Crucible of Reconstruction: War, Radicalism and Race in Louisiana* (Baton Rouge, La: Louisiana State University Press, 1984).

Vorenberg, Michael, *Final Freedom: The Civil War, the Abolition of Slavery, and the Thirteenth Amendment* (Cambridge: Cambridge University Press, 2001).

Wang, Xi, *The Trial of Democracy: Black Suffrage and Northern Republicans, 1860–1910* (Athens, Ga: University of Georgia Press, 1997).

West, Elliott, *The Contested Plains: Indians, Goldseekers, and the Rush to Colorado* (Lawrence, Kan: University of Kansas Press, 1998).

White, Richard, *'It's Your Misfortune and None of My Own': A New History of the American West* (Norman, Okla: University of Oklahoma Press, 1991).

Whites, Lee Ann, *The Civil War as a Crisis in Gender: Augusta, Georgia, 1860–1890* (Athens, Ga: University of Georgia Press, 1995).

Widmer, Edward L., *Young America: The Flowering of Democracy in New York City* (New York: Oxford University Press, 1999).

Wiebe, Robert H., *The Opening of American Society: From the Adoption of the Constitution to the Eve of Disunion* (New York: Knopf, 1984).

Wills, Gary, *Lincoln at Gettysburg: The Words that Remade America* (New York: Simon and Schuster, 1992).

Woodworth, Steven E., *Six Armies in Tennessee: The Chickamauga and Chattanooga Campaigns* (Lincoln, Neb: University of Nebraska Press, 1998).

Woodworth, Steven E., ed., *The Art of Command in the Civil War* (Lincoln, Neb: University of Nebraska Press, 1998).

Worster, Donald, *A River Running West: The Life of John Wesley Powell* (Oxford: Oxford University Press, 2001).

Wright, Gavin, *Old South, New South: Revolutions in the Southern Economy Since the Civil War* (New York: Basic Books, 1986).

INDEX

abolition movement 20, 29, 55, 60, 83, 116, 313
abolitionists:
  and 'bleeding Kansas' 89–90
  and conservative Republicans 99
  and Harpers Ferry raid 105–6, 107
  and Kansas-Nebraska Act 77
  and postwar reform 310, 316
  as minority 46
  in Civil War 194–5, 196, 202, 215, 217, 221
  opposition to Fugitive Slave Law 64–5
  opposition to Mexican War 43, 44
  southern fear of 55
Accessory Transit Company 91
Adams, Brooks 315
Adams, Dock 330
Adams, John Quincy 37
AFIC. *See* American Freedmen's Inquiry Commission
African Methodist Episcopal Church 247
African Methodist Episcopal Church Zion 247
agriculture 6–7, 8, 25–6, 27, 30–1, 201, 304, 321
Agriculture, Department of, US 305

Alabama:
  and secession 118
  antebellum 19, 20, 67
  in Civil War 159
  secession of 116
Alabama (*CSS*) 143
Alabama Claims 261
Alaska gold rush 272
Alaska Purchase 271–2
Albany State Register 56
Alcorn, James Lusk 257
Alexander, James W. 44
AMA. *See* American Missionary Association
American Equal Rights Association 316
American Freedmen's Inquiry Commission 204–5
American Missionary Association 89, 247, 253, 254
American nationalism. *See also* Confederacy
  celebration of 1–4
  and problems of identity 9–11
  barriers to 12–14
  appeals to 59, 60
  and nativism 82, 322
  and 1856 election 94
  northern variant of 97